LIBERALISM
The Demise of America

By
MICHAEL GALEN MARTIN, PH.D.
INTERNATIONAL ECONOMIST

First Edition

ISBN: 0988462818
ISBN-13: 978-0-9884628-1-6

Book cover designed by Ty Nowicki

I want to thank my parents, Dr. Eugene Martin and Martha Martin, for a wonderful upbringing that made learning fun and encouraged intellectual curiosity. I also want to thank my wife, Graciela, and my daughter, Cecily, for their patience and support while I worked on the book. Fred, my black lab, also deserves credit for giving me emotional support as he faithfully curled up next to me as I worked on the book.

CONTENTS

PROLOGUE

∽

People don't understand what a great country we have. Americans have not traveled enough to realize what we have here. They don't understand the poverty and misery that surround us. We are the envy of the world, but our own citizens look down on our country. Civilization is tenuous. We can easily lose what we have. I remember my high school teacher telling me repeatedly how easily liberty can slip away from us, that we must be continuously vigilant to protect it. I didn't understand it then, I do now.

In my work as an international economist and my travels as a private citizen I have traveled to over one hundred countries, and each time I returned home I was more and more convinced that this is the best country in the world. We should appreciate what we have.

The Founding Fathers sought to create a country protecting the rights of citizens from the government. The Constitution was predicated on this principle. For the liberals of today, like Obama, this is anathema. They don't like the Constitution. They see it as only a constraint on what the government can do. Their interest is in expanding the rights and powers of government—to the detriment of citizens. The War of Independence, the Civil War, and the two World Wars were fought to preserve our traditions and ideals, but liberalism is now surreptitiously taking them from us from within.

Part of the impetus for writing this book was my frustration at understanding how liberals think the way they do. Queen Juliana once said, "I don't understand it. I can't even understand the people who can understand it." This is the relationship between liberals and conservatives nowadays; political discourse has broken down. It has become a waste of time. It's like liberals and conservatives live in different worlds. Liberals are simply different than those of us who describe ourselves as *conservative*—but how and why? This book searches for underlying factors shaping our thoughts and behavior.

Why am I suited to writing this book? In my thirty-five years of work as an international economist I worked firsthand with many different political and economic systems. As a Ph.D. economist, I understand the theoretical and empirical issues underpinning political economy, but my career has uniquely enabled me to have direct hands-on and personal experience too. I not only have seen and worked with senior foreign country officials to better manage their macroeconomic policy, but have shaped actual policy. I have worked thirty years for the International Monetary Fund, two and a half years in research at the Federal Reserve Bank of New York, and two and a half years as an international economist at Chemical Bank of New York. I lived in Mongolia for three years as the IMF Resident Representative and saw how policies worked at the grassroots level. Early in my career I was a social worker in the Bronx of New York— an invaluable experience. These have all given me insight into why policies work and don't work, and how they affect people. But this book is only in small part about economics. It's about political economy and culture in a broad sense. I have read widely in philosophy, epistemology, psychology, and ethics, and have brought this to bear in the text.

As an economist by training, I was first troubled by the perverse and counterproductive economic policies of liberalism. However, I soon realized that the problems with liberalism were much more pervasive and threatening. Liberalism has entangled our entire culture from top to bottom and is damaging our whole culture. This is what prompted this undertaking to look at the roots of liberalism in virtually all aspects of our lives.

I believe that this country and Western civilization are heading down a dangerous path. The book is different than most books looking at liberalism in that it's pitched at a philosophical level, looking at the underpinnings of liberalism rather than getting mired in fruitless superficial discourse and ad hominem political attacks. The book seeks to explain the enduring failure of liberalism by looking at it from a variety of different angles: political, economic, historical, philosophical, epistemological, cultural, institutional, psychological, moral, and from the standpoint of justice. It will unveil the baneful nature of liberalism's origins, means, and consequences.

It's not focused on the people in politics, and only slightly on the issues, but rather it looks at underlying forces shaping events and prefiguring our future. However, while the book is philosophical in tenor, it's not philosophy for the sake of philosophy. The book is intellectual, but not pedantic; it's aimed at the common man, bringing big ideas down to earth and providing guidance through our current political-economic-social morass.

Western democracies are rapidly destroying themselves. This destruction is not only manifested in large-scale societal developments, but also in the mind and spirit of man. This is not surprising as it would not be possible for democracy to be self-destructing so rapidly if there were not something terribly wrong at the level of the individual. Liberalism is degrading not only democracy and society, but man himself. It is bankrupting us financially, but it is bankrupting us in other ways as well. This book will illuminate the real perils posed by liberalism. The nation needs to wake up before it's too late.

What I find truly frightening is that many well-intentioned and bright people are buying into even the most egregious and unsupportable polices of liberalism, for instance, the massive increase in government spending and debt. The government is spending forty two percent more than the revenue it is taking in and accumulating debt on a massive scale. Obama has borrowed more in four years than all other American presidents combined. This is an existential threat to America, but the threat is not confined to America. Western European liberalism already has those countries on the brink of bankruptcy. The fact that something is wrong is even more elemental than basic arithmetic. It's simply a matter of common sense. So why is liberalism not only allowing this to go on, but in fact actively promoting it? I could understand it if these policies served the interests of liberals, but such policies hurt everyone, including them. It is like some strange, intoxicating force has taken control of their minds, and they can no longer think for themselves. Liberals push their platform with guilt and emotion, not reason. This is because reason would shed light on their disturbing policies and agenda. In fact, they dismiss reason as a tool of oppression. Liberals have abandoned one of the principle tools which has contributed to the advancement of mankind. For the longest time I wasted time trying to understand liberalism rationally, but this is impossible. It's like trying to understand the irrational or the absurd through reason.

Liberals believe our best days are behind us. They don't believe America is a great country. They don't respect our heritage, but rather are embarrassed by it. Besides the damage wrought by a growing culture of dependency, liberalism is eroding the values which have underpinned this country since its founding. It's even destroying our history. In schools, they teach that America is really not a good nation. We abused and killed the Native Americans, are damaging the environment, cause militarism in the world, and are too material and self-consumed. Capitalism and business are evil, and greed creates social distortions and injustice.

George Washington said, "Our greatest enemy is the criminal and the state; the latter is a greater threat than the former and moreover transforms itself into the former as well." Liberalism is doing more damage to our country and our democratic values and traditions than Osama bin Laden could ever have dreamt of doing. Our system won the Cold War, triumphed over communism and socialism, but now we are destroying it ourselves. It's ironic, but we're using the ideology we defeated to defeat ourselves.

* * *

CHAPTER 1

INTRODUCTION

———◆———

You need only reflect that one of the best ways to get yourself a reputation as a dangerous citizen these days is to go about repeating the phrases which our founding fathers used in the struggle for independence.

~Charles Austin Beard, Historian

Liberalism is weakening all of the foundational pillars of the enlightenment and bringing about a decline in Western democratic traditions. Liberals are wantonly tossing aside the factors that made western democracies great: the Constitution, federalism, limited government, reliance on the market, a balanced and objective press, a system of checks and balances between the various branches of government, the rule of law, the separation of economic and political power, the independence of the private sector, the strength of the family, Judeo-Christian values, and an independent judiciary (the arm liberals now use to craft social policy). Liberals even pervert the philosophic foundations of reliance on reason, the pursuit of truth, and the concepts of justice and morality. More fundamentally, liberalism is intent not just on reforming the current system, but destroying it. Only through its destruction can liberals construct their utopian collectivist state and a transnational government.

America and Western Europe are not just facing a problem of political failure. Everything is tied together. We are facing economic failure, epistemic failure, institutional failure, cultural failure, psychological failure, and moral failure. Liberalism is responsible in large part for these failures in every domain of our lives; its influence is much more pervasive than just politics.

Liberalism is undermining the foundations of America in many ways. First, the liberal elite places the growth of the State above that of the individual, striving to seize power and destroy anything that gets in the way of their power grab, be it religion, capitalism, the family, the Constitution, the rule of law, moral values, the vitality of individuality, or the role of reason and the pursuit of the truth. Second, liberalism is destroying our economy through reckless spending and debt, and destroying democracy as the size and scope of government expands, power is centralized, and the ruling class becomes more and more detached from the public. Third, liberalism is fixated on income redistribution. This nation was founded on the principle of equal opportunity for all, but liberalism strives instead for equal outcomes. In robbing Peter to pay Paul, the government gains power and influence in the distribution process, so it is in effect *complicit in legalized theft.* Fourth, liberalism prioritizes support for those who demand government services over those who contribute to society, encouraging a taker mentality. Fifth, it sacrifices the pursuit of truth for pursuit of agenda. Sixth, it leads to institutional bloat and bureaucracy, encouraging corruption and dependency. Seventh, conformity is prized over difference, so free speech and thought are stifled in the name of harmony and political correctness. Eighth, its means and modus operandi are inconsistent with achievement of its purported objectives.

Our country is at risk. The virus of liberalism that infected the USSR, despite its failures there and elsewhere, is threatening destruction here. We won the Cold War, but this is a disease from within, arising out of the human psyche. Unfortunately, the world created by Hume, Locke, Adam Smith and others—namely that of democracy—is in danger of destruction from within. China and Asian-type autocracies are likely to prevail. Unlike the Soviet Union, which failed because it couldn't achieve its goals, the American experiment is failing despite its successes, because of internal inconsistencies in its political make-up.

I remember visiting some of the former USSR countries in the early '90s. I was fascinated by the spectacle of people facing their world turned upside down. Everything they believed in and depended on was gone. Communism was defunct; their economic system was in disarray; they had been living a lie and were suddenly aware of it. They were taught that capitalism was bankrupt and America was evil, but suddenly discovered that it was communism and the USSR that were bankrupt and evil.

The same liberal ideas at the heart of communism's demise are at work now to bring about failure in the West. Liberalism, like communism, subscribes to a belief that an enlightened ruling elite has the knowledge, the expertise, the superior moral strength, and the wherewithal to bring about desired outcomes in the environment, the economy, society, and even in our psychological nature. And it dismisses God, nature, the accomplishments of the past, simply believing that through its enlightened wisdom and intervention it can force the world to conform to its wishes. Liberals don't want to deal with the world as it is, but rather impose their idea of reality on the world.

Liberals think they know best for everything and want to tinker and micromanage everything. Though they continually profess themselves egalitarians, liberals don't think the common man smart enough to lead his own life or even to know what is really in his own best interest. Liberals think they need to intervene to make the lives of the masses better. Liberalism is about control.

The outcome of the American experiment with capitalism may not seem that appealing to some given differences in income distribution and material well-being. Poverty still exists, but there is no question that America is the best country in the world in which to live, even for the poor. Liberals and those who criticize capitalism as unfair should look at countries that have tried to impose social justice, for example Cuba, Venezuela, the Soviet Union, and China. Almost everyone, including conservatives, would love to see a society in which everyone is well off; but the fact is you can't impose such outcomes from above without causing serious problems, including economic stagnation and a loss of liberty and social injustice. The bottom-up, invisible-hand approach of capitalism leads to a much better world. To abandon a system that has proven itself as the best in the world for systems with a historical record of dismal failure would border on criminal. It simply makes no sense.

Liberalism preaches compassion for the poor. Most of the world's population lives on only two dollars a day on the brink of starvation in uncertain and frightening conditions under brutal governments. There is no question that this is a serious problem that we should all be concerned about. The liberal feels he takes the high ground, and that anyone who opposes his policies is uncaring, immoral, and selfish. The problem is not that poverty is not universally recognized as a problem to be urgently dealt with. The problem is how to effectively address that problem. The liberal is at a loss here. He wraps himself in a cocoon of intentionality, believing that as long as his intentions are good, good results will naturally follow. He is unwilling to look at history and learn the lessons of the past about what works and what doesn't.

The issue is not whether we should help the less fortunate. All reasonable people agree on this. The issue is how to help them. The liberal approach is to expand government, throw money at the problem, redistribute wealth, increase government regulation, and toss aside equal treatment under the law. Fundamentally liberals want to turn our culture upside down. They don't like the materialistic nature of our culture or its competitive and self-interested psychology.

Of course, it's natural to want to be protected; to want a risk-free future; to desire income, wealth, and services without having to earn them or to have to work hard, and not to have to take on challenge and compete. Sloth and apathy beckon us all with their seductive call. Hard work, challenge, and risk are surely not the easy way, but they are the life-affirming way. All creatures and plants on this earth must struggle and fight to live. Man is no different. This is a fundamental point of difference between liberals and conservatives. Conservatives understand that struggle is an intrinsic part of life, whereas liberals do not see it that way. For them struggle can and should be eliminated. Sure, it sounds good not to have to worry, work hard, or meet challenges, but this is what life is all about, what makes it worth living. Liberals dream of a utopia without want and desire where we wouldn't work and where happiness would be delivered rather than earned. It's almost like they are striving for a semi-comatose state, an escape from life. Most of us in some way find it attractive to be looked after and provided for. But does it make more sense to entrust one's welfare to a responsible or irresponsible party? Would you want to entrust the welfare of a child to a drug addict or an irresponsible adult? As a citizen, does it make sense to entrust our welfare to politicians and big government? Do they have our best interest at heart? Is it not better to be responsible for one's own welfare than to be under the control of an irresponsible party? Government can't manage its own budget. Do we want it controlling our economic future?

The Left is continually trying to convince the public that they are the victims of concealed oppression which they describe as the hegemonic control of the current economic and social order. This is the guise under which the Left is trying to overthrow the current system. In any game, whether the game of life, chess, or baseball, there are going to be some who do better than others. Not winning does not mean failure or oppression. The real world is tough. The Left would effectively like to eliminate social and economic games and control the outcomes, making everyone the same. Only sameness and homogeneity would rule. There would be no winners and losers, so the incentive to succeed would be minimal. The quest for conformity would squash individuality.

Using the concept of oppression, the Left is saying if you lose the game, the rules need to be changed. The game must be unfair; it couldn't be you. But more importantly, is that not the purpose of a game to have winners and losers; to encourage people to interact positively and to foster individual effort and success?

The purpose of a game is to ensure fairness in play, giving all participants an equal chance at succeeding. It is not to ensure that all participants achieve the same outcome. Only in games of chance, where only luck and no skill is involved, would outcomes be expected to be the same over time. Liberalism seems to see the game of life like roulette or that of slot machines, not games which involve striving, effort, and skill. It's the latter type of game that leads to successful societies. Viewing society as a game of chance leads to a demoralized and debased society, devoid of morality and values. Even more ominous, under the Left's envisioned dream, an elite ruling class would determine in their discretion who the winners and losers would be. It's not hard to imagine the sycophancy and corruption that would surround such a system. Of course, just looking at the experience of the Soviet Union, we have an idea of what it might look like.

Liberalism is caught in a vortex of dysfunctionality; it derives its strength from dysfunctionality, so it seeks to create more, not less, of it. The purported purpose of liberalism is to help those unhappy with the current system and not faring well under it, but if it were in fact to fulfill its promises its reason for existence would vanish. Those in power behind the movement would lose their power and influence. This is why the liberal ruling elite don't care that their policies fail to help their supporters. This is why their poverty programs and education policies don't work. It is also why they don't care that they have not passed a comprehensive emigration bill. During Obama's first two years in office, the Democrats had the Presidency and both houses of Congress, so they could have passed an emigration bill, but they didn't, as this could have weakened their political support from the Hispanic community since they would no longer be needed. They want the issue alive, not resolved. Liberalism also undermines moral values and the education of the public, creating a greater need for government and strengthening their hold on power. Dependency is the life blood of liberalism, so liberalism is institutionally incentivized to create weakness and dependency. The ruling liberal class also is incentivized to create crises as this bolsters support from those unhappy with capitalism. Thus rather than trying to solve problems, liberalism has an incentive to make them worse.

This dynamic creates pernicious side effects. Given that liberal policies actually work against the interests of their supporters, they are forced to engage in deceit and dissimulation to maintain political support. This serves not only to undermine the moral climate, but also to reduce reliance on reason and dialogue. Given that they have something to hide, it is not surprising that the liberal ruling elite want to avoid dialogue and the light of reason.

Nation-states are the foundation on which Western democracies have built their success. Liberalism is destroying the nation-state through open immigration and disrespect for law. What is a nation if it's not defined by its citizens and their culture?

Aristotle recognized the threat of excessive immigration to a nation-state. A state without borders is not a state at all. Liberalism is trying to bring about the decline of nation-states in favor of rule and organization by transnational bodies. For liberals, an enhanced United Nations or supranational bodies like the EU are the way forward. Supranational bodies gut democracy in favor of bureaucracy and huge, distended government bodies with little or no accountability. Such bodies are infested with misguided efforts, nepotism, and corruption. They are notoriously ineffective, even counterproductive, yet the Left holds out this path as the way to their utopia.

Moral relativism is destroying the values that have underpinned our society and way of life. All values are said to be the same, none better than another. Morality is weakened. Social behavior is increasingly dysfunctional, and people are losing trust and confidence in one another. Liberals somehow overlook and condone the atrocities and oppression in countries like Afghanistan, Syria, Zimbabwe, and so on, but are outraged at "inequity" in America. It's one thing to recognize that different cultures have different values based on different contexts and different underlying views, conventions, and traditions, but this isn't grounds for abandoning all values. It's natural that different cultures should have different values, but it's important that citizens in each culture believe affirmatively in its own values. It's important to respect other cultures and values, but one should not allow one's own values to dissipate. Unfortunately, moral relativism today is used as an excuse to abandon all values. This corrodes the vitality and strength of our culture. It's important to believe in something. Without beliefs a culture corrodes from within. Cultures need to compete with one another so that those that serve the needs of people best replace those that don't. People should be allowed to choose.

It's of critical importance to keep religion separated from government, and the public sector out of the private sector. This has been a signal factor accounting for the success of Western democracies. Liberalism is weakening the influence of organized religion in American life, and the incursion of government into the private sector has increasingly become problematic. Moreover, as the State is weakening the grip of traditional religion, it's establishing the cult of government. Thus we are dealing with a double threat: first, a merging of government and religion, and second, increasing intrusion of the government into the private sector.

Liberalism is destroying not only the foundations of our economy, but our national security too. It's wreaking havoc on our economic system through excessive fiscal spending, debt accumulation, and stifling over-regulation of the private sector. As a bankrupt nation we can't afford the military that we've had in the past.

The threat of liberalism is all the more dangerous because it works through deceit. Its totalitarian and collectivist agenda is cloaked in democratic rhetoric, but it's really inimical to the traditions of democracy, liberty, and justice. Its face is benign, and its words sound beneficent and caring, but the undertow toward totalitarianism is powerful—and it threatens our way of life. Moreover, in the end liberalism would also destroy itself as its fundamental disconnect from reality is a recipe for chaos and inestimable misery.

The enemy from within can be a bigger threat than a foreign enemy. By cloaking its intentions and objectives, it isn't recognized as a threat. It's hard to fight something if it does not appear evil. Americans are trusting by nature and don't deal effectively with dissimulation and malefic intent.

During the Cold War, we recognized the threat from communism, both from the military and economic standpoints. Now that we have seen the Soviet Union's demise, we are lulled into viewing the threat of liberal thinking implicit in communism as dead, but it's very alive, despite having been discredited by history. It's like AIDS or cancer; you think you've put it into remission, but out it pops again, transmuted and just as dangerous as always.

The book is organized into two sections. In Section I, we begin by carefully identifying liberalism. The term is employed to mean so many different things that it's important to understand what we mean by *liberalism*. In this connection we will look at its objectives and goals, its basic motivations, perceptions and concepts. We will then examine the philosophic foundations of liberalism and how it differs from the liberalism of the eighteenth century. Chapters 4 and 5 will look at the role liberalism is playing in the decline of America in particular, but Western civilization too. Then, in Chapter 6, we will address the weaknesses and vulnerabilities of democracy that make liberalism especially lethal. Having established the perniciousness of liberalism, the book will turn its focus in the next section to the pillars and foundations of liberalism, and explain why the misconceptions underpinning liberalism are prefiguring its failure.

Specifically, in Section II, the book will seek to show how liberalism fails across the board. It fails the test of sound economics, the test of history, and in its understanding of institutions and the nature of man. It fails in the methodology by which it is applied and implemented. It tosses aside reason and the pursuit of truth, the foundations upon which civilization is built. And, despite its professions of commitment to a high moral and ethical plane, it is immoral in essence and effect. Its modus operandi—the ends justifies the means—is the antithesis of morality. It's a politics of false promises and deceit. Its concept of justice is fundamentally misguided and upside down. In short, it's flawed throughout, but this does not make it any less dangerous. We need to understand it if we are going to survive it.

* * *

SECTION I:

IDENTITY AND EFFECTS OF LIBERALISM

CHAPTER 2

THE IDENTITY OF LIBERALISM: ITS OBJECTIVES AND GOALS, BASIC MOTIVATIONS AND PERCEPTIONS AND CONCEPTS

———◆———

Tyranny seldom announces itself.

~Joseph Sobran

Liberalism seems to be related to the distance people are from the problem.
~Whitney M. Young

Liberalism is financed by the dividends of conservatism.
~Craig Bruce

A liberal is someone who feels a great debt to his fellow man; a debt he proposes to pay off with your money.
~Gordon Liddy

Liberalism in the eighteenth century during the period of the Enlightenment and the founding of Western democracies was a movement in support of individual rights and freedom against the tyranny and oppression of government. Conservatism during this period, on the other hand, supported the status quo and the power of the reigning authorities.

Today's liberalism, beginning in the twentieth century, has reversed these roles. Despite using the rhetoric of freedom and liberty, it is the party of big government. Although it speaks out in behalf of the little guy, minorities, and women, its method of operation is to address these issues by expanding the government at the expense of individual liberty. Conservatives, on the other hand, have become the party of the market, the defenders of capitalism, and the traditions and rights that originally underpinned American society.

Liberalism was and is the political philosophy of change. It opposed the monarchical and authoritarian governments of the eighteenth century and in the end succeeded in replacing them with democracies based on individual rights and freedom. Now, however, it's militating against the democratic values and traditions it helped create, instead advancing a tyranny of collectivism. What we call a *liberal* today is very different than the liberal of the eighteenth century, but they would have you believe otherwise. Not even many liberals really understand the true nature of today's liberalism. Its dissimulation has beguiled our culture into dropping its immunologic defenses, and this virulent mutation of liberalism is growing like a cancer, metastasizing, and systematically destroying all that has made this country great.

To clarify the identity of today's liberalism it's useful to contrast it with the liberalism of the eighteenth century, which is known as *classical liberalism,* or what we now call *conservatism.* The schema below does this with regards to policy objectives and defining features.

POLICY: CONTRAST BETWEEN LIBERALISM AND CONSERVATISM

Today's Liberalism	Conservatism (eighteenth-century liberalism)
Top-down management of economy	Economy driven by the markets and the invisible hand
Expanded role for government	Limited government
Redistribution of income and bailouts	Reliance on individual initiative and hard work
Belief in transnational government	Nation-states
Government regulation	Limited regulation
Anti-business	Pro-corporation
Weak foreign policy (only carrot)	Strong projection of foreign policy (both carrot and stick)
Weak approach to law enforcement	Assertive law enforcement
Political correctness	Unconstrained freedom of speech and thought

DEFINING FEATURES: CONTRAST BETWEEN LIBERALISM AND CONSERVATISM

Liberalism	Conservatism
Rule by the elite	Reliance on the commonsense of the public
Reliance on arbitrary discretion	Reliance on system, the market, rule of law
Monistic, noncompetitive	Binary, belief in Hegelian dialectic, back and forth argument
Responsibility resides with the State; no individual responsibility	Individual responsibility
Managed freedom	Individual freedom
Collectivistic	Atomistic
Compassion-driven	Reason-based
Helping hand, subsidies and bailouts	Incentive-based
Equality of outcome	Equality of opportunity
Emotion-driven	Pragmatic
Idealistic	Grounded in reality
Teleological (goal-driven)	Process-driven
Agenda-driven	System- and rule-based
Perfectible human nature	Flawed human nature

The ideological approach of liberals is grounded in a collective mentality and the role of the State. This contrasts with conservatives who emphasize the individual. Liberal political philosophy is organic, placing the whole above the parts, whereas conservative political philosophy is atomistic, placing the individual or parts above the whole. Given the different starting points, it's not surprising that liberals and conservatives arrive at vastly different conclusions, and that they have difficulty conducting political discourse with one another.

Whereas conservatives are concerned with policy outcomes and efficacy, the focus of liberals is on the moral content and objectives of policy, not on the outcome of policy. Liberalism is based on an emotional venting and a sonorous public expression of intentionality, rather than on the exercise of reason. Liberals don't want to look at why liberal policies and programs fail, only why they are needed.

Liberal perspectives are emotion-based, while conservatives are disposed toward formulating thoughts on the basis of reason. The liberal mantra is "Because we care," as if others don't. They are saying *we feel your pain, sympathize, and empathize.* Because they care, they assume the moral high ground. Anyone opposing them is considered immoral, uncaring, and deserving scorn. Their fight is a moral fight, not a rational one.

Somehow liberals think that caring about some abstract goal is in and of itself enough. Liberals love to assume righteousness, saying, "We care," but they don't care about the analytics or the actual consequences of what they espouse. Even during the Cold War, when the Soviet Union and China were brutalizing their citizens, many liberals continued to espouse the virtues of communism. That communism's purported goal was to improve the plight of the masses was enough for liberals. The fact that these governments murdered and deprived their citizens of basic rights like free speech and thought did not deter liberals. That the citizens of these countries were willing to risk their lives to escape to the West also did not phase the liberal mind.

Liberals believe in big government, whereas conservatives see big government as a problem. Liberals are idealistic, while conservatives are pragmatic. Liberals talk in high-flown moral terms, while conservatives are grounded and reality-based. Liberals talk in universals, while conservatives are interested in the particular and pragmatic.

Liberalism is teleological. It's oriented toward an end goal, namely the redistribution of income and moving the economy away from capitalism. Conservatism, on the other hand, is process-driven: it's concerned with how we conduct ourselves and live day-to-day, rather than focusing on some abstract end goal. For liberals, the ends justify the means, whereas conservatives emphasize the means. Liberalism has a linear and progressive sense of history versus the cyclical sense of the ancient Greeks.

Liberals are focused on equality of outcomes for all people. Conservatives, on the other hand, believe in equality of opportunity.

Liberals are not strong adherents of the rules of the game or of law, whereas conservatives are. For liberals laws and rules of the game are viewed as oppressive and so are to be circumvented. Conservatives, on the other hand, think the rules of the game and the rule of law are the glue that holds our way of life together.

A fundamental difference between liberals and conservatives is their view of human nature. Liberals think people are good and perfectible, while conservatives believe man is fundamentally flawed and imperfectable. Thus, liberals are against restraint and control. They are preoccupied with the "toxicity of affect control and inhibition," and so favor "openness and tolerance for intrusions of the irrational, of the Dionysian."[1] The conservative, on the other hand, viewing human nature as flawed, sees the "importance of controlling affects in the interest of morality, achievement, piety."[2] Given this view, conservatives stress the role that should be played by rules and norms, whereas liberals bristle at the mere thought of rules and norms.

Liberals can't resist goals attached to overarching good intentions. Save the planet! Who can oppose that? Of course their policies would do no such thing, but this is irrelevant to liberals. Why are liberals focused on green policies? It is a means by which to expand the size and scope of government. They would impose onerous carbon taxes to feed government and impose regulatory controls reaching deep into yet another key sector of the economy.

Liberals support green policies and the environmentalist agenda. Their environmental policies restrict drilling, coal emissions, and new nuclear projects, resulting in curtailment of supply, engendering energy insecurity, and high energy prices. Their proposal for dealing with energy independence and the environment is conservation and the development of new energy technologies, but this can at best have a limited effect and adversely affects growth. Conservatives recognize the need to limit damage to the environment, but believe that oil, coal, and nuclear energy should be developed while we wait for green technologies efficient enough to meet our energy needs.

Liberals claim they want proper education for everyone, but support the current inefficient system and the teachers' unions. They oppose vouchers and charter schools. Conservatives support vouchers and charter schools; they recognize that the current system is not working and believe that experimentation and competition will improve education.

Liberals throw around the word *fairness* instead of using reason. Who can be against fairness? They want to make a world fair that is not fair. *Life* is not fair. Conservatives recognize that the world involves struggle, adversity, and unfairness.

Liberalism, like communism, is against family and religion, anything that supports the current system gets in the way of the expansion of State power. They want to bring about the demise of capitalism and America as we know it. Their god is the State. For conservatives, family and religion are very important.

Liberals think the free market economy overproduces luxury goods and private goods, but undersupplies basic goods. To them, public goods are undervalued. Conservatives, on the other hand, believe in the private sector, in allowing people to decide for themselves what goods they want.

Liberals believe government regulation is the cure for all problems. They believe that government oversight and regulation works, even though experience shows this is folly. For them, business people are only after money and are not to be trusted. Conservatives oppose regulation and government interference in the private sector.

Liberals believe in the decline of the nation states. They don't believe that the world should be broken up into nation-states. They are globalists. They think that multinational corporations are too powerful and are not controlled by anyone. They have a distrust of business and corporations, really of anything and anyone with money. In contrast conservatives highly value the nation state.

Liberalism subscribes to moral relativism. It's negative, trying to take apart and diminish existing values. It has nothing to replace existing values except moral relativism, which provides no real guideposts at all. Conservatism, on the other hand, puts values at the core of its philosophy.

Liberals are continually touting political correctness over free speech, while conservatives adhere to the latter as a fundamental right. Liberals literally shout down conservatives like Ann Coulter, with whom they disagree.[3] They only want to hear themselves.[4] If you can only say certain things, namely those things that are not offensive to the majority—or for that matter to anyone—do you really have free speech? If the government can determine what you can and can't say, is this free speech? Is this not what has happened to our First Amendment rights? Another cornerstone of individual liberty has been slyly removed through the forces of liberalism.

Once you can't say certain things, this spreads quickly, and soon you can't even think certain things, and then the "*Thought Police*" have accomplished their objective. Liberals in congress during the Obama Administration were pushing for the Fairness Doctrine, with the objective of creating a "fair" division of news coverage over the radio and television. For years, of course, including during Obama's campaign, liberals have never been concerned about the strong and obvious liberal bias in the media, particularly in newspapers and television news. However, with the success of conservatives on AM radio and the Fox News Channel, suddenly they *are* interested in intervening in the coverage. The SEC Chairman was quoted on December 7th, 2010, saying that the Federal Government should look closely at whether to renew the news licenses of channels that could be considered to have offended public sensitivities. Numerous Democrats, including Jay Rockefeller of West Virginia, also called for shutting down Fox News. The administration was considering trying to go the administrative or regulatory route, since passing legislation to muffle the media seemed increasingly unlikely. What offends one person may not offend another. Who decides what is offensive? The government?

Liberalism professes support for overarching principles—even though they are eternally looking for exceptions and dispensations for their favored groups—versus conservatives, who tout overarching principles and rules that are meant to apply to everyone equally.

Liberals believe in selective justice versus the rule of law. A free society works best under the rule of law, a rule of law that limits the actions of government according to general principles and treats everyone and all situations equally. This is problematic for liberalism, as it limits the government's arbitrary exercise of power. It makes it hard for them to help their friends and penalize those in opposition. This is why liberalism is constantly working to erode the rule of law in favor of a more flexible and discretionary system that accords government the scope to decide what is best. They favor discretionary action over the rule of law, although they won't admit it overtly (for example, immigration law and affirmative action in the Ricci Supreme Court case regarding firefighters in Massachusetts).[5] Over time liberalism works to find exceptions to the rule of law to move toward their goals. This starts out as change around the fringes and minor modifications, but the cumulative effect over time undermines the rule of law and replaces it with the rule of men. This, of course, is completely antithetical to the survival of freedom and the thoughts and principles that guided the Founding Fathers.

Liberals favor affirmative action where justice is dispensed by court, not law. They also see the Constitution as an interpretative document. They see it as a living document subject to the reading of jurists. Liberals don't like the Constitution because it's dedicated to stipulating what the government should not do, circumscribing the government's action and ambition.

Liberals have difficulty connecting to reality. Questions are the best way to try to get liberals to connect to reality, but even this approach usually fails. The trouble is they always revert back to their stock answers and mantras. For example, you can get them to admit that there is a fiscal deficit and debt problem, but they will then invariably say that we need all of the entitlement benefits we currently have and need even more. If you ask them if they are concerned about too much government intervention in the lives of people, they will say yes, but they don't draw the connection that an expansion in the role of government will mean just this. If you ask them if they think government is more efficient than the private sector, they will say no, but it does not register that expanded government will mean reduced overall efficiency and economic growth.

Who are the liberals?

Most liberals are wonderful people. There is nothing wrong with being idealistic and wanting to help other people. This is an essential part of our humanity. The problem is that liberalism takes advantage of this good nature and uses it for bad purposes. Today's liberalism, as mentioned, uses the language of Enlightenment liberalism, talking of freedom, liberty, and the advancement of individuality, but it is destructive of all three. While liberalism professes compassion and says it is all about helping others, it actually is about power and leaves those they say they are trying to help worse off. While many liberals are good-natured and well-intentioned, they are infected with an ideological disease which is working to harm the entire community. Good and kind people are all the time afflicted with diseases like yellow fever, whooping cough, the flu and the common cold, so it is not surprising that good people can be carriers of evil ideas as well as bad diseases. In the 20th century well-intentioned people were afflicted with the collectivist ideologies of fascism and communism which resulted in catastrophic and massive misery. In today's world the collectivist ideology of liberalism has hijacked the good intentions and idealism of people for ill purposes. Indeed it is interesting and ironic that liberalism works to bring misery upon the world, primarily by tapping the energies of good, well-intentioned people. Of course, it plays off unhealthy emotions as well, but it could not survive without the support of good people.

The politicians are at the top of the liberal ruling class. They are trying to convince the masses that they are for them, but their real interest is in the accumulation of power. The ruling class is trying to take control and is out to advance its position of power and wealth. The political elite, the establishment politicians like Charlie Christ of Florida and Murkowski of Alaska, can't give up power. They work to keep their jobs rather than work in the interest of all Americans.

The intelligentsia and academia are heavily liberal and play a key role in supporting the ruling class. Some of them are in fact part of the ruling class. The intelligentsia and academics have never adjusted to the realities of the world, never had a real job, and they disdain business as something beneath them. Of course, they wouldn't have their jobs if others did not create jobs and generate wealth so that their children could go to university, but they don't recognize this, much less appreciate it.

Some have spoken of "an alliance between experts and victims." Experts gain if there are others who cannot control their lives and need assistance. Experts can enhance their power and financial well-being as they take control of the lives of others and place themselves in the role of decision maker. The intelligentsia see themselves as smarter than lay people. There is a sense of elitism and a longing to control and manage the outside world which are very much the markings of those in the liberal movement. For them the world should be different than it is. This alliance between experts and victims is a marriage that empowers both the intelligentsia and those seeking assistance from others.

In the '60s when I went to school, the object of a university education was to teach students to think for themselves and to pursue independent inquiry to wherever that may take them. The liberal establishment has taken over universities so that independent inquiry is no longer fostered—it's discouraged. The liberal establishment now tries to inculcate the young with liberal dogma and politically correct thinking, which is not thinking at all but rather intellectual servitude. Students and teachers who voice opinions or pose countervailing arguments are harshly dealt with. There is little to no tolerance in the liberal community for any thoughts that are not consonant with theirs. This is why it's amusing to hear liberals so often talking about the need for tolerance. They have none, but they are always trying to cast those who are trying to use reason or independent inquiry as intolerant. They prefer to hide in their ivory towers, theorizing and proselytizing.

The media is also an important part of the liberal establishment. They get to participate in the power game by allying themselves with the politicians. They join the politicians in trying to control the perceptions of the masses. Like academia, the media also looks askance at the business world. They are not part of it, have never understood it, and have a certain envy of it as it's where wealth is created. The media should be fulfilling their role as the fourth estate, protecting the Constitution, but instead they are out to advance themselves and improve their own positions to the detriment of the rest of the citizenry, including the consumer and other labor.

You also have those who benefit directly from government spending and the give-away programs of the liberal establishment. These are the poor, the disadvantaged, labor unions, lawyers, government sector workers, the inside-the-beltway contractors of Washington, large businesses with big government contracts, and others who vote their self-interest over the general welfare.

There are also those who benefit from government regulatory policy and influence on the judiciary. This includes big businesses. Most small businesses don't have the influence to benefit from government regulatory activity and hence in most instances are hurt by it. Liberal influence on the judiciary benefits mostly minority groups, like blacks and the gay community, and those who in general prefer to see the rule of law diminished and bent to serve their interests. Lawyers, bureaucrats, legislators, and lobbyists are also beneficiaries of a complex legal and regulatory environment.

Liberalism also has the following supporters: African-Americans who vote en masse for a Party that has them entrapped in dependency; youth voting out of ignorance for fiscal policies that will destroy their future; those wanting to consume beyond their means; the disgruntled who blame the "system" for their failure; immigrants fleeing tyranny and bad economic circumstances at home, but voting to create it in their refuge country; those who dislike this country, believing it to be unfair, racist, materialistic, and imperialistic; those misinformed by the media and the uninformed; and those who want only the benefits of liberty, not the responsibilities.

Then there are those who support the liberal agenda, not out of self-interest, but out of sympathy with the liberal call for compassion. This group votes out of good intentions: they swallow the liberal line that they are out to help others, particularly the disadvantaged. They don't understand that the policies espoused by liberals really hurt the groups they claim to help.

A prominent constituent of this group is the Jewish community, who are hurt by liberal policies, but vote out of good intentions. It should be noted that since 1928 Democratic presidential candidates have on average attracted 75 percent of the Jewish vote.[6] Norman Podhoretz, a well-known Jewish pundit, has offered some views as to why Jews vote for liberals.[7] Perhaps in the past when Jews felt like a minority, Jewish support for liberal politics was consistent with their own interests, but this is no longer the case. The Jewish community votes overwhelmingly for Democrats and liberals for a variety of reasons. They have a deep sympathy with human rights and a tendency to associate with underdogs, perhaps on account of their own history. The Jewish community also had a strong affection for FDR, because he helped defeat the Nazis in World War II and hence helped save millions of Jewish lives. The Jews also have a long history of sympathy with socialism. The Jewish community is highly educated, so perhaps their exposure to institutions of higher learning, which are highly liberal, has contributed to this thinking. The Jewish people also are a generous and charitable people. They are compassionate and caring. Also liberalism trades in feelings of guilt and for some reason guilt plays a strong role in Jewish culture and family life.

What is remarkable, however, is not that a large number of Jews support liberal causes and candidates, but that the preponderance is so large. It's almost like the Jewish community votes as a block. In this connection I think there is momentum from their past alliance with the Democratic Party and liberal causes. Also the Jews are quite a tight-knit and cohesive community so this may explain why they vote in such unanimity. Jews may find groupthink appealing because it enhances their social cohesion, which is important to them.

Liberals and Conservatives are Different

As mentioned in the introduction, liberals and conservatives have trouble understanding one another. It's like each is living in different worlds with different realities, speaking different languages. As

Groucho Marx once said, "We have all been created the same except for Democrats and Republicans." These differences will be more fully dealt with later in the book, but let's take a brief look at some of the evidence underlying these differences, including evidence on the role played by brain structure and personality.

Brain Structure

Genetics and biology may play an important role in determining political stance. A study conducted by Ryota Kanai of the University College of London found differences in brain structure between liberals and conservatives. The study, based on MRI scans, found liberals have a larger anterior cingulate cortex, a part associated with decision-making, while conservatives have a larger amygdala region, which scientists associate with emotional learning and addressing fear.[8]

Also in October 2005, a study by Neuropolitics found evidence supporting the right-hemispheric cognitive style of liberalism. Conservatives, on the other hand, were found to have left-side-cognitive dominance. The right-side of the brain plays a larger role with emotions, and the left-side with reasoning. The study also found that left-side hemispheric dominance is associated with binary models of morality involving good and evil.[9]

In addition, the Neuropolitics's study found support for the feminine leanings of liberalism: "Conservatives and liberals vary, on average, in their testosterone-estrogen ratios, with conservative males higher on the testosterone side, and conservative females higher on the estrogen side. This means that the liberal females and males are closer to each other in their testosterone-estrogen ratios, and the conservatives further apart."[10]

When I first began to delve into neuroscientific research, I was frankly shocked by these findings. They're more than a bit scary. Care, however, must be exercised in evaluating these studies. Caution is required in looking at studies analyzing personality differences on account of the wide array of different definitions for liberalism and conservatism. In addition, the studies don't tell us whether brain structure determines political disposition or whether political disposition determines brain structure. It's natural, for example, for brain development to follow the needs and stresses put on it by individuals. One who spends a lot of time and energy writing poetry will find his brain develop differently than someone focusing on mathematics. Also, the studies are not categorical, for example, suggesting that *all* conservatives are left-brain oriented and *all* liberals right-brain oriented; the findings merely find a significant correlation, not an all-encompassing one. In conclusion there is no sound basis for concluding that genetics or our biological make-up predestine or prefigure whether we will become liberal or conservative. Nevertheless, even if the chain of causation does not run from genetics to political disposition, the fact remains that difference in brain structure and function may make the chasm between liberals and conservatives that much more difficult to bridge.

Personality

Personality has been found by numerous studies to be a strong factor determining political disposition. A recent study concluded broadly that liberals are more given to openness; conservatives to conscientiousness. According to this study, "Liberals are more open-minded in their pursuit of creativity, novelty, and diversity, whereas conservatives lead lives that are more orderly, conventional, and better organized."[11]

Moreover, this study also surveyed the literature and found the following additional differences between the personality traits of liberals and conservatives: liberals are ambiguous, life-loving, unpredictable, creative, imaginative, excited, sensation-seeking, uncontrolled, slovenly, complex, impulsive, and inclined toward novelty and diversity. Conservatives are tough, masculine, reliable, trustworthy, stable, consistent, careful, practical, methodical, self-controlled, moralistic, simple, conscientious, and concerned with rules and norms.[12]

The results concerning openness and conscientiousness were corroborated by a study of five European countries (Italy, Spain, Germany, Greece, and Poland). Openness—meaning curious, original, intellectual, creative, and open to new ideas—was associated with liberal temperament, and conscientiousness—meaning organized, systematic, punctual, achievement-oriented, and dependable—was linked to conservative behavior.[13]

Another study by the University of Nebraska found that liberals tended to be more attentive in following the gaze of others than was the case for conservatives. This is suggestive of the herd-like tendencies displayed by many liberals and the penchant for autonomy displayed by conservatives.[14]

Liberals are idealistic and emotion-driven, whereas conservatives recognize the complexity of issues and hence are pragmatic and cautious and disposed toward careful and rational analysis before committing to an action. Liberals in particular find appeal in the idealism of the young. Conservatives, cognizant of the failures of previous idealistic experiments, are resistant to any change that is not carefully thought out and does not take into account historical precedence.

Daniel Kahneman won a Nobel Prize in 2002 for his neuroscientific research which emphasized different dispositions towards thinking. Last year Kahneman published a book, *Thinking, Fast and Slow*, making the case that we have two basic modalities of thinking. Fast thinking is intuitive, while slow thinking is deliberative; fast thinking is spontaneous, while slow thinking is cautious; fast thinking is easy and without strain, while slow thinking is arduous; fast thinking is almost automatic, while slow thinking involves a sense of control; and fast thinking almost arises from the subconscious, while slow thinking takes place more at the conscious level of the mind. Studies are not available showing the breakdown of fast versus slow thinking regarding political disposition, but based on the other studies cited, indicating less commitment to a rational approach for liberals, it would seem that liberals would probably fall more into the fast thinking classification, whereas conservatives would fall into the slow thinking category.

Liberals are loners according to a study by Drs. Storm and Wilson. According to this study, liberal teenagers felt more stressed than conservatives, especially when it came to deciding with whom to spend time. The liberal teenagers were also loners, spending more time alone than the conservative teenagers. In addition, the study found that the conservatives preferred the company of relatives to non-relatives, whereas the liberals were neutral.[15]

Another difference between liberals and conservatives is that liberals tend to live in urban areas with high population density, while conservatives prefer rural areas with more open space. Conservatives have a preference for territory associated with testosterone and family and child-rearing. High testosterone is generally thought to boost territorial requirements and enhance defensive behavior too. Strong family ties and bonds between members of the group are characteristic in rural, conservative areas. On the other hand, in cities, personal connections are shallower, more transient, commoditized, and distant. Liberals are inclusive and flexible, welcoming people from outside their immediate ethnic group and group of friends, while conservatives are most comfortable with family and friends.[16]

Conservatives have also been found to be more polite, according to a recent study in the University of Toronto Magazine. The study suggests that conservatives' concern for politeness is consistent with their respect for authority and preference for order and tradition. It may also explain why after Tea Party rallies the grounds are clean, almost in the condition they were before the rally, whereas liberal rallies are tumultuous affairs, given to ventings of rage and sometimes violence, and leave a tremendous mess afterwards. This is not surprising because liberals don't like authority and feel uncomfortably constrained by tradition and order.[17]

Liberals even watch different television shows than conservatives. According to a study by the media research company Experian Simmons, the favorite television programs of Democrats are *Madmen*, *Dexter*, *Breaking Bad*, and *30 Rock*, while the favorite programs of Republicans are *Glenn Beck*, *American Idol*, and *The Office*. The programs favored by Democrats feature troubled people: these shows try to look at the better sides of the troubled. They focus on understanding troubled people, not seeing them as simply bad. Contrast this with the programs favored by Republicans, which focus on family and relationships, the past and prospects for this country, and achievement and competition, like *American Idol* and *Dancing with the Stars*. While liberals focus on failed individuals, elitists, and criminals, conservatives direct their interest to achievement, reality shows, competition, relationships, and the Glenn Beck program, which looks at the history of this country and concerns itself with our traditions. Liberals are also into crime-procedural shows like *Law and Order* and shows of interest to women. Liberals are involved in feel-bad shows, while conservatives are involved in feel-good shows. Perhaps it's not surprising that liberals are into feel-bad shows because most want society changed because they aren't happy with it.[18]

Conservatives and liberals even have different sleep behavior and disposition toward dreaming. In his book, *American Dreamers: What Dreams Tell Us about the Political Psychology of Conservatives, Liberals, and Everyone Else*, Kelly Bulkeley found that conservatives tended to sleep relatively soundly and not have many dreams, whereas liberals tended to be "troubled sleepers and expansive dreamers."[19] He also found that religious people slept better and had fewer dreams than non-religious people.

There is also significant evidence that liberals and conservatives think differently about morality. Jonathan Haidt in his work on political psychology, focusing on the moral roots of liberals and conservatives, concluded that liberals base their morality on only two moral foundations: harm/care and fairness/reciprocity, while conservatives base their moral philosophy on all five foundations, including also in-group/loyalty, authority/respect, and purity/sanctity. Liberal psychology is distinctively more feminine in nature than conservative or libertarian psychology, according to Haidt.[20] Liberals focus selectively on fairness: it's a one-dimensional, narrow-minded obsession. Liberal morality will be discussed more fully in Chapter 15 (on the immorality of liberalism), but it is clear that a difference in moral values can translate into very real political differences.

Democrats and Republicans tend to have friends who share their political perspectives. According to a study by Huckfeldt and Sprague, about two out of three friends for both Democrats and

Republicans shared their political views. This is also apparent in the political map, where defined "Red States" and "Blue States" appear clustered with like-minded people.[21]

Since personality traits are established early in life, one's political disposition is likely also determined early in life. Numerous prominent psychologists, including Freud, have found that personality is determined early in life, perhaps even by genetics. This has also been validated by several recent empirical studies. In this connection the American Political Science Review presented a study in 2005 looking at identical and non-identical twins that found "political attitudes are influenced much more heavily by genetics than by parental socialization." In addition, the Journal of Research in Personality in 2006 contained a study examining the political disposition of twenty-three-year-olds who had been subjected to psychological examination in nursery school. The study concluded that the personalities of the twenty-three-year-olds were similar to what they had been in nursery school and were an excellent predictor of political disposition.[22]

* * *

CHAPTER 3

THE PHILOSOPHIC FOUNDATIONS AND NATURE OF TODAY'S LIBERALISM

———

Liberalism is totalitarianism with a human face.
~**Thomas Sowel**

So what are the philosophic origins of the liberalism-progressivism of today? What are its connections to fascism, socialism, and communism? How does it differ from the conservative and libertarian political philosophies?

Today's liberalism-progressivism, as mentioned, is almost the total opposite of the classical liberalism that was instrumental in setting up our country. Unlike the early liberalism of our history, the liberalism of today puts the individual in subordination to the State. It's all about government and planning. It has much in common with socialism and communism, and fascism too. Many on the Left have tried to make the argument that fascism is really a product of conservatism, but, as we shall see, its nature is fundamentally connected to today's liberalism. Some writers, most notably Jonah Goldberg, have documented in detail the close connection of today's liberalism to fascism.[23] I find myself in accord with Goldberg, but feel that today's liberalism is even more closely akin to the liberalism of Rousseau during the French Revolution.

I have always found it difficult to make sense of the liberal position. Perhaps this difficulty arises from the divergent origins of Western democracies: the French and the British philosophic traditions. Both are very much intertwined in the origins of our democracy, so there is a tendency to mix the two, but they are very different in character. The British philosophic tradition tends to enhance liberty and promote atomistic, laissez-faire societies, while the French tradition limits individual liberty and fosters collectivistic tendencies. The French tradition is inclined to socialistic and totalitarian democracies where the role of the individual is sharply curtailed and circumscribed.

In the French rationalist tradition, liberalism is utopian in character. In this tradition there is an abiding faith in the powers of rationalism, in the power of reason. In their view the human mind can shape institutions and civilization. Society is best when it's organized from above through the power of reason. Hence they believe society should be highly organized and that the government should play a large role. They believe in a society of government interference. It is doctrinaire and collectivist and goal-oriented, with the intent to shape both the nature of human individuals as well as institutions. Individual freedom is seen as anarchic, chaotic, and in need of control and shaping. It's not valued, but deprecated.

This contrasts sharply with the British tradition of liberalism, which is not top-down, but bottom-up. According to this tradition, liberty is a by-product of the growth of institutions and established traditions. This growth and evolution of institutions is not planned, but develops naturally under certain conditions and traditions. It appears as a helter-skelter process, but is guided by half understood forces and the invisible hand of the market. Government interference generally results in untoward outcomes in this model, as we do not fully understand the forces that we are seeking to control. Institutional development proceeds due to Darwinian laws of competition, trial and error, and relational strength, not by the design of the elite or empowered bureaucrats.

This approach to liberty is deeply unsettling to those who subscribe to the French rationalist tradition. These people think they must control their life and their future. They feel they are smarter than the natural laws and forces of societal and economic development. Elitism and arrogance are very much a part of this tradition of liberalism.

It's interesting, however, and difficult to understand how the liberals of the French tradition, who subscribe so strongly to the power of human reason to shape society and civilization from above, abandon it when it comes to discussion of policy issues in actual day-to-day policy management. This perhaps explains why the French Revolution dissolved into a reign of terror under Robespierre, whereas in England the foundations were already laid for an individualist democracy. The French liberal tradition, despite professing allegiance to reason, allowed emotion to take control. They seemed completely unbound from empirical evidence and history. There is a distinctly anti-empiricist stamp on the character of this tradition. It was all untested and ungrounded. Liberals don't want to be bound by the real world or by empiricism.

Perhaps it's this divergence in perspectives and underlying assumptions that has made serious discourse between liberals and conservatives all but impossible. The French liberals want to be unbound by empiricism, reality, and history. They want to soar, to follow their aspirations, to impose their view of reality on the world. They think they have the power and intelligence to do it. But their views place a heavy emphasis on interference and curtailment of individual liberty

The French approach places too much faith in the power of the government to change society, even to manage it. They do not see the virtues of the current arrangements and do not appreciate the contributions of the past. They are willing to cavalierly toss aside all that has been done in the past, however successful, for what they think might be an improvement.

They're overly impressed with their own abilities and perspectives. They think that they know better than all who have gone before them as to what is best. They readily dismiss the past. They think that the times too are different, which, indeed, is true, but still we are connected to the past. To disconnect from it too readily is at our own peril.

In the United States it was the English form of liberalism which took hold and played a pivotal role in the construction of our democracy. In the twentieth century, beginning with the presidencies of Teddy Roosevelt and Woodrow Wilson, the French tradition began to assert itself and has grown at the expense of the English tradition ever since.

Although a Republican in name, Teddy Roosevelt had a profound distrust of free markets and big business and expressed on numerous occasions his dislike for the wealthy. He favored heavy government supervision of business, the creation of universal health care and universal health insurance, as well as a program much like the Social Security program later put in place by FDR. In the 1960s LBJ advanced this agenda further, passing a massive anti-poverty program and introducing Medicare.

All of these liberal presidents believed the Constitution was too constraining and sought ways to see it amended more easily and interpreted more liberally. They were opposed to strict interpretation of the Constitution. FDR even tried to pack the Supreme Court to get his way with the Judicial Procedures Reform Bill of 1937. He tried to expand the number of justices by up to *six* new justices, who, of course, would be picked by him and do his bidding. Fortunately his attempt failed, but liberal-progressives have ever since sought to scuttle the Constitution by appointing liberal judges who agree that the document is outdated and in need of liberal interpretation.

During World War I, Woodrow Wilson helped pass the Espionage Act and the Sedition Act, which made free speech, to the extent that it was against the war, a crime. In effect the First Amendment was tossed aside and many were arrested for voicing opposition to the war. Likewise, FDR imprisoned many Japanese-Americans during World War II.

Rousseau played a primary role in the development of French political philosophy during the Enlightenment. In Rousseau's earlier works, he had accorded individual liberty primacy. For example, in *The Origin of Inequality* he introduced his now well-known notion of the noble savage. "Men in a state of nature do not know good and evil, but only their independence and this along with the peacefulness of their passions, and their ignorance of vice, prevents them from doing ill." With the growth of civilization and the development of institutions, individual liberty was suppressed. In *On the Social Contract*, Rousseau encapsulated this view with the statement: "Man is born free; and everywhere he is in chains." He went on, however, in *On the Social Contract* to subordinate individual freedom to that of the "general will."

The French Enlightenment form of liberalism was organic and collectivist. Rousseau was the chief exponent of this philosophy, most succinctly expressed in his notion of the *general will.* Rousseau was clear that the general will is not just an aggregation of individual wills; in instances where the general will is in conflict with individual wills, Rousseau declared that the former should prevail. In such circumstances, Rousseau said, the individual should "be forced to be free" so as to be in conformity with the general will. In *On the Social Contract,* Rousseau said, "The less relation the particular wills have to the general will, that is, morals and manners to laws, the more should the repressive force be increased."[24] Such a constrained notion of freedom is of course completely antithetical to the British tradition and concept of liberty.

In *On the Social Contract,* Rousseau wrote, "Each of us puts his person and all his power in common under the supreme direction of the general will, and, in our corporate capacity, we receive each member as an indivisible part of the whole."[25] The whole is given clear primacy over the sum of the parts.

Like the French genre of liberalism, today's progressive-liberal movement has the germ of collectivism firmly embedded in its core. *Á la* Rousseau the individual is placed in subordinance to the collective. There is an abiding faith in the State. The role and power of the government should be expanded, and it should exercise almost complete control over social and economic developments. Today's liberal subscribes to government planning, not the invisible hand of the market.

Rousseau distrusted the masses and their capacity for self-government through a representative democracy. Like the liberalism of today, he saw the essential need for elite rule. This is highlighted in Rousseau's words in *On the Social Contract*: "How can a blind multitude, which often does not know what it wills, because it rarely knows what is good for it, carry out for itself so great and difficult an enterprise as a system of legislation?"[26] This stands in sharp contrast to the British liberal tradition, which held an abiding faith in the individual to conduct his life and participate constructively in the democratic process.

This is a dangerous notion: that people don't know what is best for them, that a certain more-knowing elite knows what is best for others and is entitled—indeed obligated—to see that they do what the ruler deems best. Coercion, even violence, is appropriate where necessary. This is nothing but despotism, although purportedly benevolent despotism. However, how is one to discern whether it is in fact benevolent or malevolent? Rousseau tried valiantly and elaborately to argue that this is not an encroachment on individual liberty, but the contradiction is manifest. Rousseau's liberalism is similar to today's liberalism also in that he was a populist. He railed against the rich and the powerful. The ruling class he saw as oppressors. Yet Rousseau, like liberals of today, had no faith in the ability of the masses to know what is in their own best interest. It's not surprising that he believed rule by an elite class was necessary.

The modern resemblance to the French liberal tradition is also striking as it regards the role of reason. Like the former it purports to put reason on a pedestal, but in fact pretermits and diminishes it. Rousseau distrusted cold logic and the counsel of the so-called learned class. For both Rousseau and the modern-day liberal, morality and spirit offer better guidance than rationality. Certain people just know instinctively what is right and wrong and, fortunately, at least in their view, most of us can recognize those with this capacity.[27]

Rousseau's democracy and that of today's liberal are idealistic, not pragmatic or rational. Good intentions are enough for them. That liberal policies, whether small or large, have an unambiguous empirical and historical track record of failure does not concern them. Certainly the inefficacy of its policies has not in any way prompted them to consider policy modification.

Rousseau recognized that the general will could only be adequately put in place if there were not factions or associations within society that had their own interests at heart. At first glance this appears to contrast sharply with the liberalism of today which is based on division and identity politics. But this is merely a short-term expedient liberals are using to gain power. In the medium-to-long term, liberalism is very much consistent with Rousseau regarding factions. This is why liberalism puts strong emphasis on achieving conformity, repressing reason, and squelching opposing views. The founding fathers of this country were very much aware of the dangers implicit in this approach.[28]

Rousseau's freedom is slippery and elusive. For him there is no morality without freedom. Man must be free to make his own judgments; if he is not he is not a moral creature but rather one responding simply to external forces. For Rousseau, man is of two natures: a higher one and a lower one. The higher one is selfless and oriented toward self-sacrifice and abnegation in the interest of society. The lower-self is driven by forces in our environment and is focused on meeting our material needs for satisfaction and pleasure. For Rousseau we must suppress the lower self so that the higher self may surface and flourish. The liberalism of today shows a similar contempt for "the lower self" as it holds materialism and the satisfaction of needs in the low regard.

For Rousseau, men ineluctably try to bring about the good, and the pursuit of the good for one man does not conflict with others. He sees only harmony, like today's liberals, no conflict, no trade-offs. This is because he sees the common good as universal, benefitting all men. He realizes that not all men perceive the common good. Man in his day-to-day activities may not be aware of the common good at a conscious level. But at a deeper, subconscious level, Rousseau supposes that most men do have a sense of the common good. Thus Rousseau believed that men would be absolutely free because the exercise of their freedom would be in harmony with the common interest. Where this would not be so, the State would have to force individuals to the common interest. It would be, in his view, in their interest that the State would do so.

This, of course, is a blueprint for totalitarian abuse. Rousseau provides the philosophical framework leaders are looking for in the exercise of coercion and oppression over their citizens. On the basis of Rousseau's views, they can comfortably say they are doing what they are doing for the good of the people, even though the people don't agree. The leaders can say, and they do, that the people are not smart enough or do not know enough to know what is good for them, so the leaders need to supply their "enlightened" vision. It's bad enough for a citizen to be abused and/or tortured by a State, but it must be that much tougher to have to hear that it's for your own good.

For Rousseau the general will can never be wrong, but he does acknowledge that it can be misled or misrepresented. He does not have an easy answer, however, for dealing with an abusive government.

Comte, a utopian socialist, is another philosopher who presented a view of the world strikingly similar to that of modern liberalism. Like the liberalism of today, he exalted morality above all else and believed in the perfectibility of man. Liberals believe in the "perfection of our moral nature." For example, Comte in *A General View of Positivism* emphasized that moral progress is more important than intellectual progress. "We find two qualities standing above the rest in practical importance, namely, Sympathy and Energy. The whole tendency of Positivism is to encourage sympathy; since it subordinates every thought, desire, and action to social feeling. It reveals the true dignity of man, and it supplies an unceasing motive for individual and collective action."

Comte, in the same work, spoke of the religion of humanity. "Love, then, is our principle; order our basis; and progress our end. Such is the essential character of the system of life which Positivism offers for the definite acceptance of society; a system which regulates the whole course of our private and public existence, by bringing Feeling, Reason, and Activity into permanent harmony... Life in all its actions and thoughts is brought under the control and inspiring charm of Social Sympathy." "By the supremacy of the Heart, the Intellect, so far from being crushed, is elevated; for all its powers are consecrated to the service of the social instincts, with the purpose of strengthening their influence and directing their employment. According to Comte, "By accepting its subordination to Feeling, Reason adds to its own authority."[29]

Comte puts mutual love over self-love. For him Positivism is a religion which should reign over politics. Morality is accorded the most exalted status; politics is but its handmaiden. Social sympathy should guide us all, not self-interest. Modern liberals also accord primacy to morality and social sympathy. This sounds thoroughly constructive and benign, but these ideas of Comte and Rousseau served as philosophic preludes to the development of fascism.

Fascistic roots and tendencies

Fascism and its evils come from the Left, not the Right. Jonah Goldberg in his excellent book, *Liberal Fascism,* documents this very well. It's important to understand the roots of this evil so we can prevent it from developing and flourishing. The pain and suffering caused by fascism in the twentieth century shouldn't be so easily forgotten. Look at the similarities of today's liberalism to fascism. Like fascism, it puts the State above the individual. Like fascism, it's organic, not atomistic: it puts the interests of the whole of society above the individual. Like fascism, it sees individual liberty as constrained to those actions which are consistent with State interests. Like fascism, it buys into myth, not reason. Like fascism, it's monistic, believing in unity, and is very hostile to opposing views. Fascists, like liberals, believe in the efficiency of the State. Both believe in massive government undertakings like healthcare. Both fascism and liberalism believe their goals and objectives should reach beyond the nation state.

There are, however, dissimilarities as well. Liberalism is compassion-based, fascism is not. Liberalism is more in the mind than in action. Fascism is very much action based. Liberalism diminishes individuals to automatons. Fascism believes, on the other hand, in the full development of the individual, although this development should be fully consistent with the interests of the State. Fascism desires to have active, inspired citizens, whereas liberalism seeks to have a passive, obedient citizenry. Fascism believes in hero worship, namely that of the leader, whereas for liberals it's the State that should be worshipped; individuals should play a low-profile supporting role. Fascism believes in war, militarism, and sacrifice, which liberalism is passionately against. The notions of sacrifice, cost, and trade-offs don't factor into liberal thinking; for liberals, we are entitled to certain things and simply should have them. Fascism is not against religion, whereas liberalism views religion with suspicion. For the Left religion is part of the past and it's a hindrance to the development of the State. Fascism does not seek equality, whereas liberalism does. Liberalism subscribes to cultural and moral relativism, whereas fascism believes in an absolutist value-laden morality. Fascism buys into history and connectedness of the past, present, and future. Liberalism, on the other hand, seeks to throw away the present and the past and replace it with a utopian dream. Liberalism fails to understand the importance of the past and the present.

The distinguishing feature shared by both is their belief in the organic nature of the polity, the power of the State, and a disregard for reason as a beacon. Both fascism and liberalism are emotion driven. These features are also in the DNA of communism.

Socialism, on the other hand, still has roots in atomism. It sees the State as set up in the interests of individuals, in contrast to fascism and liberalism, which see the organic, collectivist whole as more important than individuals. Socialism, though, is a precursor of fascism and communism, as it increases the power and influence of the State and diminishes individual power. Thus, while in name socialism is atomistic and for the individual, in fact it is not. Fascism is merely more overt and explicit that the State should be exalted above the individual.

Another difference between socialism and both liberalism and fascism is that the latter regard reason as a relic of the past, whereas socialism holds it in high regard, at least officially. Thus, liberalism in general seems to have more in common with fascism than with socialism.

* * *

CHAPTER 4

Pathologic Aspects of Liberalism

———◆———

*A moment's reflection shows that liberalism is entirely negative.
It's not a formative force, but always and only a disintegrating
force.*

~Francis Parker Yockey

*This and no other is the root from which a tyrant springs; when
he first appears he is a protector.*

~Plato

*I'll say this for adversity: people are able to stand it, and that's
more than I can say for prosperity.*

~Kim Hubbard

The purpose of liberalism is to destroy old norms, traditions, and institutions that stand in their way. The priority of the liberal ruling elite is to undermine other competing bases for power. In this connection liberals seek to destroy the power of the private sector. In a market economy, people and firms can thrive in an economy free of the influence of government. Liberals want to rein this in. They strive to eliminate or seriously weaken the underpinnings of the market economy and capitalism. The liberal ruling elite also seeks to reduce the influence of democracy itself, by making the government more and more detached and remote from the voter. Elitists do not trust the common man. More fundamentally, the new elite, taking over in the name of liberalism, are debasing laws and rule-based systems so as to give more space to their discretionary power.

This liberal agenda of destruction targets religious values, or for that matter values period, as it seeks to promote moral relativism. This opens the door to an anything-goes world. Under liberalism, values should come from the State; liberals do not want religious institutions or individuals challenging the authority of the State. There can be no doubt that liberalism is striving to weaken the family and religion as basic cultural pillars.

In this section we will look at some of the distinguishing features of liberalism in order to better understand it. Its pernicious, destructive nature will be laid open so that we can see how it works to undermine the foundations of our democracy and way of life.

Identity Politics

Liberalism bases its strategy for expanded power on *identity politics*. It's a strategy of divide and conquer. Its approach is one of pandering to the interests of certain groups which are its core constituencies. The policies espoused are meant to benefit these groups, not the entire polity. These groups vote out of base self-interest. They have no regard for the entire community. Thus there are teachers' unions, government employee unions, minorities, and gay rights, and so on. Unlike in a market economy where people may benefit by meeting the needs of others, the liberal game is a zero-sum game in which the favored constituencies take from the system to the detriment of others. It's legalized theft. It is said, "Why work for a living when you can vote for a living instead." The pandering involved in liberalism appeals to the baser instincts of man. In the liberal world, and in the incentive structures it creates, man is not out to see the community better off, only himself; in fact in the long-term he is making both himself and others worse off.

Labor unions play a key part in the liberal disease. Union leaders and their members profess a dedication to the working man, but in reality are in it for themselves. It's not about what the unions can do for labor, but what the public can do for the labor unions and its members. It's partisanship in spades.

The purpose of the unions is to jack up the wages and benefits of members above what the market mechanism would yield. Where it's successful in doing so, it disadvantages other workers who then either work for less or else lose their work entirely. Also to the extent that the unions are successful in gaining above market wages, the public as consumers are hurt by higher prices, diminishing their standard of living.

Unions have seriously hurt many industries. For example, strong labor unions, by artificially pumping up wages and pension benefits have pretty much destroyed the steel industry and the auto industry in the US. This, of course, hurts the interests of labor in the long run. The gains unions seek are myopic, short-term.

Thus unions gain advantages at the expense of others. It's intrinsically selfish. Gain is extracted through force and cabalistic practice. This contrasts with the market, where exchange is voluntary and everyone gains; the market is not selfish, contrary to popular belief. Gains are achieved not through force, but through merit and the benefit of the community.

It's important to note the California Nurses Union's role in the defeat of Whitman in the recent California Governor's race, and the role of the teacher's union in the defeat of Mayor Fenty in the District of Columbia. Whitman had signaled that she was going to be aggressive in dealing with the budget deficit in California and the unions did not like this. Similarly, Mayor Fenty in Washington had made education reform a priority for his administration and, according to numerous sources, the teachers' union fought to defeat him. The teachers' union was allegedly against reform because the reform program was seeking to hold poorly performing teachers accountable.

Education performance in Washington, D.C., is deplorable. According to the National Assessment of Educational Progress, only twelve percent of eighth grade students are proficient in reading. Yet despite the urgent need for this reform and accountability, the teachers' union fought it. Thus in pursuing its self-interest the teachers' union may be sacrificing the welfare of the students whom they are committed to serve.[30]

By 2007 most union members were in the public sector. Even Franklin Roosevelt recognized that the rationale for unions is largely confined to the private sector.[31] A strike by public sector unions could wreak tremendous damage. Public sector unions have an interest in seeing growth in government and seek to minimize their accountability. The biggest campaign contributors are the public sector unions.[32] The AFSCME – the American Federation of State, County and Municipal Employees – contributes massive amounts of funds to political campaigns. For example, in the 2010 campaign, AFSCME allegedly committed to spending $87 million dollars to support Democratic candidates. The NEA, the National Education Association, also provided heavy financial support to the Democrats. These contributions entail significant conflicts of interest, because the contributions are tax dollars that are channeled into campaigns supporting politicians who work for expanding government and protecting their union benefits. The union leadership spends member dues on campaigns without receiving the approval of members—even without disclosure. Basically, the rank-and-file union members are financially disenfranchised.

The internecine relationship between unions and liberal or Democratic politics is striking and troubling. There are laws against federal workers campaigning, but the intent of these laws is circumvented by unions. It's not surprising that public sector employees are now estimated to be earning significantly more than comparable employees in the private sector. Their bloated and unfunded pension benefits will weigh heavily on the economy and the private sector. Essentially public sector employees are robbing taxpayers and those in the private sector. It's pure self-interest, nothing more.

This was made all the more clear recently. Unions played a big role in funding the election of Obama. He has repaid the favor through treating the GM and Chrysler union workers favorably in the government buyout. Union workers at Delphi, the largest US supplier of auto parts, were reportedly able to maintain one-hundred percent of their pension, health, and insurance benefits, while non-union workers lost up to seventy percent of their pensions and all of their health and life insurance. At the same time Chrysler bondholders who should have been accorded first priority over equity and other claimants were stiffed. Chrysler bondholders only recovered twenty-nine cents on the dollar, while Chrysler's union workers did much better, even though bankruptcy law gives them much lower priority. Essentially, the Obama Administration ignored and overrode bankruptcy law—they broke the law.

For the 2012 presidential campaign the AFL-CIO has said that it will seek to provide four hundred million dollars in support to the Obama campaign.[33] The leadership apparently felt that its support in 2008 was amply repaid, so it's going all-out to support him again. Not only will it provide money, but it will also provide boots on the ground in the campaign, so it's a powerful and influential political group. It must be more than disconcerting, however, to those union members who have different political views and don't want to support Obama. They feel as though they have been disenfranchised. Their union dues are going to be spent by the leadership against their wishes. These funds could, of course, be used to directly support benefits for workers, but the leadership clearly sees a better outcome in committing them to the political arena. Of course, the union leadership might gain more than the rank and file, as they get to play with the ruling elite class.

In early 2011 when Governor Scott Walker of Wisconsin tried to rein in his state budget and slightly reduce the extravagant wage and benefit package of teachers in the state, Obama jumped in and said it "seems like more of an assault on unions." The Democratic National Committee, together with Organizing for America, assisted in helping to coordinate union demonstrations and protests intended to kill the "anti-union" effort in Wisconsin. Union leaders from across the country united to stop the effort to rein in teachers' pay in Wisconsin.[34]

Governor Walker wanted the Wisconsin teachers who contributed nothing to their guaranteed pension to contribute 5.6 percent of their salary. He also wanted them to contribute twelve percent of their salary toward health care benefits, give teachers the right to decide whether they wanted to be a union member or not, and limit their collective bargaining rights to wages. The Governor said he needed to take hard decisions to close a budget deficit estimated at $137 million in the current state budget and at $3.6 billion for the upcoming two years.[35] Continuing with the status quo was not an option. Teachers who earn about $89,000 dollars a year responded by walking off the job and cancelling school for days while they protested at city hall.[36] Is their priority not educating the children? Their actions suggest benefits are more important to them. Teacher salaries and benefits are much higher than pay in the private sector, but yet they went into a frenzy over proposed small cuts to their pension and health benefits. Apparently it's too much for them to pay five percent of their salary toward their own pensions; instead private sector employees, many with no pension or health benefits, should pay for their teacher benefits.

You would think public sector employees would feel a sense of embarrassment once the spotlight had been on what they'd been doing and how they'd been acquiring unfairly high wages and benefits. But this wasn't the case. Unions nationwide gathered together an estimated $31 million dollars and used it to try to recall (throw out of office) Republican state representatives who had supported Governor Walker's bill. Governor Walker was also subjected to a recall election.

State budgets throughout the country are seriously out of balance, in large part due to bloated compensation packages for public sector unions. Many states are likely to approach the federal government for a bailout. Some responsible governors are attempting to avoid this and bring their budgets under control, but it seems the president, who won't take tough measures himself to deal with the federal budget imbalance, is also opposing those seeking to take responsible action in the states.

The government is also seeking to bolster the strength of labor unions in the private sector. In 2011 the National Labor Relations Board registered a complaint against Boeing, which was attempting to set-up a non-union plant in South Carolina, moving it from Washington State where the plant was unionized. The company cited problems with strikes as one of the reasons for moving. The National Labor Relations Board argued in its complaint that this unfairly sought to penalize workers for their right to strike. Boeing is challenging the complaint. This is just another attempt by the government to intervene in the private market. There is no historical precedent for the government to get in Boeing's way about where it wants to locate its plant.[37]

The relationship of labor and government in the United States differs from the European socialist model in that it's not as structured, but the negative effects are not that dissimilar. In the European socialist model, wages are in many cases set from above by agreement between labor, business, and government. This is the approach favored by the Left. It circumvents the market and meets with their inclination to impose outcomes. But the result has been stifling rules, high structural unemployment, and slow economic growth.

Likewise liberals are pandering to ethnic groups, particularly the blacks, but now also the Hispanics. Liberals push welfare expansion and entitlement programs to gain their support. They also push affirmative action and pledge to put liberal justices in the court system to favor those dependent on government. The liberal elite are willing and in fact enthusiastic to even break the law—all to court the Hispanic vote. Hence they favor illegal immigration, and even favor illegals voting and getting benefits that they shouldn't be entitled to. Liberals also want to see criminals vote. To enhance the likelihood of illegal alien and criminal voting, liberals and Democrats favor lax identification requirements at the polls. In fact Attorney General Holder is actively fighting states which are trying to curtail illegal voting through increased voter identification requirements.

The liberal agenda also benefits lawyers, teachers, journalists, the media, and special interest lobbyists. Lawyers are big supporters of the Democratic Party and the Democratic Party is likewise a big supporter of lawyers. Their involvement in our society, where lawsuits are everywhere, makes living life and doing business a great deal more difficult. Liberalism ties us up, limiting our freedom to act. The outcome for the general public is an overly litigious society, sowing distrust and the pursuit of unearned gains. Lawyers raise the cost of medical care and intimidate doctors, who in turn overprescribe medical tests to protect themselves from suit. Excessive legal suits raise the cost of consumer goods. Environmental restrictions and regulations make doing anything complicated. We have not built a nuclear power plant in over thirty years. Government regulations and the legal morass surrounding them encumber us all.[38]

Society suffers from this blight of lawyers, while liberals pad their political campaign coffers and hang on to power. This unhealthy relationship also means that too many of our talented young people are going into law. This hurts not only the country, but the practicing lawyers as well. It's hard to derive satisfaction from a life which essentially hurts society.

Journalists and those in the media have been largely co-opted by the liberal establishment. The elite went to the same schools as the liberal political elite and shared in the same inculcation of liberal views. Also to the extent that the media remained impartial and neutral, they failed to share in the power of the liberal establishment and failed to do as well financially. The incentive to throw in with liberals and participate as a power player and gain financial support has been too hard to resist for most.

People don't trust the press and media; their reporting is highly biased. Suffolk University, a liberal university in the northeast of America, recently conducted a survey in which they asked students who they regarded as the most trusted newsman. "None" received the most votes. Bill O'Reilly of Fox News came in next. Fox was rated by the students as the most trusted news organization. Other news organizations were far behind.[39]

Since the founding of America, the press was meant to play a key role in keeping the spotlight on government. The role was meant to be adversarial, but under the Obama Administration the mainstream media have actively supported him and his agenda rather than report objectively. This is problematic enough, but the Obama Administration was not satisfied even with this. For them apparently all the news should be favorable. They essentially declared war on Fox News, trying to diminish them by saying that they are not a news organization, but an advocate for the agenda of the right wing. They limited access for Fox to Administration spokesmen. In 2011 they also went after the Boston Herald limiting their access to a White House press briefing because the Administration was not happy with their coverage.[40] The White House even threatened legendary liberal Washington Post writer Bob Woodward, because he revealed that Obama had deliberately given false statements. The White House also threatened to remove White House credentials for The Washington Times, unless it discontinued Lanny Davis' column, because it did not like something he had written concerning Obama's policies.[41] This is not the way a president should act in this country. The president should not bully the press; he of course has the right to express his disapproval of reporting, but he should not take action to penalize news organizations criticizing him. Freedom of the press is fundamental to our liberty and is a part of the American democratic process.

Liberalism is based on conquering by dividing. Although it professes to work for the benefit of the community, it's actually based on a politics of *dis*unity. It's alleged that some prominent liberal leaders, including some African American leaders, don't want the race issue to fade away: this is how they make their living.[42] Obama and the Democrats depend on racial politics; they are continually raising the specter of racism and pressing blacks to vote for them.

Identity politics is what you get in third-world countries where the winner politically favors his tribe or those who support him politically. It's a primitive form of politics that guarantees poor governance, poor economic performance, and diminished freedoms and rights for those not favored. An effective form of politics is one in which the political leader is committed to improving the lot of all citizens, not just those who support him politically.

Interest-group liberalism and identity politics is fundamentally predicated on a flawed model. For example, it presumes that the government holds one hundred goodies and there are one hundred interest groups; the problem is that each of the one hundred interest groups wants all of the one hundred goodies for itself. Socialism is that system of government wherein each group and each person tries to get someone else to finance its standard of living and lifestyle.

Conservative perspectives, on the other hand, are committed to general rules and principles (such as the invisible hand of the market or free trade) rather than identity politics. Conservatives see the world in a positive light. They see prospects for overall gain and growth for the community, not a fight over limited spoils. Indeed it's the free market and free trade which has led to the huge expansion in material well-being since the nineteenth century. Economics and life are not zero-sum games for conservatives; we can all benefit if we play by the rules and adhere to certain principles.

Liberalism bases its political prospects on securing the support of that part of the electorate who are high demanders of government output. The objective of liberalism is to render people dependent on government and thereby garner their support. Liberalism is creating a class of parasites, sucking the lifeblood out of the rest of society. Conservatives have to base their support on the rest of the electorate, those who aren't reliant on the government.

Thus liberalism is not just a zero-sum game; it's a negative-sum game. Not only does one group of citizens usurp the wealth of another, but the whole economic pie is diminished. There is less to be shared which contrasts sharply with capitalism which grows the pie. Liberalism involves a taker mentality, not that of a giver. They want something from the system and others. They are not looking to contribute to the social good. It's parasitical and metastatic, sapping the strength and vitality of society and the individual human beings who constitute it; it's spreading insidiously throughout the interstices of the economic, political, and social fabric, and human psychology as well.

Liberalism, based as it is on identity politics and the politics of division, is not suited to the welfare state that is its stated goal. For the welfare state to be successful, consensus is essential. Everyone must be pulling in the same direction. Groups and individuals should not be trying to gain at the expense of the polity. The politics of division practiced by liberalism, however, fans tension between groups. It's based on discordancy and strife, not harmony, and thus is not consistent with creating a successful welfare state. In fact it's egregiously inimical to it.

Nordic countries probably have been the most successful in creating a socialistic welfare state, although they too are confronting the need to cut back to fend off public debt problems. The key factor contributing to the relative success of the Nordic countries is that they are consensus-oriented. Their populations are quite homogeneous and not characterized by ethnic diversity. The small size of these countries, their governments, and institutions have also been conducive to success. The latter have helped to keep their governments largely free of corruption. This contrasts starkly with the circumstances in the US. Here we have a high degree of ethnic diversity, making it more difficult to effectively implement a welfare state. The large size of our government also makes corruption much more of a problem.

Basically we have moved from the macro-politics of the twentieth century to the micro-politics of the twenty-first century. It's important to avoid the tyranny of the majority, but we now are experiencing oppression by a collection of minorities. Forget Christmas, now no one can celebrate anything. The politics of division practiced by liberalism is succeeding in destroying the culture of the majority, but is incapable of replacing it with anything constructive.

Does liberalism promote a sense of solidarity and community togetherness by pitting classes against one another? It seeks to create harmony through a politics of acrimony and envy. Does this make any sense?

Elitism

The strategy of the Left has been to co-opt and bring into their fold as many members of the elite class as they can. Thus, as mentioned, they have taken over the educational institutions and almost own the educators. They also control the media, the press, lawyers, many top businessmen, and the entertainment industry. Even labor leaders, who purportedly represent the non-elite, have been bought. The elite class has been largely co-opted by the Left, leaving depleted ranks to support the values which helped make this country great. In effect the talent pool is now dominated by the liberal ruling elite class. Potential adversaries have been bought out and assimilated.

The elite political class organizes to exercise power over the unorganized masses. Those seeking power or trying to justify its use need to cloak their drive for power with other motives. Thus, they divert attention from themselves and claim they are doing it for the "good of others." There are thus frequently heavy moral overtones (save the planet and help the poor) in their rhetoric. But underneath liberalism is nothing more than aristocracy in disguise. It's an aristocracy not built on class or merit, but on pure power assembled through guile and deception.

The fact that liberals see themselves as better than the great unwashed masses is a disturbing trait, which ineluctably leads them to desire power. They don't see the masses as able to fend for themselves. They don't see them as able to make decisions on behalf of even their own welfare, much less that of others. Given that they don't hold the common man in high esteem, it would not be surprising that they would not treat him well should they succeed in getting power over him. The common man is but a pawn worthy of sacrifice for the intended aims of the liberal elite. This is why in China and the USSR so many were abused and murdered; it was for a "good cause," the creation of a State that would purportedly serve the interests of the common man. This perverted logic would be laughable if it were not so real and dangerous.

Liberalism has fought against tyranny by the majority by fighting for the rights of minorities. But it appears it's not so much tyranny or oppression that it's against, but rather who imposes it on whom. We now are seeing tyranny by the minorities. Liberals harshly try to suppress any criticism or opposition to what they are doing. Essentially, what we have are authoritarian progressives with the ends justifying the means. One would not expect the pursuit of an egalitarian agenda by non-egalitarians to be successful, yet it's amazing how well they sell it to the public.

Hobbes, the famous political philosopher, was also an elitist. He saw people as basically bad, prone to corruption and abuse of power, yet he believed that a dictator should rule, as strong law is better than no law. The progressives see human nature differently than Hobbes. They see people as basically malleable and capable of perfection through education and indoctrination. Unfortunately this benign view of human nature is not even reflected in their leaders. Their leaders are not sincere and do not follow what they advocate for the rest of us. The ruling elite have demonstrated that they accumulate wealth and power and do not contribute or distribute their wealth to others. Liberals want to give away other people's money, not their own. Leaders are prone to corruption and abuse of power, so the amassing of power becomes a problem for everyone. The only solution is to limit the power of leaders and government, but liberals are averse to this.

Even if liberals were right that there is one true order of society that is better than others, it would make no sense to pursue it if the means to achieve it were not available, or if such means were fraught with peril. We would need to find the sage or elite class who could in fact find that one true order of society better than others. How would we do this? As the public are presumed to be people of lesser intelligence, it would seem counterintuitive, if not impossible, to achieve this. Even if we were to accomplish this task, how would we invest the proper people with the mantle of power? It would be hard to see how a significant part of the public could agree on whom to give power to. It would also be necessary to have the right political structure and institutional constraints to ensure that the elite would in fact do "what is right." It's hard to understand why liberals deny that power corrupts. Somehow they see an elite class that is not susceptible to the temptations and corruptions of power, despite the clear historical record to the contrary.

A fundamental part of the credo of liberalism is that most men are not smart enough to run their own lives, so the elite need to take control of them. Edward Abbey highlighted the perils of this kind of thinking, noting that "anarchism is founded on the observation that since few men are wise enough to rule themselves, even fewer are wise enough to rule others."

Abraham Lincoln recognized that the notion of a ruling elite is not compatible with democracy. He said, "As I would not be a slave, so I would not be a master. This expresses my idea of democracy."

Expanded Role for Government

President Reagan's admonition in his farewell speech in 1989 that "man is not free unless government is limited," is readily apparent to all who know history. He noted that liberty and individual freedom contract as government expands in a relationship that is clearly causal. This is why the size of government is so important. It's not simply a matter of efficiency; it's critical to the preservation of liberty.

Liberalism in its relentless push to expand the size of the central government is crowding out the private sector. There are fewer and fewer resources—labor, capital, and land—available for use in the private sector as the government gobbles these resources up. There are also fewer financial resources available to the private sector as the government now finances about forty percent of its spending through borrowing. In addition to this physical and financial crowding out, there is also a moral crowding out of the private sector as the government takes on a larger and more intrusive role in educating our children and in providing assistance to the less advantaged.

Liberalism leads to top-down economic control. It's predisposed toward planning and government control of the economic system. This stifles creativity, entrepreneurship, innovation, and private sector economic vitality. Liberalism's planning and control start on a small scale, but once they start growing it's difficult to stop. As a particular planning activity encounters problems or developments that are not in sync with the plan, the scope of the plan is broadened, made more encompassing. It tends to metastasize throughout the economy. The planners are in all probability not driven by bad intent; in fact they are mostly driven by good intentions, but this doesn't mean that the impact is any less harmful. As Milton Friedman noted, "Concentrated power is not rendered harmless by the good intentions of those who create it."

Von Hayek wrote extensively on the perils of planning. In his book *The Road to Serfdom,* he saw the expansion of government planning as not only bringing about the demise of capitalism, but also spelling an end to personal freedom. He believed it would lead to modern-day serfdom. Those who rise to positions of power in an economy and government based on planning are able to arbitrarily shape the fates of others. A modern-day feudalism replaces the hurly-burly of a market-oriented economy, where individuals control their own fates.

Vaclav Havel, an anti-communist and a former president of Czechoslovakia, also warned of the dangers of excessive growth in government and bureaucracy. The West defeated communism, but some of the same pathologic tendencies that brought communism down are also deeply entrenched in democracies. Like the USSR and communist China, we too are increasingly convinced that we are smart enough to understand and control everything. Top-down, heavy-handed government stifles and smothers individual growth, encouraging sameness. It's driven to "ultimate solutions," and to choice minimization. This "era of systems, institutions, mechanisms and statistical averages" is deeply flawed and cannot succeed. The world is too complex to be either understood or controlled. Life is just not that simple.

Government uses force as its method of operation to accomplish its objectives. Markets, on the other hand, are based on voluntary interactions between individuals and organizations. While markets rely on freedom, government relies on constraint. While markets foster the development of individuality, government diminishes individual development in the interest of the development of the State or collective welfare.

As government expands, fraud and corruption become more and more of a problem. Benjamin Franklin once said, "There is no kind of dishonesty into which otherwise good people more easily and frequently fall than that of defrauding the government." Whereas most people have scruples about defrauding or hurting others, even if they don't know them, this does not apply to artificial entities like the government. In fact, many feel entitled. If other people are ripping off the system through entitlements, they think, *Why not me?* Also believing that the government is taking too much from them in taxes, they think it's only fair to get some back. It's a drop in the bucket for government, and the bureaucrats don't really care. No one will miss it.

Obama's health care reform bill, his take-over of some of the auto industry, his vast expansion of financial regulatory reform, and his attempt to pass a broad-based energy reform package based on cap-and-trade all represent a serious threat to our country. In Obama's case the expansion of government has not been gradual; it has been a wrenching change in our economy.

Government is the problem in most instances. It's not the solution to a problem, but rather it makes the problem worse. Reagan used to say, "Government does not solve problems; it subsidizes them." He went on to say, "It throws more and more money at a problem and entangles it in more and more regulation and oversight, making the problem more and more expensive and intransigent to improvement." Reagan also said that "the statist wants to tax everything that moves, if it slows down regulate it, if it stops subsidize it."

Liberals want to see a new set of incentives replace those embedded in capitalism. Rather than the incentives of the market, they want to see the government offering a carrot and stick for behavioral modification. Liberals disdain materialism. They see man chasing money and think this a demeaning weakness. The pursuit of the glory of the State is a more worthy goal. Somehow they are able to dispel the specter of past State catastrophes: China, the USSR, Nazi Germany, and Mussolini's Italy, and a litany of other failures. Fidel Castro is a hero to them. Their fairy-tale land is somehow uninfected by the past.

Liberals live in a world of temporal disjunction. The past and present are somehow not connected to the future. Is it not important to examine the results of past social experiments with collectivism and the aggrandizement of the State? Apparently not for liberals. This is another reason why liberals dismiss the value of traditions, customs, and institutions. The past is simply irrelevant to them. Worse, it's repugnant. They want a new world. Unfortunately, they don't have a clue how to create it. Their skill is in destroying the world they are living in, creating a dystopia for everyone.

It's well known that the government is less efficient than the private sector.[43] Multiple objectives, organizational bloating, and a lack of incentives help make this so. Also the more talented people tend to go into the private sector. As Ronald Reagan said, "The best minds are not in government. If any were, business would hire them away."

Gridlock is good. Efficient government is the best we can hope for, but it's a distinctly unlikely outcome. Given this—and the outlook that a strong, excessively large government is the likely outcome based on the propensities inherent in democracy—and given that such a strong government can lead to adverse outcomes, a weak government hamstrung by gridlock may be the best we can do.

In his book, *Bought and Paid*, Charles Gasparino lays out the case that Wall Street was a big supporter of Obama, showing that Wall Street contributions to Democrats in the 2008 elections far exceeded that to Republicans.[44] The big banks and Wall Street know that big government is good for them. Not only does it pretty much guarantee that "too big to fail" will continue to protect them against downside risk and bail them out when needed, it opens the door for them to gamble, taking on big risks, as they know they can't really lose.

We don't really have two political parties; both parties are for big government. The Tea Party is the only real force trying to constrain the growth of government. It's a bottom-up, not a top-down movement. It's grassroots, individuals acting out of their volition and sense of commitment to the country. These are good, concerned citizens.

Thomas Paine had it right when he said, "The government is best which governs least." Thomas Jefferson said the "fore horse" of the decline of society is a rise in public debt which leads ineluctably to higher taxation and oppression.

Liberalism is addicted to ad hoc adjustments by government to correct purportedly unfair and unjust outcomes. This ad hoc, arbitrary interventionist approach works against even-handedness. There is an aversion to being guided by general principles and rules that apply to all. The liberal cannot help himself. He thinks in his wisdom that he can do better and should. However, it's the commitment and discipline to adhere to broad rules, principles, and laws that apply to all equally that is the safeguard of individual freedom and liberty. Liberalism thus is continually undermining the basis of liberty.

As Edward Abbey is famously quoted as saying, "No tyranny is so irksome as petty tyranny." Tyranny on a grand scale of course is devastating, but petty tyranny can also be highly damaging. The officious demands of policemen, government clerks, and electromagnetic gadgets can exact a heavy toll in terms of the quality of our lives. An excessive amount of rules, regulations, and government intervention is not only a nuisance, but also deprives us of the sense we control our lives.

Mania for Spending

The liberal seems to be content with throwing money at a problem. Perhaps it satisfies his need to feel like he is doing something. It shows he cares. It does not trouble him that the money is wasted and has no or little beneficial effect and results in an accumulation of debt which future generations will have to pay back. The sins of the liberals—prodigality, irresponsibility, and a lack of concern for efficaciousness—are unpaid for by liberals. They pass the bill for their sins on to future generations. They set up a ticking time bomb of debt that threatens the culture that they and others live in.

Liberals are intent on appropriating certain social objectives, such as poverty and the environment, as their own. They claim to have the moral high ground, being concerned about these issues while they claim conservatives and others do not care. Of course conservatives and others care, but rather prefer to address these issues through the market. Liberals, on the other hand, want to throw massive amounts of money at these issues and, in the case of the environment, impose strangling regulations. Both the money and the regulatory authority involved would lay a tremendously enhanced power base for the liberal elite. Is there any doubt what their real objective is?

The massive unfunded pensions of the bloated government bureaucracies both at a national and local level and the unfunded liabilities of the liberal social programs (Social Security, Medicare, and so on) were largely created by the liberal establishment. The liberals' story-book world of entitlements and self-created rights carry a huge price tag, a price tag they cannot afford. They want others to pay for their utopian worldview, namely, those who have created real wealth. Those suckling on the public tit, working in public bureaucracies and inhabiting the upper echelons of the liberal establishment in the media and in universities cannot pay for these programs, but they demand with a sense of righteousness that others who have actually participated in creating wealth and growth in the economy do so. They do this moreover with a sense of high dudgeon.

Liberals are trying to build a utopian castle in the present at the cost of a dystopian world in the future. *Spend, spend, spend* is what liberalism is about, and it's eroding the basis of the capitalist system which creates the wealth and the growth. The future looks bleak with the trajectory of spending and liabilities mounting at an alarming rate, while our growth potential and our ability to meet these mounting liabilities diminish. This is a recipe for crisis and a clear and present danger to our democratic traditions—but this may be what the liberals want. It's not, however, what most Americans want.

Liberals can't grasp that we cannot keep spending. For example, when I was in Mongolia the IMF was opposing an effort to double government salaries at a time when the government was in the midst of a financial crisis and the budget deficit was out of control. I tried to explain to UN representatives that we too would like to see higher government salaries, but that it would be detrimental to do it under the prevailing circumstances. They couldn't grasp this reality, and continued pushing for a massive increase in government salaries even though this would have led to serious problems.

Here in the United States, Obama and the liberals are still pushing spending as the cure for the 2008 financial crisis. Excessive government spending and debt is a large part of the economic problem, but liberals inexplicably see it as the cure. They want more of it. Their complete disconnect from reality is a danger to the nation.

Compassion and Pragmatism

Compassion is at the core of liberalism. It's the purported principal force of motivation behind it, ostensibly directed at helping others who are less well-off than they. As I will discuss later on in the chapter on the pathology of liberalism at the individual level, liberal morality is generally driven almost entirely by compassion, whereas conservative morality is driven by several different forces, including compassion.

Compassion clearly needs to play an important role in society. The strong and wealthy should try to help those who are less fortunate, but force and coercion only lead to the immisseration of everyone, including the poor. Moreover, if the government usurps the exercise of compassion for itself, it steals it from the private sector. It's depersonalizing giving—disconnecting people from people, the givers from the recipients. One of the truly good things an individual can do is give to help another. This is part of our humanity. Centralizing compassion in the hands of government is just one more way in which liberalism is bringing about dehumanization and reducing the bonds between us.

Everyone is in favor of seeing the poor do better. This is not the issue. If the real objective is to see the poor do better, why does the assistance have to come through an expansion of government? Why does the government have to get in the middle? If you want to give to a charity, would you rather give to one that eats up ninety percent of what you give in administrative expenses or one that would eat up, say, ten percent? Obviously you would prefer the latter, so why then do we have the government get involved with welfare and social assistance? Charity could be delivered better through the private sector. If the objective is to increase charity, the government could give a tax credit, rather than a deduction, for charitable donations or require that everyone give at least two percent of their income to charity. This would be cheaper, more targeted, and more effective than having a massive government bureaucracy get involved.

When a liberal sees an alcoholic beggar on the street, he wants to give him money. A conservative might want to give him money as well, but understands that if he does the money will just go to feed a bad habit, one that is killing the man. If the conservative does not give money, the liberal would call him uncaring and hard-hearted. The liberal thinks throwing money at a problem is enough. The conservative is willing to spend money for a remedy to a problem, but is averse to encouraging and supporting bad habits.

It's well known in microeconomic theory that an individual's economic welfare is higher if he is accorded choice over how to spend his money rather than if the government makes the decision for him. For example, an individual is almost always better off if he is given cash rather than a physical good of equivalent value. Thus, a person would generally be better off if the government gives him one hundred dollars in cash rather than one hundred dollars in food stamps. It's hard to believe, but almost forty-seven million people (one in seven) are now on food stamps in the United States. In the Cash for Clunkers program sponsored by the Obama Administration, the government offered up to $4,500 for people trading in old cars if they would buy a new one. They did not offer this money for people buying other goods, only new cars.

Liberals are focused on certain objectives they regard as grounded in morality. Their sense of righteousness gets in the way of common sense. Because they are dedicated to helping the poor, they think that the rest is straightforward and requires no thought; for them it's simply necessary to create a government program dedicated to doing this by redistributing income (rent control, unions, welfare, minimum wage, and so on). They don't allow their reason to determine if the policies actually work. For example, liberals are not troubled by the fact that rent control leads inevitably to less available and less maintained housing for the poor. They are not troubled that unions produce higher pay for those in the union, but freeze out other workers. They are not troubled that the teachers' unions hurt education and kids trying to rise out of poverty in inner city ghettos. They are not troubled by the fact that minimum wage laws lead to unemployment and make it difficult for entry level workers to gain access to the labor force.

It's a dangerous mix to live in a fantasy land and be filled with self-righteousness to do something dramatic at the same time. Being divorced from reality means bad policies are unlikely to change, because they are not critically evaluated. It means constituencies for untruths and bad policies, which only lead to more of the same. In effect it locks people and the Democratic Party into unsustainable, bad policies; it also locks them into forever failing to commit themselves to the pursuit of the truth and sound policies. Liberals supported ObamaCare. When it's pointed out that this will bankrupt an already bankrupt system of entitlements and cause economic havoc, they offer no response.

Thus, an important shortcoming of liberalism is its failure to translate compassion into favorable consequences. This in and of itself is a devastating and fatal flaw given that it's at the core of liberalism. But liberal compassion is much more fundamentally flawed than this. The pathology starts at its origin. The compassion of the liberal is dehumanized, focusing on man in the abstract and not on individuals. It's a detached compassion, not connecting to people as individuals. It also helps to explain the cavalier attitude liberals have toward abortion. An individual life is simply not that important to them. But even more fundamental than this, liberal compassion is dishonest and dissembling.

In his book *Who Really Cares*, Arthur Brooks documents statistically that liberals give far less to charities and the less-fortunate than do conservatives. Conservatives give about thirty percent more to charities than do liberals per household and this is adjusting for income differences (in fact liberal households earned about six percent more than conservative households). Moreover, liberals are far less generous in general. Conservatives donate more blood yearly than liberals, and more of their time as volunteers.[45] Another finding of the study, according to Thomas Sowell of the Hoover Institution, is that "young liberals make the least charitable contributions of all, whether in money, time, or blood. Idealism in words is not idealism in deeds."[46] Moreover according to Charity Navigator, a national survey in 2002, "tells us that monetary donors are nearly three times as likely as non-donors to give money informally to friends and strangers. They are also significantly more likely to give food or money to a homeless person, or to give up their seat to someone on a bus."[47]

The states that generally vote Republican also donate more to charities than do the northeastern states that generally vote for Democrats. The Chronicle of Philanthropy also conducted a survey based on Internal Revenue data corroborating that Republican states give more to charity than Democratic states.[48] The seven least-generous states (including heavily liberal Maine, Vermont, Massachusetts, and Rhode Island) supported Obama in 2008. Essentially liberal rhetoric does not match actions. Bleeding-heart liberals who are continuously putting down conservatives as hard-hearted and uncaring are, in fact, the uncaring ones.

So, liberal compassion, which is the core of liberalism, is really not compassion at all. It's nothing more than posturing. The actions of liberals betray their lack of real compassion: theirs' is nothing more than a phony compassion, which helps to explain their lack of concern for the failed consequences of their "compassionate" policies and programs. Thus not only is liberal compassion bankrupt of favorable consequences, but it's bankrupt in the originating emotional driving force as well. The liberal is living a lie; liberal compassion, the purported essence of liberalism, is not really compassion at all. It's empty, hypocritical, and deceitful—and it underlies and pervades liberalism.

Although the compassion liberals continually express is a false one, I am sure many feel genuine and sincere in expressing it. But it is clear that it's more about them than it is about helping people. If the compassion were real, we would see it translated into deeds and action. It's not enough to talk the talk; you also need to walk the walk. Perhaps it fills a need to feel morally righteous, to feel connected to other people and to express strong emotion. Or perhaps it's a cloak for their guilt at pursuing selfish wants or not having given more.

But this false compassion is more than a benign lie. Conservatives tend to chalk it off as something naïve and misguided, but well-meaning. But it's not something to lightly discount or dismiss; it is, I believe, founded in the disease of self-hatred and guilt that pervades liberalism and much of our culture today. It's not benign, but rather pernicious and corrosive—and is working to destroy the foundations of Western civilization. It cloaks the greed and drive for power of the ruling elite who are intent on transforming America.

It's also worth noting that, although the Left is continually criticizing this country as hard-hearted capitalists, Americans are more generous than citizens from other countries. For example, "Americans gave, per capita, three and a half times as much to causes and charities as the French, seven times as much as the Germans, and fourteen times as much as the Italians."[49] Also whenever there is a crisis in another country, the American government and its citizens are usually there first and also with the most commitment of assistance.

Inefficiency and Corruption

Inefficiency and corruption are recognized as serious problems with government, yet liberalism strives to commit ever larger parts of the economy into the public sector. It's well known that government employment rolls are bloated. A bureaucrat's power increases as he expands his turf, both in employees, spending, and terrain covered. His incentive is not efficiency, but the expansion in his power base and authority. A government employee does not have to worry about being fired or disciplined as a private sector worker does, so it's not surprising that they are generally less efficient. As Charles Peters said, "Bureaucrats write memoranda both because they appear to be busy when they are writing and because the memos, once written, immediately become proof that they were busy." Most individual government workers do not have the opportunity to be tempted by corruption, but the large scale of government contracts with business does provide such an opportunity. As P.J. O'Rourke noted, "When buying and selling are controlled by legislation, the first things bought and sold are the legislators." Medicare and defense contracts, for example, are rife with corruption. Medicare fraud alone is estimated at about one hundred billion dollars annually.

According to an IMF publication, *Why Worry about Corruption*, the following can be said about corruption:[50]

"Throughout the world bureaucrats and people in authority are indefatigably maneuvering to position themselves in a tiny monopoly where they can be bribed for issuing a license, approving expenditure or allowing shipment across a border."

"Corruption is most prevalent in infrastructure projects. High-level corruption induces countries to increase the quantity of infrastructure because of the bribery potential of new infrastructure investment. Corruption increases the number of capital projects undertaken and tends to enlarge their size and complexity."[51]

"Since much public corruption can be traced to government intervention in the economy, policies aimed at liberalization, stabilization, deregulation, and privatization can sharply reduce the opportunities for rent-seeking behavior and corruption."[52]

Of course, liberals oppose curtailment of government; in fact they stand full square behind those policies mentioned above which contribute to corruption. They are for market interventions, trade restrictions, subsidies, price controls, increased regulation, and so on. The IMF study also found that "divisions along ethnic and linguistic lines were also highly correlated with corruption." Hence, liberal and Democratic policies which are based on the politics of division also create an environment where corruption flourishes.

Corruption hurts society. Reduced economic growth and an unfair distribution of income is just part of the cost. The moral implications and damage are profound. It's also clear that corruption tends to lead to pernicious political outcomes as well.

Democratic Party-the Party of Big Government, Big Business, and Big Labor

The Democratic Party is becoming the party of big business. Many large corporations like Google, Wal-Mart, General Electric,

Goldman Sachs, the big banks, and Microsoft gave large campaign donations to the Democrats in 2008. This is because these corporations benefit from large government. Why make money the old fashioned way, by earning it, when you can get easy money from the government.

Google only paid 2.4 percent of its profits in taxes in 2009.[53] Apple makes the iPhone in China, without unions and paying as little in the way of taxes as possible. In 2011 Apple allegedly paid an effective tax rate of only 9.8 percent in the United States, far below the corporate tax rate. And, according to the same source, General Electric paid no taxes in 2008, 2009, and 2010 on profits earned in the United States.[54] It derives a lot of its income from government projects, such as wind and solar power. It also owned part of NBC News during the 2008 presidential elections, and reportedly gave favorable coverage to Obama, the Democratic nominee.[55] Obama has close ties to Immelt, the CEO of General Electric. The fact that GE shipped a lot of jobs overseas does not appear to bother Obama as he appointed Immelt the head of his Council on Jobs and Competitiveness.

Microsoft was taken apart and attacked by the government because it focused on business, not on lobbying. It spent very little money on lobbying before the Justice Department assault; now it spends hundreds of millions of dollars on lobbying to protect itself. In effect it seems that in today's world you have to pay for protection, not much unlike the days when businesses had to pay the Mafia for protection.

The Republicans are the party of small business; its constituency is those who aren't on the federal gravy train. The Center for Responsive Politics documents that many of the largest industries are giving more campaign contributions to Democrats than to Republicans. Wall Street, which generally is closely identified with Republicans in the minds of the public, actually contributed more to the Democrats. Law firms have given more than any other donors, almost one hundred million dollars, and this favored Democrats by three to one. Lobbyists, who Democrats usually argue support the GOP, also donated more funds to the Democrats. [56]

Crony capitalism has become a serious economic and political problem. Banking and Wall Street's connection to government is causing serious threats to our economic system—as was underscored in the 2008 financial crisis—and is corroding the foundations of our democracy. Banks and Wall Street contribute massive amounts to political campaigns and are rewarded with bailouts and financial security. They are allowed to make huge mistakes and receive government bailouts. The moral hazard created by government support for bad policies and practices is transmuting free-market capitalism into casino capitalism. It's become a game of no-risk roulette. Under the system, the incentive is for banks to place high risk bets. If they win, they win big; if they lose, the government bails them out. I only wish I could go to Vegas with this kind of support.

Unfortunately, this is a problem with big government—it inevitably becomes entwined with big business and big labor, and the relationships become incestuous, pernicious, and corrosive. This is why limited government is the only real option.

In the 1960s, young people seeking power and money were told to go to Wall Street; now they are told to go to Washington. Is this what we really want—money, power, politics, and government all mixed together?

Strangulation by Regulation

The government wields power and influence not just through spending, taxing, and its role in the financial markets, but also through regulation. Liberals have succeeded in bringing about a tremendous growth in the government's regulatory power. According to Cindy Skrzycki in her book *The Regulators*, big business has learned to play the regulatory game. Their lobbyists in Washington sway legislators in their favor and also monitor closely how government rule making is likely to influence their business. Small firms cannot afford high-priced lobbyists, so they are left out in the cold. According to Skrzycki, small businesses bear most of the financial burden of government regulations, paying about $7,000 a year per employee versus about $4,500 for large firms.[57] The Small Business Administration puts the impact on small businesses even higher, estimating the cost at $10,585 per employee.[58] These are large numbers. Moreover, Skrzycki's estimate was for 2002, about nine years earlier than the SBA's estimate, so this also suggests that it has grown substantially. Since 2009 when Obama took the presidency, regulations have grown dramatically; under his Administration Federal staff engaged in regulatory activity has grown by 13 percent.[59] The public does not realize how costly regulations are to the business community and how much this raises consumer prices as these costs are largely passed on. According to the Economist, "Each hour spent treating a patient in America creates at least thirty minutes of paperwork, and often a whole hour."[60] In fact according to Skrzycki the annual cost of government regulation ranged between $520 billion and $620 billion in fiscal 2001 which was about the same order of magnitude of the federal government's discretionary spending in that year. [61] Moreover, the problem has grown significantly worse since that time. In 2008, according to a Small Business Administration study, the cost of regulation to the US economy amounted to a staggering $1.75 trillion which was larger than the $1.3 trillion in pre-tax corporate profits in 2009.[62]

Donald Trump said, "Getting things done in this country, if you want to build something, if you want to start a company, is getting to be virtually impossible with all of the bureaucracy and all of the approvals." Referring to the United States, the Economist Magazine said, "The home of laissez-faire is being suffocated by excessive and badly written regulation."[63] The United States used to be one of the best countries in the world to do business, but this is no longer true as we have lost ground to other countries.

According to the Office of the Management and Budget, there are one hundred federal agencies involved in the exercise of regulatory power, and together they issue about forty-five hundred new rules annually.[64] This role of government has seen explosive growth. In 1936 under the Roosevelt Administration, the Federal Register, which contains an account of all federal government regulations, was about 2,620 pages long; by 2001 it had swelled to 69,591 pages.[65]

The extent to which government regulation reaches into our lives has hit absurd levels. Skrzycki noted, for example, that the federal government now regulates what size prunes should be and also regulates the size of the hole in Swiss cheese. Moreover, it's not just the federal government that gets involved in regulation. The regulatory reach of state and local governments is also much felt in our lives.

Who are the regulators? They are anonymous, behind-the-scenes bureaucrats who are not elected and are not accountable for what they do. Moreover, it's well-known that there is a revolving door between the regulatory establishment and the businesses that they regulate, so there is conflict of interest. Regulators are interested in taking actions favorable to certain firms so that they can get jobs in those firms. Likewise many employees of the regulated firms like to curry favor with the regulators so that they can get some regulatory experience. The relationship is heavily incestuous and prone to corruption.

Moreover, the regulatory system is not effective in accomplishing its purported objectives. Did it stop the financial collapse in 2008 or the BP oil spill? No, it did not! Shortly before the financial collapse, Democratic Congressman Barney Frank said that Fannie Mae and Freddie Mac were in great financial shape and the regulators gave BP the highest safety rating only days before the oil spill.

The excessive growth of the regulatory role of government hurts economic growth by discouraging investment, and has added to business costs, boosted unemployment, and increased prices for consumers. For example, the Dodd-Frank bill passed recently by Democrats will add up to four hundred regulations on financial firms. It's estimated that just the technology-related compliance costs will amount to about $3.8 billion for financial firms between 2011 and 2013.[66] This comes at a time when we are trying to encourage banks to lend and keep their lending rates low to encourage business development. This bill will do just the opposite as it adds significantly to bank costs. It also adds uncertainty, as only about one quarter of the regulations have thus far been written. Congress has outsourced the job of writing the remaining regulations, and, since the regulations have not yet been written, banks are uncertain what it will mean for their future operations.

Not only do regulations have these direct effects, but the indirect effects also have wide-ranging impact. Regulations can be used to intimidate those in the private sector. Firms that are not talking nice to the ruling class may be threatened with increased regulation and tax audits. For example, when certain insurance companies were expressing concerns about ObamaCare, the Obama Administration made implicit threats of increased regulation.

Skrycki says, "We are now as much a nation of rules as we are of laws." This is yet another way that liberals are devaluing the rule of law. Also to the extent that regulators are largely under the control of the executive branch, the regulatory environment further centralizes power in that branch to the injury of other branches of government. When Obama realized that he could not get his Cap and Trade (Tax) environmental bill through Congress, he sought to bypass the legislative process by having the EPA effect the "desired changes" through regulations.

The General Will

The deep roots of liberalism in Rousseau's concept of the general will lead to potentially troubling political outcomes. According to Rousseau, the general will should not be directed to a particular person or object. It should be abstract and deal with subjects en masse. However, history shows that this is not how things work out in practice. Power is inevitably directed at opposition and its particulars.

In addition, Rousseau maintained that a "blind multitude, which often does not know what it wills, because it rarely knows what is good for it, cannot carry out the difficult exercise of legislation."[67] Rousseau says this job should be left to legislators, "But if great princes are rare, how much more so are great legislators."[68] "The general will is always in the right, but of itself it by no means always sees it. The general will is always in the right, but the judgment which guides it is not always enlightened."[69] The public is not thought smart enough to govern. They're perceived as stupid, so decisions and judgments must be made for them. We see what has happened when the general will becomes too strong. A mob takes over and it's hard to stop as happened under Hitler's Nazi regime. In fact it's this dynamic of brooking no dissent that leads to mobocracy. Mobs are not driven by reason, but are highly emotional and given to dramatic, emotional—and sometimes violent and malevolent—swings.

Decline of Individualism

Liberalism is inconsistent in that it professes interest in expanding the rights of individuals to be who they are and want to be, but engages in a modus operandi of political correctness and expansion in the intrusiveness of government that will ultimately be the death knell of individual liberty. By exalting the collective interests of the State over the interests of individuals, it's clear that liberalism works against the interests of those espousing individual liberty. This contrasts starkly with conservative and libertarian philosophies which exalt individual liberty over the collective interests of the State. Conservative political philosophy does not encourage the growth of government, but rather its constraint.

Liberalism dehumanizes man. It looks at individuals as cogs in a machine, expendable for the greater good, whatever that is and however it's defined. Liberalism devalues human life, and does this all in the name of compassion, some supposedly exalted feeling to help man in the abstract.

Liberalism's disregard for individual human life can be seen in its support of abortion. Liberals have no compunction about stamping out an individual life. To them it's but an abstraction, not something precious. The decision to end a human life is an easy calculation for them: it's but one of many lives, not something individual and unique. It's not a snowflake, but merely another replicable facsimile. In addition, support for abortion is not that surprising given that liberals don't see tradeoffs or costs to anything. For them, everything is cost-free.

This disregard for the individual human life is readily seen in the collectivist state, the ideal for liberals. History in the USSR, China, Cambodia, Cuba, and so on is a litany of disregard for the life of the individual. Many have been sacrificed in the name of progress for the State. The extent of brutality and the sheer magnitude of murder and abuse are truly stunning. It's hard to imagine how in today's world we can so easily dismiss and forget these horrors. Moreover, there was no compensating gain. At least if the collectivist causes for which people were sacrificed had achieved some measure of benefit for those who were not sacrificed or if the States had secured impressive achievements then there might be some basis for arguing that the sacrifices had been worthwhile. Unfortunately, this was not the case. These experiments were egregious failures across the board. Not only were staggeringly large numbers of people brutalized and murdered by the State, but the remaining citizens were dehumanized, abused, and left to live miserable lives. Only the few in the governing elite might have benefited, and even these were left to live lives of lies, paranoia, and fear.

Liberals do not recognize or want to recognize the totalitarian DNA which pervades their ideology. If they would at least recognize the problems involved with collectivist experiments in the past and try to come forth with solutions as to how to avoid these problems in the future, liberal ideology might have more merit. But there is no such effort. The horrors of past experiments are ignored as though they never happened. Whether it was the gulags of the Soviet Union, the murder of Russians by Stalin, the purges of Mao, or the quiet oppression of Fidel Castro, the Left simply dismisses these, charging them off as the price of progress.

When Senator Joseph McCarthy went after those in America suspected of communist ties in the aftermath of World War II, liberals were rightly upset over the threat to freedom and the right to dissent, but they seemed blithely unconcerned about the threat that communism represented. Communists were intent on subversion, in destroying the capitalist system and replacing it with a totalitarian Communist State, but liberals only were concerned with their right to dissent.

Liberalism and progressivism result in a decline in individuality and artistic expression and creativity. Collectivism squelches individual expression. Under it, art, the news, information, and truth become products of the State, not the individual. However, art and creativity arise from the individual, not from a collective society. The individual needs unconstrained space to think freely, to be truly creative, and to be able to tap the resources deep within his psyche. It's no accident that the periods in history where art and innovation flourished were those where the individual was accorded the most freedom. This was clearly evidenced in the Renaissance and in ancient Greece and Rome, as well as in Western Europe after the Enlightenment.

The uniqueness of each of us should be explored and cultivated, not squelched in the name of conformity and social harmony. Gilda Radner, a young comedian who died tragically of cancer, captured this well, saying, "It seems to me the only tragedy is to allow part of us to die—whether it's our spirit, our creativity, or our glorious uniqueness."

Liberalism devalues and diminishes the heroic. Heroes are not respected. Under the culture of liberalism, celebrity is instead exalted as it's empty of individual strength and virtue. It's largely aleatory, unmerited, and valueless.

Not only does collectivism harm the individual, it also hurts relations among individuals. In the Soviet Union family members spied on family members and children reported parents to the authorities if they said things against the State. There was a children's song taught in the schools of Bulgaria to the effect that children were heroes if they reported their parents to the State for unpatriotic thinking or statements. An easy way for divorce in the USSSR was simply to report a spouse as having said something against the State; in doing this the spouse would be summarily whisked away by the authorities and placed in a gulag or sequestered to Siberia. In the end, of course, nobody trusted anybody. I remember walking down the streets of the former Soviet Union in the early '90s; everyone walked with their eyes to the ground. No one would look anybody in the eye.

Liberalism also undermines individuality through its depreciation of sex. Sex is no longer intimate and personal. Its role in bonding males and females has been substantially eroded. Sex is no longer the lynchpin of marriage and family life. Sex is now everywhere, in the media, in advertising, and so on. Through its ubiquity, it is devalued; another important bond between humans has been weakened. Humanity is weakened as well. Only the State benefits, as individuals are diminished.

Let's recall John Stuart Mill's famous words: "The question with communism is whether there would be any asylum left for individuality of character; whether public opinion would not be a tyrannical yoke; whether the absolute dependence of each on all, and the surveillance of each by all, would not grind all down into a tame uniformity of thoughts, feelings, and actions: No society in which eccentricity is a matter of reproach can be a wholesome state."

Liberalism is disconnected from real people, from individual people; it's locked into an impermeable world of abstraction, focusing instead on *Man*. This disconnect accounts in part for the Left's willingness to accept massive purges in the march to progress; it's a price they are willing to pay, for they do not perceive the misery and loss at an individual level. The loss of life in the communist experiments in China and the Soviet Union did not bother them.

In essence liberals cry for "the poor," but they don't identify with the poor as individuals. They see them only in the abstract. In the liberal scheme of things the individual is not really real; he is only a part of the collective, the community. Perhaps liberals don't really like people, but feel guilty, and to transcend this guilt they talk of their compassion for the poor and the disadvantaged. But this is at a far remove from real life. This talk helps to relieve them of the responsibility and need to practice real compassion.

Joseph de Maistre captures the liberal view succinctly. He said, "There is no such thing in the world as man. In my life I have seen Frenchmen, Italians, Russians, and so on. But as for man, I declare I've never encountered him. If he exists, I don't know about it."[70] Of course, Frenchmen, Italians, and Russians are also abstractions, so it's more apposite if we think in terms of individuals, like Sue, John, and Fred.

Liberalism is fundamentally averse to the development of individuality and freedom. It needs to constrain and weaken individuals so that State power can be expanded unopposed. Liberals want a strong state with individuals dependent on it. They do not want strong individuals who can challenge the government and who have free reign from the State.

The traditions of self-reliance and individualism, which have played such a central role in our culture, are now under relentless attack and in decline. Liberalism is leading to bigness in all its forms: in government and in the business world. Organizations are getting bigger and bigger. A different culture is emerging, one of subservience, dependency, and bureaucracy. The individual is eclipsed by behemoth organizations and rendered little more than a handmaiden to their interests. Dependency is corrosive of the moral fabric and creates the opportunity for tyrannical oppression. As Thomas Jefferson noted, "Dependence begets subservience and venality, suffocates the germ of virtue, and prepares fit tools for the designs of ambition."

There is an old Chinese proverb: "Don't stand above the crowd, or you will be hammered down like a nail sticking out." Individuals should not shine or stand out, but rather blend in. This is the opposite of the meritocratic standards which have driven this country since its founding. It seems liberals are striving for a State founded on mediocrity and conformity rather than achievement.

Increasing Dependency

Increasing dependency on government is evident in America. According to *USA Today*, the following is true:

> "Americans depend more on the government assistance than at any other time in the nation's history. Eighteen percent of the country's aggregate personal income was made up of payments from the government for Social Security, Medicare, food stamps, unemployment benefits

and other programs in 2010. Wages represented only 51 percent of total personal income, the lowest share since records were initiated in 1929. Americans got an average of $7,427 in benefits each in 2010, up from an inflation-adjusted $4,763 in 2000 and $3,686 in 1990. From 1980 to 2000, government aid was roughly constant at 12.5 percent. The sharp increase since then, especially since the start of 2008 reflects several changes; the expansion of health care and federal programs generally, the aging population, and lingering economic problems."[71]

A study by the Heritage Foundation corroborates that dependence on government is the highest in the history of the United States. Government assistance in the early 1960s was extended to only twenty-two million citizens, now it goes to about sixty-seven million. According to the study, "The average individual who relies on Washington receives benefits valued at $32,748, more than the nation's average disposable personal income of $32,446. A full seventy percent of the federal government's budget goes to pay for housing, food, income, student aid, or other assistance with recipients ranging from college students to retirees to welfare beneficiaries."[72] This represents a twenty-three percent increase just since 2008.

William Boetcker once said, "You cannot help men permanently by doing for them what they can and should do for themselves." By their actions and policies, liberals clearly do not believe this to be true.

Lower Standards

Liberalism lowers the standards of not only the strong and successful, but also of the weak and vulnerable. Would we really be better off in a society with lower standards? We could lower the standards in school so that it's easier for students to get good grades and it would be almost impossible to fail. In fact we've already done this. Is this really good for our young people? The weak and those who have been mired in failure need to be encouraged to do better, not comforted in their weakness.

Our sports and games have always stressed success and prowess. These games also stress good sportsmanship. Should the nature of these games change so that they provide a means of expressing compassion, rather than for encouraging success and prowess? Perhaps feminine games, like playing with dolls, should replace the masculine games where physical strength and dominance is highlighted.

We could change the rules of baseball so that poor batters would be equal to good batters. Should the bat of a homerun hitter be shortened, softened, or made heavier? Should one who strikes out more often be allowed more strikes so that he wouldn't strike out more than other players? Would these changes really improve the game? Would poor batters really feel better about themselves? This would be so only if they no longer had standards of excellence. Is this what we really want? It seems this is what liberals want. It seems that liberals want to see life as a game of chance or roulette, rather than of merit and striving.

In the *Give Me Your Money* film the rules were changed so that everyone was given the same grade in class: before doing this some were getting A's, and the average was a B. After the rules changed, the average fell to a C. The next exam the average fell to a D, and after that to an F. This deterioration in student performance is not surprising, as the incentive of the good students declined and so did that of the bad students.

If two kids are selling lemonade, and one works hard and long while the other takes it easy and commits only a short amount of time, should both kids earn the same money? If the hard-working kid made thirty dollars and the lazy kid made ten dollars, should we take ten dollars away from the hard-working kid to give to the lazy one? If we did, would it not be clear that the hard-working kid would think it unfair and decide not to be so industrious in the future? Is this not what socialism and communism has taught us over and over again? How many times do we need to relearn the lesson?

In a game of monopoly, would you feel more comfortable in playing a game where the rules are binding on all players or in a game where one player can arbitrarily alter the rules without the consent of others? Who do you think would end up the winner in the latter scenario? Is it not better to play a game where the rules predominate and not the will of a particular individual? Where the will of an individual or the consensus of a small group or elite is allowed to prevail over the rules of the game, most people will come out losers.

Essentially liberalism seems committed to celebrating mediocrity and penalizing those who seek excellence and achievement. Some schools in Kentucky are reportedly eliminating the practice of valedictorians; they don't want to make other students feel bad. Basically those who don't want to compete are against seeing others who do and are interested in achievement and success. It seems the laggards and those content with mediocrity want to impose their values on others. Those who are hard-working and successful are not trying to impose their values on those who are not. People should be free to be unambitious and lazy, but they should also be free to strive and work hard.

Redistribution of Wealth

The redistributionist model is based on coveting and not excelling; it's based on reaching equality in outcomes, regardless of performance or even striving. Rawls, the liberal philosopher, argued that everyone should be equal in terms of life outcomes. Van Jones, one of Obama's czars, stated much the same. He said society should be structured in such a way that each citizen would feel comfortable reaching into a hat to select a life; in other words all lives should be about the same, so that no one could draw a bad lot. Apparently sweat and hard work should not play a part. We each should have a life where we would be relieved of choices, hard work, and sacrifices.

The roots of liberalism go back to Marx and are deeply rooted in communism which sees everything through the prism of class struggle. Liberalism has an almost monomaniacal fixation on class differences in wealth and income. It sees only injustice in income-and-wealth inequality, and cannot see other aspects or benefits of such differences. For liberals it simply is not fair that some have more than others.

Liberalism favors the redistribution of wealth. Liberals advocate progressive income taxation, taking money from the rich and giving it to the poor. This is not a dispassionate and analytically-arrived-at perspective. Liberals harbor a venomous hostility for the rich. They view the rich as uncaring and see them as living off ill-gotten gains.

This view is held strangely enough even by many wealthy liberals. But perhaps it should not be surprising that many wealthy liberals support redistribution. Some wealthy businessmen also are no doubt embarrassed by their wealth. They are self-conscious about appearing greedy and uncaring, so as a cover are given to professing support to liberal causes. This helps to ward off scrutiny and attacks by the liberal community. The super wealthy are also big businessmen who are likely to have substantial dealings with the government, so they are inclined to support government as it enhances their likelihood of getting government contracts. Also if they do not mouth the words liberals want to hear, they would be concerned about adverse government regulatory pressure being brought to bear on them.

It's a great misconception that the rich do not do good with their money. In addition to creating jobs and prosperity and new technologies—such as the Apple Computer and Apple products which make our lives easier, richer, and more interesting—the wealthy do substantial philanthropic work. They can only consume so much. Warren Buffet eats at McDonalds almost every day and H.L. Hunt, an oil billionaire, used to brown bag his lunch. You cannot eat a billion dollars of caviar a year. Bill Gates has created a multi-billion-dollar foundation to help the poor, and Warren Buffet has contributed a substantial part of his fortune to this foundation. Ted Turner, a successful American businessman, gave away one billion dollars to the United Nations. In short, these geniuses of capitalism use the funds much more to our benefit than the government, which merely throws the money at ineffective redistributive programs.

As part of my professional experience in Africa and the South Pacific, I became aware of the central role played by communal distributionist practices. In these cultures if one person worked hard and got ahead earning more than others, he was expected to contribute to others in his tribe. This represented a considerable deterrent to working hard and getting ahead, as the gains were largely reaped by others. It thus was yet another factor contributing to the economic stagnation plaguing these countries.

People have the right to be lazy and indolent. Everyone should be able to choose how much leisure they want to have relative to work. Everyone should be able to decide how much and how hard they want to work. But if they choose not to work or not to work hard, they should not then claim the product of the industrious, of those who have worked hard.

Who should have something, someone who earned it or someone who didn't? Should it be someone who merely takes it or receives it gratuitously or someone who creates something (value added) which did not exist before? Should it be someone who works for something or merely someone who wants something but won't work for it? What is the measure of want? Is it not one's willingness to work for something, to pay for something through labor and effort? For the liberal none of this matters.

This corrodes the moral fabric. We see in Sweden, a highly developed social welfare state, for example, a high incidence of sickness. One in five workers call in sick each day. Why go into work if you can get the same pay and benefits by not going? Why not stay in bed or indulge in recreation? Those who work and are diligent feel they are taken advantage of. There is an increasing lack of trust in others who are trying to get a free ride. Essentially immorality is fostered, and it's festering. When one gains as a free rider by getting others to work for him, others are clearly hurt. It amounts to another form of legalized theft. Is this morality?

Nor are liberals concerned that the money taken from the hard-working is channeled into unproductive government programs. For example, they argue that taxes should go up on the wealthy so that they can fund anti-poverty programs to help the poor. The fact that government-run anti-poverty programs are completely unproductive in ameliorating conditions for the poor is not a fact that they want to even look at.

Efficiency in government is not something that interests them. The money would have yielded better results, even for the poor, if it were left in the hands of the private sector where it could have produced jobs and economic growth, improving the lives of everyone. This would be a better outcome than having the money thrown away by an inefficient and bloated government. Looking at the issue in this way, however, is totally alien to the liberal. The only thing in their mind is "helping the poor" and striking a blow against the rich. It's a "fairness" issue pure and simple.

A more progressive income tax does not hurt the wealthy so much as those *aspiring* to be wealthy. It hurts those seeking the American dream. The rich already have their wealth. It's those lower down the ladder of wealth who are hurt most by stepped up progressivity in the income tax. Liberals are limiting the future upward potential of these people. They are basically stomping on the American dreams of those lower down the economic ladder, while they proclaim to help them.

It seems, however, that in the end they don't really care what happens to the poor. The results of their programs aren't as important to them as having programs addressing the purported purpose. It's the process or the motivation behind it rather than the end result which is important to the liberal, although he would not admit this. It's clear that this is the case, based on their continued adherence and promotion of programs that have poor performance outcomes. In fact in most instances the programs are counter-productive, leaving the intended beneficiaries worse off.

One of Einstein's famous dictums says it's insane to keep doing the same thing if you are constantly getting bad outcomes and expect to get different results. According to this, the continued persistence of liberals to pursue counterproductive poverty programs is insane—but is it? Just because their announced objectives are continually not met by their programs does not mean that liberals are insane or stupid. It's more likely that dissimulation is at play here, that liberals are cloaking their real objectives, perhaps not consciously but unconsciously. Their real objective is to satisfy their unconscious need and desire for the State to control their lives and the lives of others. They are uncomfortable with the uncertainty of the market and the uncertain outcomes involved with a free and open democracy. They are uncomfortable with making decisions in a complex world and would prefer if their lives were managed by a paternalistic government.

The redistributionist argument can be extended from the nation-state to the world, from national citizens to citizens of the world. Why should someone benefit in terms of material well-being merely because he is born in one country rather than another. Surely there is no merit in this. There is some truth to this argument, but from a pragmatic standpoint implementation would be deeply problematic. In the case of shifting income on a global basis from those in rich countries to those in poor countries, this would penalize societies that have worked well and reward those that are rife with corruption and inefficiency. It would mainly be to the benefit of corrupt dictators. Such a policy would foster bad government and dis-incentivize good government. Following the oil crisis of the 1970s there was a large financial infusion into developing countries, but this financial transfer led to major debt problems and lingering economic misery. Money was not the panacea it was seen to be for economic development. In fact, it caused even greater problems. As P.J. O'Rourke once noted, "You can't get rid of poverty by giving people money." Poverty is a symptom, masking underlying pathologies and problems.

Fairness to liberals is about equalizing, knocking down the high achievers, the successful. Recently Obama said, "If you've got a business, you didn't build that. Somebody else made that happen."[73] His view, almost Marxian in its tone and implication, seems to be that those who have wealth really don't deserve it. They are living off the efforts of others. High achievers are the people who have played a critical role in the success of western democracies. To hurt them is to undermine ourselves.

Liberals believe that everything should belong to everyone. They do not see the criticalness of private property to the proper functioning of an economy. They are also blind to the poor performance of communal farms in the USSR, and the poor condition of their public housing. In the case of the latter, light bulbs are not even replaced in the hallways, so the hallways are dark and dirty. Public housing in the USA, also, is run down and poorly cared for.

For liberals, fairness means equal outcome across people in wealth and material possessions. It's fairness in distribution, not fairness in production or contribution. If two men each have an apple farm, and one works hard and produces a bumper crop, while the other is lazy and lets his land deteriorate and his crop fail, the liberal does not care. To them the industrious farmer should share the financial reward of his crop with the failed farmer. They do not see the unfairness of penalizing the hard worker, who is contributing not only to himself but to society, while rewarding the farmer, who is unwilling to work hard and unwilling to contribute to society.

Obama and liberals criticize top-down, trickle-down economics; but it works better than bottom-up economics. Obama argues that in spreading the wealth around people will have more money to spend so business will prosper. These policies have been a dismal failure when tried both here and around the world. Liberals believe you can assist the poor by hurting the wealthy, but this just brings everyone down.

Alexis de Tocqueville, the famous French historian, noted, "The American Republic will endure until the day Congress discovers that it can bribe the public with the public's money." He also astutely observed that, "A democratic government is the only one in which those who vote for a tax can escape the obligation to pay it."

Equality

Man is essentially hierarchical, as are most creatures. It's not natural that everyone is equal. Moreover we are all different. John may be better than Steve at one thing, but Steve may be better than John in another. If we make both John and Steve equal we have to aim for the lowest common denominator, making both of them worse off. If everyone is to be made the same, who is to be the leader? Social status would take over from money as the scarce commodity. Is it better to be driven by power than money? One of the strengths of the capitalist system is that money and power are not vested in the same people or groups, so that one is a check on the other. It helps to prevent an abuse of power because power is decentralized.

What classless societies have we seen in history? There are always leaders and followers. Those societies that have come closest to this classless ideal are countries like the USSR, Mao's China, Fidel's Cuba, and Chavez's Venezuela. Are these models which anyone would want to seriously follow? The masses are galvanized into action with the illusion that they will gain influence and power. In reality, of course, just the opposite happens. They are manipulated like pawns in a sad game. Their actions and energies are involved only in changing those in the ruling class. A well-known political theorist, Gaetano Mosca has noted that rule by an organized minority is inevitable. Hierarchy is unavoidable as the masses are unorganized and never prepared to rule. [74]

A principal goal of liberalism is to equalize wealth by taking money from the rich, confiscating money from those who have earned it. It does not matter if you have earned it, all should have the same—except of course the ruling class, á la the USSR, where they all had special privileges, special places to shop, overseas travel, dachas.

But man is driven not just by money, but also by sex, power, and intellectual and moral superiority. Perhaps the smart should have some of their brains excised in order to put them on an equal footing with less well-endowed people, or they could take a drug to slow their mental processes. Similarly, those with more sexual prowess could be given a drug to diminish that prowess. Perhaps the attractive could have blemishes put on their faces or have their hair removed, so that they would not look better than those less physically attractive. Where does this stop? There would always be some people who are less attractive than others, even if one brought the particularly attractive down to the median or average level of attractiveness. One would have to set the bar at the level of the least attractive if we wanted to give everyone the same level of attractiveness. This makes no sense.

Liberalism criticizes capitalism for its success at creating a cornucopia of goods and services unequaled in human history. Yet they recommend socialist and communist alternatives that have had disastrous historical outcomes. During the height of the Cold War, when citizens of the USSR, Cuba, and China were willing to risk death to emigrate to the West, liberals still supported communism.

Liberalism criticizes the material emphasis of capitalism. They say material happiness is not happiness. This reminds me of an experience of mine in Central Park in New York City. In 1968 I was sitting on a bench and this attractive young girl comes to sit next to me on the bench. She promptly asked me, "Are you happy?" I said "Yes, I am." And she said, "You only think you are happy." That was the end of the conversation for me. I stood up and walked away. I believe she was one of the Hare Krishnas. Liberals are like this in that they believe most people are not smart enough to know what is good for them.

Around the world people have demonstrated that they want material things. People are voting with their feet, immigrating to countries which have higher material standards. Who is to say what people should want? Do we really want an elite class, or anybody telling us what we should want?

It's not really that liberals don't like materialism, but rather they don't like others to have what they don't have. It seems driven more by envy than anything else.

Liberals appear unhappy that some people are enjoying themselves. A life of pleasure and happiness is not enough for them. For liberals, man should not dedicate himself to his appetites and pleasure, but to some grander, more elevated striving. The Statist is bothered by individuals pursuing their appetites. Appetites are set by nature and individuals, not by the State. Statists do not like it that something is set beyond their control. When individuals are pursuing their appetites, they don't need leadership.

A life driven by the appetites and the pursuit of happiness is simply too unguided for liberals. It disturbs their sensibility for order and top-down control. A life devoted to developing the self is not worthwhile for them; rather one should sacrifice oneself for others, or more importantly for the State.

Liberals seem to seek an ataraxic state. They want a laid-back, worry-free world where wants and desires have been largely extinguished. Work and pain should not be a part of their world. We should all just have what we want. Life in their world should be easy, free of striving and want. We should not have to achieve or seek excellence. Being should be enough.

Complexity, pluralism, uncertainty, and discomfort are anathema to liberals. Liberals tout pluralism, but really don't want it. They want homogeneity. For them the world needs to be simple, monistic, risk-free, and pain-free. Everything has to be in order; everything has to fit together; there should be no conflict or disharmony; we should all be alike, none better or worse than another; there should be no risk of adverse outcomes; none of us should have to worry; none of us should have to suffer; none of us should really have to live. We should all be like domesticated animals or pets, coddled and sheltered, like the parakeet that can't fly free or the dog that can't run wild in the woods.

It was H.L. Mencken who said, "It's not materialism that is the chief curse of the world...but idealism. Men get into trouble by taking their visions and hallucinations too seriously." One virtue of materialism is that it's grounded in basic human appetites and needs. It's grounded in reality, in the here-and-now. Liberalism, on the other hand, is disconnected from reality and the here-and-now, and makes the satisfaction of human wants and needs more difficult. Reinhold Niebuhr, the famous 20th century American theologian, also saw clearly the "liberal fallacies of optimism and progress," which throughout history have led to the creation of unsustainable societies. Obama's "Hope and Change" mantra is yet another manifestation of this. Niebuhr recognized that one of the greatest threats to democracy is the moral idealist. The idealist fails to see the flawed nature of man, or thinks he can just wish it away. The idealist is enamored with the agglomeration of power as this is necessary to realize his utopian experiments in collectivism.

Idealism is good but it is essential that it is grounded in reason and reality; otherwise it becomes a loose cannon, creating the potential for doing much harm. Liberalism unfortunately has broken these links. And, more importantly, it has subverted the good intentions of idealists for the ill of society. Idealists, and Americans in general, are trustful and look for the best in people. This trusting nature makes them easy prey for those wishing to use this trust for bad purposes. Liberalism, driven by a hunger for power cloaked in the language of idealism, does just this. It transmutes the goodness of idealism into a baneful force.

Guilt

Liberals are preoccupied with guilt, because they cannot live up to their altruist (collectivist) morality. They feel a sense of shame and are embarrassed by anything smacking of self-interest or self-advancement. They feel guilty that they are selfish, so they try to mitigate these feelings of guilt through loud and highly vocal expressions of compassion for people in the abstract. Some liberals seem gripped by a palpable, almost desperate need for catharsis. It might also reflect itself in the form of self-destructive behavior, like drug addiction, which is so prevalent in America today; self-destructive behavior is a form of self-punishment.

Many liberals don't really like other people, but they feel guilty about it, so they compensate by espousing liberal policies of compassion. But, as mentioned earlier, if you look at the actual behavior of liberals, most give much less to charity than do conservatives. Liberal compassion is feigned, not real, and it is directed at man in the abstract, not particular people they know. Liberals are only comfortable with giving away other people's money, not their own. It is thus not surprising that they would have feelings of guilt.

Happiness

According to the Pew Research Center, only thirty-four percent of adults in America consider themselves to be very happy, fifty percent say they are pretty happy and fifteen percent say they are not too happy. Many explanatory factors—for example, marital status, religion, age, gender, ethnicity, and political affiliation—

were found to contribute to happiness. With respect to political affiliation, the Pew Research Center found the following:

> "Some forty-five percent of all Republicans report being happy compared with just thirty percent of Democrats and twenty-nine percent of independents. This finding has also been around a long time; Republicans have been happier than Democrats every year since the General Social Survey began taking its measurements in 1972. PEW surveys since 1991 also show a partisan gap on happiness; the current (February 2006) sixteen percentage point gap is among the largest in PEW surveys, rivaled only by a seventeen point gap in February 2003. Could it be that Republicans were so much happier then because their party controlled all the levers of federal power? Not likely. Since 1972, the GOP happiness edge over Democrats has ebbed and flowed in a pattern that appears unrelated to which party is in political power."[75]

Liberals do not understand that happiness comes from within. It comes from having the right values, moral and otherwise. It comes from individual effort, from setting objectives and accomplishing them. It comes from contributing to the community. It comes from fulfilling one's potential as a human being. It's not something manufactured, something provided, something received gratuitously. As George Bernard Shaw once said, "We have no more right to consume happiness without producing it than to consume wealth without producing it."

Liberals do not understand that happiness comes from self-reliance and achievement; it's not given or bestowed. They are not happy themselves, so they do not comprehend what it takes to become happy. They do not understand that happiness comes more from self-respect and liking one's self rather than from external circumstances.

There is a pathology here, stemming from a toxic mix of some of the famous seven deadly sins. *Sloth*, the failure to use one's abilities and gifts, is key—many have become spoiled and don't expect to have to work for something. We see ample evidence of this in the children raised today, particularly those of affluent parents. *Envy* is also a source of unhappiness. It arises from resentment of others for having something they don't. Thus, they are not only unhappy with themselves as they lack something they feel they should have, but they are unhappy with others who do have what they want. They feel a profound sense of "unfairness"—a word the Left is always throwing about tirelessly. This sense of unfairness and injustice naturally gives birth to *anger*, which ferments and boils, creating the basis for a festering and profound unhappiness.

Liberals believe people cannot control their own destiny. They feel the need for government help. They feel dependent and unable to help themselves. Those who feel they are able to control their lives generally are happier than those who feel feckless and helpless. This is not surprising, and it explains in part why conservatives are happier than liberals.

Marx himself led a miserable and unhappy life. He was a loner with little connection to other people, only to the concept of man in the abstract. He led a life of grinding poverty as he was unwilling to work as others did for a living. Only with the financial help of Engels was he able to make it. At the end of his life Marx himself said, "I am not a Marxist."

In Marxist ideology, all is about human suffering; they look to changing the world, not themselves. They expect happiness to be delivered on a plate. They don't think that one has to earn success or wealth. It should be a right, not a product of effort. The social and political system should deliver happiness to them; it's not something that they should have to get or find.

Liberalism reflects the mentality of the drug culture. If you are depressed or troubled, don't try to do something about it, just take a pill or inject something into your veins. Liberalism is a disease like drug addiction. Human potential is destroyed rather than bolstered and developed. Life is miserable. Rather than immersing oneself in life and developing one's potential and contributing to the community, this drug culture mentality seeks to hide from life; it contributes to a diminishment of life and is a drain on the community.

Liberals think that if you have everything, you will be happy. But as Bertrand Russell noted, "To be without some of the things you want is an indispensable part of happiness."

It's also not surprising that liberals are unhappy, because they are unhappy with the world. They see the world as a miserable place suffused with injustice. They see unfairness and victimhood everywhere. Victimhood is not an easy place to find happiness.

In contrast conservatives feel blessed to be alive and to have been born in the United States in particular. They understand that life is difficult, full of challenges and distressing events, but they see this as an intrinsic feature of life. Conservatives recognize that you cannot simply wish away what you don't like. Life is what it is—and it's beautiful. In essence conservatives feel lucky to be alive, whereas liberals feel aggrieved. That liberals are less guided by rationality than conservatives may also contribute to their predisposition to unhappiness. Horace Walpole once said, "This world is a comedy to those that think, a tragedy to those that feel." Rationality helps people maneuver their way out of difficult circumstances and deal with reality. Liberals are trapped by their emotions. They cannot handle feelings of failure or losing, because they feel they have no tools to extricate themselves from difficult circumstances. Their sense of fatalism and their lack of reliance on rationality make them feel entrapped. They believe only the government can rescue them from bad situations; they themselves are helpless.

I remember asking a successful liberal friend of mine why he and his wife had not had children. He said he would not want to bring anyone into "this miserable world." It is difficult to forget those words.

Everyone has a different equilibrium point with respect to happiness. The moods of some people fluctuate around a disposition of happiness, whereas others are gloomy all the time no matter what happens. Everyone has a different equilibrium point, in part determined by temperament and genetics. My father, a psychoanalyst with a sense of humor, had a nice anecdote capturing this psychological predisposition:

A psychologist performed an experiment on two boys, one an optimist, the other a pessimist. He put the pessimist in a room with electric trains to play with, and the optimist in a room full of horse manure. After a period of time he visited the two boys. The pessimist instantly complained about the trains. He didn't like the way they looked; they were not fast enough; and he thought they were cheap. As the psychologist entered the room with the optimist he was puzzled to find the boy digging frantically in the middle of the pile of horse manure. What are you doing, he asked? Oh, the boy said with a big smile on his face, there must be a pony in here somewhere.

Another psychiatrist, Thomas Szasz, noted, "Happiness is an imaginary condition, formerly attributed by the living to the dead, now usually attributed by adults to children, and by children to adults." Our system of government seeks to guarantee us the right to pursue happiness; it does not guarantee us happiness. No one can do that. Happiness is determined in large part by temperament and genetics. Some people, unfortunately, are destined in life to be miserable and unhappy. This simply cannot be changed. It makes no sense to turn the world upside down in the vain hope of bringing happiness to everyone. Happiness comes from within; it cannot be imposed.

There are defects in any production line, including the human production line. In a production line producing widgets, televisions, and cars there will be ones that just don't come out right and fail to meet basic performance standards. Some cars are simply lemons. Regarding humans there are sometimes just bad seeds. We all know some children who are brought up with everything going for them—a loving family, intelligence, good looks, good health, money, educational opportunities, and good people who care about them—and yet they grow up to be a burden to themselves and society. Some people are not going to be happy under any circumstances. It's not possible to save everyone and for everyone to be happy. It's an unrealistic goal.

With respect to the world of living creatures, Darwin tells us that those who are weak or unable die out, allowing the species to continually become stronger and enhance the survival prospects of the species. One should surely have compassion for the weak, but it would be a grave mistake to rewrite the rules of society to prioritize their interests over the interests of the achievers and the successful.

In Arthur Brooks' book, *Gross National Happiness*, he concludes that "efforts to diminish economic inequality—without creating economic opportunity—will actually lower America's gross national happiness, not raise it."[76] Opportunity is key, as job satisfaction and a sense of contributing value to society is fundamental to feeling content and happy. Opportunity allows people to seek out and find jobs that match their abilities and dispositions. The greater the opportunities, the less likely that one would settle for a job that isn't a great fit. Such an environment allows one the freedom to develop his potential.

Liberal attempts to intervene and micromanage will not increase happiness, much like their attempts at intervention in the economy will not enhance economic performance. But, once again, this should not surprise, since the real goal of the Left is power. They are not really interested in happiness, and certainly not the happiness of others.

In fact the most critical thing is not to have the government presenting itself as an obstacle to the pursuit of happiness. It should not impede its citizens in the pursuit of happiness. Unfortunately, under liberalism this is precisely what is happening. For liberals, if they can't be happy themselves, or manufacture happiness for those of their choosing, they are content with taking it away from others. As Russell Baker once said, "Misery no longer loves company. Nowadays it insists on it."

Greed

Liberals dismiss capitalism, claiming it is consumed by greed. They essentially make the argument that capitalism equals greed, and, since greed is bad, capitalism is bad. But greed is in wealthy countries and poor countries alike, and its manifestations are uglier and more malefic in the latter than the former. As Milton Friedman said, "The problem of social organization is how to set up an arrangement under which greed will do the least harm; capitalism is that kind of a system." In fact there is a great interview with Friedman where he's asked, "Isn't capitalism driven by greed?" He responded, "Do you think communism isn't driven by greed? Do you think socialism isn't driven by greed?" We can't cure greed or make it go away, so the best we can do is to harness it. Capitalism does that.

Moreover, capitalism is built on the psychological model of human nature that assumes humans are driven by self-interest, not greed. Greed is not equivalent to self-interest, so the liberal argument against capitalism doesn't hold water. Under capitalism, the pursuit of self-interest, as well as greed, yields benefits to others and to society. This cannot be said of other economic systems. Societies with large governments and with power centralized in the hands of a few without the checks and balances of democracy and without a large private sector subject to competitive forces are much more likely to suffer the ill effects of greed, and even of self-interest.

In addition to greed for money and wealth, there is also greed for power, social status, and sex. Overindulgence in any form is bad. Who should determine or define what greed is? Who should determine what others may or may not have? The liberal elite would like to do this, but who are they? And why should they have this right and control over others? As mentioned earlier, liberals are not really so much against materialism, only that others are more materially well-off than they are. The liberal obsession with greed is more a reflection of envy in their hearts than anything else. Why be so outraged over another person's circumstances? This rage was very much evident during the recent debate on increasing taxes for the rich.

Pessimism

The Left believe our best days are behind us. America is in decline. This is their hope, and they are trying their best to see that it becomes a reality. They are the enemy from within and are much more dangerous than external threats.

During the 1970s Democratic President Jimmy Carter characterized the country to be in a state of malaise. He said we would have to set our sights and expectations lower, as the future would not be as good as the past. His policies produced a toxic mix of inflation, slow economic growth, and high unemployment. Public confidence and expectations plummeted. It took Ronald Reagan to once again instill a sense of optimism in America. Like Carter, Obama (another Democratic President) has again cast the country into a funk. Pessimism is rampant, and few now expect the lives of their children to measure up to what they have enjoyed.

Hypocrisy

The Left is mired in hypocrisy. Liberals impugn moral imperatives by advancing moral relativism, but for them moral relativism has itself become a moral imperative. For example, for liberals the end of don't-ask-don't-tell policy or gay marriage simply should not be opposed.

Liberals are always complaining about intolerance in society, but intolerance is a prominent feature of liberalism. Liberals say people should not discriminate, for instance against gays or minorities—but in academia, the media, and the entertainment industry, conservatives are essentially blacklisted. Liberals complained about Senator McCarthy blacklisting communists following World War II, but now they're practicing it themselves.

Liberalism decries materialism, but what they really want is the wealth of others. Democrat Congressman Rangel, holding a prominent position, and well-known for his calls for social fairness and income redistribution, was called before Congress and censured for eleven ethics violations, including "submitting misleading financial statements and failing to pay all his taxes."[77] Geithner, Obama's Treasury Secretary, also had problems with his taxes.[78] Democratic Senator John Kerry, the Democratic presidential candidate in 2004, did not register his yacht in his home state of Massachusetts where the taxes are high, but instead registered it in Rhode Island where there was no tax liability.[79] Vice President Biden, who said of the rich that it's their patriotic duty to pay more taxes, even charges the Secret Service $2,000 a month to use a cottage on his property to protect him.[80] The term *limousine-liberal* is well-worn for a reason. Oliver Wendell Holmes said it best, "Redistribution or fairness is really just a form of legitimized envy." It's also, of course, an easy road to political power.

Liberals claim to be the party of the little guy, the common man, but they're full of elitist snobs, Harvard-educated snobs. When a little guy runs against them, like Sarah Palin or Christine O'Donnell, they run them down, dismiss them as uneducated, outside-the-beltway hicks and idiots. Democrats are the party of big government, big business and big labor; the little guy gets screwed; he is out of the game. When he thought the microphone was off, Obama was heard dismissing the common man and rural America as obsessed with clinging to guns and religion.

Barack Obama defunded the DC school voucher program that afforded inner-city kids and Afro-American kids a chance to escape the DC public education system, one of the worst in the country. Obama did this while he sent his own children to super-elite, expensive private schools, and while also supporting teachers' unions that oppose education reform, which could bring about improvement in education. To be fair to Obama, he is not unusual in this regard; the liberal establishment opposes school vouchers, and many other prominent liberals also send their kids to private schools and oppose reforms that could improve education for inner-city kids.

Conflict Avoidance

Liberalism, subscribing to cultural relativism, does not believe in good and evil. For the liberal, supposedly, one culture is as good as another. Ronald Reagan called the Soviet Union an "evil empire" and fought to defeat it; liberals were aghast at such language. For them the only sensible approach was one of accommodation. It was the same with the war on terror. George Bush called it a war; liberals do not see it that way. For them it's a matter of dealing with criminals. They scrupulously avoid using words like *war* or *terrorists*. Of course, it's interesting that they enthusiastically accuse conservatives of conducting a " war on women," while they refuse to use the term war in connection with Islamic terrorists and Osama bin Laden.

Courage and confrontation are not part of the liberal's vocabulary. Conflict and tension are to be avoided, except of course with conservatives. Compromise is their approach and talking about issues is their way of working, even when it's clear this leads nowhere. They are not willing to fight for anything. They do not recognize that there is such a thing as evil. The liberal does not understand the cost of *not* standing strong in the face of evil or exercising courage. Liberals think that everything should be easy and essentially free.

It almost seems that liberals want to take the passion and ardor out of life. Perhaps they see it as a potential challenge to the State. They want to see energy and direction coming from government, not the individual. It's best to keep the individual quiet, obedient, and devoid of passion.

For liberals anyone who believes in anything is a fanatic. In schools, religion is taught by comparing different religions. The idea is that each is okay in its own right, but no one religion is any better than another. Those believing in one religion and discounting others are typecast as fanatic. It's curious and ironic, then, that liberals are drawn into total faith in the liberal credo. Their fervor has the distinctive marks of fanaticism all over it. They don't tolerate other views, yet they freely hurl the word *bigot*, *fanatic*, or *extremist* at anyone who disagrees with them.

So liberalism has a strong strain of schizophrenia running through it. There is an asymmetry to their behavior. While liberals call on all others to exercise tolerance, they lash out with the fury of a bigot or fanatic when they are challenged in anyway.

Liberals believe in the absolute need to reduce tension. "Peace at any cost" is their motto. Nothing is worth fighting for. With this credo, the value of everything is reduced. It needs to be reduced; otherwise it would be worth fighting for. This is one of the reasons behind their drive to demolish traditional values. By disarming the public of their values and their passion, the public is rendered malleable, defenseless, and easy prey for subjugation. The disarmament is unilateral, however, as the ruling elite do not disarm themselves; the latter are driven by a single-minded passion to advance their agenda of political and cultural hegemony over others and respond aggressively to anyone opposing them. Essentially the game plan seems to be to deconstruct and weaken the moral values of others, while pushing their own values hard.

Incentives and Moral Hazard Problem

Perhaps the Left does not believe in the efficacy of incentives at all. To the extent that most of their policy prescriptions are based on perverse incentives, it would seem that they do not. Their policies reward the irresponsible and those who make mistakes, and penalize those who are responsible and succeed. The moral hazard in this policy approach is strong: these policies clearly encourage people to be irresponsible. Yet liberals aren't bothered by this. I am sure they don't raise their children rewarding them for bad behavior and failure and penalizing them for responsible behavior and success.

The entire liberal model is built on the sands of moral hazard, yet liberals keep trying to build their edifices higher and higher into the sky, even though failure is inevitable, based on previous experience, history, and common sense.

Their redistributionist welfare policies, bailouts of those unable to make their mortgage payments, bailouts of profligate state governments, and unions are all suffused with moral hazard. Despite the fact that Fannie Mae and Freddie Mac primarily caused the financial and mortgage crisis, Geithner and the Obama Administration in December 2010 were urging these institutions to decrease the principal on underwater mortgages. This would necessitate yet another bailout of these institutions which already have cost taxpayers billions and would saddle those who have been responsible home owners and taxpayers with still greater financial burdens.

Remaking Man

Psychology and history have shown that man is driven by self-interest and the pursuit of pleasure, but the liberal does not like this. He feels guilty about being self-absorbed and driven by pleasure. He thinks we should have more benevolent feelings toward one another and be driven by more exalted goals than pleasure. The liberal believes the nature of man can be changed, and he feels he is the one to reconstruct the nature of man. God or nature did not, apparently, do a good enough job.

Liberalism is about the prettification of behavior and morality, but it's a hollow and pallid morality without depth or strength. Liberalism sees man as flawed and miserable, but capable of being transformed into a better, altruistic being, an automaton in the service of the State. Liberals find strong appeal in eugenics. The hubris and arrogance of the liberal carries over even into the creation of man himself. He wants to recreate man, stripping the aspects of individuality and pursuit of self-development from his nature.

For liberals man can be changed principally in two ways; first, through behavioral modification via education and incentives, and, second, through eugenics. Thus liberals have placed great emphasis on getting control of our educational institutions. In this regard, they have been quite successful. The creation and advancement of teachers' unions has been instrumental to this success.

They also look to behavioral modification through changing incentives as part of their toolkit for change. They see the capitalist system's incentive structure as encouraging the pursuit of self-interest and competition rather than collaboration. This is one of the reasons why liberals feel the need to destroy capitalism.

Liberals see man as responding to the incentives of profit and materialism. They surely have to understand that removing these incentives will bring about a decline in activities motivated by profit and materialism, yet liberals will not acknowledge that this will bring about economic decline.

For liberals freedom is bad because it affords individuals the scope to follow decadent self-interest and not the grand, perfectionist, altruistic ventures of collectivism. The only way to reach the latter grand objectives is to eradicate freedom and with it individualism. The whole of society needs to be transformed from top to bottom and even the nature of man totally changed, but for the liberal this is not a pie in the sky fantasy, but actually a plausible and desirable option. It's so groundless and outlandish that it's no wonder that it's hard to have a reasonable discourse on anything with people who buy into this.

Liberals are against people exercising or having sovereignty over their own lives. They speak of freedom, but it's an empty freedom; where people are told what to think and what their values should be. They are also told what their goals should be. The goals should be those of the State, not the individual. Consequently, liberalism would disenfranchise the vast bulk of the citizenry. Citizens would continue to have nominal voting rights, but essentially the country would be run by the elite. Not believing the public is smart enough to run their own lives, much less guide the nation, the elite would seek to gain more and more control over the unwashed masses. Moreover, the elite do not feel beholden to them. They don't feel like they need to represent the voices of the public. The elite no longer think of representing "we" the people; the elite think they are superior to the people. They violate the will of the people, but think it's justified, as they consider themselves benevolent.

Liberalism believes in improving man, changing him; it does not accept man as he is; it ignores reality and is interested in imposing its fantasy. Jonah Goldberg in his excellent book *Liberal Fascism* chronicles and documents the close association of progressivism with eugenics. Eugenics has led to the horrors of genocide and racism. The thinking is some people are obviously better than others, so the deficient ones need to be eliminated. Eugenics leads to the dangerous meddling of man with his own biological make-up and development. Are we smart enough to handle this? Is it worth the risk? It's interesting that liberalism is constantly touting its interest in the underclass as its primary motivating force, yet it holds these classes in utter disdain and would basically like to see them as little more than slaves.

The Liberal Mind, Reason, and Discourse

The inconsistency between their stated goals and policies explain in large measure the aversion liberals have to reasoned discourse logic. Many liberals, of course, rely on reason and logic in the conduct of their personal lives, so they are in effect compartmentalizing their lives—some parts within the domain of reason and others not. Thus it would be hard for the liberal not to know underneath, or subconsciously, that his political positions run contrary to the principles of reason. This is why the liberal becomes so exasperated when others try to engage him in reasoned discourse on political issues.

The liberal is innumerate; he cannot understand that there are limits and that budgets have to add up and be funded in one way or another. The concept of trade-offs or quid pro quo isn't something he can grasp. Anything provided by the government seems free to a liberal. Why not have more of it?

Liberalism cannot be scrutinized. It's full of incoherencies and inconsistencies. It's not founded on logic or reason, but on fantasy. It's a world constituted of abstractions and the verbiage of collectivism. In the liberal's mind, the particular, the individual, and the real are shelved and dismissed as if they do not exist. The world we live in and see and grapple with is not the world of the liberal. It's hard, if not impossible, to connect the two. This again is a reason why the discourse between liberals and conservatives has broken down. It also explains the tension between the two: these worlds are not reconcilable.

Liberalism is replete with idealistic grand ambitions, but curiously is not oriented to action, only to moral posturing and pontification. It wants to see transformation and the exercise of power, but appears unconcerned if its goals are not achieved. The exercise of power inspired by idealistic vision is sufficient to satisfy the liberal, underscoring that it's the exercise of power and not the alleviation of poverty which is the real agenda of liberalism. Liberals criticize those in a capitalist economy for being too concerned with money and materialism, but they are intoxicated with power.

The liberal mind is afflicted with tunnel vision; there is only one right way. They are oriented toward a goal, and are not concerned with means or process. The only goal for them is a social welfare state with egalitarian outcomes.

Western civilization is based on struggle, competition, and the free ventilation of ideas. There is a Hegelian understanding and approach to reality. There are alternative perspectives and arguments. Liberalism, on the other hand, is opposed to struggle, competition, and the free ventilation of ideas. For liberals life should not be a struggle; it should be easy and harmonious. There should be no striving, no pain, no frustration, only easy bliss.

The ruling class is against thinking, except for the elite, as it could cause trouble. For liberals, the common man is not prepared to handle thinking responsibly. Liberals are against the use of reason, seeing it as part of the established order that has contributed to the oppression that they are so opposed to. Western civilization has been built on reason and skepticism, understanding that there are always multiple ways of looking at any issue. We always have to be careful to examine any issue from as many angles as possible. Liberals, however, are diametrically opposed to this approach. For them there is only one right way, and they want to be able to say what that way is without other points of view contravening them. They are also opposed to looking at evidence. For them the scientific approach of looking at evidence and using the tool of experiment is again part of the baggage of the age of reason.

Progressivism seeks to banish the world of individualism and reason and replace it with a collectivist, organic world order where reason is replaced with the enlightened judgments of the ruling elite. If this sounds like enlightened, or perhaps unenlightened, despotism, it is.

Intellectuals and Reason

Minorities and intellectuals buy into liberalism as it gives them short-term benefit. In the case of minorities it yields personal economic dividends and also protection of their rights. In the case of intellectuals it gives them a sense of power as they support the educated elite in their quest to control the unwashed and uneducated public. This comes, however, at a long-term cost as collectivism ultimately diminishes the rights and powers of both minorities and intellectuals.

Perhaps this commitment to liberalism arises out of ignorance or blindness to the trade-offs. Perhaps it's just another manifestation of selfishness or what's-in-it-for-me thinking. Perhaps it reflects a revealed time preference for today rather than tomorrow. Or perhaps, it reflects a genuine belief in the words of *hope* and *change* coming from the liberal elite.

It's interesting that many intellectuals and those populating academia buy into the liberal credo. You would think that these people would employ their critical mental faculties to analyze the liberal agenda and look at its strengths and weaknesses. Academia, however, like the media, has tossed rationality and critical thinking aside and has become an ardent unquestioning supporter of the liberal agenda. This perhaps should not be surprising as history has shown that intellectuals have played a key role in bringing about many totalitarian states. We need only look at the Soviet Union, Venezuela, and Cuba to see this. In China this, of course, was not the case. Intellectuals paid a heavy price there: they were hunted down and killed in the aftermath of the takeover.

Intellectuals and academics have paradoxically become anti-intellectual. They now are driven by agenda, not ideas. This has serious implications for our political future. As Abraham Lincoln once said, "The philosophy in the school room in one generation will be the philosophy of government in the next."

This is troubling not only because of its effects on the political process, but also because it signifies that man's capacity to use rationality for his benefit is much diminished. Man is distinguished from other creatures by his capacity for reason, but we seem almost desperate to throw this away. It's most interesting that the educated class is leading the way. It seems that the emancipation of the mind, which has received a big boost since the eighteenth century in America and Europe, is now threatened.

Rather than seeking guidance from reason and rational discourse, liberals pursue the politics of destruction. If someone is in their way, they are not interested in discourse, analysis, or compromise. The object is to destroy the other side. Slash and burn is their method of operation. You are either with them or against them. Conservative political leaders and Supreme Court nominees are routinely subjected to vicious attacks by the Left and the media. George Bush and Dick Cheney were called "war criminals" and Supreme Court nominee Bork was torn apart. The staff of Bill Clinton, a professed supporter of women's rights, allegedly tried to destroy the women who came forward with charges of sexual harassment. A Clinton aide reportedly called them "bimbo eruptions."[81] Moreover, a recent Wall Street Journal article noted that an Obama campaign website "took the extraordinary step of naming and assailing eight private citizens backing Mr. Romney."[82] The website said of these citizens that they are "wealthy individuals with less-than-reputable records." According to the author of the Wall Street Journal article, about a week after the website attacked these individuals, a former employee on the Democratic side of the Senate Permanent Subcommittee on Investigations was found requesting court records on one of the individual's divorces and on a dispute he had with a former employee. Although no connections were found between the investigator and political players, this is a troubling chain of events. Shortly after that, this Romney supporter became the target of two federal audits.[83] Apparently, it's no longer enough to go after just political opponents; liberals are also going after those who support their opponents. Are these not the unmistakable markings of totalitarianism?

To further remove the people from a say in the policy choices of governing, liberals hide behind complex technocratic solutions and legislation that defy understanding even by most of those who play a part in crafting them. For example, the Obama Health Care Reform package bill was about 2,700 pages, full of complex legal language. Even the legislator primarily responsible for the bill admitted that he had not read the whole thing. Nancy Pelosi, the House Majority Leader, said that we will only know what is in the bill after we pass it. Most members of Congress were only given seventy-two hours to read the bill. A deliberate attempt to hide behind a lack of transparency was clearly a key part of the liberal strategy. The Dodd-Frank financial reform package was similarly non-transparent.

Top-down planning plays a central role in the liberal approach to political economy. Liberals do not want those from below getting in their way. In addition to hiding behind complexity and a lack of transparency, liberals also lie about what they are trying to accomplish. For example, Obama repeatedly stressed that he was not interested in the government single-payer option and that most people would be able to keep their private health care insurance. He also emphasized that his plan would not add a dime to the budget deficit. These are clearly lies. He ran as a centrist for the presidency realizing that he couldn't win if he revealed his true ideological character. Apparently lying is okay if done for the "right" purposes and goals. It also underscores Obama's and the Left's contempt for the intelligence of the American people that he repeatedly lies in the face of clear evidence to the contrary and expects us to buy it.

Abraham Lincoln famously said, "You can fool all of the people some of the time, and some of the people all of the time, but you cannot fool all of the people all of the time." Unfortunately, in a democracy it is only necessary to fool enough of the people some of the time. Dissimulation has been working well for liberalism, but creating an agenda and a world where deceit prevails over truth cannot end well.

In favoring rule by an elite class over others who do not even have the legitimate right to resist, liberalism puts the bulk of humanity at risk of being controlled like puppets. People outside the ruling class would have no power to resist oppression. This is the historical record of experiments with collectivism. In the Soviet Union, those who disagreed with the ruling party were institutionalized in mental asylums. In China they were simply killed.

Demolition of the Constitution

The primary principle guiding the founding fathers in writing the Constitution was to guard against excessive and unwarranted government power. This after all was the reason behind the revolutionary war. In this light the founding fathers drafted the Constitution with the intent of limiting the power of the central government through separation of power, enumerated powers, and federalism.

Regarding the separation of power, the Constitution created three branches of government: the executive, the legislative, and the judicial. Given that no one body of government could write the laws, enforce them, or judge them, power was effectively dispersed. Checks and balances were built into the system to thwart tyranny. By enumerating the powers of each branch the framers also took care that each branch would not interpret its authority too boldly. Finally, by casting the form of government in federalism, significant powers were accorded to the states, thereby also limiting the authority and power of the central government.

Over time the Executive Branch has worked systematically to diminish the roles of Congress, the judiciary, and the states. Power is very centralized now in the Executive Branch. The institutional size of the Executive Branch has grown to mammoth proportions and now dwarfs the size and influence of the other branches of government. Congress has delegated much its legislative power to the Executive allowing faceless, unelected bureaucrats to craft regulations which have the effect of law. The Obama administration, as well as other administrations, also has bypassed the Senate's role in confirming appointments of the Executive branch through the use of unjustified recess appointments and the appointment of Czars.[84] In addition, the judiciary which was supposed to serve as an independent arbiter has been packed with political partisans, so its constraint on the power of the other branches has been significantly eroded. States also have only a vestige of the power they once had.

Liberals do not like the Constitution. They see it restricting the government too much. The Constitution was enacted to restrict the government, not the individual—but for liberals it should be the converse. Obama, before he took office, explicitly stated his dissatisfaction with the Constitution. In his view the Constitution is outmoded; it looks only at what the government should not do, not at what it should do.

In the Declaration of Independence it was written, "We hold these truths to be self-evident, that all men are created equal, that they are endowed by their Creator with certain inalienable rights, that among these are life, liberty, and the pursuit of happiness." Liberalism is compromising the liberty of individuals, and has turned the pursuit of happiness upside down. As mentioned earlier, the pursuit of happiness is not enough for liberals. For them we should be guaranteed happiness. It should be the obligation of government to make us happy.

The guiding principle in forming this country was equality of opportunity, not equality of outcome, but liberals emphasize only the latter. Equality of opportunity is inconsistent with equality of outcome. If you have the former you will not have the latter. The liberal government is working to render its citizens completely dependent on its arbitrary decisions. Why strive if there is equality of outcome? Individuals are at risk of losing the capacity to shape and influence their lives. Increasingly, government is able to coax and intimidate its citizens into submission and doing what it thinks they should do, not what they would like to do.

The government has forgotten that it works for us, not the other way around. The government believes that we work for the government. The ruling class no longer cares what the public thinks and wants. It's all about them now. Liberals in fact are pushing for a new bill of rights, calling for an expanded role for government.

The Obama administration has used the power of government against those expressing opposing views. The Internal Revenue Service beginning in 2010 began targeting conservative groups, particularly the Tea Party. It targeted the political opposition, especially those groups touting the importance of the Constitution, the Bill of Rights, limited government, and fiscal responsibility. It also targeted groups opposing Obamacare. There is no doubt about this, as the IRS has publicly admitted its culpability. The IRS specifically sought to deny tax exempt status to these groups, while it expedited such status for groups with liberal views. The IRS also harassed conservative groups with tax audits, and divulged confidential information submitted by them to liberal media sources.[85] It is interesting that the Obama administration vigorously protects the rights of terrorists, insisting on Miranda rights and legal protections, while it seeks to take away rights from citizens believing in Constitution and America.

In addition to this devastating attack on the First Amendment right of free speech, the government also has been assaulting the rights of the media. The Obama administration secretly obtained the phone records of the Associated Press. The CEO of the Associated Press said that this has already "had a chilling effect on journalism," making "sources less willing to talk." The government cited national security reasons for the seizure, but the Associate Press withheld the story for 6 days and only released the story when two administration sources said it was no longer a problem for national security.[86]

Attorney General Holder also personally signed off on a warrant allowing the Justice Department to search the personal emails of Fox news reporter James Rosen. To justify the warrant, it named Rosen as a co-conspirator in a crime to obtain classified information from the government. Essentially the government designated the pursuit of investigative journalism as criminal activity. This is almost unprecedented in American history, and represents a gross transgression and a violation of our right to privacy and the freedom of the press.[87]

The Obama administration has also massively expanded secret surveillance programs under the NSA on American citizens. It has collected huge amounts of information on phone calls and internet communications in gross violation of the Fourth Amendment's protections of the right to privacy.[88] Just one NSA program alone collected one trillion internet metadata records in the five years ending 2012, with half of this coming in 2012.[89] The Fourth Amendment, which protects against unreasonable search and seizure of the personal effects and papers of citizens, is no longer respected. The relationship between individuals and government has been fundamentally altered. It is one thing to use secret surveillance to target terrorists and quite another to employ blanket surveillance of all Americans.

Moreover, with the introduction of Obamacare the IRS is now mandated to collect the private medical records of Americans.

This represents yet another insidious intrusion into our personal lives. The government will have access to personal information which clearly could be used to intimidate and silence people. This would, of course, be wrong and it shouldn't happen, but the IRS has already shown that it cannot be trusted.

The Left wants to restrict what people can say under its "political correctness" juggernaut. Free speech is fundamental to our way of life, but it has been under full-scale assault. Under the "Fairness Doctrine," the Left has been trying to restrict the right of conservative radio to present opposing views. The Left also has largely co-opted the mainstream media and the press, so that the latter are no longer providing the public with independent views and unbiased reporting. Unbiased reporting is pivotally important to the proper functioning of a democracy.

As mentioned, federalism is a prominent feature of our government, but it has been under relentless assault by liberalism. The Tenth Amendment to the Constitution was intended to preserve state's rights and limit the power of the Federal Government. According to this Amendment, "The powers not delegated to the United States by the Constitution, nor prohibited by it to the states, are reserved to the states respectively, or to the people." Does anyone doubt that this amendment has become largely meaningless, as the Federal Government routinely and relentlessly has ignored it and pushed to expand its influence? Over time the power of the federal government has grown exponentially and now dwarfs the powers of the states. This is a threat to liberty and it erodes the power of citizens to influence policy. Each state and locale is different. Each has different population mixes and different needs and interests. When states have power, they can address these needs and interests directly. They are closest to the needs and wants of their citizens. Each state can have different policies to address their different constituencies. On the other hand, once the federal government has largely usurped the powers of the states, this is no longer the case. With the federal government playing the dominant role, policy is now set on a one-size-fits-all basis, so there is no recognition of the diverse needs of citizens from different states. The federal government is not as close as the states to the needs and wants of citizens, so it's less attuned to those needs and wants. In addition, monitoring the implementation of programs has become more difficult as the federal government is further from the impact of those policies.

There is much virtue to the federal system where states are accorded considerable autonomy. Each can solve problems in different ways. Each can learn from the experience of others. For example, each state approaches policies to health care insurance differently. Governor Romney introduced an approach to this issue in his state of Massachusetts which differed sharply from those in other states, but this has been a useful learning experience for all states. Now, however, liberals wish to take over this sector of the economy as well and impose a one-size-fits-all solution to the states.

Thus nowadays the states are largely subservient to the federal government. Federalism has been seriously eroded and diminished and is now only a pale shadow of what it once was. Not only does the federal government exercise powers which the Constitution meant states to exercise, but if states protest and attempt to challenge the Federal Government, the latter browbeats them and threatens to withhold their share of federal revenues.

Many representatives and constituents of states argue that it's unconstitutional for the federal government to force states to pick up the bill for federally designed and established programs. Basically the federal government is seizing control of state budgets. For example, Obama's health reform program, by lowering the bar to access Medicaid, is expected to boost enrollment by up to twenty-five percent. This is going to put a huge financial burden on the state governments. States are free to withdraw from Medicaid, but this is unattractive because taxes on its citizens wouldn't be lowered, but federal benefits would.

Liberals have undermined the judicial branch of government by appointing judges who interpret the law liberally. In so doing, liberals have circumvented the intent of the founding fathers. Where they have had trouble pushing their agenda through the legislature, liberals have sought to bypass the legislature completely and make law from the bench.

The individual insurance mandate in the Obama health care law requires citizens to buy health insurance. The government argued that it has the power to do this under the interstate commerce clause (Article I, Section 8, Clause 3). But this clause regulates interstate commerce, whereas laws in the United States prohibit purchase of health insurance across state lines. Moreover, the interstate commerce clause applies regulation on activity, not non-activity. If the government can regulate even non-activity, its authority has no bounds. Individual liberty would be severely threatened. If the government could order a citizen to buy health insurance, why not a GM car?

Chief Justice Roberts voted to sustain ObamaCare, ensuring its survival by a 5 to 4 vote in the Supreme Court. His vote was the deciding the vote. Four other Justices voted to invalidate ObamaCare in its entirety. Roberts was nominated for the Court by George Bush, but he voted with the liberals on the bench. Why?

Roberts said it was not his job to protect the citizenry from the consequences of its political decisions. This is true. But it is his job to protect and defend the Constitution, and he failed. His vote was result driven, not process driven. Even he agreed that the Administration's argument for the law on the basis of the Commerce clause was not valid. Even he argued that the mandate was not a penalty as argued by the Administration, but a tax. As Justice Kennedy said, the Supreme Court should not be in the business of rewriting law, but that is precisely what Roberts did. The law was passed with pledges from Obama that it was not a tax. The bill would not have passed if it was considered a tax. Yet Roberts said that despite the fact that the Obama Administration steadfastly maintained that it is not a tax, it nevertheless could be considered as a tax. Roberts seemed more concerned with the outcome than in the process. Justice Anthony Kennedy dissented, saying Roberts was "guilty of vast judicial overreach" and of attempting to "force on the nation a new act."

Roberts appeared cowed by the attack that he knew the Left was preparing to launch against the Court. After the Court's involvement in the Bush-Gore presidential election, the political profile of the Court has risen. He seems as though he was trying to preserve the stature of the Court as above politics. But in trying to preserve the stature of the Court, he has abandoned the Court's mission which is to protect the Constitution. What is the Court if it has sacrificed its mission? What has Roberts preserved? If he did not have the courage to defend the Constitution, he should not have accepted his nomination to the Court.

The liberal justices are never driven to protect the Constitution. They don't like it, even though they have sworn to defend and protect it. They are driven by agenda, not law or the Constitution. They do not back off. Their votes are never in doubt by the Left. All four of the liberal Justices on the Court voted to sustain ObamaCare even under the Commerce Clause as this would give virtually unlimited power to government. The problem with moderates and conservatives is they still believe in compromise; the Left does not. This means that slowly and steadily America as we know it is being dismantled. The State is growing like a cancer and destroying America.

This country is being fundamentally transformed by ObamaCare which was pushed through Congress in a highly partisan way, using questionable legislative techniques, and is now being validated by the Supreme Court in a 5 to 4 decision. Is this really the way we want to move our country forward?

ObamaCare (the Patient Protection and Affordable Care Act) asserts that the Independent Payment Advisory Board that it created to contain health care costs can make "legislative proposals" which become law unless Congress passes a law with a supermajority, including sixty percent of support from the Senate, which would save at least as much money as the proposal of the Independent Advisory Board. Essentially this appropriates the legislative authority provided to Congress by the Constitution and expands the powers of the executive branch. It further centralizes power. It reflects the view of the progressive mind that issues are too complex to be handled by the people. Issues of complexity in their mind need to be handled, not by the people, but by experts. Of course, these experts would be picked by the progressive elite and of course they would be "impartial and objective." Of course, they would not allow politics or power to influence their decisions. Of course, we are supposed to believe this. [90]

ObamaCare also violates the Constitution in that it limits the power of subsequent congresses to amend the law. Under the law, Congress cannot introduce a resolution to eliminate the IPAB before 2017, and the law would have to be enacted before August 15th of that year.[91]

All three branches of government now have powers vastly in excess of that originally envisioned by the founding fathers. Each branch was meant to be a check on the power of the others, but this restraint on power has eroded. The executive branch is now much more powerful than the other branches. Moreover, the executive branch has tried to use the judicial system to transform our society. Liberals realize that it's difficult to bring about change through the legislative process, so they try to bypass that branch. They appoint judges who share their political agenda, rather than judges interested in interpreting the law.

The founding fathers also did not anticipate the huge growth in the size of the government and the massive workforce that must staff it. The federal bureaucracy has become another important branch of government, affecting how policy, legislation, and regulation is both formulated and implemented. Its self-interest is in seeing further growth in the federal government. Its interests are not those of the citizenry, but its own.

Respect for the law is fundamental to civilized society. The Left is undermining the current social order by devaluing and disrespecting our laws. We clearly see this with respect to immigration laws and also drug-use laws, and by the liberal effort to put liberal judges in the courts so that they can bend the law to move their agenda along. The liberals are very close to their goal of achieving dominance on the Supreme Court. There are currently four solid liberal justices on the Court; with the appointment of only one more liberal judge, they will succeed in gaining control of the Supreme Court and it will become almost impossible to stop the liberal juggernaut.

Voter fraud is another diminishment of democracy engendered by liberalism. Allowing illegal immigrants to vote is a major manifestation of this. ACORN, a group sponsored by and staffed by liberals including Obama in the past, was allegedly caught engaging in voter fraud all over the country. Apparently, deceit is okay if it's for a "good" cause.

The Heritage Institution has a paper on the "Over-Criminalization of America" in which they put a spotlight on the excessive rules, regulations, and laws on the books. The rule of law is depreciated through the excessive creation of new laws. In addition, the rule of law is devalued as the government selectively picks and chooses which laws it wants to enforce or not enforce. Herbert Hoover, once said, "If the law is upheld only by government officials, then all law is at an end." Nowadays, incredibly it is the government that is not upholding the law. Max Weber, the famous sociologist, noted that respect for the rule of law is fundamental to the survival of democracy as is faith in rationality in creating rules and laws.

Liberals are continually attacking the Second Amendment, which gives citizens the right to bear arms. The right to bear arms gives individuals strength and the capacity to defend themselves. Liberals are averse to strengthening individuals, so it's not surprising to find them trying to take the right to bear arms away from citizens.

Recapitulating, it's of fundamental importance that we preserve the Constitution and limit the power of the judiciary to interpret it and read into it what they want. It's better to be governed by a system of laws and rules than to be governed by men. Liberals are averse to laws and the Constitution as it limits what they can do. But this is precisely why we need the Constitution and the rule of law. It's akin to why liberals also do not like the free market; it's because the market is based on ruling principles and forces that the ruling elite cannot control. But, again, this is why we need it. Abraham Lincoln noted, "Don't interfere with anything in the Constitution. That must be maintained for it's the only safeguard of our liberties."

Affirmative Action

The Left believe that all interest groups should be represented proportionally in desired positions of employment and in college enrollment. This is one of their priority objectives. This was first embodied in affirmative action programs for blacks, but it has now been extended to women. Merit and qualifications don't factor into their thinking; they simply want to see a certain proportion of jobs filled by blacks and women. Blacks have predominated in sports, particularly basketball and football. Relative to their numbers in proportion to the population, they are way over-represented in these sports. Jews, on the other hand, have excelled in other occupations, principally medicine and law. Based on the logic of the Left, we should mandate that a certain percentage of basketball and football teams be manned by Jews and a certain percentage of brain surgeons be blacks. Wouldn't this make for a better society? Of course, over time one would expect more proportional representation of different ethnic groups in various vocations, but this should be allowed to evolve naturally. It should not be forced or imposed. If Jews prefer to be doctors rather than football players, so be it.

The liberals have cast this emphasis on proportional representation in employment and housing as a right subject to legal protection. This is great for the Democratic Party's constituency of lawyers as it affords them a great source of income as they can bring massive suits against firms charged with not upholding these rights. It is of course difficult to prove one way or the other, but it can cost firms dearly and of course the lawyers win no matter who loses.

This, of course, is not constructive for society. It raises costs, limits flexibility in the work place, and constrains efficient production practices. It also exacerbates divisiveness and takes the focus off merit. Various groups vie for the designation of *victim*. Better to be a victim than an industrious employee in their new world.

Affirmative action is a major plank in the liberal platform. It originates from looking at society in terms of division and separateness rather than looking at society as a whole. Beginning in the sixties, liberals pushed for affirmative action for blacks, saying that universities had to favor (or prejudice) their decisions to admit blacks into school. Likewise, businesses were pushed to favor blacks over white candidates of similar qualifications, and were even pushed to hire those with inferior qualifications. Affirmative action is based on the thinking that we need to redress past injustices and inequalities by introducing policies predicated on treating people differently, not the same. Shouldn't the solution be to treat everyone the same?

Affirmative action is just another form of liberal interference in the private sector. Affirmative action and legal protections have expanded to cover not only race, but religious minorities, gender, and the handicapped. The question is, where does this end? A prominent member of the liberal media actually argued that we should seriously consider offering affirmative action to the ugly.[92] He noted that ugly people, according to research, earn ten to fifteen percent less than attractive people. Over a lifetime this amounts to $230,000 less in earnings for ugly people. In the District of Columbia and California, discrimination based on looks is already prohibited by law.

Where does this end? Some men prefer blondes, others brunettes and others redheads. Do we consider this discrimination? Should we not require by law all men to date women without regard to hair color or, for that matter, ethnicity? Should men showing a preference through behavior be subject to discrimination lawsuits?

Have affirmative action policies been effective and have they served the public good? This is an open question. Certainly, the number of blacks enrolled in college has gone up and we see blacks representing a larger proportion of the labor force in some sectors of the economy, particularly government. But perhaps this was going to happen anyway.

I know people in the restaurant industry, and I've asked some of them why they didn't have more blacks on staff. The preponderance of their staff was Hispanic or from other ethnic backgrounds. The restaurant owners said the big problem for them is affirmative action; if they hire a black and he doesn't perform well, they cannot get rid of him for fear of a lawsuit. Thus, they simply choose not to risk hiring blacks. This is a big negative for affirmative action that is not often discussed. It scares business owners and actually may reduce the number of jobs offered to blacks. Consequently, affirmative action may be doing more harm than good. Certainly, unemployment numbers for blacks are high.

In addition, does it really help blacks to get into college with lower standards than other ethnic groups? Does it really help them if schools treat them more leniently than other students? In lowering the bar for them are we not expecting less out of them? Are we not encouraging them not to measure up to the standards of other students? As an employer looking to hire someone, would you not be concerned that the college diploma of a black applicant is worth less than that of a candidate from another ethnic group?

Even more fundamentally, affirmative action probably adversely affects the self-esteem of blacks. Many probably think they would not be where they are today if they hadn't been treated more favorably than others, if the bar had not been lowered for them. It diminishes their sense of achievement and satisfaction. In summary, are blacks really helped by affirmative action?

A strong case can be made that liberal policies are keeping the black community dependent and subjugated. Liberal policies hurting the education system are keeping the school system poor, particularly in the inner cities. Welfare programs have enhanced black dependency by discouraging participation in the work force and by breaking up black families. By hurting job creation, liberal policies are keeping blacks reliant on government hand-outs. Liberal politicians are always proclaiming that they want to see blacks get ahead, but what they really want to do is keep them dependent on liberal policies and big government. By keeping them on the plantation so-to-speak, they can count on their votes. If blacks were to break free of reliance on government, liberals might lose their political support and see their power base diminished. They clearly don't want that, so their seemingly contradictory policies really do make sense from the standpoint of their own self-interest.

Liberty

In a speech on behalf of Barry Goldwater on October 27th, 1964, Reagan said, "This is the issue of this election, whether we believe in our capacity for self-government or whether we abandon the American Revolution and confess that a little intellectual elite in a far-distant capital can plan our lives for us better than we can plan them ourselves."

Reagan went on to say, "You and I are told increasingly that we have to choose between a Left or Right, but I would like to suggest that there is no such thing as a Left or Right. There is only an up or down to man's age-old dream—the ultimate in individual freedom consistent with law and order—or down to the ant heap of totalitarianism."

Invoking the spirit of Thomas Jefferson and the Declaration of Independence, Reagan said, "Our natural, inalienable rights are now considered to be a dispensation of government," he declared correctly, "and freedom has never been so fragile, so close to slipping from our grasp as it is at this moment."

In the *Empire of Illusion*, Hedges, a far-Left philosopher and thinker and winner of the Pulitzer Prize for this book, sees corporations and business as the big threat to individual liberty. He sees corporations as enforcing a kind of servile sameness on the public, dampening creativity and freedom of expression. But is not big government a much greater threat to liberty and individualism? In fact it's business and the private sector that create the pluralism necessary to offset political power; it's necessary for the business and private sector to be strong and independent in order to prevent too much agglomeration of power in any one place. It's only in those countries where political and economic power are separate that there is real liberty.

There is a threat to liberty where government gets too large and engages with the business community too much. In such circumstances government can and does co-opt the business sector. The two sectors become inextricably linked to the detriment of society. Business no longer directs its energies to satisfying the market; instead it focuses on siphoning off money from the government. The government indirectly obliges businesses to channel money back to the politicians. An oversized government not only impinges on the private sector directly, but also indirectly, and adversely impacts individual liberty.

Is not the pursuit of an altruist political philosophy an intrinsic threat to individual liberty and freedom? When the whole of society, not the individual, is viewed as the target for how policy should be formulated, is this not clear?

Freedom for liberals is not individual freedom, but freedom to reconstruct history, create fictions, and play games with the mind of man and his future prospects. Liberals are so engaged in the sequestered world of their beliefs that the influences of the real world seem not to touch them. They live in a world of their own virtual reality, immersed in a drug-like high on the myth of progressivism.

It's sometimes said, for example in Michael Novak's *Two Wings* and Roger Scruton's *Liberty and Civilization* that the concept of freedom is of two types: the Greek concept of man as owner of himself and the Judeo-Christian notion of freedom as the unconstrained space for independent thinking and making responsible choices.[93] The liberals, according to Scruton, have bought into the former, whereas conservatives subscribe to the latter. I don't know that I agree; it seems to me that liberals are headed not toward freedom, but tyranny and totalitarianism. Their behavior is not so much oriented to staking out territory for the individual as it is to tearing down the foundations on which individuality has flourished. It's true that some naïve liberals actually try to stake out and expand the space for their own lives as they want to live them, but their methods and mentality are militating to the destruction of individuality from a societal standpoint. There is irony here: liberals are contributing to the decline of individual freedom in society as they pursue its expansion in their own lives. But perhaps this should not be that surprising as the wellspring for the motivation of liberals appears to be selfishness, not the altruism that they so vocally express. It's a what's-in-it-for-me mentality. Their focus is short-term and myopic; they don't really care about the consequences for others or for future generations.

Political Correctness

One of the fundamental pillars of our democracy and our Constitution is free speech. Political correctness sponsored and supported by the Left is a direct assault on free speech. Saying the wrong thing can get you fired, sued, and socially ostracized. Political correctness is strangling not only free speech, but free thinking. The Left is trying to legislate morality and speech.

Political correctness is nothing more than censorship by the Left. If they do not want to hear it, you cannot say it. Moreover, it's not only that they don't want to hear it; they do not want others to hear it. Thus, they strive to get the opposition to censor themselves. Meanwhile they push their views through the liberal-controlled media. The penalties are extreme for violating their sensibilities: boycotts, attempts to have people fired, ostracism, ridicule, and the politics of personal destruction.

It's tyranny exercised by a conglomeration of minorities. McCarthyism is not dead. Jimmy "The Greek" Snyder, a television sports commentator, was fired for saying that blacks have a genetic advantage over whites in football.[94] The Left, through protests, have often tried to keep Clarence Thomas, the conservative Supreme Court Justice, from speaking on college campuses, because they do not like his political views. Ann Coulter, a prominent conservative, has also been shouted down and prevented from speaking by the Left.

Juan Williams was fired from NPR, a liberal radio station, allegedly for a statement he made on the O'Reilly television show indicating that he felt nervous on an airplane if he saw people wearing Muslim-style dress. In commenting on his firing, Juan Williams, an African American journalist noted for his liberal views and strong support for civil rights, said the following:

"To say the least this is a chilling assault on free speech. The critical importance of honest journalism and a free flowing, respectful national conversation needs to be had in our country. But it's being buried as collateral damage in a war whose battles include political correctness and ideological orthodoxy."[95]

The CEO of a fast-food restaurant chain called Chick-fil-A made a public statement that he believes in traditional marriage and not same-sex marriage. As a result of the statement, liberal mayors in Chicago, Boston, and the District of Columbia said that Chick-fil-A was not welcome in their cities. This was done despite the fact that the CEO was simply expressing his opinion as an individual and made clear that his company in no way discriminates against anybody who has different beliefs or life style choices. In effect liberals were not only exhibiting intolerance regarding free speech, but also freedom of religion, and even freedom of commerce.

Political correctness is really about thought-policing. It's against independent thinking and trusting one's own internal dialogue. Liberals say they're all about tolerance, but in fact it's just the opposite. The hypocrisy is all-enveloping.

Political correctness, widely espoused by the Left, has been undermining not only free speech, but free thought. If one utters a "wrong" word about race, ethnicity, or sexual orientation and gay rights, the media and the Left goes after them with a vengeance. Liberals buy into the modern-day version of public lynching. An apology or the possibility that one was misunderstood is not enough for them. They want to destroy the targeted person. Certain radio personalities, like The Greaseman in Washington and Don Imus in New York, specialize in saying outlandish and comical things, so it's natural that on occasion they cross the line. The Left got The Greaseman fired for a race joke and Don Imus dismissed and pilloried for the use of inappropriate racial slang.[96] Both apologized and admitted their mistake, but this wasn't enough. It seems that we must now be guarded in our speech. Even joking is fair game for the Thought Police.

Certain highly-funded leftist groups monitor each word conservatives like Rush, Hannity, and Mark Levine say on the radio. They are just waiting for someone to make a statement that they think they can use to punish them.

George Allen, a prominent and highly respected ex-governor running for the Senate seat in the State, was destroyed for using one word: *macaca*. It was not even clear what the word means or what the governor meant to imply in using the word, but the Left and the media destroyed him for using it as it can have racial connotations.[97] One word, even an ambiguous word, can be fatal in this politically correct world we live in.

Moreover, what makes this all the more egregious is that it's completely asymmetric. If a person is liberal, he may utter the most politically incorrect words, and it's OK. It's only if the person is not one of them that the standard of political correctness is upheld.

Our sexual orientation has deep biological, psychological, and social roots. Most men and women have deeply ingrained and visceral unconscious feelings about sex. Most men feel disgust and repulsion at the idea of having sex with another man; they cannot help this. It's their biological nature. Yet in this age of political correctness, a man cannot say this. If he says it, or even thinks it, he is labeled a bigot. When the culture gets to the point where it can suppress a truth as fundamental as this, it's in deep trouble. Truth is dead, as this is almost the ultimate truth. It's not just truth at an intellectual level that is dead, but truth at a visceral level.

Of course, if a person is homosexual he should be able to say this openly, as this is his truth, and liberals are rightly strong in their support of this. But they are wrong in denying someone who feels a visceral repulsion to homosexuality to express this as well. Discrimination based on likes and dislikes is one thing and should be thwarted, but speaking one's mind and expressing one's views is another.

The Obama Administration has not only tried to constrain free speech, but political activity as well. An important component of free speech is the right to make financial contributions to the politicians and party of your choice. In 2010 the Supreme Court ruled that "corporations and unions can pay for political ads anonymously." Obama was upset with this ruling, as he has been at odds with the Chamber of Commerce. He vented his anger at his "State of the Union" address, with some of the Supreme Court Justices sitting right in front of him. To counter this, the White House has circulated a draft executive order that would require "companies with federal contracts to disclose their political contributions." This clearly runs counter to the Supreme Court's ruling and represents a serious threat to political liberty in this country. The government can strong-arm and intimidate companies with government contracts to support the party in power, in this case the liberals. Not only does the draft proposal require companies to disclose their financial contributions, it also requires the top officers of the companies to do likewise.[98]

Government is the negation of freedom. Freedom granted is not freedom at all. To grant freedom only if the consequences are in line with what the authorities want and expect is not real freedom; it's circumscribed and constrained. Freedom needs to be allowed without thinking what the consequences will be. Individuals should be left free to make their own decisions.

Moral Freedom

Inconsistency marks liberal views with respect to economic and moral freedom. While they profess support for freedom in morality, they are opposed to freedom in the market place. They do not believe in economic freedom and do not understand its connections and implications for other freedoms, including moral freedom.

Despite their declarations, however, the Left does not really believe in moral freedom either. Liberals say that personal and moral values should not be determined by politics or government. Of course, in practice they violate this credo.

It should be noted that conservatives also are inconsistent with respect to freedom in the market place and freedom of morality. They favor economic freedom, but religious conservatives are inflexible concerning, for example, abortion rights. But are not morals important? Should we really take the position that anything goes? Libertarians are consistent; they favor freedom in both markets and the moral sphere.

Liberals like to bathe themselves in moral righteousness, but live lives of immorality. Numerous prominent liberal leaders have treated women poorly, but claimed publicly to be big supporters of women's rights. For example, Democratic presidential candidate John Edwards cheated on his dying wife.[99] Why can't liberals live the lives they preach: donate to the poor and divest themselves of wealth? Liberals say there is too much materialism, yet they ensconce themselves in luxuries.

Liberals say they care about people, but their policies hurt people. They are hiding behind "good intentions" and label anyone who opposes them as having bad intentions. This seems to be their way to avoid debate. They are non-analytic, given to emotional posturing and exhibitions of self-righteousness.

Many prominent liberals have little regard for people, only for power and are given to posturing and bombastic self-righteous rhetoric. For example, Ted Kennedy cried about women's rights, but his private life was different. After a party once, he drove his car off a bridge, causing the death of Mary Jo Kopechne, a young lady in his car. Afterward he left the scene before seeking help or even notifying the authorities. Incredibly, Kennedy did not report the accident until the next morning.[100] Yet he remained a hero of the Left and of the women's movement. Behavior of this sort clearly does not bother the Left.

Liberals like the demagogic charge and electricity of the stirred emotions of the mob, but they don't care for those who constitute it. They appear deficient in their private life in human connections and hence try to reach their connection on a mass or collective level through groups of people. This is their way to feel good about themselves and to express their emotions to people. It also serves as a screen to hide behind; it conceals their less-than-benign feelings from themselves and from others.

American Exceptionalism

American exceptionalism does not mean that people in this country are any better than people in other countries. People are people. Our DNA is not different. What *is* different is our culture. What is exceptional here is that we are not living under the tyranny, oppression, and economic misery that now characterize most of the world. We owe this to our unique history and the founding documents which underlie our system of government, keeping tyranny at bay and fostering economic plenty. My travels convinced me of this. The evidence is clear, if one will only look around the world at the disastrous situations resulting from out of control, bad government. Why would one want to experiment with failed models when we have something that works, something that has proven itself?

Our sense of identity is being obliterated, both as a nation and as individuals. Liberals have never been comfortable with nationhood, particularly for big powers like the United States. The only time you see an American flag at a liberal rally is when it's being burned. The Obama Administration is trying to diminish and change the role of the United States in the world.

Liberals appear uncomfortable with liberty, economic achievement, and the pursuit of excellence, which have been the strong points of American civilization. In their place liberalism can only offer conformity and mediocrity. An attempt to impose harmony will exacerbate social divisions, rather than ameliorate them. Subservience to the will of the ruling elite would provide "constrained" liberty (government-determined) and economic decline.

Transnational Objectives

The Left stresses world government without acknowledging the failure of world government or its shortcomings and lack of accountability. It fails to acknowledge the problems, for example, of the United Nations with nepotism, corruption, and incompetence. The bureaucratic morass that the United Nations has become signals that there is no hope of anything constructive emerging from it. The European Union is struggling and in danger of coming apart. It's beset by massive debt and bureaucratic deadlock. Why try to move to a system that does not work? The US has been a constructive force in the world. Why give up its role to countries or multinational institutions that cannot fill our shoes?

Historical Failure of Liberalism

We know based on history that liberalism has failed. The question is why has it failed? Although liberalism espouses egalitarianism, it fundamentally calls for government by the elite. The elite almost always hijack society. They take over and disenfranchise the rest of the populace. It's not surprising that power concentrated in the hands of a few is prone to misuse and works to the detriment of the society. This is a major reason for the failure of liberal experiments. Those seeking power are the ones who are likely to acquire it. Such people do not have the best interests of society at heart. They are driven by a personal need for power, and they relish being able to exercise it. It is power they are interested in, not the interests of others. We can see the abuses of leaders of the liberal movement. Given that liberalism puts the interests and welfare of society in the hands of a few, and this elite body of rulers does not have the best interests of society at heart, it can hardly be surprising that the outcomes are not favorable.

Collective Cultures

Some cultures are more collectivist in mentality than others; Japan, Germany, and Venezuela come to mind in this respect. It should not be surprising that in collectivist cultures we have seen more inhumanity to man than in cultures placing high emphasis on the individual. During World War II, the Japanese and the Germans are well known for the brutality with which they treated other people. The Soviet Union and China also have a history of brutally treating their own people. Even marriages in these cultures are more formal; there is a distinct emotional distance between spouses and family members.

These cultures differ fundamentally in character from American culture. Collective cultures have beautiful aspects as well, but we are different. Countries like the United States, Great Britain, and Australia were built on the strength of the individual. We should not deny our heritage. It has brought us success and benefitted the world.

Collectivism has led to totalitarian nightmares, dystopias of epic scale, not to the utopias promised. Liberalism leads to a collectivism which is inimical even to the values and objectives publically espoused by liberals. Collectivism leads to inhumanity to man, and intolerance. It leads to a lack of diversity and constraint on individual development and liberty.

Obsession with Security and Aversion to Risk and Uncertainty

Liberals suffer from a fear of freedom. They are uncomfortable with the choices that are required of them and the risks entailed. The energy, responsibility, and thinking required to make good decisions doesn't appeal to everyone. Many prefer that decisions are made for them. Many also do not want to assume the risks entailed in making a bad decision. The abdication of individual responsibility and accountability is attractive to such people.

Risk-taking was what defined the character of this nation in its early years. Early settlers had to fight the wilderness and the unknown. Risk-taking is what made this country great. It is why this nation achieved prominence in the 20th century. But in killing the environment for risk taking and attempting to provide a security blanket for everyone, liberalism is destroying it. The liberalism of today seems phobic of risk and failure and appears determined to engineer and legislate them out of existence.

American culture has historically been masculine, valuing prowess, independence, competition, and individuality. In a male culture people are willing to undertake risks and bear the consequences. Liberals are trying to take us away from this to a culture fundamentally feminine in nature. A feminine culture reflects the interests mothers have in protecting their children. It's oriented towards avoiding risks and adverse consequences. Such a culture seeks to protect people from the risks and realities of the real world; it seeks to shield people from the real world leaving them in a cocoon of unreality, a childlike world of false assumptions.

Liberals want to take the "if" out of life. They want a non-subjunctive existence in which people are not exposed to risks and don't have to worry about the future. An aversion to any kind of uncertainty and a fear of risks appear paramount.

The Left is opposed to pain, effort, and failure. Essentially they want to anesthetize the public from the realities of life. Under their utopia people would go through life almost in a haze, similar to a drug-induced state brought about by anti- depressants, without feeling pain and without struggling—because they would not have to worry about failure. This almost seems like euthanasia. Perhaps the latter would be more attractive.

An early American sports hero, Babe Ruth, is famously quoted as saying, "Don't let the fear of striking out hold you back," and "You just can't beat the person who never gives up." In the climate of liberalism that prevails today, the fear of striking out prevails, and the white flag is raised in the air well before effort is tried.

Respect

In the new world order of liberalism respect has been accorded a diminished role. Respect implies looking up to someone and this is against the credo of liberals, who want to see a great leveling. Respect implies hierarchy, and liberals are against this; they want to see equality. Thus in our world today, children do not respect teachers or even their parents. Those who have something, whether success, high moral standards, wisdom, academic achievement, or wealth are not respected. This reflects the almost complete destruction of values in the West. People are almost embarrassed in today's world to acknowledge that they have values or have achieved something.

In place of respect, liberals have put compassion. We are supposed to feel sorry for those who have less than we do, rather than look up to those who are stronger and more successful than us. In essence what we have is equality for equality's sake. Without values and something to respect or aspire to, we have an empty world desolate of values and aspirations.

Discipline and Accountability

Liberalism is both a progenitor to and a by-product of the entitlement culture. According to liberalism, we should not have to earn something. It's ours by right and should be given to us. This is the case whether it's money, food, health care, or world peace. Our parents worked and sacrificed for these things, but why should we? We live in another world, right? According to liberals, ours is a world where there are no trade-offs, no quid pro quos. Things don't and shouldn't cost anything. Life is simple in a fantasy world. Unfortunately, it does not conform to reality, and trying to live as though it does leads to serious problems.

Liberalism appears to be an outgrowth of permissive parenting, a lack of a sense of accountability and responsibility, an aversion to authoritarian forms, a lack of a sense of moral constraints, an excessive accent on the self, and a profound and righteous sense of entitlement.

In schools there is no longer discipline. Teachers and administrators are running scared that if they discipline a student they will have to deal with a lawsuit or a charge of discrimination of one sort or another. So children are brought up without discipline, unable to learn as the environment in school is not conducive to it.

It seems we are now living in a culture that rewards the irresponsible and those who make bad decisions, while it penalizes those who behave responsibly and make the right choices. We are in an upside-down world. Would anyone think this is a good way to raise one's kids? Would anyone expect that kids raised with perverse, upside-down incentives would turn out well? I think not, but yet liberalism is doing this in society. We are penalizing those who pay their debts and mortgages, while we bail out those who do not. We are rewarding those who have the nerve to think that others should bail them out when they do stupid things and screw up, while people who do not expect others to pay for their mistakes are left paying the bills of those who do not. Those who struggle to pay their bills and meet their financial obligations are victimized. Reckless risk takers are rewarded, while the cautious and conservative who carefully husband their resources are expected to pay for the prodigality and foolishness of the reckless. How can we expect to teach our kids responsibility, when the government is treating us as if we have none? In fact the government is treating us as though we should not be expected to act responsibly. Of course the government is acting irresponsibly itself, failing to even pass a budget in the last four years and running up the national debt, so perhaps it's only right that it should not expect citizens to act responsibly. The government in fact sets an example of irresponsibility that is hard to beat.

The government is quite happy with the prospect of most of the citizenry reliant on it for support and guidance. Indeed, judging by its actions, a citizenry living in a state of dependency seems clearly to be the objective of government. The successful are seen as victimizers, whereas those who have failed are exalted to the status of passive victims. Passivity seems to be prized by the Left; they do not see those who have failed as having contributed to their own circumstances; others, of course, inflicted their problems on them. This is the view of the Left, and it's corrosive and damaging.

Entitlement programs are needed to help the poor and those who cannot take care of themselves, but increasingly others are taking advantage of the system to find an easy way out of the rigors of responsibility. Program costs are ballooning as more and more people game the system.

For example, women can have illegitimate children and refuse to provide the name of the father and are rewarded for this behavior with public support in welfare payments, food stamps, medical care, and even free education. The system encourages this type of behavior, and it's a reason why we now see an explosive growth in this behavior. Meanwhile a family or a single woman trying to make it on their own is penalized. Does this make sense to anybody?

What about those who feel they should take care of themselves and not burden others? What about those who do not even think of asking for a hand-out? Do these people deserve better than to have to pick up the bill for those who enthusiastically and with a sense of entitlement try to extract as much from the public coffers as possible? The culture of liberalism ignores these people; it seems driven to reward adverse actors at the expense of the conscientious and responsible.

Our country was founded on the principle of everyone pulling their own weight; if you did not succeed, you died or were in big trouble. Now the founding principles have been turned upside down. It's no wonder that the country is upside down as well. In rewarding losers we are becoming a nation of losers, of parasites, and of people looking for a way to game the system and hurt others for their own gain. It's interesting that this is the opposite of the altruist morality of trying to help others. This is the morality of screwing others for your own gain. At least with the objectivist morality of Ayn Rand, there was only the pursuit of self-interest constrained by not hurting others. We have found the worst of all worlds—and it's a road to oblivion. It's interesting and ironic that liberals who tout their moral superiority and their altruist objectives are the ones inflicting this upon us.

The aversion of liberals to accept individual accountability and responsibility is reflected in their views on criminal justice. Crime is not the fault of the individual, but the culture which caused him to do what he did. Given that it's the fault of the cultural environment and society, liberals say we need to change society. Once again, the liberal approach is to change that which works to accommodate that which does not work.

It's also reflected in liberal views concerning fiscal responsibility. Responding to the economic recession of 2009 and 2010, the liberals pushed for massive government spending to spend our way out of the recession. Even though debt and excessive spending were primary factors causing the financial crisis, they nevertheless wanted to spend our way out of the recession. They wanted to go the debt route, rather than try to bring the fiscal house back into order. The Obama Administration pushed relentlessly to have the debt ceiling raised. As an individual would you push to have your credit limit raised if you had run up too much debt?

Liberal Rage

Conservatives think liberals are sweet, naïve, and dumb, while liberals think conservatives are evil, greedy, and uncompassionate. This explains why conservatives are usually kind in dealing with liberals, while liberals often find themselves gripped by rage in dealing with conservatives.

Rage is prominent in the liberal temperament. We see it when liberals explode with moral indignation, often charging those of contrary views with bigotry, racism, and social unfairness. Of course, this is a generalization: many liberals are of even temperament and are not given to outward manifestations of anger. Even in the latter, however, one can often see a glimmer of anger in their eyes, even if they try not to show it.

Where does liberal rage come from? Perhaps, it originates from a sense of injustice and unfairness. Liberals seem frustrated, feeling failure while others succeed. In contrast to religious conservatives who see the world as a beautiful and wondrous place, liberals see the world as meaningless, full of misery. They see unhappiness in life. Liberals are angry at not getting what they think they deserve. They don't understand why the world isn't the way they would like it to be. Perhaps it also comes from an aversion to introspection, an inability to look at themselves.

Where is liberal rage directed? It's directed at anything and anyone who has a different view or gets in the way of their agenda. It's interesting that it's not so much issues-oriented as it is against those opposing them. For example, liberals don't feel moral outrage at Bill Clinton or Ted Kennedy for how they treated women, but they go into a frenzy over any suggestion, however baseless and insignificant, against a conservative, such as was the case with Clarence Thomas. In fact Thomas had the following to say about his Senate confirmation hearing:

> "This is a circus. It's a national disgrace. And from my standpoint as a black American, it's a high-tech lynching for uppity blacks who in any way deign to think for themselves, to do for themselves, to have different ideas, and it's a message that unless you kowtow to an old order, this is what will happen to you. You will be lynched, destroyed, caricatured by a committee of the US Senate rather than hung from a tree."[101]

Why is liberal rage so strong? Liberal rage is strong because liberals presume those opposing them are immoral, selfish, greedy, and of maleficent motives. That liberals are averse to logic and rationality also means that they cannot see counter-arguments or other views. For them all issues essentially come down to morality, so they have no tolerance for those with different views. Moral outrage is, of course, much stronger than the sense of disappointment that comes from disagreeing with someone on an issue of reasoned discourse. When emotion predominates over one's rational faculties, it's not surprising that outrage is the product.

More fundamentally, however, anger arises almost by necessity out of the moral and epistemological stance of liberalism. Moral relativism and constructivism are used by liberals as tools against those adhering to rationalism and to prevailing cultural views. These are the key weapons in the liberal arsenal, which they use to deconstruct and assault establishment views and culture. The problem is that there is no legitimacy in using moral relativism asymmetrically and hence its use as a political strategy has no foundation or justification. While it can be used to discredit prevailing cultural and political views, indicating that there is no justification for valuing them higher than alternative liberal models, it can also be turned on those pushing the views of liberalism. Hence, when challenged, the liberal has no foundation to stand on, so his only defense is to lash out in anger. Also the failed record of liberal policies cannot stand up to reasoned analysis, so liberals really have no recourse but to defend their agenda through emotional outbursts.

Planning

Liberals suffer from a fatal conceit; namely, from the notion that the only order is order imposed by planning. For them the alternative to planning is chaos. They do not understand that there are natural forces creating order. We see this in nature. The forces of nature are self-balancing and equilibrating. Likewise market forces are largely self- balancing. If there is too much supply of a good, the price falls, sending a signal to producers to supply less of it. Similarly if there is strong demand for a good, this would lead to higher prices, which would provide the incentive for producers to increase supply to meet demand. There is no need for planning in such a system; in fact planning interferes with the working of the market, leading to unfavorable outcomes.

Liberalism is obsessed with authority and control and in the process stifles creativity and spontaneity. Liberals see government as the solution to all problems, espousing an expansion in the size and influence of government regardless of the circumstances. Obviously there are some circumstances that the government is ideally suited to address, but there are many areas where its interference is uncalled for and damaging. As Reagan said, "The most feared words in the English language are 'I am from the government and I am here to help.'"

Despite their unhappiness and pessimism about the current state of our country, liberals have an abiding optimism about the future. They take a leap of faith that they can improve the world. They presume that it's a simple and easy undertaking. In the liberal mind, mistakes would not be made. There are no real costs or risks involved in attempting the change. Rationality and history does not provide any foundation for this optimism, but this does not register with liberals, as they dismiss rationality as a tool of oppression and history as a thing of the past, irrelevant for the future.

In constructive political activity the result corresponds to the intent. Intentionality and consequence match. In perverse activity the outcome is contradictory to the desired outcome. Liberalism is highly perverse, but this does not register with liberals.

Concluding Remarks

Perhaps it's as Johann Wolfgang von Goethe once noted, "Everything in the world may be endured except continued prosperity." It has been said that man is that unique creature who will invent an illness if he doesn't have one. Liberalism is a pathology, a man-made cancer, which poses an existential threat to American and Western prosperity.

Of the many factors leading to the decline of democracy, liberalism is behind most of them: the increasing interconnection of government to private sector, of unions to government, and of big business to government, and of lawyers to government; the sabotage of the judicial branch; the debasement of the media and education; the diminishment of the Constitution; the abandonment of reason and truth; the increasing divorce of government from the will of the people, creating government for government's sake; pandering to constituencies and ruling by division (completely contrary to the notion of unity implicit in collectivism); and undermining the rule of law in favor of arbitrary judicial discretion.

Liberalism and collectivism is all about power and control, not compassion. Given that liberals believe people do not know what is in their best interests and cannot be expected to do the right thing, they believe that an enlightened elite ruling class needs to tell people how they should live their lives. The essence of liberalism is anti-democratic and anti-egalitarian. Its DNA is about the amassment power, the abridgment of freedom, and the subjugation of ordinary people.

A great threat to democracy arises once people recognize that they can use the State to take other people's money. They can earn a living through voting rather than working. Margaret Thatcher said the problem with socialism is that sooner or later you run out of other peoples' money. Europe is on a disaster course of mounting deficits and debt, having pushed the welfare state too far. Europeans now recognize their mistake, but it's too late as they are having big problems reversing it. Do we really want to go down this road?

Liberalism is a pathological condition that is seriously damaging the body politic. It's an illness arising out of envy, anger, indiscipline, ignorance, and immorality. It ignores the social, political, and economic lessons of history, which are a litany of outright and cataclysmic failures whenever liberal experiments have been tried.

* * *

CHAPTER 5

FISCAL AND MONETARY TREASON AND LIBERALISM

———◆———

A nation can survive its fools, and even the ambitious, but cannot survive treason from within. An enemy at the gates is less formidable, for he is known and carries his banner openly. But the traitor moves amongst those within the gate freely, his sly whispers rustling through all the alleys, heard in the halls of government itself. For the traitor appears not a traitor; he speaks in accents familiar to his victims, and he wears their face and their arguments, he appeals to the baseness that lies deep in the hearts of all men. He rots the soul of a nation, he works secretly and unknown in the night to undermine the pillars of the city, he infects the body politic so that it can no longer resist. A murderer is less to fear. The traitor is the plague.

~Marcus Tullius Cicero

It is hard to imagine a more stupid or more dangerous way of making decisions than by putting those decisions in the hands of people who pay no price for being wrong.

~Thomas Sowell

Do not accustom yourself to consider debt only as an inconvenience, you will find it a calamity.

~Samuel Johnson

Debt is a prolific mother of folly and of crime.

~Benjamin Disraeli

This used to be a government of checks and balances. Now it's all checks and no balances.

~Gracie Allen

As Cicero famously noted, the most dangerous enemy is not the outsider. Liberalism is like a cancer, in that the destructive cells are not recognized as a threat by the immune system. The liberal agenda is taking us toward economic ruin.

The economic ruin stems not only from the deleterious effect of liberalism on the vitality of the market and the private sector, but also from the colossal mismanagement of the government sector itself. The government's appetite for spending and borrowing is crowding out the private sector physically and financially. There is simply less in the way of resources available for the private sector to grow and thrive.

Government annual budget deficits are way above sustainable levels and the amount of public debt is becoming alarmingly high. Federal debt at the end of 2008 was equivalent to forty percent of GDP, marginally above the forty year average of thirty-seven percent, but since then it has risen dramatically higher to about seventy percent of GDP as of this year.[102] Moreover, according to the Congressional Budget Office, it's possible that public debt will rise further to one hundred and one percent by 2021 and to one hundred and eighty-seven percent by 2035.[103]

Even these projections are too rosy. For example, Obama sold his health care reform as fiscally conservative, even though it's clear that it will lead to massive deficits. One of his fiscal tricks was to embed in the calculations a seven-hundred-billion-dollar cut in Medicare payments to doctors. This proposal was recognized as one that would not be implemented, as many doctors were already refusing to see Medicare patients because their payments were too low. So everyone recognizes that Congress will reverse this, which will add another three quarters of a trillion dollars to the deficit. The Obama Administration also incorporated the student loan program in with healthcare so as to make the budgetary impact of healthcare reform look better. This, of course, is not honest accounting.

Government hides behind bad accounting. Fiscal and financial mismanagement is ruining the country. Not only is the government spending far more than it can afford, but it's lying about what it is doing. If a business CEO were doing this, he would be jailed for fraud. Unfunded liabilities of government are estimated at above eighty-four trillion dollars.[104] These are not included in the budget. Who is to pay for it? The government also involves itself in significant loan guarantees to other levels of government and to public enterprises and to the private sector. These are contingent liabilities that are off-budget. At the time a guarantee is given, no expenditures are booked in the budget— but it's a contingent liability.

Interest rates are at historic lows, so the seriousness of the budget situation is consequently understated. Once interest rates rise (and they will), government payments for interest will rise substantially, putting even more pressure on the budget. The increase in debt payments will take place not just because rates are higher, but because of the vastly expanded outstanding government debt.

Sooner rather than later, both domestic and foreign investors will lose confidence in the fiscal management of our government, and the government will have to offer higher interest rates to compensate investors for the higher risks. As investors flee US assets, the value of the US dollar will plunge in foreign exchange markets. In response, the government will have to raise interest rates to stem the run on the dollar.

The Federal Reserve Bank is guilty of complicity, accommodating the fiscal prodigality. It is printing money with abandon and buying up large amounts of the new debt the government is issuing. Since 2008 the Federal Reserve Bank has purchased $2.3 trillion in bonds.[105] It has been through several rounds of quantitative easing, flooding the economy with money and bringing about a decline in the value of the US dollar. The Federal Reserve System is a secretive organization. It does not open its books for audit. Meanwhile it is secretly bailing out many financial and non-financial organizations, but there is no accounting for where the money is actually going.

Not only is the Federal Reserve accommodating irresponsible fiscal policy and understating the true seriousness of fiscal borrowing and debt, but it is laying the foundations for another financial crisis. It is ignoring the long-term implications of its policy aimed at repressing interest rates to historically low levels. By repressing interest rates, it is hurting the financially responsible; savers are hurt while borrowing and debt accumulation is rewarded. Such policy is encouraging investment which may well become unsustainable once interest rates adjust to market levels. Banks will also be hit with a financial shock once interest rates begin to rise to normalized levels as their cost of funds will shoot up relative to returns on their assets.

In flooding the economy with money, the FED is depreciating the value of the US dollar. If the authorities decide to resort to inflation as a means of easing the burden of government debt, the US dollar will face further significant decline.

The US dollar has been the centerpiece of the global financial system since World War II. This has conferred tremendous advantages on the United States, and has served the world well. Unfortunately the fiscal and monetary prodigality inflicted upon us by the liberal establishment will likely bring about an end to the privileged status of the dollar.

In August 2011, Standard & Poor's downgraded the US Governments credit rating from AAA to AA-plus. This is the first time in history that this has happened. The action was prompted by the poor fiscal management and the worsening debt situation and the poor prognosis. Rather than deal with the cause of the downgrade—poor fiscal management and mounting public debt—the Obama Administration attacked Standard & Poor's and initiated an investigation of the company.

In addition, the sustainability of debt depends on the ability to pay. If the economy were to grow strongly, revenues and the ability to pay would increase, making it easier to bear the debt burden. But the Obama Administration's anti-business attitude and its anti-market policies are curtailing the strength of the economy, which will mean less revenue in the future. Moreover, the addition of Obama's health care entitlement program to already unsustainable entitlement programs is seriously aggravating the financial problem.

Democrats alone are not responsible for these fiscal trends, but it's now clear to all that the fiscal imbalances can wreak tremendous damage on America. Despite this, Obama and the Democrats expanded spending and debt sharply since 2008. The national debt rose from about nine trillion dollars in 2008 to over fifteen trillion dollars by May of 2012.[106] This increase is more than the increases for all previous presidents' terms combined. The debt amounts to $50,267 per citizen and is going up by $3.96 billion per day for the country as a whole. At the International Monetary Fund, fiscal deficit spending above five percent of GDP is seen as a serious risk to a country, as are public-debt-to-GDP ratios above seventy-five percent. The United States fiscal-deficit-to-GDP ratio was twelve percent in 2011, far in excess of the warning threshold of five percent, and its debt-to-GDP ratio was also very close to the warning threshold and, as mentioned, projected to rise sharply. Nevertheless, Obama has continued to press for even more spending. As President Reagan said, "They say Democrats [liberals] are spending like drunken sailors, but this does a disservice to the sailors; at least they are spending their own money."

It's clear that these policies, if left unchecked, could destroy capitalism and the bedrock of our economy, yet liberals keep pushing their destructive policies. There are two explanations for this: either they are incompetent or they are deliberately trying to destroy America as we know her. Of course they could be both, but it seems highly improbable that they could be so stupid as not to recognize what is happening. Given this, it's likely that the intent of the liberal establishment is to destroy capitalist America so they can rebuild it on new utopian socialist foundations.

Obama certainly harbors resentment toward colonial powers given that his Kenyan father was subjected to abuse by the British.[107] He attended Reverend Jeremiah Wright's church, in which hatred toward America and toward whites was preached regularly.[108] As a constitutional law student he was clear that he did not like the Constitution. Obama has surrounded himself with those who don't like America.[109] He began his political career associating with Bill Ayers, one of the founders of the Weather Underground, a self-described communist revolutionary group that allegedly bombed public buildings, including police stations in the sixties.[110] Obama's wife also said upon his election that she was proud of her country for the first time.

Another explanation is that this behavior represents a form of addiction denial. Liberals are debt junkies. Like drug addicts or alcoholics, they don't recognize that they have a problem. The addiction of liberals to spending is a disease. Liberalism shares much in common with other addictions.

Still another explanation is that it constitutes a rational pursuit of self-interest to the detriment of others. Perhaps liberals are pursuing goals of short-term political and personal benefit. So what if others have to pick up the tab for their prodigality and pursuit of self-interest.

So there are a myriad of explanations. I believe each plays a role. The conscious intent to destroy capitalism certainly cannot be dismissed, as frightening as it is to accept. Before taking office, Obama said, "We are five days away from fundamentally transforming this country." No one bothered to ask what the transformation would involve. Intent was clear on Obama's part.

For the first three years of the Obama Administration, Congress did not pass a budget as required by law. Obama has recognized in press interviews that entitlement reform has to be a part of any meaningful attempt to get the budget under control, but he has made no proposal to do so. Congressman Ryan, a Republican, did make a proposal, which Obama promptly attacked as "likely to kill grandma" and hurt the disadvantaged. As president, it was his job to present a budget and his job to propose a solution to the ballooning budget imbalance, but rather than do so, or even attempt to productively engage the Republican opposition (who did have the courage and sense of responsibility to do so), he chose the route of political demagoguery. Obama has no interest in dealing with this clear threat to our economic vitality.

President Kennedy, often lauded as a liberal, was really a conservative. In his inaugural address he said, "Ask not what your country can do for you, but what you can do for your country." He lowered taxes and was strong on national defense. Today's liberal mantra is, "Ask not what you can do for your country, but what it can do for you."

Deficit spending is not just bad economic policy limiting growth prospects, but is downright immoral: we are consuming at the expense of the next generation. Liberal greed in the name of moral compassion for our generation is but theft from our children. It threatens the best system of government on earth, and it limits our ability to operate an effective national security policy. This hurts the world too, given that the USA has been the chief instrument of peace over the last one hundred years.

Given that interest rates are expected to rise in the future, monetary policy cannot help alleviate the debt burden on government by lowering rates. Also, as mentioned, enhanced economic growth is probably not going to happen, as fiscal mismanagement is discouraging private sector investment. Investors like to have confidence in the economic management of government. When this is missing—and it's missing in spades now—investors and private sector participants are uncertain, and they curtail investment and consumption decisions and plans. The huge surge in public debt dampens confidence and the economic outlook because higher debt contains the threat of high future taxes to pay for the fiscal prodigality.

So the debt situation is not going to be alleviated through lower interest rates or enhanced growth; in fact these factors will likely worsen the debt problem. To deal with the fiscal crisis in America, and in the democracies of Western Europe, government is left essentially with two options: to boost inflation and thereby depreciate the value of its debt, or to make fundamental changes in its taxing and spending policies. If we are to avoid crippling and destabilizing inflation, government is going to have to put its fiscal house in order.

Because we are in a recession, it will be hard to rely much on tax increases. These would only exacerbate recessionary tendencies. Unemployment is high and higher taxes would only make it worse. Moreover, the Democrats are pressing in particular to increase marginal income tax rates on those earning over $250,000 a year. According to most estimates the Obama proposal to increase tax rates on the wealthy would only generate $80 billion a year. This does not even put a dent in the annual budget deficit which exceeds $1 trillion, so it is really nothing more than a distraction from the real problem.

Moreover, a higher marginal income tax rate hurts most small businesses, which are the primary job creators in the economy. In a global economy, high marginal rates also push jobs and firms to move overseas. High-income-tax states like California and New York are losing businesses and wealthy people are leaving these states—and the same thing happens on a global level. Essentially higher marginal rates hurt incentives, investment, and growth and bring in very little additional revenue as the behavior of tax payers changes resulting in less revenue than the authorities anticipate. Taxing the rich takes money out of the private sector and transfers it to the less productive government sector. Usually the government wastes the money, so increased taxes just creates more waste. Moreover, by curtailing economic growth, higher taxes hurt the poor as unemployment goes up. Broader based taxes with lower rates hurt economic growth much less and are more successful in raising revenue, but liberals rail against this approach as it means higher taxes for everybody, not just the rich. This does not accord well with the class-warfare rhetoric of liberalism.

Higher corporate taxes are also not the answer. Based on a World Bank study, out of 183 countries examined, 164 have lower effective corporate tax rates than the United States.[111] Among the industrialized countries the United States has the highest level of business taxation.[112] In a global environment high corporate taxes simply cause some of the revenue base to physically leave the country, so it does not help the revenue picture.

The liberal rhetoric on solving the budget imbalances and debt by taxing the rich reflects their comfort with a politics of deceit and their contempt for the intelligence of the electorate, but it does not seriously address the fiscal problem. Current tax revenues are only about $2.5 trillion while expenditures are about $3.7 trillion, and the fiscal debt now stands at $16 trillion, up about $6 trillion since Obama took office four years ago. On top of this is a staggering $87 trillion in unfunded liabilities which hardly anyone is even talking about.[113] Medicare and Social Security alone have unfunded liabilities of $42.8 trillion and $20.5 trillion, respectively. According to one study by a former congressman, annual fiscal revenues would have to be raised to about $8 trillion annually just to keep fiscal debt from rising as a result of the additional impact on expenditures of these unfunded liabilities.[114] This revenue potential is simply not there. Even if congress took all of the earnings of those making over $66,000 annually, leaving them with nothing, and all corporate profits, it would amount to only about $6.7 trillion.[115]

Thus, spending has to be a big part of the solution, but liberals refuse to acknowledge this. Entitlement spending has been growing substantially faster than GDP, and is projected to continue to do so. This is not sustainable, so the brunt of adjustment is going to have to come in expenditure curtailment, although this will have a recessionary influence. It is the sharp increase in spending that has produced this crisis, so it makes sense that the source of the problem should be addressed. In order for public trust and confidence to be restored, the government must show that it can gain control of its profligate appetite for spending. To avoid a recessionary impact the spending cuts could be targeted principally at the medium and long-term, but some cuts need to be made immediately for purposes of credibility.

The government is trying to do all things for everyone. It has gone beyond the bounds economically justified. It's on a binge to increase its power and influence. Now the time has come where it must draw back and dedicate itself to functions that are essential for government to perform. It must husband its resources and direct them to the most important needs, namely those needs that the private sector cannot meet. The time has come for government to prioritize. Government now should look at the functions and roles that it should be properly undertaking. Despite spending trillions annually, the government rarely evaluates its programs to see if they are effective. Moreover, if there are evaluations, they are done by the implementing agencies, so evaluations tend to be self-serving and unenlightening.

Unfortunately, liberals can't see this. Their approach is to repeat what brought us into this crisis. They want to spend their way out of it. For example, in September 2011, Obama announced a "new" plan to put the economy back on track. It was essentially a new stimulus package, similar to the one that he introduced after taking over the White House. The first package failed miserably, so what does he do but try more of the same; except that this time, he calls it a "jobs bill." This bill would add $450 billion in new taxes during a recession, and if passed, would hurt an already struggling economy. According to Administration estimates, the cost per job created is at least $200,000, and the jobs would be only temporary, ending once the subsidies in the bill expire.[116] However, the debt issued to create the jobs would remain and have to be serviced and paid off by taxpayers. Does this make any sense?

Since taking office every action and step taken by Obama has created job losses, hurting those seeking employment. His health care bill threw the health care sector of our economy into uncertainty about the future. It was one of the strong sectors in performance before he decided to throw the monkey wrench of government intervention into it. The bill made it difficult for firms to hire, as they could not determine what their health care responsibilities would be for workers. Costs could be dramatically higher. The irresponsibility of fiscal and monetary macroeconomic management has served as a strong deterrent for business expansion and hiring, as has the ballooning public debt. In addition, increased regulations and tough enforcement of discrimination laws has made hiring and firing more difficult, and thus has militated to discourage employers from hiring. The liberal push to pass a cap-and-trade (tax) bill is also deeply unsettling to the business community. And, lastly, the anti-business rhetoric which is a staple of the Obama Administration and the liberal establishment has weakened confidence in government and hurt the economic outlook.

* * *

CHAPTER 6

THE ACHILLES' HEEL OF DEMOCRACY: FLAWS IN DEMOCRACY MAKING IT PARTICULARLY VULNERABLE TO THE CANCER OF LIBERALISM

Tyranny naturally arises out of democracy.

~Plato

The urge to save humanity is almost always a false front for the urge to rule.

~H.L. Mencken

Let the people think they govern and they will be governed.
~William Penn

Remember, democracy never lasts long. It soon wastes, exhausts, and murders itself. There is never a democracy that did not commit suicide.

~John Adams

Liberalism is a disease, but like most diseases it's opportunistic, thriving better in some hosts and environments than others. Unfortunately, the democracies of America and the West are particularly vulnerable to the ravages of liberalism. Democracy is predisposed and geared to pandering, and liberalism is its vehicle. There are several points of vulnerability accounting for this.

A major weakness of democracy is its tendency to succumb to excessive spending and growth in government. As a result, democracy is deficit-prone and the size of the public sector relative to the private sector is destined to increase, threatening the private sector, its capitalist base, and individual liberty.

In a democracy each bureaucrat and politician wants to see his own turf expanded. It's in his interest to see this happen. He does not care about the cost in tax-payer dollars. The more he gets, the better for him. Unlike in the market, where efficiency is the key, the bureaucrat is not concerned with efficiency. In fact inefficiency may actually work better for him, because he can get a bigger power base in employees and funding support for a given goal if he is inefficient. If a bureaucrat has excess funds at the end of the year, he will spend it even if it's wasted, because he does not want to be penalized with a smaller budget in the next year. He does not consider that, given limited resources, an expansion in his operations will mean retrenchment in another sector. The bureaucrat does not, in other words, take into account the broader picture, the opportunity costs associated with pursuing his objectives in his sector. In a market economy these interactions are captured and the right balance can be achieved, but in a politically driven economy this is not so.

The incentive for an elected representative is to maximize his best interest, not that of the electorate. If the electorate could hold the representative truly accountable, their best interest and objectives would be pretty much the same, but they can't. Once elected, a representative is insulated from the effects of public opinion. The political machine of public bureaucracy now accords each elected representative a large staff and a large budget, which gives him a significant advantage over any opponent. Moreover, he has the advantage of name recognition and discretionary control over some government expenditures, which he can then claim credit for. Redistricting has made some congressmen virtually undefeatable, even after the most egregious transgressions. For example, Charles Rangel, a prominent Democrat working in Congress on tax issues, was censured by Congress for not paying his taxes with due diligence and yet was reelected. [117]

As the government sector expands, civil servants become a larger and larger part of the voting population. To the extent that they benefit from a larger government sector, they then vote for those candidates and political parties who support an expansion of government. This in turn creates a still stronger force, lending momentum to the expansion of government spending and influence.

In a democracy, those who get the benefits of the political system are not those who pay for them. As Margaret Thatcher once said, "Everyone in a democracy is trying to get others to pay for their standard of living." This contrasts with a market economy, which requires people to earn their standard of living.

The asymmetry between benefits and those who contribute the resources to government is the Achilles' heel of democracy. The productive and the wealthy contribute the vast bulk of the revenue to the government, but the unproductive and the poor receive the most benefits. To the extent that the latter become a majority, democracy can be transmuted into a system of legalized theft. Mencken astutely observed that "Every election is a sort of advance auction sale of stolen goods."

Essentially democracy becomes a cleptocracy. Moreover, the ruling class under these circumstances enhances its own position in power, influence, and wealth by serving the needs of those pushing for a transfer of wealth to themselves. Only forty-seven percent of the public now pay income taxes; the majority no longer cares if income tax rates go up. In fact they support it because it helps to fund programs that serve their needs.

These biases in democracy open the door to the excesses of liberalism. The door is open to the expansion of government and to excessive levels of spending and debt. The door is open to the temptation to make promises to the electorate that cannot be kept. The door is open to prodigality and theft from future generations. Politicians have their eyes on a close horizon, namely the next election. They don't care if they kick the can down the road and leave the country with big problems; their concern is getting reelected.

It's usually the median voter, not the voters at the extremes, who determines election outcomes according to public choice theory.[118] According to this theory, politicians seek to get the vote of the median voter by offering him something for nothing. The politicians seek to get their vote by offering to reduce the taxes or increase the government benefits for this group of voters. The politicians don't offer their most ardent supporters benefits, as these voters are essentially already in the bag; they go after the median voter as these are the voters who swing elections.

Median voters are frequently the least informed, so their awareness of the broad spectrum of policy issues is wanting—but politicians can draw their attention by offering them highly public benefits. That median voters are not well informed makes them particularly vulnerable to pandering, propaganda, and media bias.

To the extent that the media is subservient to the ruling class and those who wish to see an expansion of government, the public is likely to be denied coverage of what is really going on. Inefficient and harmful electoral outcomes can result. An adversarial press has played an important role in our history as a nation by operating as a restraint on the abuse of power. The co-opting of the media by the liberal establishment is thus yet another way liberalism is striking at the Achilles' heel of our democracy. Abraham Lincoln captured this well when he said, "I am a firm believer in the people. If given the truth, they can be depended upon to meet any national crisis. The great point is to bring them the real facts." He went on to say, "He who molds the public sentiment…makes statutes and decisions possible or impossible to make."

The extremists who are most ardent and involved tend to exercise more influence than moderates in selecting party candidates. In recent years in America, the Democrats in particular have shown a tendency to nominate politicians on the Left side of the political spectrum (Obama, Pelosi, Reid). The Democratic Party is way to the Left of the body politic. Only twenty one percent of the electorate identify themselves as liberal, while forty percent see themselves as conservative and forty percent as moderate.[119] Despite this Democrats find themselves in charge on occasion and during these periods they have caused a lot of damage. It's said that Democrats are put in charge once in a while to remind us why we don't want them to be.

The problem is compounded by legislative representatives who no longer have the benefit of independent thinking; they are no longer given the scope to follow their own conscience. Thirty years ago many Democrats and Republicans would vote their conscience, even in opposition to their party leadership. This is no longer the case. Now party leaders exert much more control and force those lower down the ladder to follow their lead. This was certainly evident during the Obama Administration's push to get ObamaCare through Congress. There are numerous reasons why there has been this shift and increase in the authority and control of party leaders at the expense of clear thinking. Railroading and political bribery and pressure have become rampant and almost impossible to resist.

The impact of gerrymandering and seniority is making the legislature a body of extremists and has exacerbated the damages of liberalism. Gerrymandering has been important in the drift towards extremism. Voting districts have been redrawn to ensure safe seats for certain incumbents. For example, certain politicians have been given districts where the preponderance of voters is either strongly liberal or strongly conservative. These politicians have been essentially protected from losing office as long as they tow the line of their extremist political constituencies. Consequently, by surviving for a long time they tend to become powerful party leaders and head up the most powerful committees. This is particularly pernicious given the almost total control that party leaders now exercise.

Government is not just controlled by the president and the legislature. Over time bureaucrats become entrenched and develop considerable control over what happens. Issues are complex and the management and control of programs are at a considerable remove from the president and Congress, so bureaucrats exercise strong influence. The interests of bureaucrats one would expect would not coincide with that of the voting public, so it's not surprising that the latter is not always well served.

Bureaucrats exercise considerable regulatory power. Again this grows over time because the bureaucrats have an incentive to see their base of power expand. Regulations, although done in the name of the public good, really more often than not serve the interests of the regulators more than the citizens. Over time these regulations become excessive and burden the business community and the public.

The two-party system works by keeping the party in charge honest and accountable. It's natural that, after a period in office, the party in power makes mistakes, whether real or perceived, and is voted out of office in protest. The problem arises when the opposition party is extremist and irresponsible, as has largely become the case in the United States. When Bush was voted out of office in 2008 on account of the wars' unpopularity and the financial crisis, Obama was swept into office with a large plurality in both the Senate and the House. As Rahm Emanuel is famously quoted as saying, "Never waste a crisis as it's an opportunity to pursue your agenda." The Democrats then pushed through legislation unpopular with the American public.

Strength is often a mixed blessing, but sometimes one's strength brings one down. The strength of ancient Athens was its accent on individualism and reliance on open discussion and rational discourse as exemplified by Socrates, who questioned everything. Unfortunately, this led to a less-than-total commitment to the tenets underlying their civilization. It led to internal dissension and lack of consensus. All this made them vulnerable to the outside threat of Alexander the Great.

America and the West are open to multiculturalism, so much so that they are overly critical of their own culture. This questioning of our culture and in fact a strongly negativistic view of it has contributed to our decline. This has led to moral relativism and a weakening of our fundamental values. Strong moral values are critically important to democracy, so this is one of the central ways in which liberalism is undermining democracy.

Excessive immigration in many cases has led to insufficient assimilation and cultural change. A nation without borders is not a nation. There is truth to this, but the problem of immigration goes beyond that. It offers those in power yet another opportunity to enhance their power by pandering to these new groups, giving them what they want in return for electoral support.

Liberals don't like America; the Left wants to tear down America and everything it stands for because they are unhappy and uncomfortable with it. They want something new. They want to build a new culture; unfortunately they don't know how to build or construct or contribute. They only know how to take apart, to destroy.

There are negative forces in any political system. Democracy merely gives them free reign, but it expects such forces to be countered. Unfortunately, in America and the West it seems that these forces are not countered or challenged but rather are allowed to go unchallenged. In fact these harmful forces are even fostered and encouraged. Albert Einstein warned, "The world will not be destroyed by those who do evil, but by those who watch them without doing anything."

Most cultures fail because of their failure; for example, the USSR and communist China failed across the board. On the other hand, the West is failing in part because of its success. The factors that have contributed to our successes now are working to our demise. The openness to self-criticism, multiculturalism, and open discourse has helped move our culture forward: it's not dissimilar to the biological mixing of diverse genes that promoted the development of our species. But while multiculturalism and open discourse has strengthened our culture, it has become excessive and opened us up to attack from foreign and endemic pathological forces.

And liberalism, like cancer, deceives its host, so the immune system does not recognize it as malignant. Today's liberalism uses the language of eighteenth century liberalism, but in reality is totally inimical to it. It uses the words freedom, liberty, and individualism, and expresses support for the disadvantaged and the masses, but in reality has a totally different agenda.

Democracy requires a strong and informed citizenry. If individuals cannot manage their own lives, they cannot be expected to make democracy work. Democracy requires strong individualism, independent judgment, and an ability and disposition to make moral judgments. Democracy will inevitably fail if the citizenry is diminished, and this is precisely what liberalism is doing. Through bailouts and perverse incentives liberalism is bringing about a diminishment of individualism and is taking away the ability of people to make moral judgments. It is trying to make individuals dependent on government, rather than government dependent on the people. If individuals are not expected to be responsible and accountable for their own actions, which is the presumption of liberals, it is no wonder that liberals favor big government. But if this is so, it is clear that they do not favor democracy, only the guise of democracy.

Liberalism is also eroding democracy by its adverse impact on our educational system. It is attempting to turn our education system into a proselytizing arm of government, rather than one of education. It is well-known that the American educational system rates very poorly against systems around the world. According to the U.S. Department of Education, U.S. students are only average in reading literacy among OECD nations and they are below-average performers in math proficiency. This is despite spending more per student than any other nation.[120] The problem of low productivity in our educational system clearly is related to the unwholesome connection of teachers' unions to the Democratic Party and the bloated bureaucratic Department of Education. Essentially liberalism has debased the quality of education as it supports teachers' unions for political purposes rather than students. Its objective is not to teach students to think independently and with an open mind, but rather to enlist them as foot soldiers for liberalism. Independent thinking and open dialogue is critically important in a democracy.

Another problem is that issues have become much more complex and technical. The increasing pace of change and the different factors impinging on it make decision-making more difficult. Consequently, even if voters were making sound judgments based on historical precedent and relationships, and even if legislators were faithfully trying to reflect those judgments in their actions, outcomes might not be in line with expectations.

Liberalism also hurts American democracy through its relentless attack on capitalism. Capitalism and economic liberty are critical underpinnings for democracy. As liberalism has weakened capitalism and curtailed the growth of the economy, the fighting to divide the pie has intensified, creating even greater class divisions, making democracy more dysfunctional and unable to address even fundamental problems. This should not be surprising; making democracy dysfunctional is probably the objective of liberalism.

Limited government has played an important role in the success of America. We were blessed, as we started from almost nothing. In the beginning we had only a small and weak federalist government, with its powers circumscribed by the Constitution. But over time liberal government has steadily circumvented the Constitution as it has built up its own power and control. Liberalism is destroying the Constitutional basis for our democracy, and is trying to circumvent the legislature through the judiciary. It is destroying America's democracy through disrespect for law. Laws and agreements are the glue that holds a nation together, but liberalism is flouting immigration law and diminishing the Constitution.

The fact remains, however, that democracy, whatever its shortcomings—and they are significant—is still preferable to alternative systems of government. That it's flexible and adaptable make it ideally suited to deal with the issues of change. This is especially so if it's driven by the grassroots, by the decisions of individuals and not by top-down dirigiste (economic planning and control by the state) planning.

Many people have noted the shortcomings of democracy. H. L. Mencken, for example, said, "Democracy is only a dream: it should be put in the same category as Arcadia, Santa Claus, and Heaven." He also said, "Democracy is the pathetic belief in the collective wisdom of individual ignorance." E. B. White noted, "Democracy is the recurrent suspicion that more than half of the people are right more than half of the time." And Winston Churchill said, "The best argument against democracy is a five-minute conversation with the average voter." All of these criticisms have an element of truth to them, but, despite its shortcomings, democracy is still the best form of government.

Some democracies work better than others. Because power in the hands of the few is the outcome most to be avoided, a government small in size and limited in power is the best option to avoid the downside risks inherent in democracy. Tyranny and abuse of power don't just characterize autocracies, they can easily happen in democracies as well. Even centuries ago Plato recognized this risk, saying, "Tyranny naturally arises out of democracy." Liberalism fights efforts to rein in the power of government and the elite; it strongly encourages growth in government and the power of the elite. So, if democracy is to work, the fight against liberalism must be joined. Citizens need to fight back before it's too late.

We need to listen carefully to the words of Reagan. "Freedom is never more than one generation away from extinction. We didn't pass it to our children in the bloodstream. It must be fought for, protected, and handed on for them to do the same."

* * *

SECTION II

MISCONCEPTIONS UNDERPINNING LIBERALISM THAT PREDISPOSE IT TO FAILURE

Let's look in this section at the misplaced predicates and pillars on which liberalism is built. First, we will look at the superiority of market capitalism over the statist model of liberalism. Second, we will look at the historical failures of liberalism. Third, we will look at the failure of liberalism to recognize the fundamental role played by reason in the advancement of man. Fourth, we will look at how liberalism's sacrifice of truth endangers our democratic traditions and culture. Fifth, we will look at the pathology of liberalism at the level of the individual and then, sixth, at the collective level. Seventh, we will look at the how liberalism's unrestrained promotion of immigration and multiculturalism is putting our democratic traditions in peril. Eighth, we will look at how the liberal approach to justice actually leads to injustice. Ninth, we will focus on the fundamental immorality of liberalism. Tenth and eleventh, we will look at the failure of liberalism to understand the nature of institutions and the adverse effect on their agenda and our way of life. Twelfth, we will look at the dirigiste folly of liberalism in trying to control the complex forces shaping our lives through top-down planning and management. In the concluding chapter, we will look at the reasons why liberalism is so dangerous and damaging and see as well why it's destined to failure.

* * *

CHAPTER 7

SUPERIORITY OF THE MARKET SYSTEM OVER THE STATIST MODEL OF LIBERALISM

———◆———

It's amazing that people who think we cannot afford to pay for doctors, hospitals, and medication somehow think that we can afford to pay for doctors, hospitals, medication and a government bureaucracy to administer it.

~Thomas Sowell

People try to live within their income so they can afford to pay taxes to a government that can't live within its income.

~ Robert Half

Remember that a government big enough to give you everything you want is big enough to take away everything you have.

~Barry Goldwater

Instead of giving a politician the keys to the city it might be better to change the locks.

~Doug Larson

Liberalism espouses a thoroughly discredited economic model. Government-run economies simply don't perform as well as market-driven ones. This is recognized theoretically and empirically. We will first look at the theoretical case—both at the micro and macro level—and then turn to the empirical. We will also look at the influence and effects of liberalism on macroeconomic stabilization policy.

Moreover, it's perhaps at least as important to examine the non-economic merits of capitalism. Capitalism plays a key role in underpinning intellectual freedom and liberty. It is resistant to oppression, mob rule, and elite mismanagement given that it's based on pluralism in power and a separation of economic power from political power. It is also endowed with a capacity to adapt to a rapidly changing world.

Price

The just price used to be mostly a religious concept before the advent of capitalism. With the development of markets, it became widely understood that price is established by supply and demand.

It's a bit of a conundrum why water, which is essential for our health and well-being, is so cheap, while diamonds which are not nearly so necessary are so expensive. The explanation is supply and demand. The supply of water is large, while that of diamonds is small. So even though the demand for water is much larger than that for diamonds, the price of water is lower than diamonds because its supply is much larger. Likewise an athlete or a rock star may get high pay, because they have unique talents and the demand is high for them.

Liberals often complain about the marketplace, claiming prices are not fair or just. For example, when the price of gasoline rises sharply, they complain that the oil companies are gouging them. The response of the Obama Administration to rising oil prices was to propose higher taxes on oil companies. They curtailed drilling due to the oil spill and increased environmental regulations on other domestic sources of energy. These policies obviously militated toward reducing supply, which in turn increased prices.

Liberals are inclined to intervene in the setting of prices— for example, with rent control and now more recently with the pricing of medicines—but past experience has indicated even to them the folly of intervention.

Rent controls, notoriously advocated by liberals, have sharply curtailed the supply of housing affected by controls. Not only was new construction of housing cut back, but landlords sought to convert many of the affected buildings into condominiums, and thus priced the poor out of the market. This means substantially reduced housing availability to those whom liberals sought to help. It means that the housing that was affected was maintained poorly.

Liberals think that pharmaceuticals are priced too high and want to limit prices for them or allow the importation of generics. They don't realize the huge investment required to put a new drug on the market. They label the drug companies greedy and see inequity in what they're doing. For liberals, producers should be willing to make the drugs available at low prices. Companies, they think, should not be driven by financial consideration. Liberals simply can't digest that without the financial incentive such drugs would not be brought to the market, particularly with the cumbersome government regulations that impede the process.

Liberals recently intervened in setting prices in the banking sector. Through congressional legislation in 2011, the Obama Administration reduced the fees on debit cards issued by banks from forty-four cents per transaction to twenty-two cents per transaction. Banks earned about nineteen billion dollars in revenues from these fees, so their profit was cut significantly. In response, banks have increased other fees; for example, Bank of America introduced a five dollar per month fee on customers for using debit cards. The Bank laid off thirty thousand workers to cope with their changed financial reality. The Obama Administration intended to lower fees for customers, but this was a short-sighted and myopic intervention in the marketplace. It caused the banks to raise other fees and, perhaps, led them to curtail the number of debit cards issued to people with better financial histories. This, in conjunction with the firings, helped the Bank of America to restore its financial position. What did the Obama Administration accomplish? Bank customers certainly were not helped, because the Bank raised other fees to compensate for the decline in debit card fees. The Obama Administration is always talking about how it wants to create jobs. Thirty thousand jobs were lost. Does this make sense?

Subsidies are another way the government intervenes in the market. By providing a subsidy to a product, say, to ethanol producers, the government ensures that more of it will be produced and that more of it will be consumed. Basically it ensures overproduction and overconsumption. The US government is doing this at the behest of the environmental lobby, but it's recognized now that the subsidy is actually causing more damage to the environment rather than less. It has also caused a significant rise in food prices. Even though the subsidy is now recognized as a mistake, it has not been repealed. Like any subsidy, the constituents receiving them don't want to give them up. The corn farmers are fighting hard to see that the subsidies are not taken away, so the politicians are reluctant to eliminate them.

When things are offered for free or at low cost, this does not mean that they are free in an economic sense. In fact overconsumption of subsidized goods can be very costly to the public at large. The greater the overconsumption, the greater would be the impact on the budget. The larger fiscal outlays for the subsidies would in turn require larger taxes or borrowing to finance them.

The virtue of the market system is that it effectively addresses the fundamental issues facing an economic system: one, what should be produced; two, how it should be produced; and, three, for whom remuneration should be distributed.

The market system ensures that the right goods are produced, namely, those that the public wants. Under communist or planned societies, the government determines what is produced, not the public. Another benefit of the market system is that it works to ensure that the most efficient methods are used to produce goods and services. Firms that are efficient survive, while those that are not fail. The market system distributes income according to how much workers effectively meet the economic needs of others. It rewards those who contribute the most. Those people providing the goods and services most sought after are rewarded the most. People who are unwilling or unable to work and produce are not rewarded.

The market economy allows the free interplay of supply and demand to determine prices. If there is a shortage, the market system works to eliminate it. Demand bids up prices for the good in short supply until the profit incentive is enough to draw people into the business of supplying that good. People who do so are rewarded with attractive remuneration. Liberalism, on the other hand, tends to create shortages by intervening in the market.

Profit is what drives economic growth and a better life. Unfortunately, liberals do not understand profit; they vilify it, seeing only greed. Profit arises when a firm meets the economic needs of the community efficiently or when it develops an innovation. These are good things: they make the community better off. Unfortunately, liberals do not see the good; they only see some people doing well financially and they don't like this. Under the liberal agenda profits are targeted through taxation and attacked through the media as socially unacceptable and unfair.

Profit is at the heart of the market system. It is how entrepreneurs are remunerated. Without it there would not be entrepreneurs. There would not be risk taking. There would only be wage earners. Moreover, under the economic system favored by liberals, even wages would not be in line with the economic contribution of labor. The ruling elite, through their discretion and planning, would set wages.

So in a market economy the price mechanism allocates scarce resources. Tampering with it creates real problems. When the government allocates resources through planning, rather than allowing the price mechanism to fulfill this function, rationing is the result. In the USSR people had to stand in long lines just to get bread. In government-run health care programs like in the United Kingdom, people have to wait a long time just to see a doctor or to receive much-needed medical treatments. In a market economy, consumers get the goods and services they want; in a planned economy they get what the government gives them.

I remember visiting department stores in the former USSR and seeing huge piles of shoes and hardly any consumer interest. The shoes were of poor quality and almost all of the same size, so they were of no use to most people. The company producing the shoes was happy because they met their government production target. It was not their problem if the shoes were useless.

Being in a market economy is tough. One has to be efficient and meet people's needs if one is to survive as a business. Efficiency is necessary. This is not the case in a planned economy. The market economy is in a continual state of change and is well adapted to handling change. A government-run planned economy is poorly suited to change and does not adapt well.

Some tout the case of China as an example of the strength of state planning, but China is feeding off our successes. The Chinese growth model is taking unfair advantage of the World Trade Organization, an undervalued exchange rate, and the use of technology created by capitalism to generate economic growth. Its undervalued exchange rate has played a key role in advancing its economy, as has its entry into the World Trade Organization. China's use of technology created by the West has been fundamental to its economic achievements. It did not and could not have created this technology itself. China is widely known to be abusing our intellectual property rights. At the same time that it's taking away our manufacturing jobs through an unfairly low exchange rate, it's stealing our technology to hurt us at high-value-added production as well.

In a market economy both consumers and workers have greater economic freedom. This freedom is not free however; it comes with a requirement for greater personal responsibility and accountability and greater risk. But the rewards are substantial: greater prosperity for everyone. Moreover, this economic freedom is the bedrock of other freedoms. It should not be seen as something to be sacrificed without dire consequences for liberty.

Government versus the Market

The market system produces something. Value is added. The government sector, on the other hand, mostly takes wealth produced in the private sector and redistributes it. But more importantly, the government sector aggrandizes itself—and those who support it—at the expense of others.

The private sector employs carrots and sticks. In the private sector, you may fire people who perform poorly, and you may reward good performers with bonuses and raises. In the public sector, bad employees cannot be dismissed and the good performers don't get much more than the bad performers. In the public sector it doesn't matter if it fails to satisfy the needs of the citizenry, the employees will be paid anyway. In fact they may even use this failure to justify the need for an expansion in the public sector. In the private sector, if a firm fails to serve the public well, it will go out of business.

Under the right market conditions, free enterprise is widely acknowledged to be the best way to organize an economy, enhance efficiency and productivity, and bring about high economic growth. The right market conditions, however, are not always present. Sometimes there are markets with increasing returns to scale that lead to monopolies, which don't provide the best means of meeting the public interests. Monopolies can manipulate prices and supplies to maximize their profits and hurt consumers. However, this argument was much more important in the twentieth century than in the twenty-first, as globalization now subjects almost all firms to the forces of competition.

Another justification for government intervention is the existence of certain public goods which the private sector cannot handle well. Certain goods, like defense and clean-air programs, benefit all citizens. In such situations the private market has problems providing these services, as some citizens could opt out of buying the services, but still benefit as others pay for them. This is the so-called free rider problem.

Perhaps the biggest factor fueling the expansion of government is social insurance. Social Security, Medicare, Medicaid, unemployment insurance, and the rest have grown explosively in this country, and social insurance has accounted for much of the growth in Europe as well. In the United States entitlement spending rose from one-third of federal government spending in 1960 to about two-thirds in 2010. In 2010 entitlement spending amounted to $2.2 trillion (Medicare $518 billion, Medicaid $405 billion, income maintenance $265 billion, Social Security $690 billion, unemployment insurance $140 billion, and other $203 billion).[121]

Three basic arguments have been used to justify government involvement in social insurance. First, there is the problem of adverse selection. Low-risk persons tend not to buy insurance; only people at high risk tend to buy insurance, and this causes high prices. Second, even if equitable private insurance is available, it's argued that some individuals do not act in their own self-interest and purchase it. Third, there is the free rider problem. Why pay for private insurance, when you know that government will pick up the bill if you don't have it.

These justifications—increasing returns to scale, public goods, and social insurance needs—are not sufficient to explain the marked growth in government in Western democracies over the last century. Government spending as a proportion of GDP has grown from about ten percent of GDP for these countries in 1870 to about forty percent today.[122] Most of this growth has occurred since World War II. This growth in spending is largely in the form of public health programs, public sector pensions, public education, and welfare and social assistance.

It's clear, however, that the government's own actions and interest in expanding its power has been central to the growth of government. Government policies have created their own justifications by creating problems in the private insurance industry. By allowing lawyers to run wild and initiate huge law suits against medical practitioners, the government has vastly increased the cost of medical care and private insurance. By not allowing insurance companies to sell insurance beyond state lines, the government has constrained competition and significantly added to insurance costs. So, government has helped create the circumstances building support for government intervention in the insurance realm.

Government encroachment into the realm of social insurance has squeezed out private sector groups that have traditionally helped the most vulnerable and those in need. With government social insurance, individuals don't get out of it what they put into it. Basically, government social insurance penalizes the responsible and hard-working citizens while it rewards the irresponsible and those who avoid working. Many people game the system to their advantage, taking advantage of the community at large. Thus there is a serious moral hazard problem with government social insurance.

As previously noted, democracies have a built-in bias toward government expansion, which is exacerbated by liberalism. The public doesn't realize the costs of programs. Hence, in seeing the benefits, they push for more of them. Moreover, groups with large numbers can push for programs benefiting them at the expense of others. It's not surprising that government services provided free to the public are excessively consumed. Much of it is not paid for out of current taxes and revenues, but is borrowed. So it appears free to the current generation.

Another cost that should be considered regarding the large expansion of government expenditures is that of reduced economic growth. This affects everyone. The higher taxes needed to finance the expansion in expenditure dampen growth. It's well documented that countries with high tax rates have lower rates of economic growth than countries with low tax rates.

It's well recognized that government cannot provide services as efficiently as the market. In the marketplace, competition demands efficiency. In government there is no such force operating to produce efficiency; in fact there are many factors militating against it. Generally countries with small government sectors relative to GDP provide public services with more efficiency than those with large government sectors.[123] The efficiency of government is an important determinant of economic growth rates. Countries with large government sectors have lower growth rates. A significant problem is that often government services are provided at too high a cost. There are better, more efficient and less costly ways to provide these services.

Corruption is more of a problem in government than in the private sector. The amount of fraud and waste in government is huge. For example, Medicare and Medicaid fraud alone is estimated at about one hundred billion dollars annually. And for social security spending on the poor, it is estimated that ten percent or about eight billion dollars annually, amounts to waste and fraud.[124] In one case they found they had been paying a pensioner who had been dead for thirty-seven years. His son had been taking the pension check. Unfortunately, by the time Social Security found the mistake the son too was dead. Essentially the government is more interested in finding new ways to spend than in monitoring and using effectively the programs they already have. Is this surprising? It's not their money. The more money that passes through them, the more power they have. This leads not only to increased inefficiencies, but also adversely affects the moral climate.

Government today tries to provide citizens with security and protect them from risk. Liberalism is averse to risk and failure. We are no longer open to failure, and this is regrettable. The fact is we learn a lot from mistakes and errors. The safe route is not the best route. One of the reasons for the big financial crisis in 2008 is that we could no longer tolerate recessions and pain. Thus like earthquakes, if you suppress them or they fail to materialize for a long period of time, eventually this will result in a big earthquake. Recessions and errors clean the system. This is also one of the reasons the economic recession in the 1970s was so deep.

The problem is compounded by the government's bailout of those who have made bad decisions. The bailout of banks in the banking crisis of 2008 and subsequent bailouts of car and insurance companies, unions, and people who contracted for mortgages that they could not afford reduces risk perception and encourages bad behavior. Perversely, this encourages high-risk behavior as market actors go after big but risky gains, knowing that if they lose the government is likely to bail them out.

The expansion of government has resulted in a large loss of economic freedom. It's a well-known axiom in economics that people are better off if they are allowed to make their own choices. If the government makes your choices for you, you won't be better off. For example, the government pretty much constrains you to send your child to a public school because you paid for this through your taxes. If you were to have the option of a voucher (equivalent to the value of taxes paid for the school) to send your child to a private school rather than have to send him to a public school, you may be better off, because you would have a choice.

The use of market failure (in the case of public goods, externalities, and natural monopolies) for justifying government intervention is overused. It fails to recognize that government itself has shortcomings that should be taken into account. It also fails to recognize that once government establishes a footprint in an area, it is reluctant to give it up. Once government employees are hired, and once government constituencies are established, there is little possibility of retreat. In fact there is an irresistible tendency toward expansion. Moreover, the impact government expansion has on private sector motivation and activity should not be underestimated. Businessmen are always looking over their shoulders, wondering what the government may or may not do. Government has a historical record of squeezing the private sector out and replacing it rather than trying to improve the performance of the market. Once the government establishes a foothold in a sector, it exercises monopoly powers which can lead to harmful and inefficient outcomes.

Government intervention in banking almost always leads to disastrous outcomes. In the development community, it is common knowledge that government development banks are bad and ought to be avoided. Such banks are destined to fail. If government intervenes it should offer a subsidy to banks to offset the added risk and reduced profit margins. In other words, they should pay as they go. Otherwise we all pay later in the form of a banking crisis. This is exactly what happened in the mortgage-banking crisis that hit the United States in 2008.

The most fundamental role for government in supporting the market is to provide a legal framework guaranteeing private property. People must have confidence that private property will not be taken by the government either through direct appropriation or taxation. This is why expansion of the welfare state and the movement toward socialism is such a slippery slope. Such expansion can have a very damaging impact on confidence in the market, which is fundamental to capitalism. In Africa many businessmen fear the proverbial knock on the door from government, from which they can lose everything overnight. While this is not the case in America and Western Europe, gradual slippage in the government's support for private property nevertheless can hurt. As mentioned earlier, the right of eminent domain is increasingly abused.

Public enterprises, like Fannie Mae and Freddy Mac, operate in an environment not conducive to efficiency. Government interference weakens efficiency. Public enterprises are usually highly unionized. The unions are often influential, and the institutions are usually overstaffed, and the salaries are too high. There is a commitment to providing and protecting employment. The public enterprises often operate in monopolistic or oligopolistic markets, and consumers have little influence over the range and quality of goods and services provided. Prices are often administered rather than set by the market, and are set on a cost-plus basis to protect the public enterprise's financial position. So there is little incentive to be efficient. Prices for social or non-commercial objectives are set below cost. Low prices can result in large budget subsidies. Budgetary support from the government compensates for inefficiency and in fact encourages it. The lack of a hard budget constraint means that the impact on the fiscal budget will likely be high. Fannie Mae and Freddy Mac illustrate all of these points.

The lack of a hard budget constraint for public enterprises is a serious problem leading to inefficiency and poor performance. In the private sector, a firm goes bankrupt if it cannot earn a profit. In government this is not the case. In government there is no hard budget constraint. If a public enterprise is having trouble meeting expenditures, the government simply gives them more money.

A major problem for government compared to the private sector is bad fiscal accounting and a lack of transparency. Obfuscation is a prominent feature of government. It's hard to penetrate the bureaucracy to find out what is really going on.

The government has a substantial amount of spending which is simply off balance sheet. It does not show up in the budget. Unfunded pension liabilities are estimated at over fifty trillion dollars. It also has many contingent liabilities not shown in the budget. For example, it backs up loans to Freddy Mac and Fannie Mae and more recently to the Solyndra Corporation, which just went bankrupt and left taxpayers on the hook for $525 million.

Its use of baseline budgeting makes it difficult to evaluate what is happening to the budget. For example, the government will say that it's cutting spending by, say, one hundred billion dollars in 2012. But what does this really mean? This one hundred billion dollars is relative to the current budget projections which involves increasing spending by four hundred billion to three trillion dollars in 2012; so in effect the cut would only bring spending down to $2.9 trillion, still three hundred billion higher than in the previous year. It would only slow the rate of increase, not represent a real reduction in spending.

Moreover, on those rare occasions when the government actually announces that it is cutting the budget deficit, it's just smoke and mirrors. For example, when Obama promised that his health care bill would be budget neutral, it was not. The health care bill in fact will have a huge cost to the budget. Obama simply built into his budget unrealistic assumptions, which the Congressional Budget Office was obliged to use in estimating his budget proposal. After the bill was rammed through Congress, the Congressional Budget Office estimated the true cost at $1.76 trillion over a decade.[125] Deceptive accounting tricks hid the true cost. If the Administration had been honest about the cost, ObamaCare would not have passed.

The government, which requires businesses and people in the private sector to follow standard accounting principles, does not require this of state and local governments. Given that these accounting systems are highly idiosyncratic and non-standardized, it's very hard for outside auditors and accountants to unearth problems. This has led to huge corruption and embezzlement because the accounting systems of state and local governments are ideal vehicles for hiding miscreant behavior.

Also there is a lack of will to address difficult issues anymore. The guiding principle is simply to avoid the spotlight and all controversial issues. This is amply illustrated by the grinding gridlock that has characterized our government for a number of years now. This is even more apparent in the European Union.

In a changing world involving difficult issues, it's critically important for a country to have in place an effective approach for negotiating the challenges of change. The market has shown itself to be very effective in this regard. Government, on the other hand, seems increasingly unable to handle the challenges ahead.

Government affects the economy and the lives of its citizens not only through taxation, spending, and borrowing, but also through its regulatory power. Regulations limit supply and add cost in the private sector. The budget includes the direct administrative costs of formulating, overseeing, and implementing regulations. The impact on the economy of regulations is, however, much wider than on the budget. Regulations and mandates create costs for state and local government, private sector firms, and the consumer. For example, regulations mandating catalytic converters for cars impose significant costs for car producers and consumers.

Liberals keep attacking the shortcomings of the market, but they never attack, or even acknowledge, government shortcomings or the deficiencies of over-regulation. In fact government and regulation is their solution to everything, even when the record of failure is glaring.

Liberals favor extensive government regulation of the private sector. They point to the banking crisis and the oil spill as an argument for more regulation, but, as mentioned earlier, they don't want to recognize that the BP oil rig received a top safety rating from the regulatory authority just a week before the crisis, and that government regulatory interference caused the banking crisis. The liberal argument, as always, is *we can do better next time,* they simply won't accept that their policies don't work.

If regulations worked, this would be fine, but they don't. If they don't work, who benefits from regulations? The only beneficiaries are those involved in government enforcing, formulating, and implementing regulations. It's quite common for the industry subject to regulation to get control of the regulatory agency and use it to their advantage. Usually the large prominent firms in the industry concerned buy influence or else get their people on the staff of the regulatory agency and use their influence against new competitors and small firms. This phenomenon is referred to as regulatory capture, and it's quite harmful to efficiency and the welfare of consumers. Regulation sounds great, but it does not work. It's another example of good intentions leading to nothing but ineffectiveness and an expansion of government power.

Regulatory obstacles now make it much more difficult to do business in the United States than in the past. For example, according to the World Economic Forum, the regulatory system in the United States makes it more difficult to get a construction permit here than in Saudi Arabia; the United States is now ranked as twenty-seventh in the world in the ease of getting a construction permit.[126]

The problem of over-regulation is not confined to the federal level; it also is evident at the state and local level. Underscoring the extreme extent of regulatory control were two actions taken by the Montgomery Council during June of 2011. During this period they issued a five-hundred-dollar fine against children selling lemonade outside the grounds on which the US Open Golf Championship was held. The children were donating half of their proceeds to help cancer victims. The County also levied three-hundred-dollar fines on homeowners who were charging people to park on their lawns.

Crony Capitalism

Liberalism significantly damages capitalism by bringing about what is called *crony capitalism*. Crony capitalism can be described as an economy in which business success depends on close relationships between business people and government officials. It's manifested in terms of favoritism in awarding government contracts, grants, permits, regulatory decisions, and in the design and implementation of the tax code, including special tax breaks. As the size of government grows relative to the private sector, and as its intrusiveness in regulations increases, crony capitalism becomes a more serious problem. Crony capitalism need not pervade an entire economy to be damaging; it may create significant problems even if it's confined to certain sectors. In America we see it particularly in the military-industrial complex and in the financial sector.

Crony capitalism has a highly deleterious effect on free-market capitalism, which is based on efficiency and meeting the economic needs of the community. Crony capitalism strikes at the heart of this, rewarding instead those with political power and large firms willing to play the game with them. Those with political power grant favorable contracts and make decisions that enhance the wealth and economic power of certain corporations, while these same corporations funnel money back to their political benefactors, further enhancing their power. Crony capitalism sets in motion a vicious circle of political power accumulation and unearned economic reward that works to the detriment everyone outside the game. Essentially crony capitalism is transforming business, making it similar in nature and character to government. The diseases inherent in government institutions are spreading and infecting the business world.

Crony capitalism favors "intentionally ambiguous laws and regulations," as it creates a favorable environment for those with political power to wield their influence within the private sector. Where the rule of law is weak or absent, firms have to be concerned with currying favor with the political establishment. This is why Congress now writes incredibly lengthy and convoluted legislation like ObamaCare and the Dodd-Frank financial reform legislation.

Under crony capitalism, big firms don't have to worry about failure. Because they know they will be bailed out if they make a bad investment, the incentive is to go after big returns regardless of risk. President Clinton, a liberal Democrat, opened the door for banks to get into risky investments when he abolished the Glass-Steagall Act. He sent another strong message to the banking community that risky investment was okay when he bailed out Mexico in the 1990s—what he was really doing was bailing out the banks. He even did this without the approval of Congress.

Crony capitalism and the associated moral hazard were a big factor behind the 2008 financial crisis. Despite this, nothing is done to address this problem. The lesson has not been learned. Even today the Fed is making almost free money available to banks, which they are using to make speculative investments. If the speculative investments pay off, the banks win big. If the investments fail, they don't really lose because they get bailed out. Moreover, the executives who are making the decisions win big: huge bonuses when speculative investments work out well, and great golden parachutes if the investments fail. It's the taxpayer who loses, always.

So while the case for free-market capitalism against a largely government-run economy is very strong, it's less so in the case of crony capitalism. Unfortunately, many of those complaining about capitalism are really complaining about manifestations of crony capitalism, like the favoritism shown to Wall Street bankers who play a major role in the Obama Administration, and who have been on the receiving end of mammoth bailouts. It's interesting that many of those complaining are liberals, but these are the same people who argue for an ever-expanding role for government, which creates an ideal environment for the growth of crony capitalism and its abuses. Liberals don't comprehend the connection. It would be hard for crony capitalism to take root if the government were small and limited in influence.

Some liberals, like Noam Chomsky, see the chain of causation running from economic to political power. They see free-market capitalism inevitably evolving into crony capitalism as large corporations try to use their wealth to buy power. There is some legitimacy to this argument, but the fact remains that if the government were small in size and limited in influence, crony capitalism could be kept at bay. Moreover, crony capitalism flourishes when there is a concentration of economic and political power. Yet this is precisely what liberals are calling for. It's the separation of economic and political power which is an inherent part of free-market capitalism that militates against this happening—yet this is what liberals want to destroy.

So when liberals are attacking capitalism, they are usually attacking the manifestations of crony capitalism, which they are in fact working to create. This is not free-market capitalism, but rather a perverted form of capitalism. Unfortunately, many are not able to discern the distinction, including non-liberals.

The Empirical Case

The market-driven economy of the United States has consistently outperformed the welfare states of Europe. The problems in

Europe of the creeping welfare state have produced lower economic growth rates and intractably high structural unemployment. Debt levels have risen to alarming levels and now represent a serious threat to their economic future. The promises for social safety net protections and entitlements are simply unsustainable. The priority placed on job protection is "already gone," as can be seen in youth unemployment rates in Spain, which exceed fifty percent. European Central Bank President Mario Draghi made clear in February 2012 that the European Union's social contract is obsolete and in drastic need of reform. He said, "You know there was a time when economist Rudi Dornbusch used to say that the Europeans are so rich they can afford to pay everyone for not working. That's gone."[127]

The economic failure of China, the USSR, and India before reform is well known. Since market oriented reforms have been introduced in China, the USSR, and India, all are now performing very impressively. Also, in the 1980s and 1990s Chile adopted market-oriented economic reforms and its performance has clearly stood out as the best in Latin America. In addition to the economic benefits, the military junta gave way to a democratic government. Thus the free-market approach helped bring about a free society of increased liberty. Contrast this to Venezuela which has seen freedom of the press and liberty diminished as Chavez imposed socialist policies and a vastly expanded role of government on the country.

Government-run redistribution programs in America and internationally are the centerpiece of the liberal agenda, but the programs have failed across the board. Yet liberals insist on doing more, even though it's clear that they have hurt the people they claim they are trying to help. More importantly, the real hurt is yet to come, when the programs go bankrupt.

The private sector works better than the public sector. Big public enterprises like Amtrak are losing money. Amtrak is losing about thirteen billion dollars a year. Similarly, the United States Post Office is running big deficits, while FedEx, a private firm, is making good money.

One can readily see the difference between liberal and conservative economic performance by looking at the performance of different states within America. California is teetering on the brink of bankruptcy, and its economy is flagging. Texas, on the other hand, is running budgetary surpluses and seeing a strong economy. California has lost 113 thousand jobs from August 2009 to August 2010. Since 2005, California has lost about 1.3 million jobs, while Texas has seen job growth.[128]

This discrepancy in economic performance has been largely due to different approaches to the labor market. Texas is a right-to-work state, which means that "the state prohibits compulsory union dues as a condition of employment."[129] California is not a right-to-work state, which has caused much higher labor costs in California than in Texas. Only about five percent of the labor force is unionized in Texas, versus about seventeen percent in California. California's public sector is heavily unionized. According to the above-mentioned study, California owes $535 billion to its public employee pension plan—more than six times the state's annual budget and thirty-six thousand dollars in debt for each household in the state. Pay for California's public sector employees is about thirty-three percent higher than the national average, amounting on average to about ninety thousand dollars per public-sector job. In Texas, on the other hand, government wages are about seventeen percent below the national average. Moreover, in California government sector pensions are largely unfunded, while in Texas they are eighty-three percent funded.[130]

The question is not why people are poor, but why they are rich. Capitalism makes people and countries rich. Hong Kong and Singapore are vivid examples of this. Look, in contrast, at what communism and socialism have done.

Capitalism frees almost everyone from the oppression of economic need and from the control of the government. Under liberalism almost everyone is enslaved to economic need and, in addition, is politically indentured to the State. In capitalistic democracies there are poor, but they are few in number compared to those under other governments. Moreover, because market-driven countries are economically more successful, their absolute poverty is less. Even the poor in these countries live well compared to the middle class in autocratic countries. In communist countries, relative poverty may be less, but absolute poverty is much worse. More fundamentally, there is not a slavery to economic need for the majority of the population in market-driven countries, but there is in autocratic ones. Where economic needs are not met, people don't care about freedom, only eating and surviving.

Liberal Economic Policy versus Market-Oriented Policy

Liberals claim an inexorable teleology: the world is moving toward a socialistic-organic society or communism, either fitfully or gradually. They see a march of history toward a certain end. They don't believe in market equilibrium, forces tending to move us back to stability, but rather are committed to a march toward progress and equality that must be imposed through politics. They distrust the market, but believe in government.

Conservatives believe in market equilibrium. However, although the focus is on equilibrium and the self-adjusting nature of the markets, this does not mean the economy is static or unchanging. The market system has brought more change, increased technology, and improvements in living standards than any other political-economic paradigm.

Liberalism touts that it favors non-hierarchical societal systems in which everyone is equal, but in reality it supports a hierarchical system with a ruling elite in charge. The ruling elite could serve the interests of the people, but history shows us they serve their own interests to the detriment of the public. Capitalism is also a hierarchical system, but unlike socialism or communism, it's a system based on merit, not patronage and nepotism. In capitalism the desire for power and prestige is channeled into economic energy that benefits the whole society through "the invisible hand." It yields benefit to society, whereas in collectivist political systems it's usually only the ruling class that benefits.

Macroeconomic Stabilization Policy and Management

The role of the business cycle is important in market economies. As Schumpeter, a famous economist early in our history, argued, the business cycle is fundamental to growth. He saw the business cycle as engaging in creative destruction. The economy needs to be cleaned out occasionally. Poorly performing companies need to fail and go out of business, so that the resources they are tying up can be channeled into more productive firms. Liberals are averse to this; they strive to eliminate the business cycle and prop up weak and underperforming firms.

In terms of macroeconomic management, liberals are locked into Keynesian economics. This fits with their disposition toward a large government role in the economy. Keynesian theory advocates large government spending increases to stimulate the economy during recessions. Liberals are always supportive of anything that involves large government spending or an increased role for the government in the economy. Keynesianism also advocates cutting government spending during boom times to cool off an economy, but of course liberals ignore Keynesianism then. The insincerity and inconsistency of liberalism with respect to Keynesian stabilization policy is highlighted in the current policy posture of the Obama administration. The administration is arguing against reducing government spending on the grounds that the economy needs support, but at the same time it is pushing for tax increases which would drain spending power out of the economy.

Liberal macroeconomic stabilization policy has not worked. FDR's New Deal did not end the depression. Unemployment in 1940 was at fifteen percent, the same as in 1932 when he took over. His own Treasury Secretary, Morganthau, later admitted the failure of Roosevelt's policy of trying to rise out of the depression through more government spending.

That it did not work to alleviate economic conditions during the Great Depression and during the financial crisis of 2008–2010 does not change their thinking. In the 2008–2010 crisis the democratic leadership was saying we must spend our way out. The fact that overspending put us in the crisis was somehow irrelevant to them. In creating an ever larger financial overhang we are limiting our prospects for economic growth and increasing the prospect of an even worse financial crisis in the near future.

By trying to avoid the costs of economic downturns through countercyclical economic management, we have increased the magnitude of economic dislocations when they do come. Business cycles help cleanse the economy and get rid of businesses that are not working. We can suppress the cycle, but in doing so we limit the benefit that these cycles confer as well. In the 1970s, business-cycle suppression led to stagflation. In 2008, the price tag was a financial crisis.

Liberals don't recognize the benefits of supply-side economics. President Reagan used these policies successfully in the 1980s to recover from the stagflation of the Carter years of the late 1970s and to generate growth. Supply-side policies are directed at improving the economic environment and incentives in the private sector. The purpose is to generate private sector growth, not growth in the government sector, which is the objective of liberals.

The depression of the 1930s gave liberals the opening they needed to expand the role of government. Keynesian economic theory justified a role for increased government spending to deal with the weak aggregate demand and high unemployment, which appeared intractable at the time. Of course, it was only later recognized that much of the problem with the economy was due in fact to inept government trade and monetary policies. Nevertheless, any time in subsequent years that there was a recession and higher than normal unemployment, liberals trotted out Keynesian theory as an excuse to expand the role of government.

It's critical to understand, however, that government economic policy often involves conflict of interest. That policy which would have the most favorable effect on the economy often is one that isn't helpful to the electoral ambitions of the officeholders and decision makers. This is one of the problems with giving government a larger role in managing the economy. Political objectives and considerations take precedence over economic ones.

This is one of the reasons why economies tend to do particularly well right before an election. The reigning office holders seek to enhance the likelihood of their election by prime-pumping the economy before Election Day. The year after a presidential election is usually one of weak economic growth and an off year for the stock market.

Sometimes it may be in the interest of the ruling party to actually undertake stabilization policies, which are detrimental to the economy. For example, the liberal agenda is to expand government and increase dependency on government. In this scenario, it may actually make sense for a liberal government to see enhanced economic uncertainty and an increase in unemployment. Likewise President Obama is pushing for an expanded role for the government in health insurance. Popular opinion is decidedly against this policy. That Obama's economic policies have been anti-business and actually hurting the economy may actually help him garner support for his healthcare reform package. As people lose their jobs, they lose their private health insurance. So they are more likely to support Obama's government approach to health insurance.

Thus for a liberal government there actually can be some benefit for carrying out bad economic policies. To the extent that the private sector is hurt, people may need to turn to the government for help. Reliance on the government will naturally increase as performance of the private sector is damaged.

Liberal politicians vastly expanded the amount of mortgage credit available to poor people. This led to a financial collapse, a severe economic downturn, and hurt the people it was intended to help. Nevertheless, the Democrats benefitted politically from this approach before the crash and have not had to pay a penalty after the crash. Obama was behind in the polls in 2008 before the financial collapse, but afterwards he moved solidly ahead of McCain and subsequently won the election. The public did not understand and perceive that it was the Democrats who were responsible for these policies. In effect they elected the party responsible for the economic collapse and denied office to the party that had opposed it.

Lyndon Johnson caused high inflation and economic instability in the 1960s when he undertook a war in Vietnam without paying for it, while at the same time initiating a vast expansion in welfare spending. The ensuing budget deficits led to a sharp increase in inflation and a subsequent recession. The liberal weakness in thinking that you can get something without paying for it had once again caught up with them, and with America.

Under President Jimmy Carter in the late 1970s the country suffered from stagflation as he tried to keep employment high (to secure the labor vote) while inflationary pressures remained unrestrained. The result was anemic economic growth, with high unemployment and high inflation—the worst of both worlds. In short, Carter created stagflation. By ignoring the nature of the markets and trying to enforce economic results from above through government policy, President Carter created an economic mess that was left for President Reagan to fix.

The contrast between the Carter and Reagan approaches highlight the differences between the liberal and conservative approaches to stabilization policy. Liberals sought to guarantee labor unions that they would maintain full employment policies. This meant that unions could push up the cost of labor without worrying about unemployment. The government in effect changed the nature of collective bargaining arrangements through its commitment to maintain full employment. It changed the nature of the way labor approached collective bargaining. Reagan had to pull the government back from this commitment to allow the labor markets to function properly without inflationary consequences.

Milton Friedman of the monetarist school began sounding the warning bells about the harmful effects of government stabilization policies in the 1960s. He maintained that most of the problems with the business cycle stemmed from government meddling in the economy. The government was the cause of economic instability in his view, not the cure.

It's bizarre that seventy to eighty years after the Great Depression, the Obama Administration is still trying increased government spending as a way to get us out of a recession. Obama tried a large fiscal stimulus shortly after taking office in 2009, but it did not meet with successful results. Yet again, in 2011, he asked for more government spending. At least during the Roosevelt period there was low government debt. Now, however, government debt is at alarming levels, as is the fiscal deficit. During a period like this it makes no sense to be pushing for even more spending. Yet Vice President Biden is quoted as saying *we need to spend our way out of our economic morass.* But excessive spending and debt is what got us where we are. For an economy to prosper, the business community needs to have confidence that the government is behaving properly and responsibly in managing the economy. When they see the government seemingly out of control, it's natural that there is going to be weakness in confidence in the private sector, and that growth will not materialize.

The Obama Administration and liberalism have tied our hands so that we really now have no options with macroeconomic stabilization policy. Normally, during a recession the authorities would be able to provide support for the economy through easier monetary policy and expansionary fiscal policy. Interest rates now, however, are at historic lows, and the fiscal deficit is already dangerously high, as is the fiscal debt. So in effect the authorities are out of ammunition. In fact, with fiscal retrenchment all but inevitable, the fiscal effect will be contractionary. Likewise, the low current level of interest rates is unsustainable, so this too will inevitably impart a contractionary effect.

Other Non-economic Merits of Capitalism

Capitalism brought profit and financial and economic gain out of the disrepute that hung over it during the pre-capitalist period. Prior to the eighteenth century, religion looked down upon financial gain. It was viewed as taking something from someone else. It was only with philosophers like Adam Smith, John Locke, John Stuart Mill, and Jeremy Bentham that the pursuit of self-interest and economic gain began to be recognized as a social good. Prior to that most philosophical perspectives looked at society first and the individual second. They focused on affecting the organic whole of society, not the individual.

The ideology of capitalism is based on this world, not another. It's not ethereal or theistic, but pragmatic and experiential. It's based on trial and error and yields productive outcomes. It's based on individual effort, ingenuity, creativity, achievement and success, not the words of an effete, disconnected ruling class. It's not based on dogma, but on what works and what's successful. It's looking for success and happiness in this world, not after death. It says that the profit or financial gain realized should go to those who produce it, and not to some who can exercise enough power to seize the gains of others.

With the development of the market and weakening of monarchies, the feudal system, and autocracies in general, the view began to develop that governments should exist to serve the people rather than the other way around. The success of capitalism helped foster this attitude because it gave individuals the means to survive and determine their own lives, rather than have them predetermined by the powers that be. This created an uneasy balance between government and the private sector.

The benefit of capitalism pertains not just to the economic sphere. It's pivotal to intellectual freedom and the freedom of speech and thinking. It provides the most fertile ground for the contest of ideas. No other ideology comes close. This is why capitalism has not only produced the most dynamic economies, but the most creative and artistic achievements. It's why technological growth has been the strongest in capitalistic economies. Capitalism is the most dynamic and flexible socio-politico-economic form of organization. In a rapidly changing world, it's much more agile and adaptable than a planned or top-down system of governmental control.

One of the essential features of capitalism is that it's predicated on competition. This emphasis on competition pertains not only to the marketplace, but to the arena of ideas as well. From the beginning, capitalism had a subversive strain running through it. With its foundation in technology and science, it challenged the reign of churches and religion. In addition, it challenged aristocracies and autocracies; capitalism began to develop in Europe when aristocracies and the feudal system were weakening, and it hastened the decline of these social organizations. Even today small firms challenge goliaths. Bill Gates went after IBM, and Apple went after Microsoft. Nothing is sacrosanct and safe from challenge.

Capitalism is grounded in the real world. It's based on trial and error; it takes feedback from the real world and is empirical in essence. This contrasts sharply with liberalism, which is idealistic, or top-down, in approach. Liberalism is more concerned with "what should be" than evidential truth.

Under a capitalist system, any idea can win the day if it has merit. All ideas have to compete in the *marketplace* of ideas. Like in science, ideas are meant to be tested to determine which work best. This commitment to free thinking is quite unique. Other economic and political organizations have difficulty with intellectual freedom, because it directly challenges their authority. Certainly aristocracies or societies run by an elite ruling class tend not to be favorably disposed to intellectual freedom. We have seen the havoc wrought by fascism and communism on intellectual liberty. Socialism also stifles the free interplay of ideas through bureaucratic oppression. Once a ruling class is insulated from those they govern, the control of information and the suppression of ideas is almost inevitable. It's further aggravated to the extent that the ruling class see themselves as smarter than the public.

There is something unique about the DNA of capitalism that makes it the most salutary environment for intellectual freedom to flourish. Ideas and reason itself depend on a competitive environment. This is why capitalism, with its emphasis on competition, is so important for intellectual liberty. Systems, like socialism and communism, depending on social consensus and harmony rather than competition, don't favor a robust intellectual environment. Honesty and the pursuit of truth are sacrificed on the altar of group harmony. The abiding principle is that anything that reduces tensions and works toward unity is good, even if it involves moving away from truth. An ideology of unity and coherence is not compatible with allowing ideas to freely compete with each other. Those with opposing views to theirs are suppressed, but, more fundamentally, the whole process of rational discourse is discouraged.

Capitalism is unique as a socio-economic-political organizational system in that it's so supportive of competition in the marketplace and in ideas that it's willing to see even itself questioned and challenged. Most attribute free discourse to democracy, and certainly it's a necessary condition—but not a sufficient one. Social democracy is not nearly so supportive of free discourse. Its emphasis on social cohesion constrains it. Capitalism is essential for truly free speech and thought.

Capitalism has a fundamental and pervasive effect on thought, not just in the economic, social, and political area, but in the arts. In supporting unconstrained thinking, it fosters creativity and artistic expression. Frequently the artistic world is critical of capitalism and its commercialization of values, but capitalism is fundamental to the health of art and the artistic community. The criticism may in large part be due to temperament. Artists by nature are different than businessmen. They are more emotional and less pragmatic. But it's these differences that make life interesting.

The commercial success of capitalism has provided the financial basis for the arts to grow. In less developed economies, the arts have a hard time surviving. In socialist and communist societies the arts don't flourish at all.

Capitalism is based on reason with its unrelenting pursuit of the truth. It's grounded in the real world. Socialism and communism turn their eyes away from the real world, creating their own worlds. Liberals and conservatives are in effect living in alternate universes. This is another reason why dialogue between the two is so difficult. Interplanetary communication is not easy.

Capitalism was an outgrowth of science and the advance of technology which helped bring about the decline of aristocracies and the influence of the church and religion. In both science and capitalism there is nothing that is sacrosanct. Both believe in following ideas wherever they may lead. Socialism and communism believe only in their idea, and try to force reality to conform to their idea. They are absolutist, like the aristocracies and the reign of religion that preceded capitalism and the reign of science. In effect liberalism, socialism, and communism are against the free reign of ideas where ideas compete with one another in the minds of all men, not just the elite ruling class. They are against anything that can potentially challenge their agenda.

So, it's clear that the capitalistic model is superior to liberal socio-economic-political models in economic theory and outcomes, political outcomes, social and artistic outcomes, and outcomes for individuals. What arguments can the liberals make against these arguments? None! Perhaps they don't care, because it's all about power. Liberals don't want to look at facts, history, or reality.

The Achilles' heel of capitalism and democracy is the lack of certitude that so many crave and in fact may need. Capitalism, based on empiricism, searches for the truth; it does not claim to have it. It looks for the truth through trial and error; it does not take it as divinely given. Moreover, capitalism exalts commercial values. It's driven by monetary considerations. Many are looking for more certain and less commercial underpinnings for morality. The historical record however of collectivist and totalitarian approaches to political economy shows that they result in much worse moral outcomes. Nevertheless, discomfort with the moral foundations of capitalist societies provides fertile ground for those longing for something more certain and more exalted to hang on to. These people of liberal temperament push incessantly for change, even though the change they seek will almost certainly bring about a worse outcome.

One cannot find one instance where liberty exists where there has not been capitalism. It seems to be an essential condition. Certainly Milton Friedman and some other prominent thinkers believe it to be a necessary—though not sufficient—condition. So, by attacking capitalism, liberalism is assaulting liberty too.

Those in political power often look grudgingly at the power of the market and seek to expand their influence in the economic sphere. They seek to do this through regulation and an expanded role of government in the economy. It's natural that power seeks to expand, but, if the vitality of the private sector is to be preserved, this encroachment must be held in check.

Capitalism, by providing a sanctuary for economic activity from the political realm, helps keep the power of the government constrained. If the government rather than the markets exercises the levers of economic incentive, it exercises power and control over the behavior of individuals. To the extent that the government exercises control over wages, prices, employment, and what is produced, individual liberty is sharply curtailed, if not eradicated. Government can, of course, be repressive through other means, so capitalism is no guarantee of individual liberty, but it's a necessary condition.

Capitalism is over-arching. Capitalism rises above national identities. For collectivist or top-down economic and political systems, one needs to know the specifics of who is in charge and what they are doing, but in a capitalist system one only needs to understand the logic of how markets work.

Regularities and laws of nature play a strong role in the natural world. We readily recognize the stabilizing influence of these laws. It is our recognition of these laws that has allowed civilizations to progress. Political, economic, and social systems are also subject to underlying regularities and patterns that give them stability. Capitalism, based as it is on market forces and the behavioral patterns of people seeking materialistic well-being, contains strong regularities and stabilizing forces that help societies cohere and prosper. Economic systems ruled over by autocrats do not offer these benefits. Such societies are largely defined by the idiosyncrasies of their leaders, which inevitably vary over time and tend to be quite unstable, particularly during regime change. Capitalism, on the other hand, imparts a law-like systemization on society that allows citizens living under it to plan and behave within a system with predictable tendencies and outcomes. This is a very important benefit of capitalism and it accounts in large part for the economic success stories it has created and the benefits people have enjoyed in terms of freedom and better lives. It is human nature to want to live in an environment with predictable outcomes and certainties. Capitalism provides for this psychological need through the rules of the market; autocracies cannot as they intercede with the will and prejudices of men.

Liberals merely wish it were not so. They don't like the world as it is. So what do they do? They wish it away. They say the world should be different. We should all be one in brotherhood. Human nature should be different. People should be altruistic, not motivated by self-interest. We should be less materialistic. Equality, not achievement or excellence, should be the goal. We should change human nature through education and, perhaps, genetic engineering. Although we will cede political control to an enlightened elite, these leaders will be beneficent and honest. They will somehow be immune to the temptations of power and the seductive call of corruption. History will be different this time.

Liberalism is affecting not just the economy, but national security. The fiscal debt makes national security more problematic diplomatically and militarily. Economic power is strength; without it we are a weaker nation.

In the socialist economic model, the economic value added or surplus would be garnered not by those who created it, but by those who want it. Does this sound like a viable model? Common sense tells us *no*, and so does history—yet liberals keep pushing, and common sense and reason aren't strong enough to impede the juggernaut of creeping socialism. Winston Churchill captured this succinctly saying, "Socialism is the philosophy of failure, the creed of ignorance, and the gospel of envy."

The ideology underpinning capitalism is secular and multi-dimensional. It does not derive its nature from theistic revelation, but from our own nature and that of the world we live in. It's not fundamentalist and intolerant of other views and perspectives. It's flexible and open to dialogue and competing ideas. It seeks truth through pragmatism and experimentation, not revelation. It's open to other views and approaches and hence values free and unconstrained rational discourse. It looks askance at those who claim with certitude to have the answers. It's revolutionary in that people with good ideas prevail.

Capitalism constrains the size of institutions. As will be discussed later, excessive institutional growth, particularly that of government, is a problem that undermines democracy and adversely affects all aspects of life. In the context of market situations, which are not characterized by increasing returns to scale (markets prone to monopoly), capitalism requires that institutions be of the size which is most efficient. Firms which grow too large would not be able to compete with those that are sized appropriately. Moreover, in the now globalized economy, markets prone to monopoly are rarer, as foreign competition keeps everyone on their toes.

The influence of capitalism is encompassing and far-reaching, exercising a profound effect on individuality, morality, and justice. Capitalism puts an emphasis on individuality. It fosters the development of strong individuals because everyone is accountable for his own actions and welfare. The culture espoused by liberalism, on the other hand, diminishes the accountability of individuals. If people fail or don't take care of themselves, they are bailed out and supported by the State. Liberalism creates a culture of dependency, where individuals depend on the State rather than themselves. Liberalism breeds weakness; capitalism, strength.

Although capitalism is often criticized as lacking morality, this is wrong as it in fact contains a very strong moral base. Capitalism encourages people to work in such a way to make the community better off. It encourages people, as mentioned, to be responsible and accountable for what they do. It encourages people to be strong, self-reliant, and to reach their potential.

Capitalism has a strong influence on the exercise of justice. It's a system whereby the rules are the same for everyone. If you work hard and meet the economic needs of others, you will be rewarded. It's a system that yields benefits for the whole community. It's not a zero-sum game like liberalism, where one party gains only if another loses. Liberalism doesn't believe in an even playing field for everyone. It wants to use government to decide who gets rewarded and who does not. It's a discretionary and arbitrary system, not a rules-based system, as is the case with capitalism.

* * *

CHAPTER 8

HISTORICAL FAILURES OF LIBERALISM

———◆———

Much of the social history of the Western world over the past three decades has involved replacing what worked with what sounded good.

~Thomas Sowell

We learn from history that we do not learn from history.
~Wilhelm Friedrich Hegel

Experiments with liberalism have failed at virtually every level, both here in the United States and abroad. In America they have failed at the microeconomic level, already discussed, the local level in the form of communes, and at the national level of redistribution policies. On a global level, national liberal experiments with socialism and communism have failed miserably. The fact that one cannot point to *any* stories of success should be of concern to liberals and to others, but somehow it's not.

Early Failures with Communes in America

Americans have experimented with communes going back to the eighteenth century. Religious sects of many types formed self-contained communities seeking a sense of community and brotherhood. One of the main purposes of the communes was to create a feeling of connectedness and belonging. Many of these communities sought to be economically self-sufficient. Another key feature is that these experimental communes were led by charismatic leaders, some of whom were revered as godlike or even manifestations of Christ. It almost seems that many of those attracted to communes were searching for another religion or god.

Collective child rearing was fairly common in communes. The emphasis was on group bonding, not bonding between individuals. In fact the latter was often discouraged. If some couples seemed too close, an attempt was made to weaken the bonds. None of these experiments with communal arrangements succeeded or lasted very long.

The social experiments of the Utopian Socialists of the nineteenth century all met with abject failure. Robert Owen created planned social and economic communities called Villages of Cooperation. These were small communities of about a thousand poor people who would work together on farms and in factories. Owen felt that, with the proper environment, poor people could be transformed and become quite successful. Children over three lived separately from their parents so that they could be "educated" with the proper values.

Charles Fourier proposed that society be organized into phalanxes somewhat along the lines of the Villages of Cooperation recommended by Owen. Workers would only work a couple of hours a day and do only work that they liked. Unattractive work would be delegated to children. Fourier injected an element of competition into his planned world, calling for workers to compete against one another to see who would be the best. His proposed system was expected to generate a significant surplus with the profit communally distributed, but, like Owen's experimental community, this scheme collapsed and failed as well.

In the 1960s, many hippie communes sprang up in America. None survive. Some lasted a couple of years, but none stood the test of time. Most of these were built on the principle that money is evil, and that all should live under the same economic circumstance. Those joining the communes were required to donate their wealth to the commune. In many instances those running the communes appropriated the money for themselves. Many of the leaders sexually exploited members of the commune. A large number of these communes used oppressive psychological techniques to control their members. So much for freedom and communal bliss!

The communes were founded on the principle that all should work for the communal good. Self-interest was deplored;

altruism was meant to play the central role. This precept obviously was not realized. It did not work in practice. Corruption was a problem, but more fundamentally they just did not work. The sought for sense of community just could not be attained or sustained.

The Failure of Redistribution Programs

Redistribution programs are featured prominently in the agenda of modern-day liberalism. These programs have failed at the national level as well as the international level.

In the late 1970s it was argued that the primary constraint holding developing countries back from successful development was a lack of funding. It happened that at about the same time oil-producing countries were generating huge surpluses which they were investing abroad. Banks, flush with funds and looking for new markets, turned to overseas markets, lending large sums to these developing countries. According to the thinking at the time, this should have led to significant growth in developing countries. Instead it led to a debt crisis for these countries because they had not used the borrowed funds well. Their indebtedness served to limit growth prospects through much of the 1980s. So throwing money at developing countries hurt them rather than helped them.

Economic growth in developing countries remained unimpressive in the 1980s and 1990s, despite substantial aid flows.[131] A wealth of studies support this disconnect between aid and growth performance in developing countries.

According to a study by William Easterly, "If all of the foreign aid since 1950 had been invested in US treasury bills, the cumulative assets of poor countries by 2001 would have amounted to $2.3 trillion." The benefits of this aid were lost in the aid process. In fact, according to Easterly's research, $3,521 in aid will only "raise a poor person's income by $3.65 a year."[132] Another research paper by Easterly found that the number of IMF-IBRD adjustment loans extended to countries did not have a material impact on macroeconomic policy distortions in recipient countries.[133] Other studies have shown that countries participating in IMF programs have tended to have weak growth performance, particularly those that have involved stop-go performance or gone off track.[134]

Moreover, the lack of growth was particularly surprising because during this period progress in policy reform was substantial. In both Latin America and Africa, many countries adopted fundamental macroeconomic policy reforms, some with the support of the IMF, but many other countries put in place reforms on their own without the support of the IMF. The collapse of the Soviet Union, and its alternative model for economic development, helped propel this shift in policy making. Despite this favorable policy shift, growth performance actually deteriorated over this period. A study by Easterly found that income growth in developing countries was nil in the 1980–98 period, versus about two and a half percent in the previous two decades.[135]

In addition, well-publicized international aid efforts like in Haiti and the Global Fund to Fight Aids, Tuberculosis, and Malaria were all dismal failures. The massive aid bailout of Haiti after the earthquake did little to help those in need. The money disappeared into a black hole of corruption. Similarly, with the Global Fund to Fight Aids, Tuberculosis, and Malaria, billions have been lost to corruption and mismanagement. These funds, which involve massive amounts of taxpayer dollars, were disbursed through the UNDP (the United Nations Development Program) to national governments in Africa and elsewhere. The UNDP is not accountable or transparent, so no one really knows where the money went. Gates and Bono were involved in this; Clinton and Bush in Haiti. All were well-intentioned, but this does not help those who needed the help. It helped the corrupt and dishonest, to the harm of well-meaning taxpayers.

Likewise, domestic welfare programs initiated by Lyndon Johnson in the 1960s did little to change the lives of those in poverty. Johnson's War on Poverty, inspired by Franklyn Roosevelt's New Deal, in fact, hurt those it intended to help. It was only with the 1996 welfare reforms driven by market principles that poverty was reduced.

The Personal Responsibility and Work Opportunity Act of 1996, which was enacted despite heavy opposition from liberals, has been profoundly successful. According to the National Bureau of Economic Research, "At the end of the great expansion of the 1990s, cash welfare caseloads had fallen by more than fifty percent and the employment rate of single women with children increased by 15.3 percentage points from 69.4 percent to 84.7 percent and the child poverty rate declined 6.1 percentage points from 22.3 percent to 16.2 percent."[136] Not only were welfare caseloads reduced, but income was increased, poverty reduced, and female headship of families reduced.[137]

The favorable impact was accomplished by doing away with open-ended entitlements and discouraging long-term dependency. The Act combined short-term assistance with job training and, unlike the Johnson welfare program, encouraged family stability and marriage. Despite the success of the welfare reform, the Obama administration incredibly took action in July 2012 to weaken the Act; the administration issued an order, bypassing Congress, giving greater authority to states to waive the work requirement provisions which have been central to the effectiveness of the welfare reform law. Once again, liberals have clearly shown that their goal is not poverty reduction, but increased dependency.

Freddie Mac and Fannie Mae participated in programs intended to give housing to those who could not afford it. The program failed, causing massive damage to the financial system and the economy. The government then had the hubris to blame the financial crisis and the economic recession on Wall Street greed. It was ill-advised government intervention in the financial markets that caused the crisis. Moreover the poor who were the intended beneficiaries of these "well-intentioned" policies lost their investments and homes. This was another egregious failure of liberalism, but liberals still refuse to learn the lesson. In the financial reform measures which they subsequently crafted, everything was directed at the financial institutions; there was no reform of Freddie or Fannie whatsoever. This is yet another example of a refusal to look truth in the eye, to look at reality, and learn a lesson. Liberals simply don't learn, or even want to learn.

So both liberal domestic welfare programs and international development efforts have failed to meet intended objectives. Capitalism is the best cure for poverty. Capitalism has moved more people out of poverty in the last fifty years than in the 500 years before that.[138] There is no question that it produces the greatest economic growth. It produces a bigger economic pie than socialism. Admittedly, not everyone gets a bigger slice of the economic pie, so care should be exercised here. But it would be a mistake to sacrifice the welfare of most of the citizenry so a small minority may see their economic position improved. Moreover, it's important to note that what we are talking about is relative (not absolute) poverty. With economic growth, the absolute poverty of the poor may not improve, but it rarely declines. What usually happens is that they may not gain as much from economic growth as some other segments of the population, so they see their relative economic position deteriorate. Moreover, the poor in developed capitalist countries in almost all cases have housing, food, a car, television, and a phone. In fact obesity is a far greater problem in America than malnutrition. It's not like it is in underdeveloped countries, where poverty is truly misery, where poverty means no shelter, no food, and where survival is at stake.

The Heritage Foundation corroborated this in a study that found that only a small part of the forty-six million Americans defined as poor by the Census Bureau suffer serious hardship. The study cited the following facts concerning the poor from various government reports:[139]

- Eighty percent of poor households have air conditioning. In 1970, only thirty-six percent of the entire U.S. population enjoyed air conditioning.
- Ninety-two percent of poor households have a microwave.
- Nearly three-fourths have a car or truck, and thirty-one percent have two or more cars or trucks.
- Nearly two-thirds have cable or satellite TV.
- Two-thirds have at least one DVD player, and seventy percent have a VCR.

- Half have a personal computer, and one in seven have two or more computers.
- More than half of poor families with children have a video game system, like an Xbox or PlayStation.
- Forty-three percent have Internet access.
- One-third has a wide-screen plasma or LCD TV.
- One-fourth has a digital video recorder system, like TiVo.
- The average poor American has more living space than the typical non-poor person in Sweden, France, or the United Kingdom.
- The average consumption of protein, vitamins, and minerals is virtually the same for poor and middle-class children and is well above recommended norms in most cases.

These findings highlight that consumer goods, once luxuries enjoyed by the relatively affluent only a few decades ago, are now widely enjoyed by many who are classified by government statistics as "poor." It is the dynamism of the market economy and capitalism that has brought the technological change that underlies the growth of these consumer goods which have enriched our lives. Liberalism fails to understand this. In addition, by emphasizing relative as opposed to absolute poverty, it distorts the severity of the problem of poverty in America.

More fundamentally, although liberals claim their number one goal is to help the poor, they fight and work against the forces that improve the lot of the poor. Liberals strive to weaken the vitality of market forces and capitalism, which are fundamental to stimulating technological development and economic growth. Capitalism provides more opportunity for upper mobility than other economic systems, giving the poor a ladder to climb out of poverty.

Liberal policies hurt the education system, which is critically important for the poor. Schools in inner cities are notoriously bad. Yet liberals resist introducing charter schools and vouchers, which would put competitive pressure on poorly performing schools to do better and give students the chance to choose their education. Instead liberalism supports teachers' unions, which block educational reform and have created a behemoth federal bureaucracy, the Department of Education. The latter is enormously expensive, but a dead weight on the education system. The money would be better spent in the classroom.

In addition, liberalism fights traditional values, which are critically important in the fight against poverty. Besides providing incentives rewarding irresponsibility and poor behavior, liberalism fights against traditional values, religion, and the role of marriage and the family. A study by the liberal Brookings Foundation in 2009 underscored the importance of finishing high school, getting a full-time job, and waiting till twenty-one to get married and have children. The study found that "young adults who followed all three norms had a two percent chance of winding up in poverty and a seventy-four percent chance of winding up in the middle class (defined as earning roughly fifty thousand dollars or more). By contrast, young adults who violated all three norms had a seventy-six percent chance of winding up in poverty and a seven percent chance of winding up in the middle class." [140]

A study by the Heritage Foundation underscored the key role of marriage. According to the study, "Married women are less likely to experience poverty, and unmarried mothers face a greater risk of welfare dependency. In fact, marriage reduces the probability that a child will be in poverty by eighty-two percent. Marriage brings a likelihood of greater financial success for men as well. Married men tend to have greater earnings than those in cohabiting relationships, and married individuals are more likely to own a home, accumulate savings and attain affluence."[141]

Failure of Liberalism on the National Scale

Nationwide experiments with organic, collectivist nation-states have a history of abject failure. Mao's Great Leap Forward in the People's Republic of China was a catastrophe for the Chinese people. Mao killed many of the intelligentsia and the elite, believing it was necessary to first get rid of bad thinking and education before trying to re-educate the people so a communist state could flourish. Millions were killed, and the country plunged into an economic abyss. Only after Mao died and the Chinese leadership instituted policies of economic liberalization did the economy and the circumstances of the Chinese people improve. The greater the shift to market-driven policies, the greater the improvement.

The Soviet Union did not gradually adopt market driven policies and liberalization in the 1980s as the Chinese did. Their economy collapsed under the weight of its own woefully inadequate performance. With the increased flow of information, it became clear even to the Soviet leaders that their economic system was far inferior to the democratic West's. Again it has only been since the early 1990s when Russia has adopted economic reform and liberalization that economic circumstances have improved substantially.

Elsewhere the story is the same. Castro's Cuba, Chavez' Venezuela, Kim Jong-Il's North Korea have all had a devastating impact on their citizens' well-being. For example, the socialist policies of Chavez are hurting the poor of Venezuela, the very people he promised to help. Inflation is already running at 22 percent and the currency was just devalued in February by 46 percent which will intensify inflation. Reportedly, real purchasing power has fallen to 1966 levels and real income of Venezuelans is projected to decline by 20 percent this year. Electricity blackouts and rationing of basic goods are all but inevitable. A once prosperous nation Venezuela has been brought to its knees.[142] It was all so predictable. Despite this all too familiar script, the Left never seems to learn.

So liberalism has a long history of failure. Can one point to even a single success? I think not. The closest success for socialism would have to be Europe, but here too the picture is not pretty. Europe realizes that it has gone too far with the welfare state. Most of Europe faces severe problems of debt and fiscal sustainability. They realize they cannot afford the welfare state they have created, and are now trying to retrench. But it's much more difficult to retrench a welfare state than to avoid creating one in the first place. Despite the clear lessons learned through European experience, the American Left is pressing ahead with massive new spending and new entitlements.

Europe failed economically compared to the performance of the more market driven US economy, but it also failed politically.

The EU moved power away from nation-states, and now they cannot effectively address their own problems. The labyrinthine EU, like Washington, has removed policy and politicians from the realities of the people. The EU bureaucrats live in a world headquartered in Brussels far removed from the life of the people they purportedly serve. The EU has become a bureaucratic leviathan and policy gridlock has become a real problem.

Any economy is going to have problems. Consequently it's important that the government is lean and flexible enough to address its problems effectively and expeditiously. Unfortunately, a meta-political entity like the EU is not suited for this.

Even the French, the Chinese, and the Russians are lecturing us on our profligate fiscal spending and debt accumulation. They recognize the danger, not only for us, but for the world.

In his book, *The New Road to Serfdom*, Daniel Hannan argues eloquently that we should avoid the European model. He points out that "while the U.S. share of world GDP has held steady for forty years, that of Old Europe—the fifteen states that were already in the EU prior to the admission of the former Comecon nations—has declined sharply."[143] Extensive employment protection and high tax rates have led to high unemployment rates and slow growth in Europe relative to the United States.[144]

It's always in the name of the people and in the name of the good that the most evil deeds are done. Yet we keep falling for the same rhetoric and tricks. Snake oil salesmen and fraudulent evangelical preachers like Elmer Gantry can wreak havoc, but when an entire nation falls under the trance of deceptive leaders with grand designs the outcome can be truly tragic.

Failed Foreign Policy of Liberalism

Liberals believe that peace is free and that war is unwarranted. This reflects the trait of conflict avoidance that so clearly marks liberalism. It is consistent with their approach to domestic policy. Liberals don't believe we have to pay for anything, whether it's domestic spending programs or peace. According to Winston Churchill, "An appeaser is one who feeds a crocodile, hoping it will eat him last." Liberals, however, abidingly believe that the crocodile will never eat them. They are oblivious to the lessons of history and the threat of evil in the world. In their fairy-tale world, the crocodile does not even exist. Neville Chamberlain, who supported the failed Munich Agreement appeasing Hitler, is a forgotten historical figure.

Amazingly, in his second inaugural address, Obama actually used the infamous phrase "peace in our time" eerily repeating the words used by Chamberlain in 1938 accepting promises of peace from Adolf Hitler in the expectation that war would be avoided. The words "peace in our time" are etched in history as a reminder of the peril of naiveté and appeasement. Unfortunately, liberalism's failure to learn from history is once again all too evident.

The liberal Democratic President Woodrow Wilson said in an address to the U.S. Senate in January 22, 1917, "There must be, not a balance of power, but a community of power; not organized rivalries, but an organized common peace." With his push and support, the League of Nations was established. This organization was meant to ensure peace, but it was a catastrophic failure, as it failed to stop World War II. It was the balance of power concept prevailing after World War II that succeeded in establishing a reign of peace in the world. It was no accident that America's strength and willingness to fight coincided with a long peace.

Does anyone believe that the United Nations, the successor to the League of Nations, caused the peace after World War II? Does anyone believe that peace would have prevailed if the United States did not countervail the power of the USSR? The USSR would have expanded had it not been for the assertive military stance of the USA.

Reagan was much criticized for calling the USSR an "evil empire." The liberals and Democrats wanted to accommodate the USSR and compromise with them; Reagan wanted to win—and he succeeded. It's doubtful that the USSR would have collapsed had it not been for the military pressure Reagan brought to bear on them.

Osama bin Laden kept increasing the lethality of his attacks on America, calling America "a paper tiger" because we wouldn't respond to his attacks. It was only after George Bush invaded Afghanistan and Iraq that Al Qaeda backed off. Since 2001 Al Qaeda has not been able to launch a significant attack on us.

Liberals believe in "moral equivalency." All nations are the same. No nation should declare itself more important or legitimate than another. Implicit in this thinking is that North Korea and Iran are every bit as legitimate and moral as we are. This is preposterous to all but the blind. It is amazing that liberals can utter these words with a straight face, and it can only be because they have convinced themselves that it is true. It seems as though they have an infinite capacity to blind themselves. There is something they really don't want to see. There is a fear of truth, reality, responsibility, and leadership.

An important part of liberal foreign policy is expanding the role of our values and democracy in the world, but this makes no sense in a world characterized by moral equivalency. If we do not believe in ourselves, how can we expect others to believe in us?

Moreover, through profligate fiscal policy and the run-up of debt, liberals are eroding America's strength from within. The strength of our economy has been fundamental to the strong role we have played in the world and this is being drastically undermined. Even if we would like to take a stronger, more assertive foreign policy stance, our ability to do so is rapidly diminishing.

George Washington said, "If you want peace, prepare for war." Reagan emphasized "peace through strength." Teddy Roosevelt said, "Speak softly, but carry a big stick." Liberals, on the other hand, are opposed to a strong military, intimations of action, or even strong talk.

One cannot just deny history. War and conflict have been one of the most enduring features of history; it is deeply embedded in human nature. We cannot just simply "wish it away," declaring that we are now in a time of peace. This blindness to history, reality, and the nature of man afflicts liberalism in foreign as well as domestic policy. Amazingly, after seeing the destruction wrought by communism, fascism, and Nazism in the twentieth century, we seem to have forgotten the very real threat.

Liberals assume there is no evil in the world, and that all are motivated by good intentions. They assume that conflict or trouble arises only because of miscommunication and misunderstanding. Only talk is needed to resolve problems. Implicit in this is that everyone has the same goals; there are no conflicting agendas. Is this for real?

Liberals want to keep talking to North Korea and Iran about their nuclear issues, believing this is all that's needed. This policy has shown no dividends. Those powers don't take us seriously. Malevolent dictators take advantage of weakness, but respect strength. They readily take advantage of liberalism's distaste for strong action and its aversion to the military. During the quintessentially weak reign of Democratic President Jimmy Carter, the Iranians seized our Embassy in Tehran and held the staff hostage until Ronald Reagan took office.

While talking, Obama has pulled almost all troops out of Iraq and Afghanistan, pulled an aircraft carrier out of the region, drastically cut defense spending, run up a huge federal debt putting the country on a path to bankruptcy, failed to respond to an attack that killed four Americans at our Embassy in Libya, and failed to support opposition fighters to Assad in Syria and still he expects Iranian and North Korean leaders to take him seriously. The consequent proliferation of nuclear weapons which will inevitably result from this weakness will change the world. A failure of leadership and courage to stand up to forces of evil will cost us all dearly.

Instances of liberalism's failure in the exercise of foreign policy can be readily seen in the experience of the EU. By overbuilding and over-centralizing the institutions of government, liberalism ties itself in knots and can't act. In effect the EU does not *have* a foreign policy. When Kosovo descended into killing, chaos, and genocide, the EU couldn't come to agreement with its member countries on how to act. In the end the USA had to take care of the problem for them. It was a problem in Europe's own backyard, but it fell to America, across the ocean, to deal with it.

The Left's agenda to move to meta-national government is in part driven by a desire to preempt conflict and to deflate tensions, but this does not lead inevitably to peace. It can in fact lead to inaction, and allow problems to metastasize. The League of

Nations and the United Nations have been notoriously ineffective peacekeeping organizations. The League of Nations, as mentioned, was completely unable to deal with the rising pressures in the world that led to World War II, and the United Nations actually withdrew its forces when genocide was taking place in Rwanda and Kosovo.

The liberal Obama too has a predilection for meta-national government organizations. Obama did not go to the US Congress to get approval for the military action in Libya, but instead to the UN. And to lead the military action, Obama devolved the command to NATO.

* * *

CHAPTER 9

THE ABANDONMENT OF REASON

————◆————

When a person is lucky enough to live inside a story, to live inside an imaginary world, the pains of this world disappear. For as long as the story goes on, reality no longer exists.
~Paul Auster, *The Brooklyn Follies, A Novel*

The neurotic is nailed to the cross of his fiction.
~Alfred Adler

There is no expedient to which a man will not go to avoid the labor of thinking.
~Thomas Edison

When men yield up the privilege of thinking, the last shadow of liberty quits the horizon.
~Thomas Paine

Liberalism has tossed reason aside out of necessity. The historical record of liberalism and its policies are marked by complete and total failure. Rational analysis of the record makes this clear, so the only way liberals can continue to promote their policies is to darken the light shed by reason. Of course, if they were really interested in their professed objectives, they wouldn't do this. But their real underlying objective is power. They seek to dismiss reason, arguing that it's a tool of oppression of the ruling class and hence must be looked upon with suspicion. The age of ideology, which some marked off as dead after the Soviet fall, is rising again.

Reason is a tool. It's the primary tool used by mankind to advance our position in the world and bring about progress. It's what distinguishes us from animals. Animals can think too, although mostly on an instinctual level, but man's rational capacity far exceeds that of other creatures. In abandoning reason we are throwing away our primary asset. Instead of reason we are surrendering ourselves to a herd-like mentality.

Reason can't bring us ultimate truth. Man's capacities and circumstances aren't sufficient for this, but we can gain a useful understanding of our surroundings and what works to make our lives better—and makes them worse. As Herbert Hoover noted, "Wisdom consists not so much in knowing what to do in the ultimate as knowing what to do next."

Socrates famously said, "The only thing I know is that I know I know nothing." He looked negatively at dogma and those unwilling to have their beliefs challenged. An aversion to or unwillingness to reason is the greatest danger to both man and society.

Aristotle thought each creature in the universe had a purpose, and consequently each life should be allowed the freedom to fulfill that purpose. For man, that purpose is to reason. As he noted in the first line of *The Politics*, "All men desire to know."

We have entered a period where we are abandoning our basic nature. Barack Obama said, "It has not always been the pragmatist, the voice of reason, or the force of compromise that has created the conditions for liberty." His agenda is set by a higher calling, one that doesn't involve pragmatism, reason, or compromise. During the presidential campaign, Obama said that he was above dogma and ideology, but this was only his way of cloaking his position and avoiding rational discourse on the pros and cons of different views.

The liberal mind isn't only disconnected from reason. It demonstrates an aversion to reason, but it's more than that. It's not just averse to the exercise of logic and the employment of the canons of rationality; it also shuns common sense and lacks basic respect for evidence. It's a full-blown disease of the mind, nothing less.

The Left is almost schizophrenic in its approach to reason. Liberals dismiss reason as a tool of oppression, and they ignore it in designing and implementing policies. But at the same time the Left argues that an elite ruling class can bring about a perfect world *through the use of reason*. They think that they "know" and can judge what is necessary to bring this about—but this is misplaced confidence. We simply don't have enough knowledge and intelligence to design a perfect world. So, they vastly overestimate the power of reason as a pretext for their policies and power grab, while at the same time dismissing it in the implementation of their policies.

Besides overestimating the power of reason in the hands of the elite, the Left makes mistakes of emotion, according it too much influence relative to reason in designing and implementing policies. So it makes two mistakes: first it delegates too much discretionary control to the elite assuming perfection in their use of reason; and second it accords too much of a role to emotion which blocks out and diminishes reason. Emotions and other biases corrupt and distort our judgment. In effect the Left is according a large influential role for reason, but then isn't using it. As mentioned in Chapter 2, studies show liberals are more "idealistic and emotion-driven" than conservatives. They rely more on emotional arguments, rather than logical arguments. Emotional appeals are pretty common concerning redistributive policies, or debates over the poor and disadvantaged.

Moreover, not only does liberalism diminish the role and influence of reason, but it suppresses and distorts emotion as it arises within us. It makes us distrust our own emotions and inner nature. It suppresses, as previously mentioned, even visceral truth. Only emotion arising out of the initiative of the State is to be trusted and is to be exempt from questioning. So, liberalism is corrupting not only reason, but the integrity of our own emotions and intuition. The beacons for sound judgment have all been brought down and diminished, leaving us ill-equipped to navigate the increasingly difficult problems ahead.

For the Left there is nothing objective and absolute. All beliefs and observations are just constructions. According to relativists, we live in a plurality of worlds and judgments, none better than another. Our culture has abandoned truth. We need it back if we are to move our country forward. Not only is there no dialogue or thoughtful approach to issues, there is outright repression and cultural balkanization. It evokes thoughts of the tactics of communist states and dictatorships. If you don't think like they do, they want to oppress and marginalize you or even destroy you. This is amply exemplified in the politics of destruction used against Sarah Palin, and Supreme Court Justice Thomas, and Supreme Court nominee Robert Bork.

The politics of destruction played a significant role in Obama's rise to power. In the 2004 Democratic Primary for the U.S. Senate, Obama was trailing in the polls, but won after the sealed divorce records of his opponent were made public by the Chicago Tribune.[145] Allegedly, Obama supporters "worked aggressively behind the scenes to push the story."[146] Afterward Obama's Republican opponent for the Senate seat met with the same fate as his divorce records were also unsealed again at the request of the Chicago Tribune. This caused him to drop out late in the race and his last-minute replacement was unable to defeat Obama.[147]

Just look at academia, which is highly discriminatory toward conservatives. Most universities, particularly the top ones, don't hire academics with conservative leanings. Courses are almost all left-leaning, and there's little tolerance for conservative views. After retiring from a career in economic development, I took a course on anthropology and development at George Washington University, thinking I would see what light another discipline could shed on the issue. I was shocked to find nothing but a leftist diatribe against the International Monetary Fund and the World Bank and their efforts to bring economic development to countries in need.

Likewise the entertainment industry largely has excluded conservatives as actors or colleagues and rarely shows conservative productions. For example, *The A-Team,* the number one rated show in the early 70s, was ostracized by their host station NBC because the show involved conservative themes and content. Despite the fact that *The A-Team* was their top show and chief revenue-maker, the cast was not even invited to the NBC Christmas party.

Liberals use relativism to dismantle our current traditions, beliefs, and institutions. This relativism discredits all absolutisms of the past, but liberalism is in essence an absolutist ideology itself. It's a my-way-or-the-highway philosophy. It's almost fanatical in temperament; it thinks it has some special relationship with the truth. It brooks no opposition or dissent; it has no tolerance for questioning or fruitful discussion. The liberal absolutist proudly touts his simple vision of the truth, "The Way." He speaks in sweeping rhetorical phrases of man, the future, and hope. He looks past the present and the particular; he isn't concerned with the now, but with the future. It's an almost religious vision of the future—but it's not a heaven in the sky, but a heaven in this world. One created by man for man—with the State as God. We can see the fate of truth with liberalism in the Soviet Union, which in many ways was the culmination of liberal dreams, at least early in its creation. Truth became a product of the State. It was not something that existed in and of itself, but something manufactured. Truths were created for a purpose; they were a means to an ends, not an end it itself. In the USSR, people would ask not whether this or that was true, but rather why is this or that trotted out as true. They would ask who is constructing the "truth" and for what purpose. Propaganda and political catechisms inculcating simple dogmas took the place of thinking and truth.

Abandoning reason means we are adrift in the world; we are surrendering control of our future to the forces of agenda-driven politics and enslavement to the State. America was founded because our forefathers sought to escape State control.

Truth on a grand scale is admittedly elusive and unattainable. But if we don't have goals or a sense of where we want and ought to go, we will be rudderless. This is certainly so for an individual and it's so for a society. If you look at individuals, those who have succeeded in accomplishing something are those who have laid goals. Those who did not know what they wanted to do have done very little.

For society as a whole, however, it's perhaps unnecessary and counterproductive to define goals. If individuals know where they are going, if they are motivated by the appropriate cultural and economic signals, they will move not only themselves along, but society as well. This is the beauty of the market system and a hands-off approach to economic and social management. If you attempt to impose goals on a top-down basis, this only hurts as it distorts and dampens the motivation of individuals.

During the Enlightenment, which formed the foundation for the growth of western democracies, there was an abiding faith in truth. Both individuals and society sought it out, but no longer. Without this foundation, our democracies themselves are seriously threatened.

Reason gained adherents during the Enlightenment, as it was a means to challenge the authoritarian culture of the time. The universality of reason made it egalitarian and anti-elite; it appealed to the masses. Its subversive potency made it attractive to those who wanted change.

It's interesting that liberals, who nowadays are pushing for change, have abandoned reason; in fact they want to see it dethroned and replaced by a system which seeks truth through social construction rather than through heuristic experiment. This undoubtedly reflects recognition that reason and conventional approaches don't offer support for their positions, and in fact bring embarrassing shortcomings to light. It's also interesting that liberals favor a top-down or hierarchical approach to the construction of truth. They seem intent on putting the determination and control of truth back in the hands of the elite and the authorities, rather than in hands of the people.

Reason is egalitarian and democratic. Anyone can use it; it's accessible to everyone. Throughout modern history reason has been used to overthrow and constrain authoritarian abuses. It was critical to the success of eighteenth century liberals. Today's liberals are trying to diminish reason as it's a threat to their authoritarian ambitions. They are seeking to wrest control of the determination of truth from the masses and seize it for themselves.

Under liberalism the mob prevails. Everyone should conform. This of course means non-thinking, except for the elite class, who are supposed to produce the "thinking" to which everyone is supposed to agree. In effect this denies the masses the right to think critically.

In history few cultures have accorded reason much clout. It's no accident that reason has played the largest role in democracies like in ancient Greece and in more recent times the democracies of Western Europe and the United States. Democracy and reason are inextricably linked. This is why the assault on reason is an assault on democracy itself.

In today's world, agenda prevails over truth. Worse than that, we aren't dealing with honestly presented agendas, but rather hidden ones. We are dealing with agendas intended to benefit one segment of society over another, not to work for the advancement of society as a whole. Agendas are put together with dishonesty and implemented with dishonesty.

Why is liberalism casting reason to the dustbin of history? The explanation is simple. Reason is based on analyzing issues and looking at issues from various angles. Its method involves looking at various arguments, not just buying into one. The liberal agenda, however, is one that only works with a leap of faith. Its essence is almost fanatical.

It's interesting how liberalism debunks religion, but really liberalism is nothing but a religion itself. It deflects attention from itself by casting aspersion on religions. Liberals attack others as intolerant bigots, while this is a hallmark of their own identity. Liberalism has a distinctly fundamentalist religious temperament to it, all the while claiming to be secular, temperate, and tolerant.

Liberalism is global and is only comfortable using abstract terms. It's averse to looking at issues on a smaller scale; it has a preference for the overarching, the almost undefinable. It has a blindness and disinterest in local politics and the circumstances of men as individuals. For the liberal the latter are a waste of time. This is because for liberals change should come from the top and it has to be all encompassing. Liberals have difficulty dealing with issues at a concrete and pragmatic level.

In the health care debate in 2010 liberals pushed through reform with no attempt to think carefully through what they were doing. Nancy Pelosi famously said *we will find out what's in the health care bill after it passes.* The ObamaCare bill exceeded two thousand pages, and even the head Democrat responsible for the bill admitted that he had not read the whole thing prior to its passage. This is a bill that affects one-sixth of the American economy and serious analysis and discussion was totally lacking. There was no honesty. The process was essentially one of deceit. The Democrats touted the bill, saying it would extend coverage to millions of people, improve quality of care, and lower cost. It doesn't take much intelligence to know that this defies common sense. The only way this could happen is if there were a tremendous improvement in efficiency—and there is nothing in the bill that would even have a minimal impact on efficiency. The bill contained nothing on tort reform, a major factor driving up the cost of health care and distorting treatment patterns.

So one of the most important pieces of legislation in American history was guided not by reason, but by agenda and deceit. In the end not even many Democrats liked the bill, even though they were responsible for its passage. Virtually no Democrat ran for election in 2010 acknowledging support for the bill. They recognized that the public didn't want ObamaCare, but they pushed it through anyway. Their agenda ruled their actions, rather than the will of the people or common sense—or even a commitment to honesty.

President Obama declared that ObamaCare wouldn't add a dime to the budget deficit, and that those who have private insurance could continue to keep it. The president obviously knew that both these statements were blatantly false, but he trotted them forth without compunction to sell the bill to the public. It would have been much better if he had told the truth. If he had said that the reform would add to the deficit and would hurt private insurance arrangements, but that in return he hoped that the overall health insurance arrangements would be better. This would have been a better basis for reaching consensus about what the best policy would be. Instead the approach was deceitful, lacked transparency, and has left us all worse off.

Liberals live in a theoretical fantasy land with no semblance to reality. They have an aversion to reality. They don't like the world as it is; they want to change it. They don't like the political or social situation as it is; they want to change it. They don't like human nature as it is; they want to change it.

Inconsistency is deeply embedded in liberal ideological commitments, actions, and policies. For example, liberals in America have strongly opposed Guantanamo and the strong interrogation techniques like waterboarding on prisoners suspected of terrorism. Yet they have no problem with drone attacks that assassinate foreigners, and even American citizens suspected of terrorism. These drone attacks by the way kill not only suspected terrorists, but innocent people, including children. Apparently killing terrorists is OK, but subjecting them to discomfort in the process of interrogation isn't. Conservatives, too, are opposed to infringing human rights and oppose strong interrogation techniques on that basis. But they see it as a necessary compromise in the war on terror. Conservatives thus temper their principles with recognition of the need to be pragmatic. Liberals tend not to temper their ideological views and commitments by any need to be pragmatic.

The difficulty with ideology is it renders thoughtful debate almost impossible. Bill Clinton said: "The problem with ideology is…you've got your mind made up. You know all the answers and that makes evidence irrelevant and arguments a waste of time. You tend to govern by assertion and attacks."[148]

The liberal's world is myopic. Liberals are averse to looking at history, perhaps because they don't like what it tells them. Their arrogance makes them think they can do better than those who preceded them, and—to the extent that they aren't happy with the present or the past—they want something different. They think they can wish a new world into existence. They think they can throw away the efforts and contributions of the past, as embodied in our institutions and traditions, and begin again to shape the world *de novo*. It doesn't matter to them that no one fully understands the forces that shape our societies and way of life. It doesn't matter to them that we don't directly control everything.

We can't simply wish the world away. The institutions which underlay society are formed by a complex array of forces and shape our lives in ways which we can't begin to fathom. To presume that we fully comprehend these forces and the roles that societal and economic institutions play in shaping our lives and futures is folly. It's naïve at best, disastrous at worst.

We have moved into a new epistemological era, in which reason and science aren't just used to understand the natural world, but are now used to understand humanity and modern society. There is no doubt that the liberal community, in its hubris, is convinced that they understand modern society and are convinced that it's a simple thing to remake it according to their preferences. The problem with this is that our knowledge of social and human psychology, economics, and other aspects that make societies function is far short of where it needs to be. An even bigger problem though is that liberals are averse to using reason and evidence-based thought to construct their policies. There is, of course, also the problem of the liberal elite trying to force their idea of what society should be like on the rest of us. As Lenny Bruce once said, "The liberals can understand everything but people who don't understand them."

Perhaps we have moved from an epistemological period during the Enlightenment when reason reigned to a time that is more complicated and no longer subject to the control of reason. Epistemological systems are not so much the conscious creations of man as they are the product of the underlying activities of man. Marx and Veblen certainly subscribed to this notion, that underlying economic and social forces were the primary determinants of thought and ideology. If this is the case then it would seem that the products and technologies created by man are now wresting control from man—if he ever had it in the first place. Reason, the instrument used by man to establish his hegemony over the world, is now taking a backseat to man's other creations. Man is becoming a servant to his creations. Perhaps Stanley Kubrik's vision in the film *2001: A Space Odyssey* of a computer taking over adumbrates our future. Are we creating our future masters?

Change is everywhere, and we need reason to help guide us through it. But although the use of reason should be the cornerstone of handling change, we nevertheless need to be cognizant of its limits. We aren't yet smart enough to understand the forces of nature or of societal change, so we ought to exercise extreme care.

In his book, *Inevitable Illusions*, Piatelli-Palmarini illustrates persuasively that we are all subject to the affliction of *cognitive illusion*, even so-called experts.[149] We all make mistakes and misjudgments, no matter how well informed or how logical we think we are. These are mistakes not of emotion, but of logic. We simply don't know enough to design a perfect world; we aren't that smart. Cognitive illusions lead us astray much in the same way that optical illusions do. So, the Left not only makes mistakes of emotion in making decisions and judgments, but makes the mistake of overestimating the power of reason.

In trying to usurp the exercise of rationality from the public and bestow its power to the ruling elite, the Left is making a power grab. They put too much faith in the elite and too much faith in the power of reason and human judgment. The beauty of our democratic and capitalistic foundation is that it exercises a constraint on both the power of the ruling class as well as on the power of discretion. The Constitution divides power, and capitalism creates another power center in the private sector, militating to prevent an undue concentration of power. The market works through the exercise of general equilibrating forces, much like in nature, so that top-down discretionary power is unnecessary, and is hence constrained.

Part of the appeal of reason is that, some have claimed, it has the potential to yield universal truths. In an *a priori* world, where there is agreement on the underlying assumptions, this is possible, but the problem is that the appropriate underlying assumptions aren't always straightforward. For example, in geometry we can say in a linear world that the shortest distance between two points is a straight line. For a long time the thinking was that the world is linear in nature. It seemed obvious. Of course, Einstein proved that the world is nonlinear and relative, and hence a straight line is not the shortest distance between two points.

Although not perfect, reason is essential to problem-solving. The problem is that there is widespread misuse. In a complex world, trying to prove things based on data and experiment and logic isn't straightforward; it's easy to twist results and yield results in line with one's convictions. So when you have a culture of heterogeneous groups with different and opposing agendas, it's not surprising that rationality is debased and twisted.

Liberals all talk pretty much the same talk. They all travel in the same circles. They are mostly inside the beltway, in academia, the media, and government—and all talk to each other and think the same way, so they are convinced that their thinking is the only way to see things. Liberals always trot out the same arguing points in an almost robotic way. When asked to look at the particulars of an issue and the merits of their arguments, it seems there is always a retreat into an abstraction.

The liberal avoids conflict. Of course, no one likes it, but one can't bury one's head in the sand. For the liberal, talk and communication (of course, not real talk, only high flown rhetoric and the ventilation of good intentions) is all that is necessary to resolve a conflict. The liberal wants to live in a world of unity and accord; he is uncomfortable with contention and argument. For the liberal, there are no hard choices or trade-offs to avoid. Everything should be free and easy. They don't comprehend that others may have different objectives. For example, the Obama Administration's approach to the development of nuclear weapons in Iran and North Korea is to talk to them, despite the failure of talks in the past. It's clear that Iran and North Korea have different objectives than the US, so how can we expect that "talk" will make these differences go away?

Hegel believed truth was unearthed through tension and conflict between two opposing ideas. This is anathema to liberals who avoid critical thinking and conflict and tension as well.

Liberalism is about the world of the abstract, not the world of the particular and the individual; it's about the world of the indefinable future and not about the more definable world of the past or present. The liberal lives in a world of the abstract, averting his eyes from the particular. He doesn't see horses, but horsiness. Everything is homogenized; differences are blurred and extinguished. The liberal's world is an airbrushed one, with the key aspects of reality edited out. It's an artificially constructed world, a falsified one.

Language and our cognitive temperament dispose us to think in terms of abstractions, categories, and groups. This is fundamental and essential to thinking, and is necessary if we are to avoid being entrapped and mired in the particular. It is critical, however, not to lose sight of the importance of the individual and the particular. The issue is one of balance. The saying, "Sometimes we can't see the forest for the trees," has much truth to it, but at present we are at risk of losing the trees. The fact that liberalism believes in rule by the elite and so-called experts lends itself to this disposition toward abstraction. Liberalism's emphasis on the centralization of power and growth in the institutional size of government exacerbates this tendency. It is also rooted in the collectivism that suffuses liberalism; the latter diminishes and degrades the particular, while placing primacy on the whole. Particularity and identity have been eclipsed by the tyranny of concepts and abstractions. We see this clearly in terms of our knowledge-based disciplines and language. Thus, it is not just its untethered idealism, but even its language and approach to thought that makes liberalism fundamentally flawed.

In a world of accelerating change, it's not surprising that our faith in a stable and ordered world is shaken. In earlier times, when the world was relatively stable, it was easier to have confidence in our understanding of the world. The idea of absolute truth and understanding was not tested like it is nowadays. Nevertheless, reason is our tether to reality and a promising future; we mustn't lose our grip on it.

Nietzsche wrote, "Truth is the kind of error without which a certain species could not live." The survival of our species has required that we have an understanding of the nature of the world so that we can adequately respond to circumstances and changes. Without this basic inclination, we would drift through time at the mercy of world. We would be defenseless. We can't hope to grasp things as they actually are, but even if our constructions of reality don't capture ultimate truth, we can live better lives to the extent that we understand how changes in the world affect us and how we can affect the world. Thus to be successful our epistemology can be off the mark, but it needs to be grounded in reality.

Experiential information and validation is critically important in making judgments and decisions. Observation, an appreciation for historical validation, and the use of empirical evidence is key to remaining connected to reality.

The seductive power of irrationality is considerable. Irrationality allows us to escape the tethers of reality with ostensible impunity. It gains us entry into impregnable fantasy lands, where all our dreams are fulfilled. There is, of course, the minor problem of what do we do when we wake up from the dream.

Some, however, claim irrationality perhaps is even rational under some conditions. The extent to which one indulges in irrationality, it's argued, depends on the price one has to pay for it. If the consequences aren't costly or painful, then the incentive to indulge in irrationality is higher. It's interesting that in the case of politics, and perhaps religion, this is the case. Because one person's vote is almost never going to be a deciding factor in an election, that person is pretty much free to take on outrageous and irrational views and not have to pay a price for it. The price for cognitive dissonance or disengagement from reality is close to zero in politics. Moreover, there are probably psychic and emotional benefits (for example, a sense of belonging to a group or the opportunity to take on moral posturing without cost) on the other side of the balance sheet incentivizing irrational indulgence. It does appear that a case can be made that there is more irrationality in politics and perhaps religion than in other areas of life, so there may be something to this argument. Unfortunately, while there may be no costs to individuals for this irrational behavior, it's not the case for society. If many people think like this, the likelihood of irrationality swaying elections becomes a cause for concern.

Facts have become a thing of the past. It used to be we would start with them and proceed through logical analysis to try to understand something. Nowadays we don't want to look closely at the factual. We prefer to grab this or that piece of information to justify our opinions, or even manufacture our own facts.

The day of reason appears to have passed. With rational discourse much eclipsed, everyone and everything is now agenda-driven. There is no concern with facts or with what policies are effective, only with pushing toward certain—in many cases hidden and undeclared—agendas.

Truth and knowledge aren't the issue so much anymore; rather the issue is what fiction we want. It has become a matter of what assessments we would like, not what is. The world has become a grand Rorschach test. It appears no longer to be about our capacities to know and the processes of knowing, but rather about goals and wish fulfillment. Liberals have certain goals in mind and don't want to be troubled by little things like facts and realities.

Factors Contributing to the Decline of Reason

What has brought about this change? Various factors are contributing to this dynamic shift toward agenda-driven politics: globalization, greater divisiveness within the body politic, a loss of confidence in reason, institutional change, enhanced media bias, and less connection to reality.

Globalization is contributing to the change in the climate of discourse. By weakening the power of nation-states, it's undermining its role as a stabilizing societal influence. Globalization and increased immigration are weakening cultural unity through the influence of multiculturalism. With the increase in globalization and multiculturalism, there is a greater need to defend one's interests. With multiculturalism, agreement has become more important than merit and truth. We have descended into an overt struggle for power.

Diminished ethnic and cultural unity within countries is an important factor. The politics of division practiced by liberals exacerbates this influence. Micro power is enhanced, while the power of the majority is emasculated. All groups are pushing their positions as hard as possible without regard for truth or legitimacy. It's a power grab pure and simple.

When societies were more homogeneous and more stable, there was not this divisiveness and groups did not feel threatened by others. The groups worked together, played by the rules of the game, and focused on what was best for society overall. Divisive liberal politics together with the more rapid change in social and economic circumstances have combined to weaken solidarity.

In the past change took place at a slower pace. As time proceeds it seems that change is accelerating. Rational discourse is easier and more likely to take place in an environment of stability and less change. So with all the pieces of society thrown up in the air, so to speak, it's not surprising that the resulting disorder is causing frenzy and less-than-rational behavior.

A loss of confidence in reason has played a role. Our societies built on reason and materialism have left many feeling empty. Moreover, there is the view that logic and reason can be used to prove or disprove almost anything. It has been misused and abused, so the result has been a loss of confidence in reason. Logic and reason are no longer providing rock-solid guidance. Given the misuse and the manipulation of reason, there is now a deep suspicion of it. The more we know, the less we know. Evidence is complex and ambiguous. Moreover, can we really trust the so-called experts who have their own agendas and are frequently in disagreement?

The use of reason generally involves a bottom-up approach to arriving at conclusions and setting policy. Liberals aren't comfortable with a bottom-up approach to knowledge as a sense of control is missing. They don't want their top-down approach to setting policy to be challenged by facts or evidence. They want and need a sense of control.

Liberals prefer an organic, collectivist approach to finding the right way to setting policy. They are committed to a top-down approach, beginning with and ending in abstraction. They want to avoid the messiness and uncertainty of reality. Testing out theories and looking at the experience of policy experiments isn't something they want to get involved with.

The erosion of the role of reason may reflect the rise in the power and influence of the government and the ruling elite. The latter don't want to be challenged by reason so they do everything to diminish its influence. When the masses gain power and influence, we generally see the role of reason ascend. Conversely, when the masses lose ground to the elites and authoritarianism is expanding its influence, the role of reason is usually in decline.

The idea that truth isn't absolute or something to be found, but rather something to be socially constructed by consensus, has led to an increase in energy input into the process of constructing a new version of the truth. Where others are throwing fictions around to advance their interests and positions, it becomes almost a matter of survival to do likewise. The environment has degenerated into a competition of who can manufacture the best facts and best distort the appearance of reality to suit their interests.

Greater media bias and less fair and balanced news have led to a poverty of knowledge and to a greater disrespect for so-called providers of truth. Some have merely thrown up their hands and given up seeking real information, while others now turn to themselves, realizing that they have to put real effort into the task. Truth is no longer something delivered on a platter, if ever it was. Free information is dangerous; truth has to be earned like anything else.

The separation of the media from government is an important part of our history, and has kept the power of government limited. Unfortunately, we have lost this. Important parts of the media have been co-opted by the liberal establishment. The fourth estate, the press and the media, are no longer what they used to be. Journalism used to be about reporting events with impartiality. You no longer see this. Media can no longer be counted on to provide unvarnished facts. It seems the media has gotten involved in the power game— they want to be players. They are more like a Fifth Column than a Fourth Estate now. Well-known Democratic strategist and pollster Pat Caddell has warned that the mainstream media has become a serious threat to democracy. The media has abandoned its responsibility to provide truthful reporting of events and to "protect the liberty of all of us from organized government power."[150]

There is less commitment to truth and the real. The view pushed by the Left that truth is oppression has contributed to this, but it runs deeper than that. Maybe we are too much influenced by television and video games. We are now inclined to live in fantasy worlds and have lost a sense for the real world. In fact we have withdrawn from the real world. We consciously seem to be withdrawing into a cocoon of fantasy which is made easier and more interesting by improved video and cyber technology. What is interesting is how most of us are willing to close our eyes to this process, denying that it's even taking place. The game though is thinly veiled and obvious to all but the blind or those in deep denial.

Institutional biases are increasing. Why should corporations work hard competing to earn money in the market place when they can easily earn money (and with little risk) from government? Large corporations living off the government sector have a vested interest in seeing the government expand. For example, General Electric, one of America's most prominent companies, is reportedly a player in this game.[151] By promoting green energy policy on NBC News, which it owned until recently, General Electric stands to make huge profits from wind power.[152] The company has not been doing well financially in its business with the private sector, so it's easy to see why it would be tempted to find a way by tapping the public sector and the taxpayers.

The government sector, as mentioned, benefits by expanding its power and influence. Its views are consequently shaped to support and accommodate government intervention and expansion of power. It looks at the world and issues to find justification for a greater role for government. So it's not surprising that liberal politicians and government are stirring fears of environmental catastrophe and global warming, as they can use this issue to raise substantial amounts of tax revenue and to vastly expand government's regulatory power via the Environmental Protection Agency.

These institutional influences aren't new. They have been a factor in the past, so why has the impact now been manifesting itself on social discourse and politics when it did not in the past? Each of these institutional factors has grown in importance, and together their combined effect has reached a tipping point.

Individuals also have their deeply entrenched biases. This was exemplified in the Clinton impeachment case. The logical arguments for or against were fairly obvious, and one could see how it was possible to come down on one side or the other. What was interesting is that Democrats invariably opposed impeachment, while Republicans felt it justified.

It's interesting and noteworthy that the judgments and assessments of most people match what they would like them to be. We all twist ourselves into rhetorical and logical knots to come up with the conclusions that we like. We will not admit that such judgments are merely reflections of our preferences, but instead try to wrap ourselves and viewpoints in the mantle of truth and sound reasoning. Even intelligent people, who know better, play this game, willfully overlooking how tenuous their positions really are.

The Substructures and Underpinnings Determining our Thoughts

It's not this that interests me so much as it is rather obvious that people try to justify the superstructure (the end results or how they would like to see the world) of their thoughts by whatever rhetorical and argumentative efforts are necessary. What interests me rather is what influences the substructure of our thoughts, the foundations. What is it that shapes and determines the superstructure? Why are my opinions different than yours? This may seem simple and straightforward, but it's not. It's not simply experience and activities at the conscious level, but rather forces operating at the unconscious level that are probably most important.

It's essential to remove ourselves from the smokescreen of superstructure discourses, as these hide the truly defining factors. Since logical discourse is so perverted as to twist and distort facts and reasoning to advance certain perspectives or agendas, logical discourse unfortunately has become less interesting and relevant. It's more important and useful to focus on and try to understand the factors determining our views, because logic isn't really the factor it once was. In understanding what lies behind differing views, we might be better able to understand the issues, or at least see them for what they are.

In this respect family life probably plays a strong role. For example, the liberal versus conservative philosophies that permeate so many areas of our thoughts may arise in no small measure from the way we were brought up; for example, the stern, authoritative father model versus the nurturing, permissive model. Do we respect authority figures or not? Do we expect rules of behavior to be explained and fair? Some, like George Lakeoff, hypothesize that the conservative mindset arises from the authoritative family model, whereas the liberal mindset originates from a permissive family background.[153]

The male-female tension in culture has undergone profound change. It used to be that men invariably had the predominant roles. Most Western democracies are paternalistic in nature. However, as women are gaining more and more freedom and their roles in society are changing, the male dominance in culture is receding. Liberalism in many ways is feminine. It stresses compassion, empathy, and emotion-based approaches to issues rather than reliance on reason. Conservatism, on the other hand, is essentially masculine in nature. So with the growth of liberalism, the feminine character of our culture has brought with it an attendant decline in reliance on reason.

It's interesting that many contemporary books and articles attempting to explain the inability of men and women to understand one another stress the point that women are fundamentally emotional, whereas men have dispositions more based on rationality. Some of this contemporary commentary advances the argument that, when a woman is emotionally venting and complaining about something, a man shouldn't try to use reason to come up with a solution to her problem, but should simply listen. The liberal temperament is much like this; they want to vent, but not hear about logic or solutions.

Morality takes root in the early stages of life.[154] Infants are possessive of toys and food. Infants resist restraint or anyone preventing them from what they want to do. Infants as well as adults naturally avoid pain and want pleasure. These behaviors express the inborn nature of man. They show him to be self-interested and self-absorbed, as well as pleasure-seeking. This is the nature of man exhibited throughout history. This accords well with individualism, liberty, capitalism and the conservative personality. Liberals see this nature, but don't like it. They believe they can change the nature of man and moreover that this would improve all our lives; in fact they see it bringing about a utopia on earth.

If this is our nature, then how do we explain the liberal personality? The nurturing mother tending to all our wants is part of our early upbringing. Perhaps the liberal personality is locked more into this state of dependency. He loves receiving care and feeling the security of loving parents. He is indulged and cared for—and he loves it. This fixation on being taken care of, loved, and provided for may well be the basis of the liberal personality. The liberal personality is averse to competition and striving hard for something. The liberal thinks he should be given what he needs; he shouldn't have to work for it. He enjoys living in a cocoon of dependency where all his needs are met.

Lakeoff, an avowed liberal, sees the father in the family as rigid and unyielding. He doesn't like the father. He doesn't see the father as loving and understanding, but somehow as estranged and unloving. He doesn't see the father trying to provide guidance in a constructive way.

Women prefer egalitarian structures more than men. A study by Jim Sidanius in the European Journal of Social Psychology concluded that "the data…showed that males were more anti-egalitarian than females, and that this male/female difference in social and group dominance orientation tended to be largely invariant across cultural, situational, and contextual circumstances." Hence, liberalism is against hierarchy, although its elitist nature belies this.[155]

Hierarchy is necessary in society. Communism and socialism like to push the idea hierarchy isn't necessary, but hierarchy is necessary in almost all realms of life, whether in the family, in business, or in government. Liberals have a problem with authority figures, perhaps stemming from a less than satisfactory relationship with their fathers.

Regarding early life experiences, the following factors could contribute to ideational proclivities and liberal or conservative personality dispositions: trauma from separation from the womb at birth, failure to cope and be self-reliant, feelings of insecurity in personal ability, a lack of self-confidence, and antipathy toward paternal authority.

Most psychologists agree that personality is established early in life, and empirical research corroborates this view. As was mentioned in Chapter 2, The Journal of Research in Personality in

2006 determined that the personalities of their sample of twenty-three-year-olds were similar to what they had been in nursery school and were an excellent predictor of political disposition. In addition, the American Political Science Review in 2005 found, based on a study of identical and non-identical twins, that genetics played a stronger role than parental influence. A study by Thomas Bouchard of twins separated at birth also corroborated the strong role played by genetics.[156]

Unconscious archetypal psychological templates shape our consciousness and determine our views in ways outside of our understanding. It's interesting whether these archetypal influences may be shifting and bringing about changes in our political views. Perhaps changes in modern society—a reduced role of the family and an increased role of technologic games and toys for children—are bringing about fundamental changes in underlying psychological archetypes.

So, people are no longer interested in the search for the truth. We, in fact, don't want to see it. We believe we can create our own truth. The emphasis in most of our lives is on the production of realistic illusions or artifice. Perhaps in the constructivist vein we think if we can sell or push our version of the truth, this is what will prevail. But as noted by Michael Crichton, "The claim of consensus has been the first refuge of scoundrels; it is a way to avoid debate by claiming that the matter is already settled."

Truth isn't simply a matter of consensus. We can't ignore the realities of the world. Truth arises out of the natural world and our social and economic circumstances. Truth shouldn't be a matter of what we want the world to be, or what we think it should be. Truth arises out of reality, not out of our wishes or our agreements with one another. As Lenny Bruce once said, "The 'what should be' never did exist, but people keep trying to live up to it. There is no 'what should be,' there is only what is."

Essentially the shift away from reason means less emphasis on pragmatic outcomes, efficiency, and materially beneficial outcomes. Dogmas and concepts are giving way to experimentalism, but it's a groundless experimentalism, detached from reality. Passion rather than reason is becoming the beacon. The restraining influences of individualism and reason are being abandoned and eclipsed. The landscape is set for an unrestrained reign of passions. This is a dangerous course.

The Philosophic Template of Liberalism

Let us put the liberal mindset into historical perspective. In an excellent book, *The Search for Meaning: A Short History,* Dennis Ford looked at several different mindsets that have prevailed over history: the mythic mind-set, the philosophic mind-set, the scientific mind-set, and the postmodern mind-set. One would think at first that liberalism would fit most closely with that which was most recently historically manifested, but let's look carefully at this.[157]

The mythic mind identifies with an ontologically different world than our day-to-day world. It's a world on a higher plane than our world and it is one requiring total engagement. It's a Don Quixote world invested with good intentions and good and evil. It's a surface world without complexities and profound ideas. It can't be subjected to scrutiny and rational inquiry. The mythic mind is a mind in a spell; it wraps the participant in a world of reverie, but he must be ever so careful not to wake up; he must be ever so careful about looking in the mirror or asking questions. He can't be self-conscious; he has to remain absorbed in the myth, the story, otherwise his belief could be shaken. Essentially he has to fight being awoken from a dream, for this would throw him into an altogether different world. Self-deception is the key. A suspension of credulity and a leap of faith are essential and provide the basis for transcending our day-to-day lives. Those of mythic mind buy into a universalistic fiction that redefines their lives and reality. The problem is, like using drugs, sooner or later one wakes up and is jolted into reality. Fleeing from reality and its harsh choices may seem the easy course in the short run, but it inevitably ends badly. Men can't fly however hard they try. The myths of communism, Nazism, fascism, religious cults, and utopian experiments have shown us the horrible consequences associated with entering dream worlds too deeply. Reality may not always be easy and pretty, but in the end we can't get too far away from it without paying a heavy price.

It's not surprising that the mythic mind-set prevailed early in history, as mankind had little understanding of anything. Without a rational and empirical understanding of his world, man organized his world through faith and fiction. This all changed with Plato who helped to initiate the philosophic mind-set. The philosophic mind-set held sway for a long period beginning around the third century BC and reaching into the seventeenth century.

Whereas faith and emotionality provided the underpinnings to the mythic mind, reason and the mind played the key roles during the period of the philosophic mind-set. Skepticism, not blind faith, was the hallmark of the philosophic mind. Plato was the major figure in the philosophic period. He moved away from emotion and faith and tried to understand the world we live in by using the mind. Philosophy tried to understand the world through the use of logic and abstraction. Plato did not see the world we live in as real. For him this world was but one of appearances. It was a shadow of the real world. The real world was one of ideal forms, whereas the world of appearances was inhabited only with imperfect representations of the ideal forms. So, "Horsiness" is an ideal form existing in the real world, whereas horses, imperfect representations of horsiness, inhabit the world of appearances. The philosophic realm of the real world was constituted of universal ideal forms, whereas the world of appearance was full of particular imperfect forms. In Plato's view only the elite, those with highly refined intellect, could hope to understand and glimpse the real world of ideal forms. This, of course, differed sharply with the mythic period in which anyone could buy into the myth. A philosophic understanding of reality and truth was perceived by a cold analytic intellect which contrasted sharply with the heated, sensual engagement with reality of the mythic mind.

The scientific period was ushered in by Aristotle. Aristotle brought Plato down to earth. He turned Plato's approach to truth and understanding upside down. Plato saw the real world as constituted of universal forms and the world of appearance as made up of less perfect forms. Aristotle viewed the world in a completely contrary way; he saw Plato's world of appearance and particulars as the real world and the world of ideal forms and universals as less real. Aristotle's view of the world was atomistic, with small molecular particles more central to understanding and life than the larger, organic whole. The former determine and make-up the organic whole. While Plato was more concerned with another world, that of ideal forms, Aristotle was concerned with understanding the world we live in. He became preoccupied with causation and the question of why things happen.

Aristotle saw the world in teleological terms, with everything trying to move from its actual state to one of achieving its full potentiality. For Aristotle everything has a purpose, so once we know the purpose we can look back and explain what is going to happen to it. So, an acorn is destined to become an oak tree.

Aristotle contributed to the birth of the scientific mind, but science was not concerned with teleology, but with causation. The scientific mind wants to know how we can control our environment and better our lives. Science sees neutral, atomistic forces of causation as explaining events. It looks at cause and effect in an objective empirical way. While Aristotle sought to find the cause for something in the effect, the scientific method wants to find the effect in the cause. In other words, it looks forward rather than backward. Through the conduct of experiments under *ceteris paribus* conditions, science seeks to explain effects and events by the causes that precede them. This is a very different ontology than that of the mythic and philosophic periods. It's focused on the daily world we live in, not some abstracted or ideal world of a higher order. It's concerned with what is, not with what we presume or what we would like reality to be. It's a view of the world as seen through the lens of rationality and empiricism. It's geared, as mentioned, to helping us understand what is happening around us, to controlling our environment, and to improving our lives.

The problem with causality is that we live in a general equilibrium world. Because *ceteris paribus* assumptions don't hold, it's difficult to secure a good understanding of reality. It's difficult to point to this or that factor as a causal influence, isolating it from other influences when looking at the big picture. Nevertheless, despite its shortcomings, the concept of causality has been fundamental to the advancement of science and the development of civilization.

Science sees causality as arising from atomistic forces from below. It's concerned primarily with the inanimate things, unconscious forces, and the material world. It's concerned with the world as it is. Liberalism, on the other hand, is primarily concerned with human consciousness as it can affect the world from above through conscious design. It's not concerned so much with what is, but what might be or should be. Liberals don't like what is, so they want to create a new reality.

The postmodern mind-set is about deconstruction, taking apart the prevailing ideologies, traditions and perspectives. According to postmodernism, we live in a pluralistic world where all truths are relative. Essentially postmodernism is dedicated to destroying monolithic versions of the truth, but it really devalues all truths and standards of value and morality.

Liberalism has largely espoused postmodernism and used it to destroy prevailing traditions and institutions that have served as obstacles to achieving its agenda. It's interesting that, although liberalism has used postmodernism to bring about an end to absolutist views of truth to foster a more pluralistic society, it's unwittingly creating another absolutist world view.

Although one would tend to associate liberalism with postmodernism, we see that the fit is not quite there since it's working against the pluralism that it purports to espouse. It is important to realize that progressive-liberalism is not rooted in postmodernism; it just uses it as an instrument to weaken anything that stands in its way. It's strange but liberalism seems really more closely associated with the mythic mind-set than the scientific and postmodern mind-set. This is because it's faith-based. It shuns reason and discourse and doesn't even really want to look at itself in the mirror. Self-consciousness and questioning are squelched, as it could break the spell. So liberalism is really not modern, but rather harkens back to even pre-philosophic periods.

Other Aspects of Liberal Thinking

Liberalism has its eyes on the distant future; in other words it's not our world, but the world of youth and their youth. In this way it's not much different from some religions which put the focus on an afterlife. Both are in some sense sacrificing the present for the future. Liberals are focused on living in another world. This one isn't good enough for them.

There is yet another anomaly here, however. To create a better future, it's necessary to save or sacrifice, but saving and sacrifice isn't in the DNA of liberals. They don't comprehend that you need to pay for things. Their time preference is much on the present which is reflected in high spending. Their big-spending-deficit ways aren't consistent with building a better future.

Liberalism is non-materialist in that its policies hurt growth and wealth creation. It thus implicitly assumes that materialism is not what people should want. Perhaps they do, but they shouldn't. Yet liberalism is essentially about usurping the wealth of some to give it to others, so there is a strong underlying element of materialism from this standpoint. Antimony and inconsistency seem ever present in liberalism, defying the penetration of reason and logic. For this reason liberalism involves of necessity a shut-down of the mind.

In the 1930s, irrationalism was essential in the development of fascism in Italy and in the Nationalist Socialist Party in Germany. During this period in Mussolini's Italy and Hitler's Germany, the critical exercise of intellect was tossed aside in favor of emotion, myth, monomaniacal passion, and the drive of pure will. For some reason irrationalism is rearing its ugly head again in a new form of liberalism. It did so before when the capitalist system struggled during the depression of the 1930s and the economic problems since 2008 now are exacerbating the expression of and impact of liberalism. This is a disease which just can't be stamped out.

Free speech and free thought are essential for the development of men. This is a central guarantee of the American Constitution. Unfortunately, there are mounting pressures on both free speech and free thought. We see this most apparently in the regime of political correctness. We can no longer talk and think freely about important issues like race relations, homosexuality, and Islamic terrorism. Clearly if our feelings and thoughts about these issues are repressed, it's unlikely that we will be able to deal with these issues in an effective way.

Not only is political correctness a problem preventing free and open discussion, it even forces us to lie to ourselves. So lies and dishonesty aren't only forced on us in the social sphere, but into our own personalities and thoughts. For example, many people have strong thoughts about issues of ethnicity, sexuality, and faith, yet when asked nowadays how they think about these issues few would reveal the strength of their feelings even to themselves—for fear of being labeled a bigot. Free internal thinking is critically important, but the Thought Police have even encroached upon this domain. An important part of reason is the process of discrimination, distinguishing between things and circumstances. Liberalism vitiates this process in its subscription to moral and cultural relativism.

So political correctness isn't just about speech, but about thought suppression and separation from our basic instincts and emotions. Reason isn't just about cold hard logic; it should connect fundamentally to instincts and emotions. William James, a preeminent American philosopher early in our history, captured the intricate connection between rationality and feeling well in his words, where he acknowledged "catching real fact in the making only in recesses of feeling, the darker, blinder strata of character." Political correctness weakens these connections with our emotional and instinctual resources and hence undermines the strength of rationality.

George Lakeoff and Mark Johnson in their work, *Philosophy in the Flesh*, buttress this view of William James, seeing rationality as deeply connected with feelings. They underscore the prominent role played by metaphor and discount the traditional Cartesian view of reason as falling entirely within the province of the brain. For them also, reason isn't the application of cold hard logic on cold hard facts by one part of the body. Reasoning and conceptualizing isn't transcendent, operating without influence from the body and experience.

Likewise concerning race, many people take ethnic pride in their own race. The Irish celebrate their ethnicity with Saint Patrick's Day and the Orthodox Jews, the Arabs, Indians, and Chinese are tight-knit, having strong and proud cultures. America is like no other country in the world. Anyone from any culture and ethnic group can be an American and is fully accepted as one, and this requires that we all treat each other equally and with respect. Most of these groups prefer to associate with members of their own ethnicity and probably consider their values and culture superior to others, but this doesn't make anyone of them bigoted. It's natural and people shouldn't be afraid of being branded a bigot if they admit it.

America is known as the melting pot of the world, where cultures and ethnic groups freely intermingle and are molded into one. It's a beautiful feature of our country and it has made us who we are. It has made us strong and more interesting. But it doesn't have to become all-encompassing, penalizing and diminishing those who would like to see their native born culture and ethnicity preserved and developed.

Moreover, even if there are a few pernicious bigots, is it not better that their views are freely expressed? Is it not better that we know? Repressing them doesn't make the problem go away, and it may stifle a healthy debate about race relations. Many, including black Americans, have complained about the lack of a free and direct discussion about race relations. One also has to think seriously about the cost of political correctness on our liberty and our ability to think and speak freely.

Liberty isn't only hurt by overt force or compulsion; the force of public opinion exercised through the tyranny of the majority in many cases is more dangerous and effective. Political correctness, in the name of the good and equality, is much used as an instrument of suppression. The suppression of free speech and thought is a clear and present danger to liberty.

It's interesting that liberals and conservatives have a different mode of arriving at opinions and beliefs. For liberals, truth is collective and consensual. Liberals speak the same language, use the same code words; they get their views from others, rather than churning out ideas themselves. They use their opinions and beliefs as a defining feature of who belongs to the group. A black who doesn't like Obama is cast out. Clarence Thomas was cast out. A liberal who disagrees with the war is cast out. Senator Lieberman, one of the most liberal members of the Senate, was pushed out of the Democratic Party.

Conservatives, on the other hand, don't approach truth through consensual modalities. Their approach to ideas and truth is individual and dialectic or conflictive. There is a distinctive Hegelian aspect to their method, an appreciation for the tension in ideas. They rely on reason, logic, and introspection, rather than strive for consensus and harmony. Tension and conflict is OK. Everyone doesn't have to be happy. Trade-offs are part of life and reality. Decisions and judgments don't have to be easy. Many are difficult, and we have to face that we risk making a wrong decision. We each have an individual responsibility for making decisions and judgments. Liberals prefer to evade the sense of individual responsibility, pushing responsibility off to a collective group. It's enough for a liberal to feel comfortable with truth if most others believe it. Conservatives aren't comfortable with truth unless they have worked rigorously through the argument's pros and cons. It's not enough to know only the pro or con arguments; one must try to know both and seriously weigh the merit of one against the other. Liberals, on the other hand, secure in their consensually arrived at truth will dismiss harshly anyone who advances a contrary view. Consensual agreements are often fragile and not well thought out, and liberals holding those positions don't want to risk having that consensuality fractured.

Liberals take their opinions from the views of others or from authority. They don't feel the need to work up a view based on reasoning and logic. For them there is no sense in doing this, since it's the group that counts. It should "feel" right. This is why the liberal gets so upset when his views are challenged. It's a threat to the group. Moreover, he is uneasy with logic and reasoning. For him this isn't the proper way to arrive at a view.

Discourse and an effort to engage opposing views are essential to finding a better way forward. To ignore opposing arguments is a grave mistake. It's important to realize the weaknesses in your position so that you can make your position as strong as possible. Moreover, it's not so much that an argument or its antithesis is right, but that a third or middle position most often is closest to the truth, particularly in a world of change.

Usually freedom of thought is defended on the grounds of individual rights and freedom, but it can also be defended from the standpoint of the community. In this connection Oliver Wendell Holmes viewed thinking as a social activity. According to Holmes, no one person is likely to have the right view, but by bringing together various viewpoints we can refine our thinking for the benefit of all. This is why it is so important to allow open dialogue and allow all people the right to express their ideas. Constrained thinking hurts not only the individual, but the community as well.

As Laurens Van der Post once said, "Human beings are perhaps never more frightening than when they are convinced beyond doubt that they are right." If this type of attitude is conjoined with mob or consensus mentality, it's a toxic and dangerous concoction. A thoughtful person, understanding the use of reason and the fallibility of all views and conclusions, is necessarily cautious and tends to reevaluate his position as events unfold and other information and perspectives come to the fore. This, of course, isn't the case with someone impervious to reason and convinced that he is right. We see this in the efforts of liberals in their continued push for increased spending and debt, even though we are now near the precipice.

Truth should have no agenda. When the agenda becomes paramount to the pursuit of truth, reason by necessity is sidelined. Facts and experiential evidence are willfully ignored. The script takes precedence over the truth.

The insincerity of liberals regarding the pursuit of truth and serious dialogue is easily seen in example after example. Liberals, as mentioned earlier, were highly critical of George Bush for waterboarding prisoners, but were eerily quiet about Obama killing thought-to-be terrorists, even American citizens, with drones. The Benghazi tragedy and the Clinton sex scandal also highlight how liberals arrive at the conclusions they want regardless of the facts or principles. This use of reasoning to advance only certain viewpoints regardless of the facts is an abuse of the power of reason. It underscores that they are not serious about using it to pursue truth, only agenda.

When truth is the object and reason the instrument, we aren't certain of where it will lead us. We become aware of our direction as we go along and learn. The destination may evolve or change. The process determines the destination and conclusion. On the other hand, when the agenda is paramount to the pursuit of truth, there is certainty about destination and destination determines process. The risk inherent in the latter is manifest. As Thomas Paine noted, "Reason obeys itself; and ignorance submits to whatever is dictated to it."

We need to look for the spark of imagination, intuition, creativity, and reason within us to guide us, not try to impose a process of logic automatically as if it's going to guide us. We need to be open-minded about the outcome of our thinking, not try to use our thinking to guarantee an outcome. Creativity, not blind submission to the rules of logic, is a principal and necessary ingredient to critical thinking.

We need to feel the spark of life. We need to probe the boundaries of life within ourselves and the boundaries with the external world. We need to feel life, not deaden it. Liberals are trying to put us in the land of the walking dead, zombies, lifeless automatons. Under their tutelage and influence, we are becoming lifeless empty creatures enslaved to our own creation, the State. What is the State for?

Liberals are into groupthink, or, as Ann Coulter calls it in her recent book, *Demonic*, mobthink. Rather than analytic thinking or pondering the complexities of issues, they are into slogans and simplistic images which they attempt to reaffirm through constant and incessant repetition. Thus, we have such sayings as "power to the people," "make love not war," "save the planet," et cetera. Those in the liberal community repeat and re-emphasize these slogans and simple perspectives to the point that they become almost mantra-like and induce an almost mesmeric suspension of critical thinking.

Liberals "think" like a mob, but usually people think like a mob when they are in a mob, but liberals are able to retain this mob-like mentality even when they are alone. The appeal of groupthink is that you don't have to think.

It was Irving Janis, a social psychologist, who introduced the term *groupthink* in 1972. He noted eight basic characteristics of groupthink which, by the way, come remarkably close to the thinking behavior of liberals today:

1. Illusion of invulnerability
2. Collective rationalization
3. Belief in the group's morality
4. Stereotyped views of those not in the group
5. Pressure on dissenters
6. Repression of their true feelings
7. Illusion of unanimity
8. Appointment of mindguards to shield the group from negative information.[158]

These traits are associated with some very real risks. Feelings of invulnerability inevitably lead to excessive risk-taking and avoidance of contingency planning like we see in the reckless spending and debt build-up of liberal governments around the world. Collective rationalization stresses conformity over critical thinking and avoids serious examination of assumptions and consequences. As a result, other alternatives aren't seriously considered and discussion is discouraged. Total and unquestioning belief in the group's morality produces an overwhelming sense of righteousness, causing members of the group not to worry about the effects of their policies. They just *know they are right*. Members of the group view those outside the group as the "enemy," so compromise and discussion is all but impossible. Those outside the group are viewed as "bigots," "ignorant," "immoral," "selfish," and "lack compassion." Having a discussion with them is fruitless. The views of the in-group are assumed to be unanimous, so dissent even from within the group isn't tolerated. Members even need to suppress their own feelings and thoughts, so as not to feel disloyal or outside the group. As Albert Einstein once noted, "In order to be an immaculate member of a flock of sheep, one must above all be a sheep oneself." To ensure solidarity, "mindguards" are appointed to prevent facts or information from outside the group which might jeopardize or compromise the cohesiveness of the group from coming into their purview. This results in cherry-picking information and a filtering of facts for what is supportive of the group's consensus. All in all, it's remarkable how closely these characteristics of groupthink fit the liberals of today.

Groupthink and the effects of collectivism are forcing individuals to the sidelines of functioning epistemology. In his recent book, *You Are Not a Gadget,* Jaron Lanier expressed concern that collectivism is squeezing individuality and humans out of the knowledge business. With the advent of the Web, he says, "the trend has been to remove the scent of people, so as to come as close as possible to simulating the appearance of content emerging out of the Web as if it were speaking to us as a supernatural oracle."[159] It's much like going to a supermarket in any advanced country where it's difficult to link meat to any real animals anymore. The uniqueness of the animal has been homogenized, so it almost seems we are not really eating meat, and that an animal isn't really involved.

* * *

CHAPTER 10

THE SACRIFICE OF TRUTH

———•———

Those who make you believe absurdities can make you commit atrocities.

~Voltaire

Integrity without knowledge is weak and useless, and knowledge without integrity is dangerous and dreadful.

~Samuel Johnson

We don't see things as they are, we see things as we are.

~Anais Nin

A lie would have no sense unless the truth were felt dangerous.

~Alfred Adler

If the facts don't fit the theory, change the facts.

~Albert Einstein

For an individual it's important to be able to examine one's own beliefs and decide if they are appropriate. Times change, and circumstances change—so it's important to be able to use reason and critical analysis to determine if a change in views and behavior or course is advisable.

Without this commitment to the search for truth, or at least open dialogue, and with an understanding that we aren't on solid ground and that our positions have to be continuously reexamined, man can easily find himself going down perilous paths. Paths which would end in adverse, perhaps disastrous, outcomes, for without open discourse and self-examination, it would be very difficult to make course corrections to avert disaster. This is particularly important in a rapidly changing world where the parameters are constantly changing.

If government ——the ruling class—becomes insulated from the people and has different interests and agendas from the people, the pursuit of truth suffers, as the government actively and covertly tries to delude the citizenry. Deceit and dissimulation become primary instruments of power. This is why the nexus between government and the people is critical for the pursuit of truth to survive and flourish. And it's why the increasing chasm between the government (the ruling class) and the people is so dangerous.

Politicians aren't interested in facts or truth, only what will benefit them in the short term. So, the bigger and more controlling the government, the more insulated the ruling class is from the citizenry, the farther we will find ourselves from facts and truth. The trend for bigger and bigger government in America and Western Europe is thus intimately connected with the fading interest in facts and truth.

As we lose our interest in, and our way to the truth, misinformation prevails. This leads to poor government and continued incentives for the government to suppress liberty and work against the interests of the people. The greater the gap between "the official truth" and reality, the greater will be the need for suppression and deceit. Moreover, one would expect the gap to widen over time, so the problem gets worse. Suppressing the liberty of an individual hurts not only that individual, but the whole of society. The sense of vitality and exuberance that comes from being able to act and think freely is important to everyone and to societal discourse and interaction.

If truth is no longer respected and sought after, this affects not just society but goes to the core of the internal lives of individuals and their families. It's hard to live in a world that one knows is false. With genuineness and honesty sacrificed for deceit and dishonesty, personal relationships necessarily become distant and untrusting. Warmth is replaced with coldness and calculation. This was well evidenced in the USSR and in China under Mao.

Judging from history, fairy-tale worlds easily transmute into nightmare worlds. A connection to reality and truth is essential for mankind to progress and flourish. Simon Blackburn in his excellent book *Truth* captures this point well in the following passage:

> "Freedom includes the freedom to blur history and fiction or the freedom to spiral into a climate of myth, carelessness, incompetence or active corruption. It includes the freedom to sentimentalize the past or to demonize others or manipulate the record. It's not only totalitarian societies that find truth slipping away from them: the emotionalists of contemporary populism or the moguls of the media and entertainment can make it happen just as effectively. This is why Plato felt that he had to forge the vocabulary of reason and truth in opposition to democratic politics. Orwell thought this, and anybody worried about such things as the ideology of those who own the press, or the Disneyfication of history, should think it, too."[160]

The moment we see warning signs that truth has been compromised, we need to energize ourselves and marshal our resources to get it back. It's like the canary in the mineshaft that alerts miners to a coming explosion. The decline of reason and truth is a sign that something else is going terribly wrong; for example, that the government is becoming too powerful and detached from the people, and that liberty and freedom of thought and expression may be at risk.

The aversion of liberals to obvious facts—and their ceaseless pattern of lying—suggests a base motive, but their dissimulation is probably not intentional or malevolent. Liberals seem addicted to fiction and myth. They are so enveloped in it, and surrounded by other liberals with similar views, that they don't realize what they are doing. There is blindness and a frenzied sense of denial. Their fear of anything which could puncture their fragile world causes them to circle the wagons anytime truth threatens to awaken them from their daydream. Instead of seeking truth, they seem driven by a fear of it as it turns their world upside down.

The Left's complete disregard and abuse of truth can be easily seen in Secretary of State Hilary Clinton's remarks before a

Senate Hearing on the Benghazi disaster in which four Americans, including the Ambassador, were killed. For weeks after the killings, the Obama Administration explained to the media and the American public that the attacks arose out of spontaneous protests over an American video defaming Muhammad. They did this even though they watched the attack in real time on video and there were no protesters outside. They did this even though the Libyan President said that it had nothing to do with the video. In Libya there was not even any knowledge of the video. It was clearly a planned terrorist attack, but Obama did not want to admit this as it damaged his narrative that he had Al Qaeda and terrorists subdued. [161]

Afterward when asked about the attack in a Senate Hearing, Secretary of State Clinton exploded angrily, "With all due respect, the fact is we had four dead Americans. Was it because of a protest or was it because of guys out for a walk one night who decided they'd go kill some Americans? What difference at this point, does it make?"[162] Does the truth not make a difference? The Administration was the only one peddling the protest as an explanation for the attack, even though all evidence, video and otherwise, showed there were no protests. No one was outside the compound before the attack. And no one ever suggested that it was "because of guys out for a walk." You don't go out for a walk with heavy artillery and engage in a seven hour attack on the Embassy. It was clearly a planned attack by terrorists. The Left is content to spin their stories of fiction to the American public and the media even when in obvious contradiction to the truth. Their brazenness is stunning and a clear and present danger to the world we live in.

Liberals are opposed to truth, because they see it as a threat to peace, harmony, and conformity which are accorded primacy in their agenda. The pursuit of truth reveals reality which is full of tension and conflict. Liberals prefer to hide from reality, suppress it, rather than confront it. Peace is more important than resolution and revelation. Their fragile edifice of forced harmony and conformity needs to be zealously guarded, if it's to survive.

According to liberalism and relativism, there is no truth, only a plurality of truths with one no better than another. This is their way of devaluing truth. It underscores their disconnect from reality and their intent to push an agenda through a new epistemology.

Architecture of Knowledge

In traditional approaches to epistemology the structure or architecture of knowledge can be considered to be of four basic types.[163] First, with a finite linear structure there are a finite number of reasons; one reason leads to another until finally there is some belief for which there are no additional reasons. Under this system none of the reasons repeats. Second, with an infinite linear structure, there is no limit to the number of reasons that can be given to support a given proposition or belief. There is thus infinite regress. Third, a structure of knowledge based on circularity differs from the linear structure in that there is a repetition of reasons. In a circular system there are a series of reasons behind a given belief until one comes back full circle to the initial belief or the reasons behind it. Finally, another approach, really a non-system, is knowledge with no structure. This describes an approach to knowledge or beliefs that involves no reasons or justifications.

Faith or religion is based on the finite linear structure; it's a foundationalist approach to the truth and this still holds considerable sway, although its purview and influence has been substantially curtailed by science. The impact of globalization has reduced the truth value of religions, as it has brought the positions of various religions into close proximity to one another, thus highlighting the inconsistencies.

The two contemporary approaches that have the most support are the coherence theory and the consensus theory. Both represent avenues of escape from the nihilistic net of relativism. The coherence theory is essentially based on a circular structure of knowledge, while consensus theory tosses aside traditional approaches to epistemology, saying that truth should be the product of consensus. Coherence theory differs from the traditional epistemic scheme founded on a structure of circularity, however, in that it's not predicated on a system involving a chain of causation running from one factor to another, but rather sees a system that is simultaneously determined.

The coherence theory recognizes our fundamental incapacity of grasping reality directly as it may or may not exist in the world outside of ourselves. Instead it concentrates on reality as it's captured in our heads in the form of thoughts. Rather than trying to say that this or that is real, as would be the case with a correspondence theory of truth, coherence theory puts together an overall picture of truth, with all the parts and pieces needing to fit together without inconsistency. Thus in coherence theory the truth of a proposition or statement can only be established in relation to a system of other pertinent propositions. This is the approach taken by science; scientists formulate theories and perspectives based on this approach. If something in the world is found that is inconsistent with a given theory or contradicts it, that theory is considered to be invalid. Non-contradiction is viewed as an essential feature or requirement of truth.

In my experience as an economist with the International Monetary Fund, coherence theory was often the basis for how we put together financial programs for member countries. We usually did not have general equilibrium econometric models that we could rely on, so we put together analysis and formulations of policies based on coherence theory. A coherent system includes whatever fits into it: there isn't anything left outside it by which to test its claims. In financial programming, all pieces of information need to fit, be consistent, and be non-contradictory. This is so at the statistical level as well as at the behavioral level and the theoretical level. Consistency, however, doesn't mean to say we really know what is going on. It simply means we aren't lost in partial equilibrium, or in myopic perspectives. We have transcended small, myopic, and hidebound perspectives, but to what?

Coherence theories generally are of two types; either the world is seen as composed of two primary substances (good and evil in the West and yin and yang in the East) or is unitary. In other words the world is either binary or monistic. In a binary world struggle and tension is involved. In a monistic one struggle is no longer necessary. Cohesion and peace is the sought and expected outcome in this world, whereas equilibrium is the best that can be hoped for in a binary world. Liberalism clearly subscribes to the monistic view of the world. Such a world is unitary, indivisible, and cohesive. Those seeing the world in such a way tend to look at the whole, not the parts or particulars.

Liberals, though, are averse to coherence approaches as they don't provide them with enough control of the truth; instead they exalt the consensus approach as the way to the truth. The consensus approach, however, can lead to tyranny by the majority. This then is yet another inconsistency implicit in liberalism. While they purportedly fight for the rights of minorities, they are really espousing an epistemology favoring the majority. This is, of course, if we take them at their word, which we have already concluded would be a big mistake. What they really want isn't a system in which truth is determined by consensus or by majority, but rather by the elite ruling class. Liberals want to appropriate the determination of truth for themselves. The State is just a cover for their usurpation of epistemological control and theft of the truth. It sounds a bit like a return to the reign of the pharaohs in Egypt centuries ago.

If one buys into the consensus theory of truth, one has to accept that the majority can't be wrong. One would have to accept that the Germans who supported Nazism were right. Only those intoxicated with liberalism and those averting their eyes from the horrors of history could find this approach viable. It's an approach which completely strips the individual of any right or role for truth determination and or moral authority. It's yet another form of diminishment of individuality wrought by the Left. Consumed by self-hatred and unhappiness, liberals seem intent on destroying individuality.

Richard Rorty, perhaps the preeminent philosopher for liberalism today, firmly rejects a representational understanding or view of knowledge, arguing that we need to abandon a foundationalist approach to epistemology. In his book *Philosophy and the Mirror of Nature* he declared that analytic philosophy had pretty much concluded that the quest for epistemological finality is beyond our reach. Accordingly, he argued, we need to find a way other than science and empiricism forward.

Representational epistemology (the correspondence theory of truth) sees the mind as trying to mirror the external world. The latter is seen to be independent of the mind. On the other hand, most modern philosophers see an intimate connection between the mind and the world. The two aren't independent of each other. For Rorty, for example, truth can't exist independently from the human mind. The world is out there, but descriptions of the world aren't. Only description of the world can be true or false. The world on its own can't.

Rorty said that "personal ideals of perfection and standards of truth were no more needed in politics than a state religion." Thus he supports consensus as the basis for establishing truth, but he argues like other liberals that this should be value free. Would this really be such a nice world: a world without personal ideals of perfection, standards of truth, or values? Some would say it sounds more like Hell!

So, Richard Rorty suggests that we dismiss our concern for objectivity and instead focus on creating truths based on community consensus. Rorty proposes the construction of truths in order to build an epistemology built by the masses. His objective seems to be to remove the tyranny of epistemology from the hands of the elite and place it in the hands of the masses.

The public should get together and, through consensus, establish what truths should be. Inter-subjective agreement, not objectivity or reason, should be the test for establishing what is true and untrue. This is difficult to understand given the concern of liberals about tyranny and oppression in the past. Truth established on the basis of majority agreement seems like a recipe for abuse and oppression. Truth was established in this way in communist China, the Soviet Union, and Nazi Germany, and this should be lesson enough for us to avoid this approach to the truth.

It's interesting that in China during the Great Leap Forward the communist leadership especially targeted the educated class for annihilation. Mao saw these people as a threat. Their thinking and mindset was viewed by Mao as too intransigent to change, so he thought it best to eliminate this class, along with a lot of the books and libraries. There was no attempt to have discourse with this class. Intellectualism was seen as an obstacle that had to be destroyed.

The liberalism of today also is fundamentally anti-intellectualist. As discussed in the previous chapter on reason, it shuns rationality and free and open debate. Liberals try to shut down free speech. For example, students shout down Clarence Thomas or the Minute Men or others with whom they disagree. The leadership of universities, whom you would think would bend over backward to protect free speech, actually encourages the protesters. Universities are no longer interested in turning out students who can think for themselves; the goal in education now is to indoctrinate students. There is overt and strong pressure on students to adopt orthodox liberal positions and views. They want them to buy into the program.

Liberal intolerance was on show at the Miss America Pageant. Liberals in the audience booed a contestant who said that, although she respected the right of people to make their own choices, she herself felt that traditional marriage is appropriate. She was not a believer in gay marriage, and for this she was booed— even though she respected the rights of gays to make their own choices.

Liberalism through political correctness attempts to suppress not only dialogue, but thought. It also seeks to suppress values that are not consistent with their values. For example, liberalism strongly supports homosexuality and gay rights. It not only tries to protect homosexuals from discrimination, but seeks to openly encourage this life style through the school system and the media. Anyone who opposes this, even in a minor way, is labeled as a bigot.

Humans, and most creatures, are programmed to be heterosexual as this is pivotal to species survival. It can't be surprising then that most men feel a visceral, instinctual revulsion at the thought of sex with another man and are repelled by homosexuality. Yet liberalism is telling us that we can't express our feelings; indeed it's telling us that we can't even have these feelings. There is no more basic feeling than this. It's instinctual, but it is also grounded firmly in many religions, so it has a faith

245 | The Sacrifice of Truth

component. It finds support at the conscious level. Why can't people express this most basic view and remain committed to their values. Political correctness attacks truth not only at the conscious level, but at the level of instinct and faith; the soul and nature of man is fundamentally under attack.

It's true that a small part of the population is born gay. They are biologically determined as such and have no real choice to be otherwise. For these people, truth is their homosexuality and they ought to be able to declare and express this truth without suppression. They have no right, however, to label others as bigots simply because they have another fundamental truth, namely, that they are heterosexual, and are conceived to think and see homosexuality as a perversion. This is another example of tyranny by the minority.

Liberal philosophers diminish truth. Michel Foucault, for example, sees truth negatively. For him it's an instrument of oppression. According to Foucault, the elite construct an artificial truth to keep the masses in subjection.

Truth isn't in our capacity to apprehend, but this doesn't mean that it doesn't exist. Noam Chomsky, an avowed leftist, said, "I'd be surprised if humans could understand all things as I would if a dog could." Quite rightly, we don't possess the cognitive equipment to understand all things, not the world, not even ourselves, but this shouldn't mean that we shouldn't try to apprehend it.

Truth isn't an abstraction. Truth is a tool that we use to connect with reality. It has allowed man to adapt and adjust his behavioral reactions to changes in the world and in the context of certain situations. So its strength isn't in deep-seated connections to underlying realities, but rather to surface connections that allow us to formulate theories about causation so that we can pattern our behavior to maximize our welfare. It's an issue of utility and adaptation.

Moreover, it's an issue of character. Immanuel Kant and other philosophers have emphasized the importance of "uninhibited truthfulness" toward oneself as well as to others. The commitment to the process and search for the truth is important, even if we can't find ultimate truth. It is essential to the development of healthy individuals and healthy societies.

The postmodern age is one of incredulity and skepticism, which is much advanced by liberalism. Yet despite this environment of incredulity and questioning of values and traditions, liberals have thrown themselves into the thrall of the big-government-liberalism myth. Liberals live in a self-absorbed world in which subjectivity is the determinant of truth.

In a world of pluralism there may be many truths. But just because each truth may be only culturally specific shouldn't mean that all truths are devalued. Each truth serves its own culture in its own way. It's not valueless.

Perhaps the bigger and more troubling problem for liberalism is that some in their own ranks call for a deliberate strategy of deceit. In other words it's not just occasional lying and misrepresentation to deal with difficult situations, but rather is part of a broad strategy to delude. For example, in Saul Alinsky's *Rules for Radicals*, which is a play book for the Left, deceit is advocated as a means of amassing power and advancing its agenda. Liberals recognize that the public doesn't support their agenda, so they realize that the only way they can advance it is to delude the people. This is OK with them for the ends justify the means. This is one of the key reasons why it's so difficult to have constructive discourse with a liberal. They don't want real dialogue and, in fact, are frightened of it. Unfortunately, most Americans don't see or understand this. Many who support the liberal agenda are like children led by the pied piper. The tactics advocated in the book, *Rules for Radicals*, and the tactics of the Left are inimical to the exercise of basic democratic activities and dangerous for democracy. Democratic institutions and Western culture is based on honesty, integrity, and the pursuit of truth. To the extent that leaders are able to deceive the public, the whole premise of democracy is discredited.

The press and the media are no longer interested in searching for the truth or facts. The death of journalism is evident everywhere. Rather the press and the media have become active propagandists for the liberal ruling elite. This is a predominant feature that distinguishes totalitarian states from democratic ones.

Totalitarian states believe in manufacturing the truth, not finding it. The fact that our media has now become largely propagandists is a very troubling sign that our democracy is in the final stages of subversion. When propaganda becomes a substitute for the truth and a sizeable segment of the citizenry actually become obsessed with the practice of deceit, this is parlous ground. A democracy requires straight-forwardness and a commitment to inform the citizenry. Once deceit and dissimulation squeeze out straight-forwardness, honesty, and integrity, democracy is doomed. Unfortunately, not only is democracy doomed, but humanity is as well. Man cannot live in a world of lies. Even the so-called winners in this world are losers. Even those who game the system successfully in this world are losers.

Collectivism defines truth even if it's known to be a lie. In the Soviet system, the lie ruled. Nobody would question the official truth put out by the State, because this was synonymous with treason. The penalty for impertinent questioning was severe. As the lie grew, so did suppression. Reagan properly characterized the Soviet Union as an evil empire. An empire built on lies is, indeed, evil.

Of course, this kind of language made the Left uncomfortable. As mentioned earlier, conflict avoidance is fundamental to the character of liberalism. The Left prefers fuzzy language and is firmly committed to moral relativism, so their approach is one of accommodation, compromise, and talking around differences. Seeing truth is difficult for them; it's against their nature, because for them it does not exist except as a matter of social construction.

Barack Obama ran as one who would be president of all Americans, not just blue states or red states. He ran against partisan politics and ideology. This obviously was an egregious deception, as he has pursued a hard-Left agenda as president and been one of the most divisive presidents in American history. He promised transparency in government; instead we got the back-room deals involved in passage of Obamacare in which even key figures on the Democratic side did not know what was going on behind closed doors. He promised to cut the budget deficit in half by the end of his first term, but instead has run fiscal deficits in excess of one trillion dollars each year, adding another five trillion dollars to our national debt. Not only has the Obama administration covered up basic facts behind the tragic Benghazi incident, but it actively fabricated lies to create a false narrative. The Obama administration also fought to cover up abuses of the IRS, with two IRS officials actually invoking the Fifth Amendment to protect themselves from self-incrimination. And, incredibly, Obama's Attorney General brazenly lied to Congress under oath about the Fast and Furious operation and about his role in bugging reporter James Rosen.[164]

In July 2011, Roger Clemens, a renowned baseball pitcher, was put on trial for lying to Congress about his use of steroids. What a farce! Lying is a well-practiced art form in Congress; members depend upon it for their political survival. Lying is a serious transgression whether committed by a public or private figure, but it's amusing to see the righteous indignation and outrage in Congress at the alleged transgressions of Clemens. President Clinton lied under oath to Congress and he is a hero of the Left.

Lies are pernicious and evil, not just because they misrepresent reality. As Socrates famously noted, "False words aren't only evil in themselves, but they infect the soul with evil." They destroy not only our ability to see the world, but ourselves as well. There is a metastatic character and contagion about lying; one lie begets another. Moreover, to sustain a world built on lies, coercion and brutality are frequently necessary.

Once the pursuit of truth is dishonored and abandoned, the ground is cleared for the reign of dissimulation, distortion, and outright lies. Reason and respect for the truth help to discipline us in terms of what we believe. Without such discipline, there is little to stop us from believing the most egregious and deleterious fictions. The quest for truth is a battle against chaos. Chaos is a favorite refuge of the scoundrel and those who want to exploit others for their own advantage, so there are those who want to see chaos win the battle against truth.

In such a world there are no grounds on which to argue for truth. Liars and dissemblers need not concern themselves with justifying their positions. It's the force of the mob which reigns and determines truth and moral authority. Force, not reason or conscience, are given the reins. Is this really what we want? Is this really likely to take us in the right direction? Reason and agreed approaches to finding truth are critically important for social order and trust.

Integrity is also sacrificed. The key to character is integrity. It's not outside perception that matters, but how one sees and feels one's self. The State shouldn't impose truth on its citizens. Truth isn't monolithic. There is no one truth for all of us. We are all different and should seek our own truths. Like in capitalism, where economic direction rises from the bottom to the top, truth should percolate up from individuals and not be forced on us as if we are all the same. One-size-fits-all doesn't work for clothing, and it doesn't work for truth either.

Liberalism, as discussed previously, has its roots in Rousseau's philosophy; its approach to truth can be best understood in the context of the tradition of the French Enlightenment as expressed by Rousseau. According to Isaiah Berlin, a prominent scholar of this period, "Rousseau puts sincerity and emotional relevance above truth and stresses the value of goodness and purity of nature and warmth of feeling above that of accuracy or intelligence." Rousseau valued moral character over intellectual approaches to the truth.[165] Such an approach to truth has a large element of mysticism and is resistant to verification and corroboration. Accordingly, it's almost impenetrable and difficult to challenge or refute.

Marcus Cicero said, "Nature has planted in our minds an insatiable longing to see the truth." It would seem that this is not really the case. Many prefer to live with manufactured reality and created fictions than to confront the difficulties of reality. The pursuit of truth is an arduous undertaking. Some prefer not to see the world as it is, but rather as they would like it to be. Moreover, many people need certainty and can't deal with the uncertainties implicit in the search for truth.

Liberalism is more concerned with moral truth than with evidential truth. In fact it seems to dismiss evidential truth as unimportant. Moral truth for liberals trumps everything else. Moreover, they don't want to question the nature of their moral truth or look at it analytically or even reflect on the best way to carry it out. One can't just wish truth. It's not an act of will, but rather the mind has to be quiet and the will held down if truth is to be found. Truth is in the world, not in our minds. The liberal's view of truth is hidebound and really no more than fiction dressed up as truth. Truth should stand on its own merits; it shouldn't have to be protected from probing eyes and inquiring minds. What is there to hide, unless there is nothing there?

Political correctness now restricts our view of even the obvious. For example, liberals don't want to say we have a Muslim problem. They don't want to admit that most terrorists are Islamic radicals, and are against profiling for security purposes at airports. Obama did not want to refer to acts of terrorism, preferring to call them man-made disasters. If we can't even look the obvious in the face and recognize it, how can we be expected to productively confront problems? Do we now have to run from facts because they are scary or difficult?

If police reports of a string of robberies describe the perpetrator as always wearing a green raincoat, police of course would look out for someone in a green raincoat. Likewise if the perpetrator is described as tall or fat, they would be on the lookout for someone fitting that description. If he is described as black, they would be on the lookout for a black man. If, however, he is described as Middle Eastern, as is the case with most terrorism, liberalism tells us that we have to pretend that this is not so. In screening at airports, grandma and a child have to be given the same screening procedures as someone of Middle Eastern background. By diminishing the efficacy of screening procedures hundreds of lives are being put at risk. Does this make any sense? The hyper-sensitivity and obsession of liberalism with racial and ethnic difference has all the markings of psychological illness.

As mentioned previously, political correctness restricts not only the way we speak, but the way we think. Even our most deep-seated feelings and thoughts are suppressed, like those relating to religion, sexual orientation, and interracial marriage.

An example of this came up in a political discussion I was watching on television where the issue came up of a black poet invited to the White House. Some were criticizing the decision to invite the poet, as he had written poems seeming to support the killing of police officers. The point arose that the poet opposed interracial marriage. The conservatives on the panel pointed out that had a conservative taken this position, he would be branded a racist. What really struck me, however, is that virtually all of the conservatives came out saying how could anyone oppose interracial marriage. It was almost as though it's inconceivable that any right-thinking person could oppose interracial marriage. I can sympathize because I know if they had come out with any less of a position, there would be calls for them to be fired. They would be immediately branded as racist.

This is bizarre. It's clear that large segments of the population don't favor interracial marriage. For example, the Chinese, Indian, and orthodox Jewish communities quite prefer to marry people of their own ethnicity and cultural background. Likewise some Italians, Irish, African Americans and many Latinos prefer to marry their own. Such people are proud of their own heritage and background and would like to see it perpetuated. Is there anything so outrageous about this? It's almost natural. Most species in the animal kingdom are driven along these lines.

It's fine if some people are in favor of interracial marriage, but those who prefer another way shouldn't be regarded as pernicious and evil because they take pride in their own heritage. Some people prefer to reach out for new experiences with other cultures; others are provincial and prefer to look inward. Neither should be regarded negatively. Both are good for society.

Even in the workplace political correctness exacts its toll. Rather than focus on merit and performance, executives have to worry about whether the workplace environment meets the standards of political correctness. Sexual harassment and discrimination must be closely monitored. Companies must be concerned about discrimination lawsuits. Even if they know that they aren't discriminatory, they have to protect themselves by making sure that a certain proportion of the staff and management are "minority" and female.

Managers have to worry not just about meeting company objectives in performance, but about surviving appraisals of their performance from subordinate staff. Thus managers have to spend their time and energy trying to avoid a bad report from an employee. Rather than trying to discipline a bad employee, managers have their eye off the ball of performance and are spending time skirting potential problems with employees. In general tension pervades the workplace, with everyone watching his step.

Nowadays people are so worried about how to speak and act in a politically correct way that they can't do what needs to be done in an effective way. We are all tied in knots, circumscribed, and worried about second-guessing. Government can't act as it should; business can't act as it should; the schools can't do their job effectively; and daily living, speaking, and thinking has become disingenuous and unduly complicated. Spontaneity in thinking and speaking is a relic of the past. We all need to guard ourselves lest we cross the line of political correctness. Would it not be wonderful if thinking could come to life again, and if we could speak from the heart with simplicity and without fear of saying "the wrong thing?"

In effect political correctness has pushed us all toward becoming our own censors. Spontaneity in thought and speech, part of what it's to be alive, are squelched. And for what?

Christopher Morley's admonitory words about the danger of herd-like thinking are worth recalling: "Read, every day, something no one else is reading. Think, every day, something no one else is thinking. Do, every day, something no one else would be silly enough to do. It's bad for the mind to be always a part of unanimity."

"Facts are the enemy of the truth," said Miguel de Cervantes. In Cervantes' book *Don Quixote*, the protagonist tilts at windmills. For Cervantes, a life of fantasy (but nobly inspired) is better and more worthwhile than a quotidian existence of sordid everyday realities. Liberals, too, seem more concerned with noble inspiration (at least on the surface) than in dealing with the everyday world. Noble inspiration unconnected to reality leads most often to folly. Folly may sound benign, but it's not. Ideas and actions have consequences.

If an individual or a society is to prosper, the pursuit of truth is necessary. Individuals or societies that turn a blind eye to the truth pay a heavy price. We ignore reality at our peril. It's built into our DNA. We can't help ourselves, although sometimes—in fact, often—we don't want to see the truth because it doesn't serve our interests. It's not surprising that the pursuit of an agenda of truth serves some people and not others, and consequently can be a source of social tension between social groups.

Liberals don't like the truth that capitalism has been so successful and has provided the foundation for material and spiritual freedom. They don't like that those who work hard and strive for high behavioral and ethical standards fair better in life than those who don't. They want equality pure and simple.

Because the pursuit of truth doesn't serve the interest of liberals or buttress support for their social and economic policies, they want to deprecate and diminish truth. They do this by relativizing it. One truth is of as much value as another. For the liberal the world is full of pieces of information with none having more priority or claim to virtue than another. By deconstructing the world and belief systems, all beliefs are devalued. In doing so, liberals are seeking to get us to emotionally and rationally disinvest in our beliefs.

Another way liberals want to diminish truth is by removing it from the realm of public discourse. They argue that social and economic issues are too complex for the unwashed masses to understand. For liberals, truth should be pursued not by the public, but by an elite and educated ruling class. For them the pursuit of truth should be the domain of technical experts who "understand the issues." Of course, technical experts are masters at hiding behind jargon and impenetrable argumentation, documentation, and institutional firewalls, so they are able to push any agenda they want. I believe it was George Bernard Shaw who said, "The professions are a conspiracy upon the laity." The liberal establishment wants to manufacture the truth, and they don't even want to reveal the production process, or how they arrived at it. They can't tolerate scrutiny.

Moreover, as issues become increasingly complex, even so-called experts can get lost in the analytics of issues. So there is a tendency to take dishonest shortcuts. The government, the media, and others look for a villain to blame, for example, the Wall Street bankers in the financial crisis. Or else they offer other simplistic explanations that serve their agenda and discredit those in opposition to their agenda. Trent Lott, a former key figure in the Senate, once noted that if you hear issues talked about in Congress, you can be sure these aren't the real issues, only a smokescreen for an underlying power struggle.

For the Left, agenda dictates truth, and it's all encompassing. Accepted members of the Left must accept without reservation all of the agenda. Deviation from even one item on the agenda can be grounds for excommunication from the group. As mentioned previously, Senator Joseph Lieberman of Connecticut, one of the most liberal members of the Senate, was pushed out of the party because he deviated from the position of the Left on the Iraq War. In the Left there is no room for critical and independent thinking. Everyone must be in lock-step.

A key feature of science, introduced most notably by Karl Popper, a philosopher of science, is the notion of *falsification*. According to Popper, it's essential for scientific theory to make predictions that could show it to be false if the predictions aren't borne out by experience. Liberals, of course, don't buy into this. They keep repeating the same mistakes. Collectivist political solutions don't work. Liberal policies don't work, but the Left keeps pushing them regardless. In pushing programs for more aid, financial assistance, and welfare, liberals are essentially forecasting that such programs will reduce poverty, despite the history of failure. Science, reason, evidence, and the pursuit of the truth aren't part of their way of working.

Liberals think in collective terms, abstracting from the individual, but they often argue or try to defend their positions by using individual references. For example, in discussing the issue of raising the debt ceiling, Obama said we need to put a face and a story on the people affected. Rather than deal with the issue analytically and logically, he sought to hide in particularity. Likewise when Paul Ryan, a Republican, introduced a proposal for dealing with Medicare reform, Obama criticized him for trying to prevent grandma from getting the nursing care she needs. Of course, once the money is raised through higher taxes, the people the liberals have used to buttress their case are rarely impacted. The objective is to expand the government empire. Money is fungible, so it goes to feed the leviathan, leaving grandma, and the poor, out in the cold.

Part of the problem with truth-seeking is institutional bias against it. As Upton Sinclair once astutely said, "It's difficult to get a man to understand something when his job depends on not understanding it." Many of our institutions get in the way of the truth and, in fact, have a vested interest in not finding it. This issue will be fully discussed later in the chapters focusing on institutions.

The inconsistencies inherent in liberalism reveal its fundamental disdain for truth. Liberals speak of unity, but practice division; they speak of the need for tolerance, but are intolerant; they assail religions, but in fact subscribe to a religion where the State is God; they speak of the future, but in their greed for spending now are destroying it; they speak of equality, but are really for control by an elite ruling class as the masses are considered too stupid to know what is best for them; they speak of free speech, but suppress it through political correctness; they speak of the need for compassion, but are driven by hate, and anyone who disagrees with them are enemies; they speak of morality, but their policies and the perverse incentives involved undermine it; they speak of justice for everyone, but are all about favoring those who support them; and they speak of prosperity for all, but craft policies that produce only economic misery.

Because liberalism is riddled with inconsistencies and contradictions, it can't open itself up to logic and the pursuit of truth. It's not only inconsistent and contradictory plank by plank, but with other planks of its agenda. So, the declared and ostensible liberalism of today really has no possibility of fruition. However, as mentioned, the real goal of liberalism is power. It operates to achieve power through deceit. It derives its energy through deceit and dishonesty, not straightforwardness and integrity. The latter have been bulwarks of American culture, so we are inherently vulnerable to those who want to use our credulous disposition to their advantage.

The problem is that achievement through deception and contradiction is ultimately doomed. It makes no sense; man can only dumb himself down so much before sooner or later he wakes up. Moreover, even if the elite were to succeed in gaining control and power, they would be torn apart, confused, and demoralized with the contradictions.

An aversion to reality translates into an aversion to the pragmatic. This in no small measure accounts for the failure of most liberal policy positions, even by their own standards and declared objectives. An illustration of this can be found in the liberal-progressive opposition to carbon-based energy. Not only are they against coal and oil, they are also opposed to natural gas and nuclear energy. The EPA puts heavy restrictions on coal mining and the government largely prohibits offshore oil drilling. Oil drilling is severely restricted in Alaska. Moreover, as a result of strong opposition from liberals and the environmental lobby, no new refineries have been built in the United States since 1983. The Left has blocked the development of nuclear energy too. A nuclear plant has not been built in the United States for over thirty years. Liberals favor only so-called "clean energy": solar and wind power; ethanol and electric cars. Of course, it is desirable to develop renewable, clean sources of energy, and we should definitely pursue this, but it makes no sense to expect that these sources will magically develop to replace our current sources of energy overnight. In the meantime, especially in light of the strong increase in world demand—stemming mostly from China and India—we need an energy policy that boosts coal, oil, natural gas, and nuclear energy production. Failure to grasp this is hard to understand, but the liberals manage to ignore reality. The consequence of this failure is to increase our reliance on foreign sources of energy. This puts our economy and our national security at risk. It contributes to rising world energy prices, and in fact to more environmental damage as energy production in China and India produces more pollution than here in the United States.

Reacting to strong rises in the price of oil in 2011, Obama blamed speculators and oil companies for high prices. He isn't stupid, and surely recognizes that his policies limiting output and rising world demand are causing oil prices to rise, but he doesn't want to be open with the American public about the effect of his policies. In fact at about the same time that Obama was blaming oil speculators, his administration informed Shell Oil, which had spent four billion dollars in preparation for drilling off the coast of Alaska, that they wouldn't be able to do so. This cost Shell Oil four billion dollars, which will obviously be reflected in yet higher oil prices and will reduce future supplies, which will contribute to even higher oil prices. In addition, in 2011 the Obama Administration loaned Colombia several billion dollars to build a refinery there, while it still opposes building one in this country. The government also loaned Brazil several billion dollars to develop offshore drilling there, while it opposes it in this country. In 2012 he blocked the development of the Keystone oil pipeline from Canada which would have brought oil in from Canada and created thousands of jobs. Does any of this make sense?

Moreover, his policies limiting energy production are just part of the effect of his policies. By running large fiscal deficits and having the Federal Reserve print excessive amounts of money through so-called "quantitative easing," he has caused the value of the US dollar to decline. Since oil is priced in dollars, this has contributed significantly to the increase in the price of oil. If one looks at charts tracking the value of the dollar and growth of the money supply, both align closely to the rise in the price of oil.

On May 11th, in a commencement address in Virginia, Obama actually said, "Information becomes a distraction, a diversion that is putting pressure on our country and on our democracy." The President said, "The class of 2010 is coming of age in a twenty-four-seven media environment that bombards us with all kinds of content and exposes us to all kinds of arguments, some of which don't always rank that high on the truth meter." He actually mentions truth, when his whole political career has been built on dissimulation. [166]

In summary, liberalism and collectivist ideologies derive their energy from emotion and instincts, not from the rational thought of independent individuals. The latter wouldn't provide the strong cement they seek for social cohesion. Liberals aren't interested in discovering or acknowledging truth. Liberalism is about the accumulation of power and its pursuit requires that truth is brushed aside. Liberalism thus represents a sharp break from the Hellenic tradition and its influence on Western culture. Socrates in particular was relentless in his pursuit of truth through open discussion, skepticism, and analysis. It was only through such a rigorous and open approach to dialogue that man could free himself from mistaken beliefs. This is as important from an individual standpoint as from that of society. What kind of world will we be living in if we succumb to an ideology committed to falsehood and mendacity rather than truth and reason? Living in a culture of lies and dissimulation would be a veritable Hell, a torture exercised on all.

* * *

CHAPTER 11

PATHOLOGY OF LIBERALISM AT THE LEVEL OF THE INDIVIDUAL

———————◆———————

Liberty means responsibility. That is why most men dread it.
~**George Bernard Shaw**

Man has to suffer. When he has no real afflictions, he invents some.

~**Jose Marti**

Freedom makes a huge requirement of every human being. With freedom comes responsibility. For the person who is unwilling to grow up, the person who is unwilling to carry his own weight, this is a frightening prospect.
~**Eleanor Roosevelt**

Remember always that you not only have the right to be an individual, you have an obligation to be one.
~**Eleanor Roosevelt**

Liberalism has problems with human psychology on three levels. First, the policies and goals of liberalism are based on mistaken assumptions and fundamental misconceptions about the nature of human psychology, and hence its assumptions lead to unworkable formulations for societal and economic policies. Second, liberalism fosters undesirable tendencies and poor behavior, while it discourages constructive behavior. Third, psychopathology underlies liberalism; pathologic psychologies are responsible for a large part of its political support. The supporters of liberalism are the dysfunctional, the losers, the free riders, the unhappy, the guilt-ridden, and the idealists untethered from reality. They are claimants on society, not those who make it strong. In sum, psychopathology is both a cause and effect of liberalism.

Perhaps the key failure of liberalism is its misguided understanding of human nature; this is at the root of many of its ill-founded conclusions. Plato and Kant saw human nature as intricately tied to reason, seeing it as our fundamental feature distinguishing us from other creatures. Marx perceived the economic basis of human nature, behavior, and thoughts, believing that the economic and institutional relations underlying our lives determine our nature. Freud, on the other hand, saw a key role for the unconscious mind as a determinant of our behavior and nature.

Liberals, like Marx, seem more interested in collective human psychology than in individual human psychology. They are more interested in the State than human beings. Liberals think human psychology is plastic; for liberals, humans are clay to be molded into a form that is consistent with the vision of the State. This is quite concordant with behaviorists like B.F. Skinner who believed human behavior was essentially determined by external conditioning. According to behaviorists, external incentives and disincentives largely shape human behavior.

Evolutionary psychologists, on the other hand, understand behavior differently than behaviorists. While the latter see human behavior as "learned from experience" and due to external conditioning, evolutionary psychologists believe that innate, evolutionary factors play an important part in determining how we behave. Konrad Lorenz, the most notable exponent of evolutionary psychology, emphasizes our evolutionary connection to other animals. Man, like other animals, has needed aggression, particularly in his early years, to survive. Without aggression, man wouldn't have survived as a species. This aggression is channeled not only to other creatures, but toward our own species. This instinct toward aggression helps explain the ubiquity of war and turmoil in the history of mankind. This evolutionary view of man doesn't easily reconcile with liberalism's benign view of man.

Conservatives subscribing to Judeo-Christian views believe human nature has both good and evil tendencies. For conservatives, the world as well as the human psyche is a battleground fought over by the forces of good and evil. Conservatives recognize the potential of humans for goodness, but they also understand the potential for evil. So in politics they believe in affording scope for the development of the good that resides in all of us, but they are also cautious about giving too much power to any of us, so as to limit the potential for the exercise of evil. Of course, the belief in evil doesn't need to be predicated on religious grounds. Joseph Conrad said, "The belief in supernatural sources of evil is not necessary: men alone are quite capable of each wickedness." Moreover, it's not just our underlying capacity for evil that is the problem, but that we seem so blithely ignorant of our own nature. Cicero recognized this long ago: "O wretched man, wretched not just because of what you are, but also because you do not know how wretched you are."

Liberals, as previously mentioned, don't believe in a binary world of good and evil, but rather a monistic world where we need to strive to create ever more harmony. They don't understand or believe in man's innate nature, but rather they believe he is a blank sheet, a *tabula rasa*, that can be written on and shaped at will. Man for them is malleable and can be easily molded. Conservatives see man shaping the State and society, whereas liberals see the State and society shaping man. This is why conservatism requires strong, thinking, rational and independent individuals, while liberalism requires weak, malleable individuals who aren't given to thinking about what leaders are saying and doing. In the liberal world, with the exception of the elite ruling class, man should be a follower.

Essentially the virtuous man is being redefined by liberalism. Traditionally, a good man was courageous, honest, hardworking, responsible and accountable for his actions, not lacking in will, irresponsible, lazy, unaccountable, dishonest, and unwilling to stand and fight for something. Under the assault of liberalism, altruism, empathy, compassion, and collaboration are exalted, while independence, hard work, responsibility, and accountability are now diminished. Self-discipline is no longer important. Conflict and competition and stress are to be avoided and discouraged. A man should try not to stand out; it's more important to get along and conform.

Liberals want to change society so that there are no longer losers, malcontents, or the irresponsible. It is strange that the policies they tout involve perverse incentives, so these bad behaviors are actually promoted and incentivized. This applies to drug addiction, hard work, sexual responsibility, and the like. Liberals think compassion will change everything. They believe people are malleable and plastic, susceptible to change—but even if this were true, it must be accomplished through the proper incentives and social and economic context. They appear to be behaviorists, but yet are employing perverse incentives to get change. This is a puzzle that defies comprehension.

It's interesting that liberals believe they can change society and the nature of individuals when they don't believe in individual responsibility or accountability for individuals. They see the life of the individual as being largely deterministic. That is to say, their behavior is shaped by social and environmental forces beyond their control. If an individual can't affect his own life, how can liberals argue that they can change the nature of society and individuals? On the scale of the collective, then, they are basically acknowledging that they escape the thrall of determinism. Perhaps the explanation is that they believe the common man is too stupid to affect his life, but that the elite— the smart people—can basically re-engineer not only themselves, but society, and the very nature of human beings themselves. Liberals are saying in effect, then, that the common man—really the stupid people—is totally malleable. He can be made into anything the liberal elite want, good or bad. There are strong assumptions here about not only human nature, but the influence of other unseen and not-understood forces that shape human behavior, as well as the ability of the liberal elite to engineer the wrenching change that they desire.

Having examined the faulty psychological assumptions underlying liberalism and its flawed assumptions concerning behaviorism, let's turn to the negative psychological traits of liberalism. Some of these negative traits are fostered by liberalism, while others provide liberalism its underlying support. Some play a role as both cause and effect. A few of these have already been discussed in earlier chapters, but I will expand upon these and explore additional traits as well.

Envy and Coveting

Envy is a primary motivating force in liberalism. Since antiquity, envy has been recognized as a vice. It's corrosive—a canker eating at the soul. With envy, one is unhappy when someone has something that one does not. The envious person sees injustice here, so, rather than being inspired to rise to the other person's level, they intend to bring the other person down.

Liberals speak of beneficent intent and goodwill, but genuine goodwill can't arise from a heart full of envy. Envy breeds hate and anti-social behavior. A heart filled with anger and hate is deaf to reason. This is a key factor behind the jettisoning of reason by the Left, and why so many liberals seem impervious to the influence of arguments. It's also a key factor behind the divisiveness of their politics.

The deadly sin of envy underlies liberal calls for redistributing income. One could argue for affecting the allocation of incomes in society on dispassionate analytic grounds, but this isn't the liberal way. Instead the liberal is outraged that certain members of society earn more income and have more wealth than others. There is a strong strain of class envy, where class is determined by income and wealth in America and not social class, as in Europe. The liberal is driven by divisions within society rather than commonality. He hates the rich. When President Obama compromised on extending the Bush tax cuts for those earning over $250,000, the Left went crazy.

According to the Tenth Commandment, "You shall not covet anything that is your neighbor's...you shall not desire your neighbor's house, his field, or his manservant, or his maidservant, or his ox, or his ass, or anything that is your neighbor's." Envy is the precursor and underlying motivation behind theft and disharmony amongst men. For Saint Augustine envy is "the diabolical sin." "From envy are born hatred, detraction, calumny, joy caused by the misfortune of a neighbor, and displeasure caused by his prosperity." It's a blight upon the human psyche and the community, but this is what liberalism promotes and encourages. It's the basis and the lifeblood of liberal politics.

People consumed by envy are never happy. There is always someone better off than they, and they are better off because of some unfairness. It's not justified. They are no better than I, but they have something I don't. Rather than look within themselves to understand what it is that would bring contentment, they look outside where no answers can be found. The thinking is *if only I could have that, then I would be happy.*

I have had jobs where there were many well-off and supposedly intelligent people, but most were consumed with envy. They saw others making more money or holding more prestigious positions, and they were unhappy. Moreover, even after working hard to attain that which they envied, they again became unhappy because, of course, someone else had even more. It's a never-ending cycle of unhappiness.

This is a fundamental and fatal flaw of liberalism. Envy is at the core of liberalism, but envy can't lead to the world of bliss that liberalism promises its followers. As indicated, envy leads to a never ending cycle of unhappiness. There is no portal for escape. Moreover, it brings down those who are the object of envy, bringing immiseration to them as well.

It doesn't matter to the liberal whether the money was earned or not. It's just not right. It's unfair. They in particular don't like people who made their money through commerce. Of course, the owners of Wal-Mart and McDonalds have done more for the poor than the programs created by liberals, but liberals don't see or understand this.

Aversion to Work and Achievement

Liberalism tarnishes achievement and the pursuit of excellence. Achievement and the pursuit of excellence distinguish some to the detriment of others. In trying to ensure that we are all more or less the same, it's a by-product of liberalism that we should try not to distinguish ourselves or show that we are superior to others. In communist China, they have a saying, "The nail that sticks out above others will be hammered down."

In the liberal world of the future, the road to personal advancement will not be through hard work and enterprise, but ingratiation to the powers that be. We will be at the mercy of those in power, so only by serving them will a good life be possible. We will avoid the discomfort of making decisions and assuming responsibility, but must find comfort in being told what we can and can't do.

In our market economy and in our society, rules and principles have been the foundational structure. This has been why games and sports have played such an important role in shaping our economy, social structure, and the individual human psyche. Liberals don't like the outcome of the game and want to change the rules or, really, do away with rules altogether and replace it with "benevolent" discretion. In fact they don't really like the idea of winners because this is elitist, and suggests some are better than others.

Legalized Theft—Penalizing the Successful

Underpinning liberalism is a desire to take from others via legalized theft. Liberals are saying it's OK to want not to pay. This is the entitlement culture. Intrinsic to this is an aversion to hard work and creating something of one's life. In this view, work is a burden; life should be easy. This is an interesting idea, since it is in many cases coming from liberals who have led lives of achievement and success. Somehow, what has worked for them—what has driven them—isn't applicable for others. They are saying it's OK not to want to work hard and achieve something. Such people should be rewarded for a lack of energy and drive. Inertia is good.

Those in government who are the engineers and the implementers of this legalized theft don't feel a pang of wrongness over what they are doing. They don't feel like "thieves in suits," but instead feel almost a moral smugness; they think they are doing the right thing. There is a disconnect from the underlying reality of what they are doing. They aren't troubled that they are benefitting from the process. They aren't troubled that legalized theft is underlying and financing their pay and benefits package, which is much higher than that of the private sector. They aren't troubled that money is taken from those who earned it to support those who did not, including themselves.

Under liberalism, the demanders of government services expect others to pay for their standard of living. This hurts our social mores, as people are no longer getting what they have earned. Those who have worked hard and contributed to the economy are penalized, while those who have not are rewarded. Moreover, given that the political system is used to commit legalized theft, the political process itself is fundamentally transformed; constructive political dialogue has given way to a divisive and fractious power struggle.

Liberals think America has moved ahead through fraud, injustice, and the expropriation of the resources of others. They view individuals who have gotten ahead in the same way; all are guilty of ill-gotten gains. Since their focus is on the vulnerable and the victims of society, the counterpart to this are the victimizers who must be those with the wealth and the power. So the wealthy are victimizers and oppressors. The liberal believes these people should give up their ill-gotten gains. If they demonstrate a reluctance to have the fruits of their labor taken from them and consumed by an inefficient bureaucracy or by people who have not earned it, they are further labeled as immoral and uncompassionate. They are expected to enthusiastically give up what they have earned. As Vice President Biden said, "It's their patriotic duty to want to pay more taxes."

In a global world those societies which limit the achievement and success of their citizens will be destined to be eclipsed and superseded by those who give achievers free reign. Liberals to the extent that they succeed will be consigning America to the dustbin of history.

Lack of Self-Esteem or Respect

In our traditional and established culture self-esteem must be earned. In contrast liberalism believes it should be given. It no longer must be earned. Liberals are pushing us away from our tradition of meritocracy. Merit is not important to liberals; in fact they distrust it. Respect in their world will come only when everyone (except, of course, the elite ruling class) is in similar material circumstances. This is enough for them. But it is a very materialistic understanding of self-respect.

In fact it seems that liberals are at war with respect. They don't seem comfortable with it. Respect arises out of admiration for achievement, extraordinary prowess, and the exercise of moral values. Liberals aren't comfortable with looking up to anyone or any set of values. This is why respect, which used to be everywhere in our society, has become a rare phenomenon. In today's world children don't respect their parents or their teachers. There is also very little respect for the law anymore, even by the government.

For liberals we should all get along and respect each other. Although by this they don't mean look up to one another. Rather they mean we shouldn't disrespect one another; we should all just let others do as they want. Essentially we should abandon value judgments. It's wrong to think that irresponsible people using drugs or having children out of wedlock are any less than we are. Essentially, it's wrong to expect others to live up to certain standards.

Respect and trust amongst individuals is declining. Government rules, regulations, and laws are replacing the religious and moral values that previously governed relations between people. The government and the justice system now intrude in the lives of people, affecting the way parents, teachers, and children interact, and even relations between spouses. A child can now sue a parent. A decline in the trust and faith between people can't be good, nor can replacing it with the control and surveillance of the State. This has all the marks of the development of an Orwellian state. This is a road toward stripping man of his identity and humanity.

Lack of Individual Responsibility and Accountability

The liberal has no faith in the strength of the individual. For the liberal, man isn't responsible for his actions. This is why liberals don't believe in punishment. Individuals are weak-willed and can't help themselves, so punishment isn't fair. Nothing is the individual's fault. It's always the "fault of the system," so this is why it's the system that should be fixed. Criminals aren't at fault. It's their background, their history, their cultural environment that cause their transgressions.

For the Left, bad behavior and bad motivation should be relieved of their bad consequences. The link between cause and effect should be severed. This doesn't mean that they don't believe in cause and effect. In fact it seems that they see everything as caught in a web of cause and effect, so that, in their view, the individual really has no control over his behavior.

In reducing our sense of responsibility and accountability, liberalism trivializes our moral agency, our self-determination, and our autonomy – what ontologically makes us humans, not animals. It doesn't expect us to make responsible choices and judgments and strips away our natural disposition to have values and make moral judgments.

The liberal idea that people shouldn't be punished because they aren't really responsible is the ultimate moral abdication, yet liberals pride themselves in their moral superiority and boast about it. Their belief in relativism leaves them without a moral compass—and without values.

For liberals it's OK that people pursuing irresponsible behavior pass their problems onto the rest of society. Others are forced to pay for their mistakes. This is the case whether we are talking about unwed mothers, drug abusers, or outright criminals. Our traditional moral code—that individuals should look after themselves and avoid encumbering others—is gone. The moral code of liberalism, however, favors those who don't care about what they are doing to others, or even to themselves.

Essentially liberalism subscribes to a system of perverse incentives. It penalizes those who succeed and act responsibly, while it rewards those who fail or won't even try. This makes some sense in their logic, since individuals aren't responsible for their own failure. It's not surprising that they don't think that successful individuals are responsible for their success. According to liberals, their success is determined by the system and forces beyond their control. Essentially in the liberal's logic, the individual doesn't determine his own fate. As Obama said to small business owners, "You didn't build that."

Childlike

Liberals have a child-like nature. They don't and won't recognize the consequences of their actions and values. For them it's enough to espouse values and try to impose their wishes on others. They aren't interested in praxis or the consequences of their actions. Liberals don't see complexity; everything is straightforward for them. Like a child, liberals are more driven by emotion and wants than by pragmatism. Really they are more like a rich child. They have a sense of entitlement. It's only right or fair that they have something. The liberal, like a child, demands that his wants are fulfilled, and is prone to tantrums of anger when they aren't. Like a child, the liberal doesn't want to be held accountable for his actions. He lives in a dream world divorced from reality and refuses to accept the real world.

Aversion to Decision-Making and Responsibility

Many people don't like decision making and choice and are averse to responsibility.[167] They prefer choice reduction or for the government to make decisions for them. This relieves them of the effort involved in making decisions and passes the risk and responsibility for making decisions onto the government. People who want to be told how to live are naturally dispositionally suited and inclined to totalitarian government. Many liberals are opting for dependency and an easy life over responsibility and self-sufficiency.

Enchantment with Celebrity

The public these days is enchanted and obsessed with celebrity. Many people, particularly the young, are fixated on becoming a celebrity, perhaps because it appears in many ways gratuitous, unearned. They don't want to work hard to earn money and fame. It should just happen. Many celebrities, perhaps because they are highly talented, make what they do look so easy, and so appear unearned. Celebrity appeals to the desire of the liberal to make it "the easy way," so for this reason they largely confine their ire to those who make their wealth in the business community. It is interesting that celebrities who are generally known for their poor values, narcissism, sexual promiscuity, financial prodigality, and ostentatious bad behavior have become our new heroes.

No Shame

There's no shame anymore in doing things which were formerly considered bad and immoral. In fact it's sometimes considered good in that it may bring attention. Celebrity is a key driving force for many people now, as it feeds the narcissism inherent in liberalism. Celebrity, even if it arises out of bad conduct, is considered a good thing. People are no longer embarrassed at having done something "bad," something which has hurt others.

Having values and morals is considered a hang-up to liberals. Free sex and drug indulgence is good in their eyes. Like anything else, they don't see the cost side of the ledger for these kinds of conduct.

Indulgence and Gluttony—Zero Time Preference

The essence of liberalism is pandering to the passions of the masses. Liberalism is served by men who are slaves to their passions, because such men can be made into slaves of the State. Liberals believe contemporary culture is too restraining of the appetites. The liberal wants his desires slaked—and slaked now. He has no patience, so he doesn't want to bide his time. His time preference approaches zero. Today is more important than the future. This is reflected in the spending patterns of Americans today. The savings rate is very low. Few are prepared for retirement.

Life involves trade-offs. If one wants a more comfortable future, he needs to sacrifice today. Liberals can't endure curtailed enjoyment or sacrifice today; society should give them everything now, even if it comes from someone else.

Edison said genius is ninety-nine percent perspiration and one percent inspiration. Hard work and assiduity is fundamental to succeeding. We all admire the achievements of the super athlete, the skilled musician, or the successful businessman, but aren't willing to strive ourselves. For liberals, work gets in the way of life. One shouldn't have to work hard. Life is about pleasure: consuming and indulging, not creating and producing.

You can't have everything. Expanded health care and a glorious metro system are nice, but at what cost? Liberals don't comprehend the cost side of the picture; it's like they're numbers-illiterate, like many of the people who took on mortgages that they could not afford.

Liberalism supports those who want to consume more than they produce, while it disadvantages those trying to live responsibly. Almost all liberal interventions favor indulgence over striving for success. Even the monetary policy of liberalism, imposing a low-interest rate regime, hurts savers and helps borrowers.

The more well-off liberal doesn't understand that, due to liberal policies in which the masses or disadvantaged are going to get more, his own standard of living is going to go down. They could, of course, give directly to improve the life of others, but in fact liberals give less to charity than conservatives. They don't understand that the policies they recommend will lead to a general economic decline, leaving most everyone worse off.

Although they publicly profess otherwise, liberals favor themselves and this generation over future generations. Just look at the excessive spending and borrowing that is such an integral part of liberalism. We are living beyond our means today at the expense of our children. The borrowing and consequent accumulation of debt is something our children and their children will deal with. We're enjoying a feast, but our progeny will be left with the bill. Although they cloak themselves in altruism and compassion, liberals are self-absorbed and narcissistic.

We even see this indulgence in our weight. For the last forty years Americans have been getting fatter and fatter. Even children today are encountering significant problems with weight. We all recognize that obesity isn't good for us and that it also carries a stigma. Nevertheless, we can't help ourselves. We are weak and slaves to our appetites. A similar argument can be used about smoking. We are trading off our future for present indulgence and gluttony.

For liberals, freedom is doing what you want to without obligation. Thus sexual liberation has freed sex from obligation and marriage. Sex should merely be for pleasure. It's an indulgence, not a responsibility, to conduct without regard for others and the effect on society. The snuffed-out lives of aborted babies are just the necessary debris of this inclination to indulgence.

Liberals tout freedom, but have essentially entered a Faustian bargain. They are trading greater freedom today for collective enslavement tomorrow. Some don't recognize the quid pro quo that collective enslavement is coming; others do but don't care or even crave it. Some are in denial. The fact that liberalism has suspended or occluded the power of independent thinking makes it hard for them to see the harsh reality of what they are doing. Of course, this Faustian bargain is almost costless for this generation, but it won't be for future generations.

Deceit and Dishonesty

There is an immorality implicit in liberal behavior and thinking in that it's rooted in an ends-justifies-the-means mentality and modus operandi; liberals are willing to lie and employ deceit to accomplish their objectives. Straightforwardness, integrity, and honesty aren't worthwhile traits, but rather points of weakness that can be exploited. We have seen example after example of this. The most conspicuous example was Obama's deceit in pushing his health reform bill through Congress, but we really need look no further than his inaugural oath. In the inaugural he promised under oath to protect and defend the Constitution of the United States. He did this even though he has made clear that he sees the Constitution as an obstacle to his liberal agenda. Below are Obama's words expressed in 2001 on a Chicago radio station.

"The Supreme Court never ventured into the issues of redistribution of wealth and sort of more basic issues of political and economic justice in this society. And to that extent, as radical as I think people tried to characterize the Warren Court, it wasn't that radical. It didn't break free from the essential constraints that were placed by the founding fathers in the Constitution, as least as it's been interpreted, and [sic] Warren Court interpreted in the same way that, generally, the Constitution is a charter of negative liberties, says what the states can't do to you, says what the federal government can't do to you, but it doesn't say what the federal government or the state government must do on your behalf."[168]

Obama clearly does not like the Constitution, and his actions show that he is doing everything in his power to marginalize it. Yet he promised to protect and defend it. In his campaign for the presidency, Obama concealed his radical views and denounced ideology, saying he would be president of all the people, but he has not lived up to his words.

On a lying scale of one to four, legendary liberal Washington Post writer Bob Woodward gave Obama four out of four Pinnochios for lying about the "Sequester." Obama repeatedly tried to pin the blame for the fiasco of the poorly designed budget-cutting legislation on Republicans, but Woodward revealed facts showing that Obama had initiated it.[169]

An interesting problem is that liars frequently end-up believing their own lies. In fact this is almost psychologically necessary in order to have a coherent vision of the world. This puts them at an even further remove from reality. Moreover, it makes them even more hostile to rational dialogue, and it creates feelings of insecurity as their world does not hang together, and sub-consciously they know it.

Averse to Reason and Uncertainty

Because liberals are so focused on achieving their goals at all costs, they dislike using independent thinking and critical analysis in arriving at conclusions. They don't look at issues from multiple angles. Commitment to independent inquiry means starting out unsure of the conclusion that you will arrive at. Liberals are afraid of taking a road with an uncertain destination.

If the goal is "good," that's enough for them. They are averse to analysis and careful consideration of the many effects a particular action will have. In this sense liberals have an aversion to complexity, messiness, and uncertainty.

Liberals are optimistic about a better future. They think a better world can be created, but they don't know how to get from here to where they want to go. They are goal-oriented, not process-oriented. It's as though they see the promised land and are simply convinced that we can magically arrive there.

Reason isn't a hallmark of liberal perspectives so this inconsistency isn't that surprising. It is passion for change, almost out of desperation and frustration with life that drives them. The daunting task of jumping over this large logical chasm between what they want and reality perhaps underscores the depth of the desperation and frustration that they feel.

Driven by Anger

There are several explanations for liberal anger: It is an expeditious instrument to fight off opposing views without having to rationally engage them. Since liberals cannot defend their positions on rational grounds, they naturally get unsettled and irritated when pressed. Moreover, liberals view their positions as principally determined by morality and compassion, so it is natural for them to get angry at anyone opposing their positions, as such views would be seen as immoral and mean. Moreover, since their positions are arrived at principally through consensuality, rather than reason, challenges to these views are seen as a threat to group cohesiveness and hence must be defended vigorously. The emotional foundation of liberal views makes them particularly prone to ventings of rage.

Unfortunately, when one is fully consumed by anger, one can't see oneself. Perspective and a sense of balance are lost. Perception, not only of external factors and issues, but also of oneself, is critical to rising above anger. This is why the abandonment of critical thinking is fundamental. Moreover, the process feeds on itself. There is a vicious circle going on where anger results in the dismissal of reason, while at the same time a lack of appreciation for reason makes it difficult to rise above anger.

Herd Mentality

As mentioned earlier, Ann Coulter in her recent book, *Demonic*, emphasized the mob dynamic in the way liberals think. It seems that what liberals need in a mob or from a mob is a sense of strength, connectedness, a sense of power, and a sense of righteousness, all things missing in their private lives. The liberal, feeling insecure and alone, seeks the comfort of belonging to a larger group, abandoning his critical thinking for the sake of security.

Moral Smugness

Liberal rhetoric and thinking is laden with moral tone and a strong emphasis on "rightness" and "wrongness." As a result, liberals easily fall into fits of moral outrage if others disagree with them or hold other views. Their commitment to stances is almost fundamentalist. Yet despite the high content of moral tone, there is almost no real moral *content*. Morality makes little sense once one commits to an ends-justifies-the-means mentality.

Need for Oneness and Collectivity

It's almost as if liberals have not gotten over leaving the womb, like they're suffering a lasting trauma from the experience. They have this seemingly unquenchable need for oneness, a need to be part of a larger collective. Perhaps this reflects a greater sense of alienation and loneliness than affects the rest of us. Or perhaps it simply reflects unhappiness and a need for change, a need to feel secure and have someone look after them. Perhaps they simply don't want to brook the onus of having to make decisions. Capitalism and market oriented economies do involve a lot of decision making. There are advantages to this, but there is the negative weight or burden of having to make these decisions. Decision making isn't easy and involves psychological stress.

Hypocrisy

Another weakness of liberalism is the intrinsic hypocrisy. Liberals decry the unequal distribution of income and wealth and continually parade their compassion for the poor, yet the vast majority of their leaders continue to live lives of luxury. Those liberals who give directly to the poor out of their own pockets and who reduce their own standard of living to help others are to be respected. Unfortunately, most liberals (as noted in Chapter 4) cry about the poor, but do nothing about it except ask others to contribute.

It's interesting that many of these liberals, like elite figures in the entertainment field and politics, lead lives of luxury that the common man would find difficult to imagine even in his dreams. Yet these same people rail against materialism and the indulgences of others. It's also interesting that many celebrities in entertainment loudly denunciate gun ownership as contributing to violence, but are part of a media industry suffused with violence. And it is amusing to hear these celebrities venting in high moral tones, while living lives of dissolution. They also fulminate about global warming, while leaving an enormous carbon footprint themselves. The hypocrisy here is stark and needs no comment.

Trivialized Lives and Commitment Problems

Liberalism fosters and supports individuals who lead shallow, commitment-free, trivialized lives. These individuals are afraid to make value judgments and averse to making themselves stand out from others. They want to be friends with everyone, but end up friends with no one. Many young people today boast of thousands of friends on Facebook, but in reality have few or no real friends. It's no accident that the seat of liberalism is in urban areas, where commitment problems are the greatest. Liberals can be seen as creating the kind of alienation that they have always ascribed to capitalism. The difference is that capitalism creates strong individuals; liberalism, weak ones.

Sex has served an important role in society: it provides new humans and connects people together in families—but under liberalism this role has been diminished. Sex is losing its power as an influence in connecting the lives of people together. Sex is now more of an individual thing. A recent study, for example, has shown that interest in sex has declined significantly in Japan.[170] According to the report, "A whopping thirty-six percent of teenage boys between the ages of sixteen to nineteen said they had little to no interest in sex, and in some cases even despised it." This is almost a twenty percent increase over the 2008. This sounds incredible, but perhaps it's not surprising since sex is no longer serving a role in connecting the lives of people together.

Liberalism breaks down families and, by making sex into a commodity, depreciates relations between the sexes. It encourages fleeting relationships and avoidance of long-term commitments. Commitment avoidance is a common feature of a liberal, and it's a direct by-product of liberal policies, and their largely urban lifestyles.

By weakening the family and enhancing the disconnect between people, as well as gutting individuality, the State is creating an environment where people will lead solitary and lonely lives. The State will control such people. Like in Catholicism, where priests are proscribed from marrying so they can dedicate themselves and their lives to the church, the State is positioning singles to dedicate themselves and their lives to the State. The individual will have no one else to turn to.

With the role of the family diminished the influence of parents and family on children is decreasing. This has reduced the extent to which parents can pass on their values to their children. The school system is increasingly taking over the role of parents in teaching about values. Liberals push their political views on children in schools.

Empty Compassion

Liberals place compassion above all else, but it's not compassion on a small or local level, but on a grand dehumanized scale. It's not compassion for a particular individual, but rather for an abstract group or mass of people consigned to victimhood status. So, relations between people are more distant. It's the State that gives and exercises compassion, not the individual. Individuals are supposed to have their bond with the State, not with each other, as the latter is a threat and an impediment to State power.

Control-Freak Personalities and Aversion to Reality

Liberals want everything in life to be neatly organized and in its place. Control- freak personalities are perfectionistic; the real world is too messy and disorganized for them, so they want to create a utopia, a perfect world. We would all like everything to be perfect, and strive to make life the best we can, but we can't deny the world as it is. The liberal mindset, however, does just this. This is perhaps why so many in academia and the entertainment industry are liberal: they have an aversion to the real world, they have taken refuge from it. They don't want to work in the real world, only in their ivory towers and the theaters. These utopians don't have an understanding of how the real world works. Moreover, amazingly they don't understand how we are supposed to move from today's reality to their utopia; they just want it, and think they should have it. And, like a baby, they throw a tantrum when they don't get what they want.

Weak-Willed Individuals

Liberals favor weak-willed individuals as they aren't able to effectively contravene the power of the State. By stripping away the power of reason and weakening the pursuit of truth, the State tries to limit the tools by which individuals can challenge the State. It also seeks to undermine his commitment to moral principles, as these too can be a threat to the ruling class.

That liberals think individuals can't make it on their own is atavistic. Early in civilization, humans did band together in warfare against other tribes and for the hunt. Individualism did not exist early in civilization. It really began to emerge with the advent of capitalism, which broke the chains and constraints on life imposed by feudalism. Under feudalism and pre-capitalist society, the individual was just a tool of those in power. Those who were not in the elite led miserable lives. Capitalism and the spread of material wealth led to a vast improvement in the lives of those outside the exercise of overt political power. Instead of recognizing this, liberals believe capitalism and its derivative materialism are evil, a blight on mankind.

Whereas Aristotle and Ayn Rand put the development of the individual as the highest goal for society, liberalism works against the flourishing of the individual.[171] Liberalism prefers the whole to the individual, the State to the individual. The altruist believes the individual should subordinate his interests to the State. The implication is that the individual is working against his own self-interest, and that he doesn't value others and wouldn't help others unless constrained or coerced to do so. Liberals are cynical that people genuinely are interested in the welfare of others and would do this on a sufficient scale in a market-based economy.

In the utopia envisioned by liberalism, the individual is emasculated, beaten down, and emptied out. The individual is already a slave to his passions, so in the liberal's world he would be better off if he were to become, instead, a servant of the State.

Liberalism works to hollow out the individual, corrupt him, take away his integrity, his sense of self, his sense of control over his own future, and his value. He becomes nothing, a mere instrument of the State. In China, and other statist societies, there is little concern about the value of a human life. Individuals are expendable, used up by the State. The March of Progress is more important. Even the elite government heads in Russia and China are faceless, almost robotic, and machine-like.

Liberalism is trying to change man into a docile, obedient creature without passions, so that he will be better able to serve the State. It is one thing for liberals to say that they are going to change the nature of man, and it's another thing to do it. Despite the significant advances in understanding the psychological and biological nature of man, we really don't know much. We certainly don't know enough to fundamentally re-engineer ourselves. Man will remain a creature with passions, driven largely by self-interest and unconscious psychological forces. We may wish otherwise, but we can't change our nature through wishes. If the liberal program tries to suppress our true nature, it will only channel it in ways we can't anticipate. Liberals want to replace competition with co-operation, but we need an environment of competition to fulfill our basic emotional drives, whether it's on the field of sport, the marketplace, or in the political arena. It's better to allow a natural expression of our drives than to see them rechanneled and manifested in less constructive ways. Suppression of our basic nature can only lead to unhappiness and pathology at the level of the individual which would result in adverse outcomes on society as well.

To the extent that liberal government is basically government for the weak, the poor, and the underperforming members of society, it's basically a government for the victims and those unable to adapt to life. In an international environment, it would tend to draw losers and those asking for a handout, rather than emigrants who could contribute to society and make it dynamic. Much like San Francisco and other cities that offer attractive social benefits for the needy and the homeless, the nation would become a mecca for malcontents and those unable to make it on their own. If the Left were successful in achieving its declared goals, we would have a society suited to and perhaps run by dysfunctionals. Of course, the real outcome would be traditional oppression by the ruling elite, but this would be done in the name of the weak and the dissolute.

By knocking down those who succeed, indeed by disparaging them and casting them in a light of injustice, liberals would not only hurt the advancement of man, but make men smaller. Those who succeed bring light and positive energy to mankind. By diminishing them and dampening their energy and luminescence, we are hurting all men.

Liberalism stifles human flourishing. Aristotle, as mentioned, felt that the primary role of government should be to allow for the flourishing of man. He wanted to see government creating the conditions necessary for unleashing the talents of men. He wanted men to reach their full potential. Liberalism stunts this growth and limits the individual expression of our uniqueness in the name of a greater state. Men are different and unique; we all have different potentials within us, but must be free to cultivate this uniqueness, otherwise we become like mannequins, superficial, and all alike. According to liberalism, men should stay in the harness of the State, working for the greater good, and not for themselves or their own development. For liberals, equality, conformity, and the ability to express and hopefully feel compassion are utmost.

In the liberal world, morality doesn't originate from individuals setting their own values and making judgments about right or wrong. Under liberalism the individual is a mere cog in the machine. The State sets the moral standards—and administers them. Moral education, or brainwashing, is applied in the public school system and the media and government constantly write and talk about what is appropriate behavior and what isn't. The State sets in law the rights which constitute appropriate behavior. It uses the court system and regulations to make sure the public acts in the right way. Essentially, in the liberal's world, the individual can't be trusted to do the right thing or to make the right decisions. He must be constrained like a horse in harness. Liberal ideology in effect reduces man to an animal. His intellect, power to reason, exercise of judgment, and his moral agency are all tossed aside as not only unhelpful, but injurious.

The State is taking a position on what type of personality and behavior is preferable. The State, through its impact on incentives, is altering the types of personalities that predominate in society. Should this be the role of the State?

Political correctness prevents us from saying or even thinking some deeply felt feelings and perspectives. We have even begun to doubt ourselves, to regulate ourselves, so that our minds, emotions, and instincts are suppressed. We now distrust our basic instincts and emotions. The natural within us is no longer natural. So political correctness isn't only affecting our external freedom, but our internal freedom; our ability to be ourselves is compromised. The essence of individuality is corrupted and diminished. This has implications for society, not just individuals.

Man Subservient to the State

Liberals think man is soulless and driven by appetites; conservatives think man is unique, has an individual soul, and is capable of transcendence. For liberals man is one of many parts; he is expendable for the sake of society. He exists solely for the sake of serving collective society. But for conservatives, each man is special and capable of truly great achievements. Each man's life is precious and shouldn't be sacrificed for society. Society lives through the individual. By debasing the individual, society debases itself.

In today's liberal world, the public mind has shifted from a sense of governing to being governed. The government no longer reflects the will of the people. The ruling class is now in charge, and they're beginning to run away with our government and, with it, our way of life.

Liberals claim to be oriented to the future and to change. But to the extent that they are intent on putting the individual back in thrall to the State, they are retrogressive. By diminishing the role of reason, they are turning back the clock. Man has an inherent susceptibility to servitude, to becoming a slave. There are always those who want to gain power over others. They do it through guile nowadays, not force. They use compassion, a false sense of righteousness, a call to serve mankind, and a call to help save the earth. They use people's inclination to do good to bind them in servitude.

Fear of Inferiority

The Left is intent on eradicating feelings of superiority and inferiority from the psyches of individuals. Some individuals shouldn't have more than others and shouldn't consider themselves or be considered by others as superior. A lot of the animus and ideology of liberalism derives from a fear of inferiority. But rather than strive to overcome perceived shortcomings, the liberal mind is intent on harming those of "superiority" to level the playing field. This is perhaps why liberals don't seem concerned about diminished economic growth prospects, which are clearly caused by their policies. For them, it's OK if the overall wealth of society declines so long as differences among members are narrowed.

Alfred Adler noted, "The greater the feeling of inferiority that has been experienced, the more powerful is the urge to conquest and the more violent the emotional agitation." The liberal political program wants to exaggerate and inflame feelings of inferiority and victimhood to advance their quest to power.

Fear of Difference and Diversity

In attacking superiority and success, liberals are basically diminishing the brightness of diversity and the development of each individual's unique potential. The liberal agenda is intent on bringing about a gray society where homogeneity is the rule. They even seem intent on bringing about a gender-neutral society, in which natural and biological differences between men and women are discounted. They don't want differences between people, economic or otherwise. It should be a society free of envy, where diversity isn't celebrated but decried.

Obsession with Security

Liberalism seemingly prizes security above all else. Is man really happy in an environment with no challenges or risks? Is an American Indian living on a reservation happier than his ancestors who lived free in the wild? Anyone who has been to an Indian reservation or who is aware of the social statistics concerning alcohol and drug addiction as well as crime and suicide rates knows the answer. Were people happy in the USSR? Mao's China? or Fidel's Cuba? Although challenge and risk have their downside, as there are losers as well as winners, challenges are what make life worth living.

Surmounting challenge is the essence of real happiness and life fulfillment: we see this whether it's a mountain climber reaching the summit, a football player winning the Super Bowl, or a scientist winning the Nobel Prize. Moreover, the public at large is inspired by those who reach great heights and overcome risk and challenge. Children are driven by dreams. Do we really want to squash the dreams of man and child?

A government security blanket isn't the answer. Fear of failure shouldn't be what drives national policy. As FDR is famously quoted as saying, "The only thing we must fear is fear itself." Rather than focus on failure, the national interest would be better served focusing on success. As JFK said, "America should strive to put a man on the moon, not because it's easy, but because it's hard."

A secure life is a boring life. Scope for spontaneity is important. Over-organization is stifling. A life devoid of adrenalin surges is a life constrained and cut short. It's like putting a bird in a cage. The bird may be safer in the cage, but he isn't living. Man, or any creature for that matter, isn't meant to be tethered and constrained.

No Heroes Anymore

There are no heroes anymore, only celebrities. In fact the bad guys are celebrated more than the good guys nowadays. Strength and success and virtue are no longer respected; they are outdated, boring, and inauthentic. This is so, in part, because the Left doesn't believe in good and evil. In the perspective of liberalism, everything is relative and all behavior is justified by external factors—so individuals deserve neither credit or blame for their actions. So, not only are there no heroes anymore, there are no villains either. Moral relativism doesn't exalt any behavior above another.

Man doesn't reach his full potential by shrinking from a challenge. He may have a fear of failure, but he isn't defeated by it. In fact it's only through failure that people ultimately succeed. No one is successful without experiencing failure. It's only through failure that we learn what we are doing wrong. It allows us to get better. Failure helps us direct our lives. A young boy may find that he isn't good at sports and consequently he may continue to search for something that is suited to his talents. Over time, and through experience, he will find the right path and vocation. Each of us has innate abilities as well as innate disabilities. The experience of failure helps to guide and direct us toward our innate abilities and to realizing our maximum potential.

Man's nature needs adventure. If challenge and development is circumscribed and smothered by a socialist nanny state, he will be driven to an interior world of fantasy increasingly disconnected from reality, particularly with the game technologies available now.

Underestimation of Man's Capacity for Evil

Man's psychological make-up isn't much changed from that of our early ancestors. Our instincts, emotional constitution, and behavior are deeply rooted in the past, while our cultural and technical environments have changed drastically. Man's capacity for both good and evil is well documented in history. We can't presume it is a thing of the past. Evil is in our nature as well as good. It can't simply be banished and assumed away as liberals would like.

The effort of liberalism to construct a new political, social, and economic polity based on a misunderstanding of the nature of man can't succeed. You can't force square pegs into round holes, and you can't force man to adapt in ways inconsistent with his nature. Virtue is acting according to nature.

Lack of Courage

Liberals lack courage to stand up to conflict. They prefer to appease and do nothing and hope the problem will go away. President Clinton did nothing to stop Osama Bin Laden despite a continued escalation in his attacks. War is to be avoided if at all possible, but liberals don't believe it is necessary under any circumstance. This lack of courage was also exemplified in the Fatwa issued against Salmon Rushdie by Arabs who felt he had put Mohammed in a bad light. The West did not stand up and say this was unacceptable.

Free Sex

In the short term, liberalism is bringing about an atomization of life, while at the same time professing the virtues of collectivism. Liberalism is promoting a form of freedom, wherein the individual can do almost anything to satisfy his hedonistic proclivities. They don't understand or care that free sex and drug use affects society. This, to a certain extent, is consistent with their idea that family life and religion don't matter.

The Left promotes sexual freedom and homosexuality. They aren't just asking for increased tolerance of homosexuality, but are actively promoting it in the classrooms and on television. Homosexuality carries with it a lot less communal responsibility than heterosexual behavior with its connection to family and procreation. The Left promotes an anything-goes, no-strings-attached sexual morality. Now there's less emotional and moral connection between people, not more. Confidence and trust in others is waning. This form of sexual freedom treats others like commodities, things to be used up and discarded. The liberal agenda brings about a lack of depth in people and in their relationships. Shallowness and triviality become the mark of individual lives.

Unhappy and Disgruntled

The liberal sees oppression and injustice in all spheres of life; economic, political, and social; he sees this in his life and in the lives of others, so he is by nature unhappy and disgruntled, burdened with grievances and the need to bring about change. The status quo isn't good enough for him; he wants something different. He, of course, isn't the problem. He doesn't need to change; it's others who need to change; the system should change. It's everything else that is out of whack; he is as well, but it's not his fault.

Liberals want to change society because they aren't happy. To propose societal change merely on the basis of being unhappy doesn't make sense. One should have a proposal for positive change based on a well thought out strategy and not proceed to seek change simply for change's sake. To propose a model that has failed historically isn't a sound basis to move forward. Nor does "hope and change" work. Obama has proven that.

In my travels I have seen much of the world, and I know how lucky I am to have been born an American. Anyone born in this country has won the birth lottery. If I had been born in the Sudan or Malawi, for instance, my life would have been totally different. The liberal has no idea how lucky he is to be an American. Amazingly, not only is he not grateful, he is actually resentful.

Self-Hatred and Unhappiness

Liberals are consumed by a dislike of themselves and those around them. Just look at the guilt that permeates their rhetoric and lives. Self-hatred is a central feature of the liberal personality. It in turn usually reflects the failure of individuals to develop the way they would like. Of course, out of a group of people you would expect to find some who are happy and some who aren't, just like you would expect some to be thin and some to be fat. Nevertheless it makes no sense to try to turn society upside down because some people are unhappy. Would such people be happy under different social circumstances? It would be highly unlikely that they would be. It's probably not possible to have a society in which everyone is happy. Moreover, would this even be desirable?

The liberal sees most people as helpless and unable to fend for themselves. They think the world is a rough and tumble place where people need help to make it. Ours isn't a beneficent world where life can be fun, rewarding, and manageable. It is a miserable place where we must band together if we are to make it. The liberal resents life and those who are able to make it and be happy.

Negativism

For liberals nothing is good; there is only suffering and victimization. Liberalism arises out of negativism, not optimism. The liberal always sees something wrong that should be fixed, righted.

Alienation

The liberal suffers from a sense of alienation and discomfort in living in the existing cultural environment. He doesn't feel connected to others, so he is driven to connect and to feel part of the crowd. He doesn't want to feel alone. He is bored and drawn to the almost electric charge of mass politics, to the smell of a mob and its irrational spell, throbbing with raw tribal emotional animus. It is like a draw from a more raw and primitive past.

Liberalism results in alienation as individuals increasingly find they can only relate to people as abstractions. In addition, people become less interesting and less excited about developing their potential and the value of human relationships wanes. A diminished sense of self-worth and confidence and a sense that people can't make it without government help naturally leaves people feeling insecure and vulnerable.

Disposed to Majority Tyranny

Liberalism encourages a tyranny of the majority. Bertrand Russell, a brilliant philosopher and socialist as well, warned eloquently of this threat: "This will only be avoided if liberty is as much valued as democracy, and it's realized that a society in which each is the slave of all is only a little better than one in which each is the slave of a despot. There is equality where all are slaves, as well as where all are free. This shows that equality, by itself, isn't enough to make a good society."[172] Although an avowed socialist, Bertrand Russell, nonetheless recognized the threat of excessive authority and control, as well as the threat implicit in the drive for equality. Today's liberals, by contrast, are blithely unaware of any potential costs or negative aspects of liberalism and the growth of centralized power. They lack caution about the fundamental changes they are bringing about. This makes them particularly dangerous, as they are operating without an analytic frame of mind and without the ballast of reason.

Philosopher Jeff Malpas captures the essence and meaning of true liberty in his work, *Death and the Unity of Life.*

To live life fully one must have a "sense of self-awareness, self-conception, and self-direction."[173] He stresses that "the having of a life is not only a matter of grasping one's life as one's own, but is also a matter of one's own making of that life, both of which converge in the capacity to understand that life within some narrative frame."[174] Life is fundamentally about making choices. This is how life is wrought, shaped and developed. Liberalism is engaged in a direct assault on individualism and liberty through its massive expansion and intrusion of government, the dismantling of rationalism, cradle to grave paternalism, and its drive for conformity, harmony, and subservience. Liberalism is about reduction of choice for individuals and about limiting the ability for self-development. Under liberalism the government is usurping choice from individuals, leaving them essentially empty vessels. Having a life is also about taking responsibility. Through its agenda of perverse incentives, rewarding the irresponsible while penalizing the responsible, liberalism is also vitiating this essential component of liberty. Without responsibility liberty can clearly be destructive to both individuals and society. The subversion of American individualism and liberty could not be clearer.

Guilt

Liberalism leaves the individual plagued by guilt and cynicism as he realizes that the altruist morality doesn't work and that he can't measure up to it in his own life. He falls far short in practicing it in his own life. He feels guilty because he pursues his self-interest—which is human nature. The liberal, however, can't accept this reality. For him there is something unwholesome about pursuing one's own interest.

But it's human nature to enjoy oneself. Humans all over the world crave the material comforts we have, but liberals think this unsavory. However, this is the will of the people as expressed in their actions. But, of course, for liberals these are the unwashed masses who aren't smart enough to know what is best for them.

Aversion to Reality

Liberals have difficulty adjusting themselves to reality. As T.S. Eliot said, "Humankind can't stand much reality." Because they don't adjust well to reality, it's not surprising that many are uncomfortable with their lives and are unhappy.

Liberalism's divorce from reality is similar to the mentalities associated with smoking and drug use. Both smokers and drug users must be aware of the statistics and the likely harm these will have on their health, but they choose to ignore it and pretend it's not real. Drugs help them to gain an even greater remove from reality. It's easier for these people to take drugs if they feel unhappy than to try to take action in the real world to address their problems. Similarly, liberals continue to overspend and run up the national debt, in effect living beyond their means, while they are in denial that this will have any adverse consequences.

Nathaniel Branden once noted, "For the rational, psychologically healthy man, the desire for pleasure is the desire to celebrate his control over reality. For the neurotic, the desire for pleasure is the desire to escape from reality. "All of us are given to the attraction of dream worlds from time to time. Dreaming is psychologically healthy. There is a problem, however, if one cannot exit the dream and re-enter the real world. Moreover, it is one thing for an individual to be lost in a dream world as the effect is likely to be largely a personal problem, but the problem with liberals is they insist that the rest of humanity become part of their dream. They insist on inflicting their "reality" on the rest of us whether we like it or not. Their dream world may have the appearance of benign idealism, but make no mistake it's a devastating pathological force driven by a need and desire to control others. It is all about control, and unfortunately their dreams have a history of becoming nightmares. As Daniel J. Boorstin once remarked, "We suffer not from our vices or our weaknesses, but from our illusions. We are haunted not by reality, but by those images we have put in their place."

Elitism and Intellectual Arrogance

Liberalism is suffused with intellectual arrogance; liberals think they know better than everyone else. Moreover, they know how other people should live their lives. People are too stupid to know what is good for them. Many liberals, especially those from the media, academia, and the political elite, have gone to elite schools and feel themselves superior to most Americans. For liberals the public can't be trusted.

This explains why the liberal media has no compunction about giving the public misleading information. Distortion and prevarication are necessary tools to bring the public to the right views. Deceit and lying is OK, particularly, if it's to infidels and the ignorant.

Moral Arrogance

Liberals think they're morally superior to the public, to conservatives, and to anyone who disagrees with them. If someone disagrees with them, they're a *bigot*. From his high perch, the liberal doesn't see the public as even worthy of engagement. He looks with disdain and contempt on the public. This rancorous patronizing attitude blocks any possibility for real discussion or dialogue. This is unlike conservatives who don't hate liberals. Conservatives see liberals as good, well-intentioned people. They simply don't agree with their policies. However, the moral and intellectual contempt felt by liberals toward conservatives is palpable. They genuinely think that conservatives are bad people. They see them as immoral and intellectually stunted. For liberals, conservatives stand in the way of achieving a moral good and need to be forcefully brushed aside.

Spiritual Deficit

Under the liberal agenda the State is to replace God and religion. Like in the USSR, however, the replacement lacks a spiritual dimension—it's essentially secular. This explains in part an almost messianic emphasis on compassion, because they need this to bring the public's emotions into the service of the State. Liberalism diminishes and destroys faith and spirituality, but isn't able to successfully replace it with faith in the State.

Suppressed Artistic Development

Artistic development, expression, and achievement are stifled in a collectivist environment, where the individual is subordinated. The arts are about the pursuit of uniqueness of self, not about conformity. When individuality was given center stage in America early in our history and through the 1960s, art flourished. In the 60s we had Hemingway and Faulkner, Louis Armstrong, Elvis Presley and rock and roll. Architecture was avant-garde and adventurous. Frank Gehry, the well-known architect who designed the Guggenheim Museum, says that the expressionist period of architecture has come to a screeching halt—now the emphasis is on functional, prosaic, and sustainable designs.[175] With the ascent of liberalism and the weakening of individuality, we have seen a general decline in creativity, artistic expression, and achievement in America. Artistic expression is important to the health of individuals and to society. To the extent that art is suppressed or adversely affected, our welfare is diminished. It's a warning sign that things aren't right.

Neuroticism and Fear of Freedom

As mentioned at the beginning of this chapter, pathologic psychologies lie at the root of liberalism. In this connection, fear of freedom and self-destructive tendencies play an unmistakably important role.

Many thinkers and philosophers have noted that man's emotional and psychological nature is still rooted to the pre-modern period, while his technical prowess and intellectual capacity is firmly established in the advanced world of today. Our emotional capacities no longer match or work well in the modern environment. It is emotionally difficult to come to grips with our newfound freedoms. We have the ability to flourish as individuals, but many are uncomfortable with the new environment and want to return to totalitarian-collectivist ways of living. Living with freedom requires strength, courage, and a sense of responsibility to others and to oneself. Many don't have this psychological strength, and are thus inclined to social and political environments where the role of the individual is reduced to that of an automaton.

If you don't care about your freedom and aren't willing to fight for it, there are those who are ready and waiting to take it from you. There are many who love power and love to control others. Whether at the national level, the community, the office, the family, or just in a meeting, there are always those who want to be top dog and impose their views or agenda on others. Unfortunately, those who are willing to cede control of their life and freedom to others inflict collateral damage on those who do value their freedom. As the power mongers expand their power this hurts and threatens everyone.

Erich Fromm, a famous psychoanalyst and socialist in the twentieth century, focused a great deal on alienation. He was concerned that many persons suffered from a feeling of disconnect from reality and uncertainty even about their own identity. Those suffering from alienation had difficulty relating to their culture and were in fact quite critical of it. These persons sought connectedness to something larger than themselves; they sought identity and were prone to idolatry and transcendence, although of a non-religious kind. Unlike Freud, who treated the individual rather than society, Fromm, a liberal, felt alienation was the fault of society and not the individual, and so wanted to see society change and move toward socialism.

Given the enormous misery brought on by totalitarian states in the first half of the twentieth century, Fromm was driven to understand the nature of personal psychologies that could allow these evil regimes to develop and become such a world force. In his well-known book, *Escape from Freedom*, he sought to provide an account of the psychological origins of totalitarian states. Essentially, he saw many men as lonely, insecure, and uncomfortable with the challenges of freedom; he saw men as willing to trade their individuality for the security, lack of responsibility, and identity offered by totalitarianism.

Fromm saw sadomasochistic and neurotic tendencies as playing a role. Both sadism and masochism stem from an inability to deal with loneliness and individual feelings of weakness and incapacity. According to Fromm, both the sadist and the masochist try to overcome their individual shortcomings by establishing obsessive, compulsive, and destructive connections to other people. This is well articulated in the quote below from *Escape from Freedom*.

"The annihilation of the individual self and the attempt to overcome thereby the unbearable feeling of powerlessness are only one side of the masochistic strivings. The other side is the attempt to become a part of a bigger and more powerful whole outside of oneself, to submerge and participate in it. This power can be a person, an institution, God, the nation, conscience, or a psychic compulsion. By becoming part of a power which is felt as unshakably strong, eternal, and glamorous, one participates in its strength and glory. One surrenders one's own self and renounces all strength and pride connected with it, one loses one's integrity as an individual and surrenders freedom, but one gains a new security and a new pride in the participation in the power in which one submerges. One gains also security against the torture of doubt. The masochistic person, whether his master is an authority outside of himself or whether he has internalized the master as conscience or a psychic compulsion is saved from making decisions, saved from the final responsibility for the fate of his self, and thereby saved from the doubt of what decision to make. He is also saved from the doubt of what the meaning of his life is or who he is. These questions are answered by the relationship to the power to which he has attached himself. The meaning of his life and the identity of his self are determined by the greater whole into which the self has submerged."[176]

For Fromm, the drive for power arises out of weakness, not strength. The individual feeling weak and unsure of himself wants security by attaching himself to something larger than himself. By annihilating his own identity, ceding it to another person or entity, he escapes the burden of responsibility.

An automaton doesn't worry about making decisions, he simply complies with orders. He, in fact, shuns reason because he shouldn't question orders or his place in society; these decisions should be made by others. The drive for conformity and sameness extinguishes freedom and individuality. Looking and thinking like everyone else should eliminate feelings of isolation, alienation, and anomie. At least this is the thought implicit in liberalism. Unfortunately, forcing sameness and the same standard on everyone almost always produces an even greater sense of aloneness. It's verboten to talk of difference. It's for this reason that many totalitarian states need to stoke up emotion and drive for a goal to divert attention from shortcomings at the individual level.

Unfortunately, these character traits that helped to produce the totalitarian nightmares of the twentieth century seem much with us today and are perhaps accounting for the resurgence in liberalism. The resemblance is striking and frightening.

Freedom involves costs. It's not easy, it's not a gift. There is no easy way out. The totalitarian-collectivist route extinguishes individuality and diminishes man to nothing but an instrument of his own creations. The collectivist route dehumanizes and degrades man. It leads to authoritarianism; it's not consistent with democracy and freedom.

The issue then is how to live with the challenges of freedom, not how to escape from freedom. Freedom carries with it the spark of life, the opportunity to realize our potentials. Not everyone is up for the challenge, and not everyone who tries to meet the challenges will be successful, but it's the best way forward. We can't and shouldn't want to hide or run from challenges, to shrink in fear, to shun the development of our potential. All species on this earth have their strong and their weak. It's the law of nature that the strong survive and bring greater glory to their species. To attempt to cater to the weak spells doom for our culture and species. We must reward those who seek the right path and not those who shrink from it.

This doesn't mean that succor shouldn't be provided to the weak. It does mean, however, that we should encourage good behavior and not penalize it. For those who can't help themselves, help should be forthcoming. We should raise up mankind by strengthening and improving the lot of those struggling, not by bringing down those who are succeeding.

The feelings of insecurity, loneliness, and alienation aren't simply an outgrowth of the freedom afforded us by modern civilization, but are also caused by the rapid change in our world today. In most of man's history an individual would die in the same socio-cultural milieu in which he was born. The world simply did not change that much during a lifetime. Life span was much shorter. In today's world, however, life span has increased markedly at a time when technology is changing the world right before our eyes. Man is an adaptable creature. He can change to address the needs of a new environment, but at the same time change is difficult. We have a threshold for the amount of change that we can comfortably and psychologically endure. We are probably far in excess of that amount in today's world. Moreover, liberalism, in its attempt to throw out the traditions, practices, and beliefs of the past, is exacerbating the already excessive amount of change that we must deal with.

Change then is a factor causing many to want the shelter and security of collectivism. Trading their individuality and freedom for the bondage of collectivism brings with it security and an illusory alleviation of the pain of alienation. Unfortunately, like pain medications and drugs, it doesn't change the underlying realities. Submission and addiction bring their own costs, which are much higher than those borne by free and autonomous men.

Erich Fromm's insight that sadomasochism may be at the root of the psychological drive toward collectivism is consistent with the dehumanized compassion that we see in liberals. It's not "love" for another human being, but rather an expressed need for connection with a larger whole. It's not care for others that drives it. The connection is to an abstract notion, not to a human being. It's in essence dehumanized. In Germany and Japan collectivist personalities predominate and these features are prominent.

The sadist needs another to feel whole; he can't exercise control over himself, but he can do so over others to the extent that he can find someone seeking dependency and submission. The masochist doesn't like himself, so he assaults his own individuality. Suicide is the extreme, but there are many gradations along the way. Both sadism and masochism arise from an inability to live with oneself. It arises out of weakness and neurotic psychological roots. It's not rooted in love or emotional feelings for others, but in a need for dependency.

Destructive Behavior

We all know people who are engaged in self destructive behavior, people who seem more intent on harming themselves than helping themselves. It is clear that a lot of man's suffering whether at the individual or community level is self-inflicted. In seeking an explanation for this, Freud concluded that we must have an instinct or drive explaining this behavior. Like the struggle between good and evil, there is a struggle between life affirming forces and destructive forces. Specifically, Freud found the explanation in the Death Instinct and the Instinct for Aggression. Freud noticed that many of his patients would become locked into re-enacting past trauma, rather than trying to rise above it and leaving it in the past. Sometimes, as James Bymes once said, "People seem more afraid of life than death."

It is also common to see these destructive impulses redirected outward to the external world in the form of a "will to power" and aggression. Late in his life and certainly in his book *Civilization and Its Discontents*, Freud was more convinced than ever of the power of these destructive forces and the important role they play in our world. Many of these forces in the twentieth century stemmed from collectivist ideologies, and liberalism is now bringing about their reemergence.

Liberalism does not recognize the darker side of human nature. It professes to see man as a peaceful creature who simply wants to live a simple life. It does not see any ill will, striving, or weakness to evil, only a benign and altruistic nature. But this blindness to human nature actually catalyzes and strengthens these destructive impulses. The perverse incentives of liberalism, along with moral relativism, are intensifying destructive tendencies. There is no shame or social opprobrium cast on those harming society or themselves. Liberalism has weakened civilizing and life-affirming forces, while it has strengthened forces of entropy and destruction. We see this at both the personal and the societal level as individuals and the State are living beyond their means without responsibility and accountability. The unsustainable rise in debt is just one of many manifestations of this moral decay. We know that it will not end well, yet we continue to do it. The debt bomb will inevitably explode in our faces and we will deserve it; perhaps we even want or need it.

Self-Annihilation

Liberalism is about the annihilation of the self. We see this syndrome throughout America and all over the world. Sickness is rampant. Self-destructive practices, like drug and alcohol addiction, are widespread. Collectivism is just another form of this. It's destroying the identity of man. Humans have conquered many forms of physical diseases, but not mental illness—and liberalism is just one of many manifestations of this.

Liberalism believes the State exists over and above individuals; individuals exist for the benefit of the State. As Bertrand Russell has noted, however, the State doesn't feel pain, suffering, joy, or despair; only individuals feel. Liberals are willing to sacrifice individuals for society, the parts for the whole, and in so doing the whole is degraded as well.

Individualism is at the foundation of democracy and liberty. It's what makes it strong. Independent thinking is a *sine qua non* for effective democracy. Yet liberalism strives to make people weak and dependent, not strong and independent. Liberalism maintains the charade of democracy even though it effectively disenfranchises the citizenry. The illusion of democracy is there, but not the reality. People go through the motions of voting, but they have no real influence. Moreover, would you even want their vote to count? A people diminished, no longer able to think for themselves or even run their own lives can't be expected to give proper direction to a country or choose its leaders. The strength of democracy must come from the ground up, from the people, not from the top-down. If the people are diminished and incapable, the government would be as well.

In sum, liberalism is destroying the mind and spirit of man. It's not just society and the economy that is being damaged; it's the heart and soul of man. It is a vicious circle, with liberalism working through the State to corrode and vitiate the character of man, while at the same time it's working through the psychology of the individual to corrupt the nature of the State. The momentum and institutional dynamic of liberalism has created a downward spiral that will be difficult to stop.

* * *

CHAPTER 12

PATHOLOGY OF LIBERALISM AT THE COLLECTIVE LEVEL: GOVERNMENT LEVEL

———◆———

Any society that would give up a little liberty to gain a little security will deserve neither and lose both.

~Benjamin Franklin

Of all tyrannies a tyranny exercised for the good of its victims may be the most oppressive. It may be better to live under robber barons than under omnipotent moral busybodies.
~C. S. Lewis, God in the Dock: Essays on Theology and Ethics

Majority rule only works if you're also considering individual rights. Because you can't have five wolves and one sheep voting on what to have for supper.

~Larry Flynt

Liberalism has a number of collective pathological tenden-cies:

(1) The tendency of government to pander to the masses, giving, giving, giving rather than doing what is best for the whole of society.

(2) Dividing and separating groups through identity politics, creating divisions rather than collective solidarity.

(3) The tendency for spending to expand, creating a Von Hayek road to serfdom, with spending leading to deficits, higher taxes, suppression of the private sector, and impoverishment of future generations.

(4) Expanding the size of government, creating a Leviathan with a huge bureaucracy, and thereby providing a safe haven for an insulated ruling and political class that threatens everyone.

(5) Government increasingly gets its tentacles around business, and rent seeking replaces market-oriented production thereby creating an ideal environment for corruption to grow and fester.

(6) Excessive and inefficient institutional growth which is increasingly remote and disconnected from people.

(7) Political greed grows ever stronger and more menacing, with short-term power goals predominating over the long-term interests of the public.

It's important to keep in mind the characteristics and conditions requisite for political systems of horror (Nazis, Mussolini, Stalin, Castro, Amin, Pol Pot):

a) Power in the hands of a few

b) Ruling class's arrogance and a detachment from the public

c) Grand abstract goals detached from reality

d) Sense that man is not good enough and should be changed; an interest in eugenics

e) No sense of cost or sacrifice

f) The electric sense of power from being part of a mob

g) Diminishment of the role of the individual

h) Diminishment of the role of reason; emotions are exalted over reason

i) A lack of regard for current traditions and institutions

j) A refusal to look at the lessons of history

k) An organic concept of polity

Liberalism shares all of these characteristics. Liberalism in the context of a democracy looks harmless at first, much like early-stage cancer cells. The problem is its dynamic tendency to grow and expand. Liberalism need not necessarily result in the political horrors that attended the totalitarian catastrophes alluded to, but one must note the similar characteristics and tendencies—and be aware of the risks.

One must ask, "Why risk the horrors?" Where is the common sense and the morality in taking on these risks? There are, to be sure, benefits as well as costs in going down the road toward liberalism. The former are always touted by the Left, but there is a complete avoidance of the issue of the potential disaster lurking at the end of this road. It seems the eyes of the Left are fixated only on moving ahead and are oblivious or in denial about the risks involved. Emotion is driving their wagon, not reason or thoughtful reflection of recent historical lessons. This lock-step mentality is truly frightening.

One can ask why people don't stop such historical disasters as Hitler, Mussolini, Stalin, Mao, Castro, and Pol Pot from happening. The problem is that the horrors involved appear only later, toward the end of the road. Early in the political journeys of these regimes, they did not look so menacing. By the time the evil nature of these political systems manifested itself, it was too late.

As mentioned earlier, the liberal mind-set is ineluctably drawn to utopias. They can't help themselves; they are fixated on creating a perfect world. If one looks at the historical record of utopias, it's a sad sight, littered with human ruin and disaster. That utopian experiments have not worked out doesn't deter the liberal, however, because he doesn't look back at history.

Despite its utopian goals, liberalism is really about sinking to the lowest common denominator; it's not about achieving new highs and excellence. So, while liberals talk of the future and hope, their policies are really retrograde. Liberalism is a throw-back to times past and outdated ideas. It's taking us back to where the few rule the majority, where the masses are subjugated and controlled.

Even if the worst outcome of collectivism is avoided, one would find petty tyranny with bureaucrats ruling even the smallest parts of our lives. They would determine what light bulbs you may use; what types of appliances you may own; what energy you may consume; what you may say and how you may say it; whom you may hire and whom you may fire, and for what reasons. The government would intervene in your health care, imposing itself between you and your doctor. It would interfere in how you raise your children. Does any of this sound familiar? If so, it's only because it has already happened. The famous quote of Edward Abbey is appropriate here: "No tyranny is so irksome as petty tyranny: the officious demands of policemen, government clerks, and electromagnetic gadgets."

As Milton Friedman said, "We all have greed in our hearts; none of us is an angel." It's better to have people self-govern than to have the government involved. At least economic greed produces something; political greed is barren.

The State and bureaucrats have never been responsible for any of the great inventions that have moved us forward; these have always come from individuals. Art is constrained and stifled under collectivist regimes and polities. So the disease of bloated and excessive government, the utopia of the Left, is nothing but reduced economic and scientific progress and an oppressive life for creative and artistic spirits.

Freedom is necessary in a democracy; individuals must be willing to stand on their own two feet, to think independently, and to take action where necessary. Liberals want to diminish individuality, emphasizing political correctness, homogeneity, and the welfare of the State. By diminishing individuality, freedom is necessarily diminished and democracy is threatened. The collectivist approach doesn't work because it weakens its own constituent parts, thereby weakening itself.

For the State the greatest virtue for individuals is self-sacrifice. It places high esteem on those individuals who dedicate their lives to others. This is because the greatest threat to the State is the individual. When an individual is willing to commit himself to a goal involving self-sacrifice, this is perfect for the State. That the State is the one that largely determines the goal to which the individual is dedicating himself strengthens the power of the State, but the most important thing is that the individual is in thrall to a collective ideal.

Individualism is a fundamental part of the foundation of Western democracy. In destroying individualism, liberalism is destroying democracy. This is an existential threat, not a minor modification to our way of life. The Left is intent on putting us in the harness of the State. Once the collective mentality and totalitarianism puts its stamp on people, it's hard to recover individuality. Witness the breakup of the USSR. Even years after its demise, the people from the former USSR find it difficult to adjust to a life where they need to take charge of their own lives. They still look to government and others to solve their problems and shape their lives. It will take generations for Eastern Europeans to adapt.

The liberal agenda is motivated in large part by an animus toward hierarchy and those with power and wealth. It's ironic, however, that the pursuit of their policies will result in a greater concentration of power in the hands of the few. The difference will be that the power will be in their hands, and not those who currently hold it. Overall the public will have much less power under this regime than they do now. Of course, liberals say repeatedly that they will rule in the interests of the public, so what do we have to fear? Oh, if we could only avert our eyes from the wreckage of history.

Liberals like to take advantage of crises to pursue their agenda. As Rahm Emanuel is famously quoted, "Don't waste a crisis to get what you want to get done." It's for this reason that liberals like to create a crisis or await a crisis: it affords them the opportunity to pursue their agenda. The public should be wary of this propensity to manufacture crises, whether it's a military war, a war on poverty, global warming, or whatever else. Liberals have an incentive to make things worse rather than better, like in the financial crisis of 2008. Rather than focusing on jobs and growth, they pursued an agenda that made things worse. The explosive growth in fiscal spending and debt, exacerbated by a new entitlement program, has seriously destabilized the economic environment.

Liberalism is clearly working to undermine the rule of law. The rule of law is fundamental if a democracy is going to perform well. Under the rule of law everyone is treated equally. Under the rule of law the powerful and the rich are treated the same as the weak and the poor. Since liberalism favors government by the elite, it's not too surprising that they would like to see the rule of law weakened. They prefer a system governed by discretion and dispensation, not iron-clad laws, as this enhances their power.

A fundamental pathological characteristic of most totalitarian societies is their obsession with surveillance of their own citizens. Unfortunately, this is a byproduct of liberalism as well. Although most liberals are strongly opposed to surveillance and incursions into their private lives, their unflagging support for growth in the State ineluctably leads to this outcome. The monitoring of phone calls and the internet as well as the recent revelations of the NSA surveillance program by the Obama administration clearly underscore the seriousness of this threat. According to multiple sources, there were "massive increases in phone and internet surveillance under the first term of the Obama administration." [177]

A salient feature of liberalism is its belief that man is not good enough. Since the nature of man is driven by self-interest, this is inconsistent with the collectivism espoused by liberals. The liberal solution is eugenics; they believe in social and biological engineering to make him suitable for their utopian state. Do we really want anyone tinkering with the genetic make-up of man? Jonah Goldberg, in his book *Liberal Fascism*, documents the historical affinity of liberalism for eugenics. Today's liberals believe deeply that the nature of man needs to be changed; thus far the emphasis has been on education, but eugenics has deep historical roots in liberalism.

Nationalism involves a love of country. It involves a sense of pride and a willingness to defend and fight for it. This explains in part why liberals love to disparage our country and look for ways to mock it. They don't see that America played a key role in defeating evil in the twentieth century: Germany and Japan in World War II, the USSR in the Cold War. Instead, the liberal believes imperialism and abuse of power is the hallmark of America's foreign policy. By undermining our pride and belief in America, liberals are advancing their cause toward transnational institutions. This is why Democrats and liberals are so reluctant to criticize the United Nations despite its flagrant shortcomings.

Liberals are also against the tribal aspect of nation-states, where one group of people bands together and distinguishes themselves from others. Liberals don't want any barriers between men. They want to see all men under one government. They are for inclusion, not exclusion. They would like to see cultures disintegrate, so that a new utopian world order could be created distinguished by homogeneity, sameness, and equality. As mentioned previously, moving toward transnationalism reduces accountability and the ability of the masses to control their futures. This feeds right into the liberal agenda of having control ceded to a ruling elite.

Liberals disparage the nation-state model, but they offer no evidence that a transnational governing body would be better. They simply say it would, and push hard to see their goal actualized. This is very dangerous and it makes no sense. If one wants to do away with a system that has worked well and replace it with a system of meta-government, there should be a sound argument for doing so. We should be able to look at evidence that it has worked; for example, we should be able to look at the experience of the EU, the League of Nations, and the United Nations. The record of the latter organizations is disappointing to say the least. What is the argument for doing away with the nation-state in favor of a transnational government? The liberal doesn't even bother to offer one.

It is well-recognized now that the EU is fundamentally flawed and unsustainable. What is truly amazing is that this massive change in Europe was created in the first place with virtually no serious thought concerning the pros and cons. This is the nature of liberalism to move ahead with grand utopian plans without thinking about what they are doing.

Political systems favoring freedom and individuality have been rare occurrences in history. Tyranny is by far the governmental form that has predominated throughout history—even today it far outnumbers those favoring freedom and individuality. Freedom needs to be fought for to be achieved and it needs to be fought for to be maintained. It takes strength to fight against the strong forces militating toward tyranny. There are always people who want to take charge and rule over others, even do them harm; if the public is acquiescent and passive they will be run over by the ruling class. Tyranny will be their fate. It's only if the public stands up for its rights and choices that democracy and freedom have a chance. The fight is against submissiveness and apathy. To be an automaton is easy; to be a free man is difficult. It's easy to be part of the herd, but difficult to find your own path.

Our forefathers have truly bequeathed us a gem. We have a gem in our hands which others have fought for, shed blood for, and died for. To allow it to be taken from us or to carelessly lose it would be a shame—and a sin.

* * *

CHAPTER 13

MULTICULTURALISM

———◆———

A nation without borders is not a nation.

~**Ronald Reagan**

L iberalism is hurting the functioning of democracy by encouraging too much immigration. Immigration is good and necessary, particularly in the context of globalization, but if excessive it is quite damaging.

Democracy works best in a society that is relatively homogeneous. This doesn't mean to say that it can't be ethnically diverse. America is a country founded on emigration. The key is that various ethnic groups all had to grapple with the same hard circumstance of survival. These harsh realities forced on them a certain commonness of circumstance, a commonness which brought them together. Even up until the latter part of the twentieth century, assimilation was no problem. We were, as de Tocqueville said, a *melting pot of cultures.* There was only one language, and that was English. This is no longer the case. Spanish is now very prevalent language in the US. Many signs are now in both English and Spanish. Assimilation is now failing. Increased ethnic diversity can bring about a diminished sense of belonging and a greater sense of social isolation, hurting not only the sense of individual well-being but also the willingness of individuals to contribute positively to society as a whole.

In 1965, Democratic President Lyndon Johnson radically altered US immigration law. He abandoned the quota system, which primarily targeted immigration from Europe, namely those countries from which we derived our cultural heritage. In its place he established an immigration policy based on family connections, which resulted in a dramatic shift toward immigrants from South America, Africa, Asia, and, later, Russia. These countries have cultural characteristics much less in harmony with our democratic and cultural traditions.

Where there is a lack of cultural homogeneity, there are more likely to be different interests and objectives in society. These divisions can make democracy more difficult and tense. If one group prevails over the others, there is a feeling of oppression and unfairness. Once society loses its homogeneity, the various groups begin to jockey to see who will predominate to get their way. Since interests no longer converge, the game changes from finding consensus and reasonable solutions to common problems to getting one's group in a position to where they can get what they want. The game changes from finding solutions to achieving power and exercising it. Rather than seeking truth through reason, the criterion becomes agreement and social harmony. Compromise reigns over real solutions and effective government.

In this context a welfare state purporting to work for everyone is a lie, because the government really tries to reward some groups and not others. A smaller rather than a larger government would be better, because the scope for groups to hurt one another would be diminished. It would be less likely that the institutions of government would be used as a club by one group against another.

In the USA, most immigrants are poor and uneducated and thus clearly have different needs than most Americans. They need more support from the State. Their dependency on the State is greater, so it's not surprising that they would like to see an expansion of the government and the benefits offered. For example, a 2012 poll by the Pew Research Hispanic Center showed that 75 percent of Latinos want a "bigger government providing more services ... while 19 percent say they would rather have a smaller government with fewer services."[178] According to the Center for Immigration Studies, forty three percent of legal and illegal immigrants are on welfare after twenty years.[179] This helps to lead to pressures on the fiscal budget and to a growth in the size of government relative to the private sector. These groups want taxpayers and other citizens to help support and improve their living standards. But other citizens naturally resist this.

This cultural divide is more pronounced because these new immigrants are disposed toward having large families, whereas the more established citizens have birth rates barely sufficient to maintain a stable population. In Western Europe the older more established citizenry are dwindling, while immigrant families are expanding rapidly. So the demographic profile is changing significantly. This leads in time to dilution and diminishment of the original culture.

Most immigrants come from countries without a tradition of democracy at least in a functional sense. In the source countries for immigration, power rather than political consensus is the dominant modality of their political systems. Power comes from the top, not the bottom, so there is a constant struggle to get to the top. The spoils and political control go to those on the top; they get to pursue their agenda to the detriment of the rest of the citizenry. There is no sense of inclusiveness, only exclusiveness. Bringing this cultural baggage to a functioning democracy is damaging indeed.

Communication is more difficult because societal groups speak different languages and access different sources of information through different media sources. This can lead to a breakdown in dialogue, especially since many of these groups isolate themselves from others.

A common language is important to cultural unity. There is too much emphasis in early education in teaching the children of immigrants in their native languages. Countries like Canada and Belgium, where two languages prevail, have underscored the disadvantages of such linguistic arrangements and the inevitable associated cultural problems. Both countries are essentially culturally divided and tensions make life difficult; in fact in Canada, French-speaking Quebec actually held a referendum on seceding from Canada.

Excessive multiculturalism is undermining the foundations of democracy and destroying our culture. We need to believe in our own culture. We shouldn't be guilty or ashamed to say what we believe. In California, they no longer celebrate Columbus Day; now they celebrate Native People's Day. Relativism is an abandonment of belief and commitment to our own culture. Cultures that are not tolerant and open seek to destroy unsure cultures.

Europeans are now recognizing the mistake they have made with multiculturalism. Sarkozy, Cameron, and Merkel now all admit it's been a failure. Foreigners immigrated to these countries and have failed to assimilate. In Australia the Prime Minister told immigrants they are welcome if they want to assimilate and adopt the culture of Australia; otherwise they are not welcome and should go back to their native countries.

It's interesting that liberals are strongly for top-down planning and control of the economy, but not with respect to immigration policy. In effect we have no immigration law. The federal government refuses to enforce the law or even to protect our borders. It in fact institutes legal action against states like Arizona and Alabama that have attempted to deal with the problem of illegal immigration. Meanwhile it condones sanctuary cities that offer protection to illegal immigrants. Nor is there even a guiding principle shaping our policy toward immigration.

In effect there is no policy. The tail is wagging the dog. Illegal aliens are determining immigration outcomes, not the authorities. One in three immigrants is now illegal. There is no attempt at thoughtful analysis about what our policies should be toward immigration. This is a fundamental force impacting our country and shaping its future, but there is no thoughtful discussion about what our policies should be. There is no thought given about what an appropriate number of immigrants should be, whether they should be skilled or unskilled, and whether preference should be given to certain countries or cultures.

We need immigration, but the issue is what kind. We need legal immigration; giving preference and advantage to illegal immigration makes no sense, and serves to undermine respect for law in general.

The problem is that such considerations are deliberately squelched by a liberal establishment bent on using immigration as a basis to destroy our outstanding cultural and democratic traditions. They are also using it to enhance their power. They are buying the votes of illegal immigrants through pandering and lenient policies. Liberals have largely succeeded in banning identification requirements for voting, so they have made it easy for illegals to vote. In addition, since most of these immigrants are under-educated and low-skilled, they are dependent on liberal entitlement policies. At the same time such immigration policies hurt US workers, rendering them more dependent on government and unhappy with capitalism.

Recapitulating, then, liberalism is pushing immigration too far, undermining even the kind of cultural homogeneity required for their utopian collective society to exist. In addition, the divisive-identity politics which the Left uses to enhance its political position is inconsistent with the welfare state they claim they want to create. So, once again we see inconsistency between the professed goals of liberalism and its tactics. This pattern of behavior reaffirms that their real goal is power, not a democratic welfare state—because their actions and tactics would then be consistent with their goals.

* * *

CHAPTER 14

SACRIFICE OF JUSTICE

———◆———

Whenever a separation is made between liberty and justice, neither, in my opinion is safe.

~Edmund Burke

We must face the fact that the preservation of individual freedom is incompatible with a full satisfaction of our views of distributive justice

~Friedrich August von Hayek

Man's capacity for justice makes democracy possible; but man's capacity for injustice makes democracy necessary.

~Reinhold Niebuhr

I beg you, look for the words 'social justice' or 'economic justice' on your church Web site. If you find it, run as fast as you can. Social and economic justice, they are code words.

~Glenn Beck

At his best, man is the noblest of all animals; separated from law and justice he is the worst.

~Aristotle

America, since its founding has been all about political justice. To this end the Founding Fathers established the democratic foundations of this country. Since FDR, however, there has been a fundamental shift in the nature of justice. Liberals are pushing hard for economic justice, and they are willing to sacrifice the pillars of our democracy to pursue it. In essence political justice is now being sacrificed for "economic justice."

By *economic justice*, liberals mean redistribution of income and wealth. For them it's not right that some should have more material wealth than others. They are uninterested in who creates wealth and of the nature of economic growth; they are solely interested in the distribution of wealth. For liberals this is economic justice. It's not justice that people get what they contribute to the economy through meeting the needs of others—which is the notion of economic justice created by our Founding Fathers and which is embedded in our market-oriented economy. For liberals it's OK if someone doesn't want to work and is a drain on the community. This person should still be rewarded.

In talking about the redistribution of income to help the poor, it's important to understand who we mean by "the poor." In talking about the poor, as mentioned in Chapter 8 on the Historical Failures of Liberalism, we are not talking about people worried about their survival. They have food, shelter, and health care. Almost all have television sets and other modern conveniences. What we are talking about then is not survival, but rather seeing to it that most everyone has the same level of wealth and material well-being. We are talking about relative, not absolute wealth and well-being. Where does this stop? Should everyone have a Mercedes? A big-screen television? A house? It was an attempt to provide housing to those who could not afford it that caused the mortgage and financial crisis in 2008.

For liberals the government is the primary tool for delivering economic justice. Through taxation, public spending, and regulatory action, government can affect the distribution of income and wealth throughout a society. The historical record shows that government has affected both vertical and horizontal equity; that is, it has redistributed income away from higher income earners to lower income earners, and has shifted income and benefits between people of equal economic status. Regarding the latter, government intervention has favored public sector employees over private sector employees, and those who willingly do not work and act responsibly over those who do. These problems of inequity between people of roughly the same economic status should cause liberals to wince, but one doesn't hear concern from this quarter.

Liberals are only concerned about vertical equity; you never hear them complaining about horizontal equity. Thus, you have public sector employees deliberately underperforming on the job and overusing sick leave, because they know they can't be fired. You have people deliberately dropping out of the labor force to collect unemployment insurance. You have people in the underground economy receiving their income in cash and evading taxes, while at the same time collecting benefits and financial assistance from the government. Liberals don't complain about this, perhaps because they don't want to draw attention to the shortcomings of government and because they don't want to risk offending some of their constituents, the parasites on society who selfishly game the system. Moreover, to the extent that this kind of inequity helps grow the government, this is to the liking of liberals who are bent on growing the power of the State and the ruling class.

The idea of a "just" price goes back to the medieval period. The price was supposed to be fair; it shouldn't be greater than the worth of the good. During this period price was not understood. It was thought that price was related to the basic and inherent worth of a good. It was not until more recent times, with the development of market economies, that we now understand price to be determined by supply and demand. Apparently liberals want to return us to the medieval perspective of a just price, and ignore the forces of supply and demand. The price of a worker's labor is equal to the amount that he contributes to the firm employing him. It's determined by supply and demand. For the government to impose "economic justice," taking money away from someone who earned it and giving it to someone who did not, violates this basic principle.

Some liberals have argued that utilitarians would support the idea of income redistribution. According to this argument, taking money away from a rich man to give it to someone in poverty would enhance overall societal utility or happiness. This would be so because the happiness lost by the rich man would be less than that gained by the poor man. A hundred dollars lost by the rich man would represent only a small portion of his wealth, so he would be less affected than the poor man, for whom a hundred dollars could be a big deal.

This argument, however, is myopic because it only looks at a snapshot in time. It doesn't take into account the dynamics. The impact of so-called economic justice, transferring money from those who earned it to those who did not, would be to pervert incentives. Over time it would penalize productive members of society and reward those who are a drain on it. This would reduce the vitality of the economy and reduce its growth rate. The size of the economic pie to be shared would shrink. It would reduce economic and political freedom because the government would be interceding in the affairs of individuals.

Bertrand Russell, the socialist philosopher mentioned earlier, supports income and wealth redistribution. He said the following:

> "Material goods are more a matter of possession than goods that are mental. A man who eats a piece of food prevents everyone else from eating it, but a man who writes or enjoys a poem does not prevent another man from writing or enjoying one just as good or better. That is why, in regard to material goods, justice is important, but in regard to mental goods the thing that is needed is opportunity and an environment that makes hope of achievement rational."[180]

Notice that he stresses opportunity, environment, and hope of achievement when talking about the production of mental goods, but ignores these with material goods. The market provides opportunity and environment regarding the production of material goods, but he wants to degrade the market and circumvent it with government interference. It's noteworthy that he speaks of production and consumption with mental goods (writing and enjoying poetry), but ignores production with material goods, focusing only on the consumption aspect. Clearly this is a serious mental gaffe. If producers are denied profit or incentive to produce material goods, there will be less available for consumption. Opportunity and environment are critically important here, just as they are for mental goods. The market for material goods is not a zero-sum game as he seeks to characterize it.

Bertrand Russell is one of the great minds of the twentieth century. He is a renowned logician and mathematician. The fact that his mind short-circuited here is symptomatic of liberals. Even those with great analytic capacities are able to turn a blind eye and short-circuit those capacities when trying to justify income redistribution. It can't be justified rationally, so they twist logic to get the conclusion they want and even convince themselves that it makes sense. As an intellectual, he clearly favors mental output (his work) over material output, displaying the ever-present liberal bias and elitist condescension.

Differences in intellectual endowment are largely a gift of nature, although here too hard work plays an important role. Why is the liberal only concerned with inequality when it pertains to material well-being? Liberals, like Bertrand Russell, don't realize that the expansion of State power usually brings about a curtailment of intellectual freedom and artistic expression. It's critical to acknowledge this link, but liberals blithely ignore it.

Nozick, a conservative philosopher, equates taxation for the purpose of income distribution to a theft of a person's labor. In paying taxes most of us are working several months out of the year for the government. This is a form of oppression and a muted form of slavery, although in this form at least we are allowed to do the work we like.

For libertarians, income redistribution is wrong even if it would increase societal happiness, which we have indicated it doesn't. For them income redistribution is wrong because it infringes on individual liberty. People shouldn't be told what to do with money they have earned. Freedom to control one's life and to make choices for oneself is of paramount importance to the libertarian.

Does the State own me or do I own myself? Do I have a right to the output of my own labor or does the State? Libertarians would answer that we own ourselves and likewise are entitled to the product of our labor. If the State can't take one of my kidneys or one of my eyes to help someone who needs them more than I do, why can it take the product of my labor to give to someone else?

It is bizarre that liberals are interested in the creation of an organic state that supersedes the individual, but espouse policies that reward people who sap the strength of the collective polity and the State. However, what liberals really want is to hurt individuals who are succeeding because they are an obstacle to the accumulation of state power.

Although they profess otherwise, liberals don't appear to believe that we all have an obligation to enhance the welfare of the community. Those that don't contribute out of volition—the indolent and the lazy—are nevertheless singled out for support by the liberal establishment. It is, of course, appropriate to help those who are weak and lack the capacity to help themselves, but liberals go well beyond this. In fact liberals don't appear to believe that we even have an obligation to ourselves, much less than to the community.

Thus, liberalism creates an environment where slackers and cheaters thrive. Parasitic, self-seeking behavior is rewarded and encouraged, while behavior that is responsible and conscientious is penalized and discouraged. Is this justice?

Moreover, as Albert Einstein once noted, "Sometimes one pays most for the thing one gets for nothing." Getting something for nothing breeds dependency and subservience. It vitiates the work ethic and disposition for striving. It undermines ambition and a sense of self-worth. It not only stifles human development, but degrades it. Perhaps the so-called beneficiaries of liberal justice are its greatest victims.

Is it economic justice that liberal welfare policies have hurt the poor rather than helped them? Is it justice for workers that liberal support for unions hurts other workers, the consumer, and the taxpayer? Is it justice that liberal support for trial lawyers adds to the cost of medical care for the public? Is there justice in the false promises which liberals continually make to the disadvantaged? Does it make sense for the government to have $87 trillion in unfunded mandates for social programs and pensions? Is there justice in making promises to people and not making the necessary provisions to see that the promise will be fulfilled?

Where is the morality in false promises, promises broken? Liberal programs and politicians continually make promises that they fail to meet. Their poverty programs, as discussed, have clearly failed. They have made promises in the form of Social Security, Medicare, Medicaid, and now Obamacare—but all are vastly underfunded. The lock box on Social Security trust funds has been removed, and the funds used for other purposes.

The foundations for Western democratic perspectives on justice and morality are found largely in the thinking of the Greeks and in the work of philosopher Emmanuel Kant. According to Aristotle, the State shouldn't be neutral about what is right and wrong. People should be rewarded based on whether or not they deserve it. Those who are deserving are those who live lives based on virtues espoused by the State. Modern philosophers, such as Emmanuel Kant and Rawls, differ with the Aristotelian view. For them the State should be neutral on moral issues and on how to live life.

The utilitarians subscribe to a hedonistic moral philosophy where pleasure equals good and pain equals bad. The objective of a government in this view is to maximize happiness for the society. This school of philosophy sees man and his nature as hedonically driven.

According to Bentham, "Nature has placed mankind under the governance of two sovereign masters, pain and pleasure...They govern us in all we do, in all we say, in all we think: every effort we can make to throw off our subjection will serve but to demonstrate and confirm it in words a man may pretend to abjure their empire, but in reality he will remain subject to it all the while."

John Stuart Mill, a subsequent utilitarian philosopher, attempted to amend this view to take into account that some pleasures and pains differ in their quality and can't all be measured equally. The question is, who should decide which pleasures are of quality and which are not? Here Mill fell victim to the temptation of modern day liberalism. It is clear that he felt that intellectually superior people like himself should be put in the role of playing God, passing judgment on how others should lead their lives. He was not really subscribing to utilitarianism, but rather revealing his own superiority and elitism and contempt for ordinary folk. He was an egghead and effete snob and felt that others who did not lead similarly intellectual lives were living on a lower and less moral level. The Untermensch, he seemed to be saying, needed guidance. The ability to enjoy simple pleasures seemed alien to him.

One key danger of the philosophy of utilitarianism is its focus on maximizing the pleasure of the entire population. This organic orientation obviously could threaten the rights of an individual. In this regard, the example is often given of a Roman circus with certain citizens thrown in the ring to fight the lions. Perhaps the crowd might find great pleasure in seeing such a spectacle, but clearly those in the ring would have had a different view.

It is thus interesting that utilitarianism—which underpins a lot of moral philosophy still today in Western democracies and underpins much contemporary economic theory and policy—has this fundamental germ of collectivism at its core.

Utilitarian theory is used to buttress free-market capitalism, because it's the best system for maximizing welfare for the overall polity. Those who contribute the most to meeting the needs of others are rewarded the most. This is economic justice. It's not justice to reward those who don't contribute.

The philosopher Immanuel Kant disagrees with the utilitarians. He believes it's wrong to base morality and considerations of justice on meeting our need for pleasure and happiness. For Kant we shouldn't be captive to our appetites, but rather should be guided by reason. Man is more exalted than other creatures that are driven by appetite and should act accordingly. More specifically he said we should be guided by a *categorical imperative* to help human beings out of respect for one another. He says, "Act in such a way that you always treat humanity, whether in your own person, or in the person of any other, never simply as a means, but always at the same time as an end."

It should be noted that Kant was unfair in his criticism of utilitarianism because he characterized it as narrowly focused on the satisfaction of basic appetites, whereas, even John Rawls in *A Theory of Justice* recognized that it could encompass "rational desires" as well.[181]

Kant was critical of utilitarianism because he felt that it accorded reason the role of satisfying the passions. In his view reason shouldn't be instrumentalist, helping to achieve the desired ends of our appetites, but rather should guide us to a higher moral plane. Here he seems to be in some agreement with the anti-materialism that marks today's liberalism.

The rejection of reason by today's liberals, however, puts them at a far remove from Kant, who puts ultimate faith in reason. As discussed previously, liberals seem now to shun reason because its use calls into question their methods and agenda.

Like the utilitarians with whom he disagreed, Kant's view of justice is not favorable to the liberal's view of justice. Liberals treat individuals as a means, not an end. For Kant, a person is not an instrument to be used by the State or anyone else. Individuals and humanity are deserving of respect and *autonomy*. Liberal collectivism, however, diminishes humanity; it glorifies their submissiveness to the State.

For Kant, freedom is not just finding the best way to a given goal, but is the selection of the goal itself. The goal should be outside our immediate interest and be determined through reason. Liberals want to arrogate this freedom to select the goals for themselves through the State, leaving individuals to find the best means to achieve these goals. Liberal ideology sees individual freedom as a small thing. It's the State that is important, not the individual.

Kant believed in social contract theory as the basis of political economy, but a hypothetical one, not an actual contract. He did not flesh out, however, what such a social contract might look like, except to indicate that it should be based on the *categorical imperative* to shape our actions and behavior in such a way to respect one another.

This task of fleshing out a social contract was taken on by John Rawls, a modern-day leading philosophical exponent of economic justice and liberalism. Rawls formulated a concept of justice based on a hypothetical thought experiment. In this experiment he assumes that we start with a situation that is not currently prevailing, but rather with an initial situation where no one would know what his position in society would be. Everyone would operate behind a *veil of ignorance*. None of us would know what class or ethnicity he would be. Nor would he know his religion or position in the economic and social strata. Under this set of assumptions, Rawls believes that we would all choose to have a society where everyone is equal, because no one would want to risk an unfavorable circumstance. Basically, Rawls presumes that we are all risk-averse. He assumes that we all want sameness, and that a nonhierarchical society would be both feasible and desirable. Essentially he presumes that fear of inferiority prevails over all other considerations.

Liberalism fails to meet even a Rawlsian concept of justice. In Rawls' view, a policy is only just if it has a favorable effect on the most disadvantaged. Liberal welfare policies, as mentioned, have not succeeded in helping the poor. This is the case at both the national level as well as the international level. At the national level, LBJ's war on poverty and its welfare policies have been largely discredited. At the international level, aid programs to help the poor have failed. The vast improvement for the poor in the international community has come about through the adoption of market-economy principles in China and East Asia. The movement away from Mao's communist regime in China to a market-oriented economy has transformed the country and showcases the bankruptcy of egalitarian policies, while at the same time highlighting the strength of capitalism.

Rawls is only concerned with inequality in income and wealth, but man is not just driven by money; he is driven by sex and power and intellectual achievement too. Why should we allow inequality in sex, power, and intellectual achievement? Why not equalize everything. For example, why not limit sex partners, ensuring that everyone has the same number. Perhaps drugs could be given to suppress the sexual appetites and prowess of those who would otherwise have more sex than others. Pretty women could be banned from wearing make-up or forced to undergo cosmetic surgery to equalize the playing field with less attractive women. Similarly, those with superior intellectual faculties could be given a drug, or subjected to surgery, to level the playing field.

Only in certain communist countries, like Cuba, the USSR, and Mao's China have the lives of the most disadvantaged been improved through higher education and an improved safety net. However, we are all aware of the horrors attending this. The damage to everyone else in these societies was extravagant. Liberty was annihilated and economic oppression enforced on everyone, not just the poor.

Rawls' view of justice is extreme in that it exalts considerations of justice over everything else. Rawls ignores the implications of trying to achieve justice as he sees it for the political and economic system as well as for the psychological and social effects. To put in place his system of justice would require a massive expansion and intrusion of government into each aspect of our lives. A tyranny of bureaucrats and an elite ruling class would be inevitable. This is hardly the nonhierarchical world that Rawls seems to long for. The damage to human striving and achievement would be devastating.

In a Rawlsian world there is a fear of failure. There is an aversion to risk and choice. The overwhelming need is for safety and sameness. It is a uni-dimensional world focused only on material well-being.

Governments don't arise out of contracts or agreement; they originate out of the interplay of a multitude of social, political, economic, and psychological forces and evolve out of the past. Governments and political economies are not the willy-nilly creations of armchair philosophers. In essence, contract theory is an unrealistic view of how societal arrangements actually evolve. This contrasts with utilitarianism, which is undergirded and actualized through the price system and the market. It's much more realistic than the Rawlsian theory—and is more practical and constructive in policy implementation.

Rawls maintains two basic principles:

"The first requires equality in the assignment of basic rights and duties, while the second holds that social and economic inequities, for example, inequalities of wealth and authority, are just only if they result in compensating benefits for everyone, and in particular for the least advantaged members of society. These principles rule out justifying institutions on the grounds that the hardships of some are offset by a greater good in the aggregate."[182]

These are constraining principles. They limit the prospects for societies to develop and grow. Surely, it would be desirable if everyone could gain from the implementation of a certain set of policies, but this is unrealistic. If the net effect is significantly favorable and the favorable effects are reasonably distributed over the population, this should be sufficient to go ahead. Moreover, it's likely that certain policies would favor certain groups, while other policies would favor other groups, so over time the favorable effects could be distributed fairly over the citizenry. This surely represents a more promising course for policy implementation.

The Rawlsian view differs fundamentally from the utilitarian viewpoint because the latter doesn't take a stand on how it would like to see the distribution of utility relating to a particular policy. The utilitarians are merely concerned with maximizing welfare for society as a whole. It's true that it would be desirable to take into account the impact on the most impoverished, but the Rawlsian approach is too extreme and would limit societal welfare in the end.

Rawls is even more extreme in that he wants social policy to offset other factors that contribute to differences in wealth and income, including natural abilities and talents. Below is a quote to this effect:

> "While the liberal conception seems clearly preferable to the system of natural liberty, intuitively it still appears defective. For one thing, even if it works to perfection in eliminating the influence of social contingencies it still permits the distribution of wealth and income to be determined by the natural distribution of abilities and talents. Within the limits allowed by the background arrangements, distributive shares are decided by the outcome of the natural lottery; and this outcome is arbitrary from a moral perspective. There is no more reason to permit the distribution of income and wealth to be settled by the distribution of natural assets than by historical and social fortune. Furthermore the principle of fair opportunity can only be imperfectly carried out, at least as long as some form of family exists. The extent to which natural capacities develop and reach fruition is

affected by all kinds of social conditions and class attitudes. Even the willingness to make an effort, to try, and so to be deserving in the ordinary sense is itself dependent upon happy family and social circumstances."[183]

If we were to treat talent and even motivation as undeserving of reward because they are determined by factors outside of our control, this would totally undermine the basis of positive and negative incentive structures that have served our political economy so well. America is a meritocratic culture: hard work and talent are rewarded. Rawls finds unfairness in this and would like to turn it upside down. He is intent on replacing our meritocracy with a culture of mediocrity.

In trying to redress even differences in motivation, the implementation of Rawlsian justice would create a strange land indeed. Clearly it would be a heaven for the indolent and lazy. Those who are disinterested in helping either themselves or society would find a very congenial environment, but the rest of us would feel very much out of place.

The fear of failure is an important motivating force not only for humans, but for any creature on this earth. Liberals want to eliminate this fear and replace it with a soothing sense that it's okay to fail. In fact it's those who succeed who should feel uneasy, because they must be benefitting unfairly in some way.

Rawls is intent on imposing an equality of outcome on society. He doesn't specifically address the fact that we live in a stochastic world. Fortuity and misfortune impose themselves on all of our lives. They are a fact of life. Presumably Rawls would like to banish these stochastic realities from our existence as well. Some of us die young or fall prey to sickness, while others are blessed with health and live long lives. Some of us might be struck by lightning, while others might win the lottery. Life is uncertain and unfair. To try to make life what it is not is folly.

Kant did not find the basis of liberty in the notion that we own ourselves or that it comes from God. For Kant liberty and freedom should derive from a respect for humanity itself. Humans should respect themselves and others.

Kant believes that morality and justice are concerned with intentionality and principles, not consequences. Liberals appear to fit this bill...but do they? Kant says it's the intention that counts, but by this he surely means more than posturing. It should be genuine intention. We have seen that most liberals, certainly the politicians, don't shape their own lives in line with their stated compassion for the poor, and they demonstrate no concern that their policies have failed time and time again.

The liberal principles of fairness, equality of outcome, and the priority of the collective over the individual were at the heart of communism—and brought about its demise. With the failure of communism, the West presumed that capitalism and democracy had triumphed. But the same liberal principles that brought about the demise of communism are now afflicting the West as well. It's a disease that we are not immune to, and it is destroying us from with-in.

Morality and justice in liberalism are teleological. It's focused on the ends, the goals. For Aristotle, morality and justice were also teleological in nature. To understand either morality or justice, it was necessary to understand the ends. But this conception is fraught with danger. Fundamentalism can have us pursuing the wrong goals. We can see this with the Islamic extremists. Killing is justified, indeed morally grounded, if it's in the name of Allah and wreaks havoc on infidels.

Does it not make more sense to rely on process, means, and individual liberty? Does it not make more sense to seek answers through reason, truth, and simple precepts for behavior? Instincts across cultures are in accord with some basic patterns of behavior, such as the Golden Rule, compassion, not stealing or killing, and not lying. Is it not better to allow individuals the freedom to decide what is moral and just, rather than seeking a collective position which risks divorce from fundamental feelings for humanity?

Liberal moral teleology is dangerous and destructive to humanity; it hurts those it purports to help. Unequal treatment under the law hurts the values of individual liberty that liberalism purports to support. Individual liberty is the real way to their goals, and still they squash it. Equality of outcome is not the answer; dignity and equality of opportunity represent a better way.

The ideas of social and economic justice and fairness are frequently thrown about by the Left and underpin the leftist agenda. Both words for the Left have everything to do with redistribution and nothing with justice. The word *justice*, at least for a conservative, means equal treatment; for the Left it means special dispensation. It means that the groups whom they favor should be exempted from the rules, principles, and laws that apply to everyone else.

According to Plato, "Justice in the life and conduct of the State is possible only as first it resides in the hearts and souls of the citizens." Liberalism, however, fans the flames of injustice in the hearts of men, as it sows the seeds of dissension, envy, and anger. Through its politics of division, liberalism is creating an environment antithetical to justice. In fact it's sacrificing justice on the altar of its agenda for power.

The liberal notion of justice is nothing more than an oxymoron, a contradiction in terms. Justice implies equal treatment and fairness, but liberals use justice as a tool, not for advancing equal treatment and fairness, but for advancing their agenda. They are not interested in equal treatment or the evenhanded application of laws, but rather in preconceived outcomes.

This is vividly illustrated by the tragic Trayvon Martin case. Early in 2012, Trayvon Martin, a young black teenager, was killed in what is alleged to have been an altercation with George Zimmerman, a neighborhood watch volunteer. Thousands of blacks are killed each year, most of them by other black men. Are liberals concerned about this? No, there is little attention paid to it. They look for a crime that can divide us, because that is the way they sustain themselves and advance their agenda of power. Before anything was known of the Trayvon Martin case, the liberal media and establishment put a spotlight on it. The Washington Post put it on their front page and called the alleged perpetrator, George Zimmerman, a "white Hispanic." To satisfy their template of division, it simply didn't fit if Zimmerman was Hispanic, so they called him a white Hispanic. They also made him out to be a racist even though he reportedly mentored black kids and, in 2010, actively protested against police corruption when the son of a policeman was not arrested for beating a black homeless man. No one knows what the facts are in this case. The criminal justice system is the forum for sorting this out.

Even if it were clear that Zimmerman killed Trayvon Martin simply because he was black, would it serve the interest of society to blow it up and cause racial tension and anger if it was one out of thousands of killings? It's always possible to look for things in society that will divide us. Is it not better to look for things that bring us together?

Liberals profess that they are against racism. They claim they want to diminish tensions between ethnic groups and work toward a society of unity. Yet their actions and methods of operation militate to fan divisions and work against unity. This is because the real goal of liberalism is power, and the politics of division are the means to achieving it.

Justice for liberals is subservient to their quest for power. They don't mind sacrificing it if it advances their power. In fact, the rule of law—equal treatment under the law—is something they are uncomfortable with because it constrains the exercise of the power of the ruling elite. The ruling liberal elite prefer to exercise discretion rather than submit to principles or laws. Thus in the economic sphere they want to decide who gets what, so economic justice for them is not served by the rules of the marketplace. Likewise, in the legal sphere, the rule of law gets in their way, so they brush it aside.

They are not concerned with justice for George Zimmerman. The media fanned the flames of racism by trying to depict him as a racist, without any information to work on. It's interesting that mob justice and vigilantism, the things that blacks were most terrified of early in this country's history, seem to have become their modus operandi in this case.

Why not let the justice system handle the case? Why try to exert outside pressure without knowing the facts? In fact it's even worse than that in that, by various accounts, the liberal media distorted the facts to make it appear that Zimmerman was racist.

Liberals love to use the word justice, but in practice make a mockery of it. The liberal view of justice is not just an oxymoron;

it's the antithesis of justice. It's not just non-justice, it's antagonistic toward justice. It's based on mob emotion arising out of anger and hatred. It's, in short, a disease of mind and spirit. With the politics of division practiced by liberals, our society is divided. Like a disease in which part of the body fights other parts, liberalism is fostering the growth of a cancer of division that works to the harm of us all.

The Left's sacrifice of truth for agenda, discussed in Chapter 10, has a direct bearing on the concept and delivery of justice. Truth and justice are inextricably linked. Horace Walpole once said, "Justice is rather the activity of truth, than a virtue itself. Truth tells us what is due to others, and justice renders that due. Injustice is acting a lie." A grounding in reality, particularity, and context is required if justice is to be effectively rendered. Liberalism, unfortunately, is lost in idealism and irremediably disconnected from reality, and has a preference for the overarching and the abstract over the particular and context. In essence justice for individuals is being sacrificed for a collectivist ideal. When the individual is not accorded primacy, justice becomes a word without meaning, much like democracy and truth. This is clearly evident in collectivist countries like Russia and China where justice for individuals has been sacrificed for the power of the State.

Fundamentally liberalism also errs by its single-minded obsession with a narrowly defined concept of "justice" and "fairness"; it ignores political, economic, social, institutional, historical, rational, empirical, and psychological realities. Justice can't be fruitfully considered in isolation from these realities. Trying to impose "economic justice" affects parameters in these other realms; perverse signals and incentives are created, setting off adverse behavioral chain reactions which reverberate throughout the system.

An agenda of redistribution fans the flames of envy. It creates a fertile environment for envy to grow and fester. It is based on and driven by an unwholesome emotion, one of the seven deadly sins. It also undermines democracy as government is perverted into an institution of pandering and theft.

* * *

CHAPTER 15

Immorality of Liberalism

Those who stand for nothing fall for anything.
~Alexander Hamilton

A system of morality which is based on relative emotional values is a mere illusion, a thoroughly vulgar conception which has nothing sound in it and nothing true.
~Socrates

Liberty cannot be established without morality, nor morality without faith.
~Alexis De Tocqueville

Is it moral to encourage bad behavior? Evidence, whether on an individual level or on a group level, clearly shows that when you reward behavior you will get more of it; when you penalize it, you will see less of it. Yet liberals reflexively bail out bad behavior and try to excuse it, while expecting those practicing good behavior to pay for the bailout.

Perhaps the real issue for liberals is that there really aren't bad behaviors, just different behaviors. This is pretty much the position of moral relativism to which they heartily subscribe. Or perhaps it reflects the liberal view that we can't really modify our behaviors because they are predetermined by social conditions. The latter, of course, is a *carte blanche* justification for abdication of moral responsibility.

Is it moral to encourage and implement legalized theft? The liberal feels it's justified to take resources from those who have earned them and redistribute them to those who have not. They don't give their resources, but rather the resources of others. In fact liberals and Democrats, as previously discussed, give less to charity than conservatives. Would it be moral and justifiable for an individual to take money from someone (theft) and give it to someone they think should have it? If not, why is it justifiable for a government to do so?

Bertrand Russell, once said, "A government with a policy to rob Peter to pay Paul can be assured of the support of Paul." Moreover, in such a scheme the government is not an unaffected or impartial actor. It gains power, influence, and wealth through this role of redistribution. The government is directly guilty of theft and benefitting along with Paul at the expense of Peter. Is this a sound basis for moving civilization and morality forward?

Is it moral to steal from the unborn? Liberalism is not content to take money from those who have earned it. This is not enough, so they now have government borrow 40 cents on the dollar to support their profligate ways. Liberals say they are about helping the weak, but they are in essence attacking the unborn who can't fight back and defend themselves.

According to Neil Howe, author of *The Fourth Turning*, the baby boom generation now dominating political and cultural outcomes "will always tend toward self-indulgence in their personal lives—but if they allow this to overflow into public life and demand generous public benefits, they will bankrupt their children financially, themselves morally."[184] The boomer generation challenged and deconstructed the moral order of their parents, but left nothing in its place. They replaced the sense of community and sacrifice of their parents with self-absorption and fractiousness. It's ironic that the *Greatest Generation*, who sacrificed in World War II to save the freedoms of this country, gave birth to children who are carelessly allowing it to slip away as they focus on their own indulgences.

The baby boom generation was energized and absorbed in moral uprisings against war and discrimination in the 60s. Their DNA involves a love for mass movements driven by a sense of moral outrage and an almost messianic sense of mission. This personality stamp reflects itself strongly in America now as the baby boomers have moved into key positions in government and throughout society. Baby boomers, although very much self-absorbed and narcissistic, need to belong to a group driving for change and miss this feeling which was such a fundamental part of their lives in their formative years. It is ironic that this generation which sees itself involved fundamentally in a moral crusade is in fact so morally bankrupt. The self-deception involved to sustain this is hard to fathom.

As mentioned in the discussion of economic justice, liberals are outraged at what they see as vertical inequity—for example, issues relating to the rich versus the poor—but are silent about horizontal inequity as it relates to income redistribution between people of similar economic status. That liberals reward people who evade hard work and taxes, who fail to save, and who shirk their individual responsibilities doesn't concern them. That they penalize those who are industrious, save, pay their taxes, and are responsible also doesn't concern them. Is it moral to bail out some homeowners and not others? Is it moral to force responsible taxpayers to pay for the mistakes of others, including the mistakes of government?

This obsession with vertical inequity and quiescent acceptance of horizontal inequity underscores the moral bankruptcy of liberalism. It highlights that they are not interested in individual morality at all. The real issue for them is power. Their focus is on government seizure of wealth from the private sector that can then be used to create a culture of dependency and a consolidation of government power.

Is it moral to make false promises, promises that you know you will not deliver on? Is it moral to promise Social Security retirement and then break the lockbox into which Social Security payments are made? Is it moral to promise high public sector pensions to public employees and not provide the funding to pay for these pensions? Government requires firms in the private sector to provide funding to back-up their pension obligations, but they have defaulted on their own responsibility. Liberals are continually promising that their programs will help the poor and disadvantaged, but the consequences are just the opposite. Yet they press for more of the same and oppose reforms that could actually help the disadvantaged. Is it moral to squander money, especially the money of others on counterproductive programs? Is it moral to abuse the public trust and fail to serve the public interest through responsible policy formulation and implementation?

It's interesting that liberals deify and exalt their leaders, but vilify and demean those who oppose or disagree with them. Hence liberals see things in terms of good and evil when trying to advance their agenda—but in terms of morality they don't recognize good and evil. To liberals an axe murderer is probably a good man who was only unfortunate enough to have been exposed to the wrong environmental conditions, whereas Dick Cheney and George Bush are evil war criminals. Regarding morality, liberals are monistic, not believing in right and wrong and good and evil. But when it comes to their agenda and what they want they are Manichean. This discrepancy is quite revelatory, exposing a raw hunger for power.

An ends-justify-the-means modus operandi is the antithesis of morality. It presumes that we are all agreed on what the appropriate ends are. It dismisses rules and ethical standards as obstacles that need to be surmounted. Anything that gets in the way of their agenda is dismissed.

The trouble with the ends-justify-the-means modus operandi is that it inevitably leads us down a slippery slope. Once authorities can get away with unscrupulous means they can dramatically grow their power. Over time the engagement in unscrupulous means becomes more and more pronounced and evilness festers and grows consuming all, the authorities and victims alike. So, while in the beginning the end is the predicate for action and policy, later on the means become the predicate, determining all. The ensuing vortex of evil sucks everyone in.

It almost seems that liberal political tactics come straight out of Machiavelli's book, *The Prince*. Machiavelli, a philosopher of the Italian renaissance period, justified the pursuit of political ends by whatever are the most effective means whether moral or not. *The Prince* was a manual on techniques for the manipulation of others for political purposes. However, although Machiavelli tossed aside moral constraints as an expensive political obstacle, he argued that it can be effective to cloak one's actions in the name of morality and virtue. Inconsistency and hypocrisy were fine if it served one's purposes.

Liberals are always arguing we need programs to help the poor, women, gays, oppressed workers, and the disadvantaged, but their real objective is to expand their own power and influence. They love to cloak their actions in false choices: we need to raise taxes so that little Johnny with the bad leg can get the care that he needs, or that grandma, who has a bad heart condition, receives proper treatment. Anyone who opposes such support is promptly and loudly labeled immoral, selfish, or greedy. Of course, any revenue raised leaves little Johnny and grandma unaffected because the raised revenue simply goes to finance more government bloat. Liberal spending on education and poverty has not improved our education system or reduced poverty. What does the Department of Education really do? Would it not be better to spend the money in the classrooms on the students?

Liberals don't see a problem with Medicare fraud of one billion dollars a year. Of course, this shouldn't come as a surprise. It's not their money. For the bureaucrats in charge of Medicare, fraud is actually a good thing. It expands their turf. It gives them more power, more money to play with. It expands their influence, so why should they try to curtail it? Liberalism actually encourages and enables freeloaders and slackers to take advantage of the government welfare state.

The negative effects of welfare are well documented. It encourages a life of dependency. It harms family life, because it has provided an incentive to break up marriage as a way to secure public-funding support. The intended impact on poverty has never materialized, but the negative, unintended consequences are blatantly manifest.

If liberals were really committed to an ends-justify-the-means morality, you would see them more concerned about the efficacy of the means they are using. However, they show no interest in whether their policies are failing or if the institutions which they have created to improve education and reduce poverty are working. This betrays their lack of real interest in their professed agenda of poverty alleviation and improvement in the life of the public. It underscores that they are not about process or efficacy, but only the enunciation of unrealizable dreams and the seizure of political power. It shows that they are about misrepresentation and deception.

Liberals support abortion. Is this moral? That millions of embryos are snuffed out and potential lives are terminated is not of concern for them. For them the key is that women should have a right to choose what to do with their bodies. If women are careless and engage in reckless sex, they should be allowed to have an abortion. Of course, the liberal says nothing to discourage bad sexual behavior. For them there is no such thing. And, of course, the fetus doesn't count. He doesn't vote.

Is it moral to push collectivism, which strips man of his individuality and dignity? Is it moral to make men into automatons, instruments of the State? Is it moral to say as moral relativism does that, all values are the same, none better than another? Does moral equivalency make sense? This strips man of his values. Those who profess to have values are ridiculed and called bigots.

Is it moral to encourage people not to live up to their potential? Nature has created in all creatures the need to fulfill their potential. Those that do survive; the others don't. Struggle is a fundamental part of nature. Liberals, however, believe that life should be easy, that struggle simply should not be part of life and so should be eliminated. Is it moral to encourage people to be dependent, to take from the community rather than to give? Is this not corrosive of the moral fiber of man?

Is it moral to strip man of reason and dissuade him from pursuing truth? Are not reason and the pursuit of truth fundamental to the nature of man? Political correctness is not only denying man the right to speak freely, but even to think freely.

Liberalism is elitist, seeing man generally as deficient and unable to take care of himself and make the right decisions. For liberals, however, man is not without hope. The Left believe that men can be re-educated to live better, more moral lives. Education is a big part of their agenda. Liberalism goes further however, subscribing to eugenics. Eugenics has played an important role in the liberal-progressive movement since the early twentieth century, as Jonah Goldberg documents well in his book *Liberal Fascism.* Fascism and collectivist political experiments have a long history of eugenics. We have certainly seen this in Mussolini's Italy and Hitler's Germany, but the American Left have been believers in eugenics too. Woodrow Wilson and Teddy Roosevelt were strong adherents of eugenics. Nowadays liberals are ardent supporters of stem cell research. They want to play God. They want to change the nature of society to fit their vision, and even change the nature of man through education and eugenics. Is this moral or is it hubris of the worst order?

Whatever became of sin? Since early Christianity there has been an emphasis on sin. Seven sins in particular were considered as fatal to spiritual progress: pride, envy, gluttony, lust, wrath, greed, and sloth. These sins now have become the vestments of liberalism. The liberal elite exude an arrogance and excessive confidence in their abilities, and disdain the way others think and want to lead their lives. They are driven by envy of others who have what they don't. The rich in particular are a focus of their envy. Gluttony drives them to consume and pander to their appetites, while sloth makes them shun work. Lust manifests itself in sexual abandon and indulgence. Nothing should get in the way of the fulfillment of their desires. They can't contain their wrath at any who disagree with them. Greed for power underpins liberalism, not the compassion they profess. And greed for wealth impels them to try to take wealth from others through the political system.

King Solomon in the Book of Proverbs spoke against a "lying tongue" and "a deceitful witness that uttereth lies." Dishonesty, though not part of the seven deadly sins, is a serious moral problem. The liberal, as mentioned, is not averse to deceit and dishonesty if it's for a "good" purpose.

The Greek philosophers of antiquity, like Aristotle and Plutarch, focused on character, not actions or policies. For them this was as essential in public life as in private life. Without character and commitment to certain values, private life suffers, but so does the ability of a government to function properly and to serve the interests of its people. The early Greek philosophers were concerned with the notion of the best way to live a good life. This is in sharp contrast to the focus of moral discourse today, which fundamentally ignores issues of character and virtue. Today the focus is on justifying actions rather than on looking at the importance of character and at the individual as a moral agent. This is in keeping with the movement of liberalism deemphasizing the role of the individual. Today's focus on moral decisions and actions puts the cart before the horse, and in no small way actually contributes to moral decay.

For the Greeks, a moral man was strong, courageous, independent-minded, honest, and committed to reason and the pursuit of truth. He was industrious, hard-working, and willing to sacrifice for the future. He trusted himself. In contrast, in today's liberal world of diminished individuality, the individual is subordinate to the State. The individual is expected to follow the herd and follow the guidance of the elite ruling class, rather than trust his own judgment. Strength and courage have been replaced by expressed compassion and a willingness to bend. Risk-aversion is now the goal, not adventure, striving or hard work. Nothing is worth fighting for.

The contrast between the early Greeks and the liberalism of today is stark. Whereas the early Greeks had a commitment to personal excellence and achievement, the Left encourages dependence and taking. Whereas the early Greeks encouraged respect for others and their achievements, the Left encourages envy. Whereas the early Greeks valued courage and taking risk, the Left encourages risk-aversion and security. Whereas the early Greeks valued hard work, liberalism encourages the easy way and an entitlement mentality. Whereas the early Greeks valued reason and openness to discussion and other points of view, liberalism is committed to irrationality, intolerance, and political correctness. Whereas the early Greeks valued the pursuit of exalted goals and self-sacrifice, liberalism is pleasure-driven and encourages self-indulgence. Whereas the early Greeks sought to see man develop his individual potential to the fullest, the Left seeks to diminish man and make him a servant of the State.

Moreover, liberalism, by shifting the center of moral decisions away from the individual to the government, exacerbates this. Without character in the center of morality and without the individual in the center of moral decisions, morality is hollowed out and empty. Government is wresting control of morality and in the process depreciating it. Without individual character, morality is an empty vessel. Without the individual at its core, it's meaningless.

It's interesting that government itself hardly ever accepts any responsibility for bad policies and the harm it does to others. Rarely does one see any evidence of accountability in government. Did Democratic representatives Dodd and Frank or others apologize or accept responsibility for the mortgage crisis and the fiasco of Fannie Mae and Freddie Mac? No, they did not. Of course, to be fair, they did not expect private citizens to exercise any responsibility either. There is this aspect of consistency in the liberal credo, but is this really the world we want to live in?

Liberalism's de-emphasis of reason hurts morality. For Aristotle, "Virtue is character concerned with choice, lying in the mean which is defined by reference to reason." It is a mean between two vices, one of excess and one of deficiency; and again, it is a mean because the vices respectively fall short or exceed what is right in both passions and actions, while virtue both finds and chooses that which is intermediate."[185] This encapsulated Aristotle's notion of the Golden Mean. For the early Greeks, virtue and moral behavior were fundamentally grounded in reason and were exercised by the individual, not the State.

Bertrand Russell also underscored the importance of reason and a scientific state of mind to morality and ethics. In his book *Authority and the Individual*, Russell said the following:

> "Empiricism is to be commended not only on the ground of its greater truth, but also on ethical grounds. Dogma demands authority, rather than intelligent thought, as the source of opinion; it requires persecution of heretics and hostility to unbelievers; it asks of its disciples that they should inhibit natural kindliness in favour of systematic hatred. Since argument is not recognized as a means of arriving at truth, adherents of rival dogmas have no method except war by means of which to reach a decision."

Some would say that capitalism has no intrinsic morality. They would say that it is limited to only commercial and monetary values. But this ignores the reality. Capitalism clearly rewards certain behaviors. It rewards hard work, dedication, educational achievement, and those who develop their market skill. It rewards those who meet the needs of others in the marketplace. By alleviating the misery and bondage of poverty, it allows people the opportunity to pursue exalted aims. Moreover, by providing a sanctuary for individual liberty, it allows individuals to develop themselves as they would like, not how some ruling elite or government would like.

With capitalism there is room for a plurality of moralities allowed principally by emancipating people from their basic material needs, as well as by its effect in promoting individual liberty. This contrasts starkly with the monolithic moralities generally characterizing most collectivist political systems.

Capitalism allows people with different moralities to transact with each other and to prosper. It's not a zero-sum game, with one party benefitting at the expense of another, which is pretty much the inevitable situation in non-market economies. Under capitalism both parties to a transaction usually benefit, otherwise they wouldn't engage in it voluntarily.

Liberals see profit as sin. They don't want to understand that profit comes from meeting the needs of others. A profit primarily comes about if one is able to provide something others want more efficiently than others can provide it. Liberals don't understand that in hurting profits, they are hurting not only those who accrue them, but the people who buy their products. Liberals declare that they are trying to represent the interests of the latter, but this is not their real intent or effect.

Liberals complain that poverty in America and the world is immoral, but poverty is not a recent phenomenon. Poverty has plagued us ever since man appeared on earth. It has only been with the advent of capitalism that the lives of a large part of the world's population has improved. But for liberals because it has not completely eliminated poverty, the solution is to destroy that which has brought us so far. Does this make any sense?

With capitalism there is hope for changing one's life and improving one's economic well-being. This was not the case before its advent. Though liberalism professes to bring hope to the masses, it is attempting to destroy the very vehicle which has allowed hope to flourish. Liberalism is but a cruel joke, raising the hopes of people while undermining the foundations of hope.

Liberalism is premised on a zero-sum-game perspective: it's about dividing the pie rather than growing it. This is evidenced in the politics of division that plays such a dominant role in liberalism. This view of the world and this divisive politics inevitably descends into an "us-against-them mentality." This is not the liberalism of JFK, who said, "Ask not what your country can do for you, but what you can do for your country." Today's liberalism is a culture for freeloaders and slackers and those who want to manipulate and game the system to their advantage. The responsible, the conscientious, and those trying to make a positive contribution to the system are left holding the bag. What kind of moral system is this?

The politics of division is basically about advancing one's interest at the expense of others. The fact that it is done under the banner of compassion and proclamations of helping others makes it even worse. Is it moral to use dissimulation to accomplish one's objectives? Is it moral to abandon commitment to truth simply because it's an obstacle to the pursuit of one's objectives? Are not truth and honesty universal foundations of almost all moral systems?

Our culture is the most successful in the world economically and in terms of individual freedom and happiness. We can see this by the number of people trying to immigrate here. Yet we don't defend our culture. In earlier generations our forefathers shed blood for it, now we just apologize and surrender it. Is it moral to squander what our forefathers shed blood for? Our ethical views compete in a global environment. We need to stand up for our values and culture, not capitulate and apologize for them.

It's good to test our moral standards against others. Competition is good here too. But to compete we need to be advocates for our own moral standards. We need to fight for them, not meekly acquiesce that all standards are equally valid. Spinelessness and obeisance to moral relativism don't serve us or others well.

Liberals have as little respect for the law as they do moral principles and guidelines. Laws and moral principles are for them forms of oppression and needless constraint. They favor lax drug laws. One shouldn't strive for happiness or pleasure when one can simply take a drug instead. Why work at it when you can take a pill or inject something? Where is the morality here?

For liberals, good behavior and moral axioms are unnecessary. Frugality and sexual responsibility are unnecessary. It's OK for those who don't save for retirement to be bailed out by the state. In other words, those who do save and work should take care of them. Likewise, in the scheme of liberalism, it's OK to have children out of wedlock. For liberals there should be no penalty for people who do this. In fact, there is a *reward* for it, in the form of tax-payer support. Some choose responsibly not to have children out of financial considerations—but it's ironic that these people must provide support to those who simply don't care to exercise responsibility.

Liberals make it clear that most people don't know what is really good for them. Liberals believe most people don't have the intellectual capital to effectively manage their lives. Given this, liberals think it is incumbent on them to shape the lives of those in need in guidance. In effect liberals want to steal the moral agency of others. Is this moral?

Essentially moral systems are of two types: they are either based on the consequences of actions or on moral principles guiding actions. The consequentialist approach says an action is either right or wrong based on the effects produced; the deontological approach, on the other hand, ignores the consequences and instead focuses on the actions *intrinsic* rightness or wrongness. In other words, actions are not judged as a means to an end, but rather are evaluated on their own merit. According to this approach, lying, cheating, incest, and killing are simply wrong.

Utilitarianism is probably the most influential moral theory based on consequentiality, whereas religion and Immanuel Kant's work are the most important deontological systems. Both of these philosophies profoundly affect moral perspectives in the West. Utilitarianism is practical and underlies economics because it looks at the satisfaction of wants and maximizing welfare. Deontological theories, on the other hand, largely are an outgrowth of our Judeo-Christian heritage, although Kant in his work sought to generate a duty-based moral system that did not need a religious predicate.

According to utilitarianism, as mentioned in the chapter on justice, the moral good seeks to maximize utility, or happiness, for the population over all. Jeremy Bentham, the founder of utilitarianism, did not distinguish between higher or lower pleasures. In fact he is famously quoted as saying, "Prejudice apart the game of push-pin (bowling in today's world) is of equal value with the arts and music and poetry." Of course, this doesn't fit with the elitism of liberals. For them the pleasures of the intellect should outweigh the simple pleasures widely enjoyed by the masses. The pleasures derived from a game of bowling should in no way be commensurate with that of watching refined theater. It's interesting that liberal sensibilities seem so dismissive of what the masses find so enjoyable, while at the same time they represent themselves as those carrying their banner and seeking to support them.

Utilitarianism treats each individual equally. The pleasure of one person is not treated differently than that of another. Thus the basis of utilitarianism is very egalitarian. Again, one would think that this would appeal to liberals, but, no, it runs against their elitist nature. For them, the pleasure of a poet or an intellectual should be accorded more weight than that of a simple, uneducated man.

Utilitarianism is a consequentialist moral doctrine that plays an important role in shaping public policy. Communism is consequentialist too. Although communism is primarily thought of as a political ideology, it has very significant moral dimensions as well. It de-emphasizes the individual in favor of the collective and takes moral (and other) decisions away from the individual and gives them to the State. Pursuit of self-interest is frowned upon. The maxim, "To each according to his need, from each according to his ability," suggests the intervention of the State and the sacrifice of individuality on the altar of the State.

Another difference between utilitarianism and communism is that utilitarianism works on an issue-by-issue basis. It's not all-embracing and encompassing, so it's less prone to abuse and usurpation. Communism, by contrast, is all-encompassing, seeking a grand overarching goal and institutional framework that lends itself to misuse and abuse. By working on an issue-by-issue basis utilitarianism is ideally suited to short-term policy formulation and implementation, whereas communism has serious shortcomings as it has its sights and focus on the long-term. As a result, communist experiments have always led to adverse short-term outcomes and poor outcomes on an issue-by-issue basis. This is one of the reasons why communism has failed. You can't get to the long term if you can't traverse the short term.

Some ethicists would argue that commitment to moral principles is more important than basing action on considerations of consequence. Indeed, philosophers like Immanuel Kant believed that consequences shouldn't be factored in at all. Kant, as noted in the previous chapter, believed that certain categorical imperatives, universal moral axioms, should be the sole guide of our conduct. Consequences shouldn't be taken into account at all. For example, even if it would save thousands of lives, torture shouldn't be used to extract information from a terrorist. This is, of course, difficult in our modern and complex world, but nevertheless there is much good to say about such an ethical standard.

One could not say that liberals are adhering to such a standard. Liberals are not driven by moral standards because they have none; they are averse to laws, rules, and standards of behavior. Liberals are instead driven by emotion, not morality. Empathy (not backed up by action or deed) and a sense of belonging to something larger than themselves drives them, not a commitment to principle or morality.

For Kant, morality comes from within. We all have a moral law within us. For him the essence of morality is to obey moral laws that we impose on ourselves. Moral law shouldn't come from a force outside ourselves. It definitely shouldn't come from the State. This internal moral law is informed and guided by reason. Nor is it moral to treat others as instruments, using them to advance our own self-interest. The nature of liberalism is fundamentally inconsistent with Kantian ethics. Although it's grounded in professed altruism, its elitist nature is geared to treating people as instruments. It doesn't see moral law as coming from within us, but rather sees it imposed upon us by social convention. Moreover, liberalism is opposed to rules and principles, because these constrain the power and authority of the ruling elite.

Leon Trotsky, one of the most prominent founders of communism, said, "The end may justify the means so long as there is something that justifies the end." The problem with this thinking is that it creates moral chaos; it strips civilization of the glue that holds it together. Moreover, how do you justify an end? And how easy is it for a leader to declare that he is seeking an apparently good goal, when in fact he is driven only to the end of amassing power and personal aggrandizement. History is littered with cases involving just such abuse.

It's interesting that liberals tout moral relativism, arguing that one set of morals can't be said to be better than another, but all the while are on a jihad for their own moral agenda. Anyone who disagrees with their policies is considered immoral and uncaring. Hence liberals are making real moral decisions without even realizing it. They cannot see themselves.

If people believe that all moral systems are arbitrary, merely products of social convention, they would no longer feel constrained to act in a certain moral way. They would think they have a license to do anything. Such thinking is destructive of individual character. It dissolves the forces that bind communities together for the benefit of all. We see the baleful effects of moral relativism all around us in today's world.

As mentioned earlier, Jonathan Haidt of the University of Virginia believes that the approach of liberals to morality is hidebound and much narrower than that of conservatives. He says that liberals are narrowly concerned about how we treat each other, and don't understand the broader role of morality as an instrument to bring about a well-ordered society. According to Haidt, morality is composed of five fundamental foundations. The focus of liberalism is only on two of the five pillars: harm/care and fairness/reciprocity. For liberals, the essence of morality is that we shouldn't harm one another and we should care for one another. Fairness for liberals, as mentioned above, means equal outcome across people in terms of wealth and material possessions. It's fairness in distribution, not fairness in production or contribution. Also, as indicated earlier, it's about vertical equity, not horizontal equity.[186]

Conservatism, on the other hand, is more encompassing. It relies not just on harm/care and fairness/reciprocity, but on the other pillars of morality, including in-group/loyalty, authority/respect, and purity/sanctity. Liberals, as discussed earlier in the psychological studies, don't favor their ethnic group or friends over others outside the group. The extent to which they buy into moral relativism probably contributes to this. It's well known that liberals have a problem with authority and respect, perhaps stemming from discomfort or bad experience from an authoritarian father. They also have a problem with purity/sanctity, because they see such notions primarily rising out of outdated religious dogma and, more importantly, constraining their sexual and material appetites.[187]

The more broad-based approach of conservatism looks at morality as integrally involving "values, practices, institutions, and psychological mechanisms" for the purpose of creating and supporting a morally ordered society. In other words, the focus is on creating a morally ordered society, not a free zone for individuals to pursue their appetites. In this context, issues like gun rights, abortion, and gay marriage need to be considered not in isolation, but in the light of an interlocking system of morality. As Emile Durkheim warned, "Man cannot become attached to higher aims and submit to a rule if he sees nothing above him to which he belongs."[188]

Compassion is an important part of what makes us human. Liberals place a high emphasis on compassion. However, by having the State take over the exercise of compassion, it's removing it from the life of individuals. It's removing part of our humanity. Likewise the State is taking over the role of instilling values and moral education in our children. Liberalism is divesting us of our values and stripping us of our moral agency.

Nowadays, when a man gets caught cheating on his wife, he blames it on sex addiction. He attributes his bad actions to a medical problem and seeks rehabilitation. Likewise drug users and smokers blame biological addiction. There is always a justification, an abdication of moral responsibility. Where is the moral choice? In the liberal mind there is none. Bad behavior, according to them, is determined by factors and circumstances outside of our control. There is no such person anymore as a *bum*. This person now is "homeless," "disadvantaged." He needs help and we shouldn't expect or even encourage any initiative on his part. We should only expect and support dependency.

In essence liberalism is suffused with immorality. Its policies and agenda are morally bankrupt. Likewise the ends-justify-the-means philosophy underpinning it is not just immoral, but dangerous and downright evil. The ubiquitous contradictions and hypocrisies that riddle liberal philosophy from top to bottom highlight its moral bankruptcy. Nevertheless, its ever-present efforts to clothe itself in the language of morality are quite successful—it has managed to fool a sizeable part of the electorate. One can only hope that such people will wake up before it's too late.

In a quotation at the beginning of this chapter, de Tocqueville noted that we can't have liberty without morality, and we can't have morality without faith. I don't agree that we can't have morality without faith or religion. There are many people who are not religious who are very moral. The work of Kant makes this quite clear, but it's nevertheless true that faith and religion play an important role in making men moral. There is no doubt that the importance of morality and respect for our fellow man is central to the preservation of liberty. In undermining morality, liberalism is destroying the foundation of liberty. The disdain of the elite liberal for the common man is also a clear danger to liberty.

* * *

CHAPTER 16

LIBERALISM'S IMPACT ON INSTITUTIONAL STRUCTURE AND PERFORMANCE

———◆———

It is difficult to get a man to understand something when his job depends on not understanding it.

~Upton Sinclair

Confusion of goals and perfection of means seems, in my opinion, to characterize our age.

~Albert Einstein

Another reason liberalism fails is it doesn't understand the institutional side of pursuing an agenda. Intentionality and objective are not enough. To achieve one's ends, it's necessary to have a firm grasp of how we get from here to there and the institutional aspects that intermediate between intentionality and outcome.

As we have seen there is strong evidence that liberals don't care that their declared objectives are not met. If this is so, it would not be surprising that they are not interested in institutions. If, however, they were genuinely interested, it would be pivotally important that they understand the institutional factors that link their declared intentions to their declared objectives.

The institution intermediating between intention and declared goals for liberals is government. The reason liberals aren't concerned about failing to meet declared objectives is that such objectives are really only a smokescreen for their real objective: the expansion of government and the powers therein. It's the only explanation that makes sense. Otherwise, why would liberals continue pursuing policies that have failed time and time again?

Liberalism, with its expanded role for government, creates inefficient, corruption-prone, and oversized organizational structures; it creates overly complex organizations and centralizes power in the hands of the few. The liberal bias is for centralized power and against federalism.

Institutional failure, particularly in the machinery of government, is exacerbated by liberalism. It's natural that as institutions age they grow too large, become inefficient, become far removed from their original purpose, become difficult to control and manage, and ultimately disserve the people they are meant to serve. Institutions over time take on a life of their own. They become living, breathing entities with their own objectives that often work to the detriment of humankind. Unfortunately, this weakness is endemic to all cultures and political systems. But, while conservatism fights to constrain these adverse tendencies, liberalism fosters and accentuates institutional dysfunction.

Stability

Liberalism is creating instability in many ways. First, by ignoring the past and the lessons of history, it is putting together policies that are destined to fail. Second, by failing to balance spending and revenues, it is creating an unsustainable fiscal and macro-economic situation which will explode. Third, it relies on intervention rather than letting markets adjust themselves. Suppressing problems only allows them to fester. Fourth, by creating a centralized power structure and diminishing the power of the states, it adds to risk. Federalism is inherently stabilizing as different states pursue different policies, so all states are not going in the same direction at the same time. Fifth, the risk of instability is increased by trying to introduce too much change too fast. Sixth, by demolishing time-tested institutions like religion, family, and traditional values, it is undermining the foundations of our country. Seventh, its reliance on mob or group-think has the herd all moving in the same direction at the same time. Eighth, liberalism's abandonment of reason is a serious mistake as reason is our best beacon into the future. Ninth, creating large inefficient institutions that are resistant to change in a rapidly changing world is a recipe for crisis and breakdown. Tenth, it hurts stability by weakening democracy in favor of strong centralized power with no checks and balances.

It's important not to veer sharply off course and enter into patterns of instability. By relying on reason, man can effect corrections when he sees trends moving too far in one direction or another. Growth and change are important and necessary, but are best achieved in a stable framework, a framework of equilibrium. Going off course too abruptly and without the check of open discussion and the application of reason, constantly questioning whether we should slow down or speed up, or change direction, is dangerous and doesn't serve the interests of anyone. Self-correction and the exercise of control on trends are needed to keep momentum from taking us too far in one direction or another.

Liberals are not students of history. They dismiss readily the past failures of similar utopian visions and somehow don't believe them to be relevant. They seem desperate to dismantle the current social and economic system and jump to their utopian vision of the future. Process and change and complexity are uninteresting to them—but dynamics are just as important as destination. Things don't just happen. Just witness the horrors that followed the French Revolution and the Russian and Chinese revolutions.

Liberals believe that they can bring about desired changes easily, although the historical record offers stark evidence to the contrary. They believe in abrupt, wrenching changes, not in small changes phased in gradually. They don't recognize the complexities involved. They don't foresee the unintended consequences that inevitably follow the implementation of new policies. Everything doesn't remain unchanged. We are not dealing with a *ceteris paribus* environment, but rather a highly complex general equilibrium economic, political, and social system.

Politicians like change. It makes them look energetic, aggressive, and like they are doing something. It's a bit like the new boss in the office. Things may be working fine, but to prove he is able, industrious, and productive he will propose change for change's sake. Conservatives are not against change, but they are aware of the complexities involved and are circumspect about large sweeping changes introduced in a short time without much analysis. Conservatives respect the difficulty of changing things and respect the potential of unintended consequences.

In his bestselling book *The Black Swan*, Nassim Taleb said, "Our world is dominated by the extreme, the unknown, and the improbable (improbable according to our current knowledge) and all the while we spend our time engaged in small talk, focusing on the known, and the repeated."[189] Taleb thinks that we underestimate uncertainty and the likelihood of the rare event. He went on to write, "Owing to a misunderstanding of the causal chains between policy and actions, we can easily trigger Black Swans (unforeseen outcomes) thanks to aggressive ignorance—like a child playing with a chemistry kit."

We are blind to randomness. We expect the past to repeat itself. This blindness is particularly significant and dangerous with large deviations or changes. Malcolm Gladwell, in his book *The Tipping Point*, emphasized how equilibrium can be thrown out of kilter if change is too fast.

It's important to respect our traditions and customs and not overturn them wantonly. To be sure, change and growth are important, so one doesn't want to be stuck in the past. But surely it's a mistake to undertake a massive overhaul of systems that are little understood and that were put together and have survived time. Change should be thoughtful, gradual.

John F. Kennedy, talking about the electoral system, said, "If it ain't broke, don't fix it." This thought is equally applicable to our current economic and political system. It has demonstrated itself to be the best in the world. We shouldn't tinker with it.

The Left tend to be against anything that represents the status quo. The system should be turned upside down. This contrasts starkly with the conservative who sees good in the world. For the conservative the current system is just and represents cumulative efforts over time to improve the lot of man. Our current traditions, institutions, and values embedded in western civilization are the best that man could offer up to this time and shouldn't be tossed aside because they're imperfect. Nothing is perfect, but our system is so much better than anything else out there that we would be crazy to throw it away for utopian dreams.

In a market economy, the business cycle, unimpeded by government, clears out the inefficient and unproductive. A competitive capitalist economy gets rid of the dead wood. Nonperforming enterprises disappear. This is not so in statist economies. Large government institutions are primarily interested in expansion and self-preservation; their mandated missions are merely window dressing. Once a government institution or program is established it's notoriously difficult to get rid of, even if it isn't performing and is a dead weight on the system. So, while a market economy makes gradual and incremental adjustments over time to keep the system running well, a statist model resists change. Government institutions are rigid and not given to adaptability in the face of change. This rigidity means that in time they get far out of touch and hence become vulnerable to wrenching change and catastrophic failure. In an age marked by rapid and accelerating change, this is a troubling and fatal flaw of the statist model. It bottles up pressures for change until there's an explosion of uncontrolled forces. It lets a disease or problem within the system fester and go untreated rather than attempt to address it when treatment could effectively deal with the problem. Thus it is prone to disease, averse to cures, and disposed toward devastating outcomes.

Liberalism is caught in a vicious self-fulfilling spiral of intervention that is highly destabilizing. It is irremediably entangled in the pathology of interventionism. First, as dislocations build as it suppresses the self-corrective forces of the market and the business cycle, this helps justify more government intervention and fix-it attempts to remedy ever-growing problems. Second, once a crisis erupts, even more government intervention is justified. Thus intervention creates a need for ever more intervention; it creates an ever increasing demand for itself and an inexorable expansion in the State. The private sector which is more adaptable to handling change becomes smaller and less significant. This destabilizing dynamic is highly destructive and difficult to stop.

Intervention engenders behavioral changes adverse to stability. In the 1970s the government's commitment to full employment enhanced the leverage of unions to raise wages and led to the problem of stagflation. On the business side, corporate bail-outs and crony capitalism have created moral hazards and incentives to engage in risky and speculative activity. As a consequence corporations are more dependent on government largesse and hence weaker and less able to compete and adapt to change.

In his most recent book *Antifragile*, Nassim Taleb noted, "the problem with artificially suppressed volatility is not just that the system tends to become extremely fragile; it is that, at the same time, it exhibits no visible risks."[190] Suppressing problems creates the illusion of stability, while it sets in motion forces which actually undermine it. Thus politicians who try to eliminate uncertainty, risk, and adverse outcomes are perversely the very ones creating these problems, only on a much grander and dangerous scale. They do this unwittingly, but this is the folly of planning. They fail to recognize that the fragility of systems is decreased by volatility and uncertainty as small and continuous adjustments help to stabilize systems. Exposure to disorder encourages adaptiveness, innovation, and strength.

Liberalism does not even look at system fragility or the basic risks involved in its hubristic approach to planning and control.[191] It looks only at the short-term, not the long-term effects of its policies. It does not acknowledge that intervention can produce harm as well as good, focusing only on the good. This willful blindness is very destructive.

Thus, to minimize the risk of existential failure, it is critically important to focus on the stability of systems. This involves decentralization, avoiding herd-like movements, not creating institutions too big to fail, avoidance of top-down management and decision-making which is prone to error and rigidity, not placing all bets on one policy and goal, and not suppressing small corrections or adjustments in the market. Unfortunately, liberalism is not only pursuing policies that are destabilizing our society, but it is also rendering our institutions less stable so that they are less able to withstand the kind of pressures that are mounting. On top of this, it is reducing our policy abilities to respond to a crisis. With the budget deficit and debt very high and interest rates at historic lows, the authorities have no ammunition left to combat a serious economic crisis. It is like a doctor throwing away his medicine bag, while exposing his patient to a dangerous virus and at the same time giving drugs to weaken the patient's immune system. Like the malevolent doctor, liberalism professes good intentions and compassion, but it is working tirelessly to destroy us. This is not just unintentional quackery. Liberalism thrives on crises, as it opportunistically uses them to expand power; it has an incentive to create crises, not to avoid them, and this is reflected in its actions.

Bias Toward Oversized Organizations

By rewarding politicians and bureaucrats, who spend more and who expand the size of government, democracy is afflicted with a congenital defect, one that bloats government and atrophies the private sector. This syndrome, when taken to its culmination, ends in a polity consumed by government. It is no longer a government of, by, and for the people, but rather one of, by, and for the government.

Increased reliance on debt, rather than taxes, to finance increased spending also expands government. Much like excessive spending in the private sector; it just seemed easier and did not involve immediate costs, given our time-preference bias for the here and now rather than the future. Why not let future generations pay for our indulgence?

Reliance on Keynesian counter-cyclical techniques has also increased the size of government. During recessions, the government boosts spending to stimulate the economy based on Keynesian theory. During booms Keynesian theory suggests that the government should curtail its spending, but in reality the government has shown no appetite for this. Thus government counter-cyclical management has over time led to an expansion of government—it swells in size during recessions, but does not contract during boom periods.

Another explanation could be that as nations and their citizens become more prosperous, citizens develop an increased demand for public goods and services relative to private goods.

There is no doubt that this could be true too, but the primary driving forces are those mentioned above.

Government expands because there are not sufficient forces constraining its growth. In a market economy, firms are limited in size by the most efficient scale of production or, in the case of increasing returns to scale, by anti-trust policies. If a firm expands beyond the most efficient scale of production, its profits would suffer and it would be placed at a disadvantage relative to competitors. The profit motive constrains firm size in a market economy. Government, on the other hand, is largely unconstrained. It's not subject to the tether of profit or efficiency. It's difficult to monitor whether it is in fact serving the public good. And even if it isn't, it's impossible to terminate a government program. The constituency benefiting from the government program, including government bureaucrats, will always prevail over the public interest. They will fight tooth and nail to maintain their benefit while the public is not nearly so motivated, because the cost to them is often hidden and most certainly more diffuse.

The bias of liberalism toward ever greater size in organizations is metastatic, it goes on and on. Governments within countries grow forever larger and more dominating, but liberalism doesn't stop there. It expands to meta-level, transnational government á la the European Union, the World Trade Organization, and the United Nations.

The problem is organizations have an optimum size beyond which they become inefficient and prone to corruption. The agenda of liberals for big government, big institutions, government interference, and regulation conduces to corruption, rent-seeking, and adverse incentives. Institutions are becoming overgrown, exceeding their optimum size and thus are increasingly inefficient. As institutions and organizations grow beyond a certain size, objectives expand to too many, and the institutions become corrupt. Is it not interesting that everyone, including most liberals, agrees that government is dysfunctional and becoming more so over time? Yet liberals seek to vest ever more power in it and expand its size.

The incentives such institutions create often are not connected to the intended or stated objectives. For example, bank regulations designed to prevent charging high interest on credit cards have caused many banks to curtail lending to poor people. Government programs at Fannie Mae and Freddy Mac intended to channel mortgage credit to poor people have ended up hurting those people. The Department of Education—set up to promote education—has siphoned money away that otherwise would have gone to the schoolroom. Food stamps and generous social assistance programs have hurt the incentive to work.

As size increases, the humaneness of the organization dies and worsens the quality of lives of those working for it and those having to deal with it. Interpersonal connections erode, while the impersonal forces within the organization grow. Bertrand Russell once wrote, "Men in control of vast organizations have tended to be too abstract in their outlook, to forget what actual human beings are like, and to try to fit men to systems rather than systems to men."[192]

There are two ways to organize an economy: it can be done through the private sector or through government. Liberals are averse to business. Academics, lawyers, bureaucrats and most of those in the media and entertainment industries would be hopelessly lost trying to make a living in business. They would hate it. They think business is dirty, unsavory, below them. So they prefer government to business.

The problem of oversized organizations is not confined to government; it applies to the private sector too. Globalization and the development of modern technology and communication have all fostered the development of larger and larger institutions, but these are kept efficient by the forces of competition. However, big government's interference in the private sector and crony capitalism is exacerbating the problem.

The Leviathan is inexorably expanding and eating all in its path. Unless it is stopped there will be little left of democracy, capitalism, or liberty. The founding fathers recognized the threat of government. In contrast liberalism today glorifies government and supports its vast expansion. Many recognize the lessons of history about the dangers of big government, yet liberals continue to push big government, even those who don't gain from government's expansion. Why? Institutional growth has a momentum of its own. Institutions have an ineluctable drive for expansion and control that is hard to stop. As they grow they are more and more difficult to control. A managing director brought in to head up a large organization, for example the World Bank, has a difficult mandate. His influence is severely circumscribed. He is more likely to be controlled by the organization than control the organization. Institutions have taken control of us rather than us of them. It's not men, but the creations of man that are now in control.

Bias Toward Over-Complexity

Liberalism is biased toward making life too complex. Lawyers support the liberals in government who in turn support them. The result is a society steeped in litigiousness and impenetrable legalisms. Obamacare was passed by Congress, and, as mentioned, not even the primary supporters of the bill knew what was in it. Nowadays not only are citizens confronted with hefty tax bills, but they must pay an accountant to determine how much to pay. The tax laws are too complex for most people to arrange payment themselves. According to Tanzi, the US tax system now contains over seventy thousand pages of laws and regulations. Tanzi goes on to say, "This increasing complexity and its consequences may be the ultimate price to pay for the expansion of the role of the state in the economy and the greatest future danger for a market economy and a democracy." That complexity will make reality progressively different from our perception of it."[193] For a democracy to function effectively, it is critical that the citizens know what is going on, but as institutions become increasingly complex, their internal workings become increasingly removed from the scrutiny and understanding of the public. It even goes beyond this however. For it's not just the public that no longer knows what is going on, even the leaders in government are clueless. For example, the bank supervisors in the Federal Reserve System and the FDIC had no clue what was going on in the mortgage industry before the financial crisis in 2008.

Bureaucracies develop a life of their own and resist control. For example, the Department of Defense is so sprawling and involuted that it's hard for the man brought in as a Secretary of Defense to understand what is really going on, much less control it. If even leaders can't control their organizations, it is clear that they have a life energy of their own, an energy to survive and more than that, to thrive. President Dwight Eisenhower once warned of the dangers of the large military-industrial complex, but these dangers now lurk in overgrown institutions everywhere as institutions have grown in size and complexity.

Bad fiscal accounting doesn't give the public a clear picture of what is going on in government and what the financial implications are for the public. The complexity of government is covered up by an equally complex and impenetrable system of fiscal accounting. Entitlement programs like Social Security and Medicare are grossly underfunded. Public pensions, too, are unfunded and there are massive amounts of other unfunded and contingent liabilities. The central bank and foreigners are financing a lot of the deficit. There is a lack of transparency and obfuscation galore. Poor accounting standards and practices are letting the government get away with gross fiscal irresponsibility and financial mismanagement—and who can stop it?

The judicial environment is too complex and doesn't serve the interest of the public well. Rather than individuals resolving issues amongst themselves, instead everyone sues one another. Liberalism, which has made the judicial system too complex, is doing the same to the health care system. Health care is more remote and impersonal as it becomes more institutionally complex. The extent to which patients and doctors talk with each other to determine the proper care is on the decline. This is a problem with the HMOs, but it's getting exponentially worse as the government expands its influence into the health sector. Increasingly, government bureaucrats have a say about what treatments doctors can provide patients. Obamacare is about to make this problem significantly worse. Liberalism is separating people from simple face-to-face contact and decision-making, even concerning issues relating to their own bodies.

Essentially, government is trying to pursue too many goals, some of which should be beyond the scope of government. It's trying to do too many things and, consequently, doing none of them well. It's compounding the problem by trying to use means unsuited to the task in the first place and forcing solutions through top-down control and micromanagement.

Alexis de Tocqueville and others have recognized that soft tyranny is the greatest threat to democracies like the USA. He was concerned with a gradual wearing down of our system of government and our human spirit. An ever more intrusive government is controlling more and more of our lives. The State is intent on micromanagement—and on reducing all challenges to its authority. Recently with the introduction of Obamacare, the government is inserting itself between patients and doctors, stripping them of discretion and authority over health care.

Einstein said, "Any intelligent fool can make things bigger and more complex. It takes a touch of genius and a lot of courage to move in the opposite direction." Unfortunately, the intelligent fools are in control.

Bias Toward the Accumulation and Concentration of Power

Liberalism leads to an inevitable concentration of power. Unfortunately, those who want and acquire power rarely use it well. Kurt Vonnegut said, "There is a tragic flaw in our precious Constitution, and I don't know what can be done to fix it. This is it: Only nut cases want to be president." And Cullen Hightower noted, "We may not imagine how our lives could be more frustrating and complex but Congress can."

There are always those who wish to rise to exercise power and authority over others, whether in government, the private sector, or in personal relationships. Many of these people who need power are unbalanced psychologically and are unhappy living a conventional life. Some want power because they love exercising control over others. In some cases they enjoy making others feel inferior, or just making them suffer. In other cases it's a way to feel superior to others. Others find they can bury their empty lives in the world of power. It's like a drug for them, anesthetizing them to the pain they feel in the realities of life. It's a form of workaholism.

Power in the hands of man is a dangerous and ugly thing. Better to live under the dominion and influence of mammon than that of power in the hands of man pursuing power for its own sake. Those who have political power frequently abuse it and don't want to give it up. If people are corrupt before acquiring power, they ineluctably become more corrupt afterward. As they say, absolute power corrupts absolutely. One only has to look at Mugabe, Hitler, Mussolini, Stalin, Chavez, and Castro to understand the evil of too much power in the hands of one man. Unfortunately those who want power and acquire it are not normal. It would be better to be governed by the common man, a so-called "normal man." This is why Ford was such a good president, and also Truman: both fell into office by chance, they did not want it.

The public has less trust in politicians than in any other vocation. Car salesmen come in second to last. Since 2000, the approval rating of Congress has stayed in the single digits. Politicians are only interested in the pursuit of power and reelection. They are willing to deceive and lie to accomplish their objectives. In fact it's almost necessary that they do so if they are to be successful politicians. The interests of the country are not high on their list of priorities. While in office, many politicians become quite wealthy. This is obviously not accomplished on their wages as civil servants. Corruption and backroom deals play a key part in the lives of politicians.

Yet the agenda of the Left is to create a much more powerful state dominated by an elite ruling class. If we know that power corrupts and absolute power corrupts absolutely, what sense does this make? This is particularly so because we would be vesting this power in people we already know to be corrupt. Nor are these people even really elite. If we look at the politicians in this country, they are certainly not the best or the brightest. Their academic and professional backgrounds are really unimpressive. Putting this on top of the fact that many are corrupt, dishonest, and have proven to be mostly interested in themselves and in retaining power, it's hard to understand why anyone would want to see more power in the hands of these people.

Politicians repeatedly say that they are only interested in the welfare of their constituents and the country, but hardly anyone believes this, including the Left. They have a low regard for the intelligence, the morals, and the wishes of the general public, so they think it's necessary to lie and deceive to accomplish their goals. In the recent reform of the health care system in this country there was zero transparency, and Obama and the democrats repeatedly lied about what was happening. Public polls showed that the public highly disapproved of what the democrats were doing with the health care reform bill, but they went ahead and did it anyway. It's interesting that they call this "serving the public."

Of course this is a flaw in any political system governed by men. This is why it's of utmost importance that the power of men is limited. Constitutional government helps to restrain the power of men, but over time these constraints are eroded. The market system plays a key role in limiting the concentration of power. Where political power and economic power are concentrated together the danger of abuse of power is greater. The market system keeps economic and political power in different hands. It limits the opportunity for rent-seeking.

The market system is just that, a system where men don't govern, but rather the invisible hand of the market does. It's governed by a system of rules and the forces involved in the pursuit of self-interest. The pursuit of self-interest in a government governed by men without the constraint of market or other forces leads to adverse outcomes for those not vested with power. The pursuit of self-interest, however, in the context of a market economy leads to desirable outcomes, involving economic growth and reward to those who meet the needs of others. The more government interferes with the market, the less this constraining force exists. This is why it's so important to limit the size of government and its regulatory power.

Liberalism is opposed to the creative economic destruction implicit in a free-market system. In free-market capitalism, obsolete technologies and inefficient firms fail. Under liberalism they are subsidized and protected. This is because under liberalism the key to institutional performance is power, not economic efficacy. As long as institutions are working to grow the power of the ruling elite, this is all they require and want.

Throughout history, cultures have had to deal with the blight of over-concentration of power. It seems that those who get a taste for it want more and more of it. Power is a well-known intoxicant, and its evil allure is well documented. Over time the accumulation of power becomes more and more pronounced, and corruption and abuse become more and more of a problem. Soon comes a breaking point in which the governed rise up to bring about wrenching change. The resulting anarchy and social upheaval is destructive and damaging. It's the price tag for letting power become too concentrated, but this is a pathologic juggernaut that is hard to stop. The lessons from history could not be clearer, but many, particularly liberals, choose to ignore it.

It's hard for individuals to engage in battle with large institutions because the latter have a formidable array of resources. So the advantage goes to the institutions and not the governed. The Tea Party uprising, however, is showing that individuals still have power, but they are up against not just a Goliath, but a whole phalanx of Goliaths.

Government Institutions Prone to Corruption

It was H. L. Mencken who noted, "A good politician is quite as unthinkable as an honest burglar." This may be a bit of an exaggeration, but it's abundantly clear that corruption is present more in public institutions than in market institutions. With the market there is government oversight and public scrutiny. In contrast, government institutions largely police themselves.

Corruption hurts not only the institutions and the people they are meant to serve, but hurts the moral climate of society. Values are depreciated and corroded. The purported aim of liberal policies is to foster communitarian psychology and culture where altruism eclipses self-interest, but the outcome of liberal polices is a direct and complete contradiction of this. Their policies work against their stated and declared aims.

A recently published book, *Why Nations Fail: The Origins of Power, Prosperity and Poverty*, seeks to explain why some nations prosper and others fail, and the author found institutional factors played a major role. Failed states were largely those beset by extractive institutions that served the interests of the ruling elite but not the masses. These inefficient, corruption-prone institutions did not develop by accident, but rather were developed on purpose by the elite to serve their interests. It's not surprising that in such institutional environments investment and economic growth doesn't fare well. Unfortunately, these institutional environments are commonplace around the world and are a significant explanation for why there is so much poverty and oppression. Where power is amassed and concentrated in the hands of a few, it's quite common to find that those holding the power intentionally create institutions that serve their interests and not the public.[194] As Edward Abbey said, "Power is always dangerous. Power attracts the worst and corrupts the best."

Bias Toward Unity and Against Differentiation Both at a Local Level Via Federalism and at a Global Level

Federalism was central to the American Constitution. It circumscribed the power of the national government, reserving considerable autonomy to the states. Unfortunately, over time, the power of Washington has grown, while the influence of the states has been severely diminished. This puts those governing at a further remove from those they are governing, but this is not a problem for liberals, because liberals think the public is too stupid to know what they want or to guide government. The result is less transparency and accountability in government, but, again, this is no problem for liberals. The elite are somehow supposedly immune to abuse of power and corruption and inherently know the right thing to do. In fact, for liberals, less transparency and accountability fits in with their modus operandi. Since they believe that the public should be disenfranchised, or at least have their influence drastically reduced, liberals naturally favor less transparency and accountability.

With the accumulation of centralized power (the objective of liberals) efficiency is lost in the delivery of services. Efficiency suffers as the bureaucracy becomes bloated and overstaffed.

Efficiency is also lost because localized programs can be better focused and tailored to local circumstances. As administrators are closer to the problems they are targeting, they are more likely to be aware of the intricate nature of the problems, and will be better positioned to see how the policies are actually working, and be better able to tweak them if necessary. Moreover, when policies are handled at the national level, it's pretty much necessary to adopt a one-size-fits-all approach, whereas this is not the case with policies formulated and delivered at the local level.

With the role of the states declining, we are losing the advantages inherent in policy experimentation at the state level. As states experiment with different policies, we get an idea as to what works and what doesn't before trying out policies at a national level.

Liberals, however, are not content to see the power of Washington grow and that of the states decline. They are not content diminishing federalism. Liberals want to see supra-national governments take over power. They want to see meta-national or international bodies take over from nation-states. Liberals believe nation-states should be a relic of the past. They look to a new world order as they see nation-states impeding the progress of liberalism.

The United Nations is notoriously inefficient and corrupt. It's wasting billions of dollars that could be used to alleviate poverty. Despite this, and in spite of their repeated claims of putting poverty alleviation at the top of their priorities, liberals and the Democratic Party resist efforts to reform and clean up the UN. Reducing funding to the UN is not enough. It should be fundamentally reformed, yet liberals don't want to use the power of the US to do this, even though the US is the primary funding source for the UN. It wastes US resources. Since these resources are so important to the UN, we could have significant leverage in encouraging reform, but the liberals resist this. It seems that the internationalist agenda of the liberals trumps their objective of poverty alleviation, though the latter is not their real objective. The accumulation of power and money is the real underlying objective cloaked in their rhetoric of compassion.

One advantage of small countries and federalism is that it allows differentiation. People with different dispositions can settle in areas with different characteristics. For example, different states could offer different bundles of government goods and services (parks, police, welfare and so on) at different tax rates and people could vote with their feet. Liberalism however is bent on destroying this. They want one size fits all government. World government is their objective. Liberalism is thus oriented to diminishing individualism not only within nations, but across nations and cultures. These meta-government organizations are even more insular and disconnected from the grassroots citizen. This greater disconnect leads to less efficiency, corruption, the pursuit of the wrong programs and objectives, and hiring based not on meritocratic considerations but on power connections. It's based on patronage politics like the UN, where unprofessional and untalented people man the organization.

Liberals want to see globalization. They want to see transnational organizations grow in influence and importance. A world government is a distant objective. Liberals don't like their own culture; even multiculturalism is not enough for them. They aspire to an ever higher level of abstraction than the collective polity they would like to see in America.

They want something even more abstract, even more collective, something that is all but indefinable, and as hard to grasp as an unattainable ideal. Transnational government—government by international organizations—would put individuals at an even further remove from government. The individual would all but disappear in the mist of an unattainable idealism and a mind-boggling bureaucracy.

* * *

CHAPTER 17

THE IMPACT OF INSTITUTIONAL FAILURE ON THE OBJECTIVES OF LIBERALISM

The disease which inflicts bureaucracy and what they usually die from is routine.

~John Stuart Mill

The government solution to a problem is usually as bad as the problem.

~Milton Friedman

Whereas in the previous section, the focus was on the impact of liberalism on institutions, this section will focus on the impact of institutions on liberalism, for example, on the failure of liberalism to achieve its declared objectives.

The failure of liberalism is attributable to many factors, but an important one is its lack of understanding of how institutions function. The Left is content to confine itself to the realm of intentionality. It believes that if you want the right things, they'll just happen. It doesn't concern itself with the process of intermediation and the role of institutions. Given that poverty alleviation and redistribution of income is accorded primacy in the Left's agenda, it's useful to illustrate specifically the institutional shortcomings that have contributed to the failure of poverty alleviation.

Before beginning graduate school, I worked as a social worker for the Department of Welfare in the Bronx of New York. I saw first- hand the failure of the system. The people who mostly benefitted were unscrupulous and smart enough to know how to game the system. The truly poor, who lacked energy, motivation, and the savvy to work through the system, were largely unhelped.

I saw the institutional shortcomings in how welfare was delivered. Staff had large caseloads, and the incentive was to avoid trouble with one's caseload. Since the poor and the weak were less able to give the staff trouble, most energy and time was devoted to warding off problems with those smart enough to challenge the system. For example, if a lady with five kids claimed that her welfare check had been stolen, and that she was threatened with eviction, the Department would bend over backward to avoid a bad headline in the newspapers. They would do this even if the lady had an established record of defrauding them. In essence the welfare system worked as a safety valve system rather than one of poverty alleviation. It bought off people willing and able to make trouble.

In addition, welfare workers were supposed to work in the office for three days a week and visit clients for two days during the week. Some workers got telephones for clients so they could avoid visiting them in the field. Instead they would go to the beach or do something else to their liking.

The failure of the welfare program is well documented and recognized. Finally, in the mid '90s, a conservative congress was able to pressure President Clinton to pass fundamental reforms. The reforms sharply curtailed the number of people on welfare, encouraging welfare recipients to get back into the workforce. The reforms had a big positive impact, underscoring the failure of the welfare system.

Because I spent thirty years working in international development as an economist with the International Monetary Fund, I will focus this section on the institutional shortcomings of international poverty alleviation efforts. Specifically, I will attempt to establish how institutional problems contribute to the failure of liberalism to alleviate poverty.

Despite significant progress in macroeconomic policy reforms in developing countries in the '80s and '90s, economic growth didn't pick up in these countries. Governance problems, including corruption, in developing countries have contributed to aid's failure to register a significant impact.

The international aid community points the finger at governance and corruption problems in our client countries, but a significant factor has been governance shortcomings in the aid community. Governance problems in countries receiving financial support are a much bigger problem than that in aid organizations. In recipient countries, the governance problem is particularly serious because it is essentially corruption. Corruption for personal gain is a manifest problem in most governments receiving assistance from aid organizations, whereas this corruption is scant in aid organizations. In aid organizations, the problem is one of incentives inappropriate for the goals sought.

Moreover, the aid community may be contributing to corruption in developing countries, not just by encouraging existing corruption as more support is to corrupt countries, but by creating incentives for additional governance problems.[195] So the aid community, rather than mitigating corruption in member countries, or even having a neutral effect, may in fact be exacerbating the problem.

To the extent that this is the case, aid givers may be institutionalizing a significant barrier to progress in growth and development for the developing world. It's a fundamental law of both nature and society that interventions—whether biological, environmental, social or institutional—have not only a direct impact, but systemic and indirect impacts too. Unfortunately, the behavior of aid recipients and others have changed as a result of the interventions of aid givers.

Thus to look at only the immediate or proximate linkages or effects of aid in general, and International Monetary Fund programs in particular, is to miss the big picture. If we are to see more favorable developmental outcomes from these interventions, we need to more carefully assess the derivative and institutional effects such programs are generating, and take action where necessary to contain adverse systemic effects, particularly with governance corruption problems.

The views expressed here were percolated slowly over the course of my thirty year career with the Fund, but in particular reflect experience over the three years I served as the IMF resident representative in Mongolia. This experience allowed me to see firsthand the "real" or grassroots interface of aid with development.

Evidence on the Relationship of Aid to Corruption and Growth

Governance problems in aid organizations are exacerbating governance problems in recipient countries and thereby curtailing the potential benefit of aid on economic growth. This argument is predicated on the following component hypotheses:

1. Despite sizeable aid, macro-economic policy reforms in developing countries in the '80s and '90s did not lead to an increase in economic growth in these countries. Aid has not been effective in increasing growth.
2. Key behind the lack of link between aid and economic performance has been corruption and poor governance in recipient countries. Corruption and governance problems have been serious in developing countries, and these problems have been adversely affecting growth.
3. Aid organizations through various modalities are enhancing the governance and corruption problems in countries receiving aid.

Let's look specifically at the empirical foundations for each of these propositions. Focus will be directed in particular at the third position linking problems in governance in aid providers to governance problems in recipient countries, as the first two propositions are pretty widely accepted.

First, aid has not been successful in boosting growth performance in developing countries. As mentioned, in Chapter 6, on the historical failure of liberalism, economic growth in developing countries remained unimpressive in the 1980s and 1990s despite substantial aid flows. Various studies were cited to support this finding. Please refer to that chapter for the specifics and references. The benefits of this aid have been lost in the aid process.

Second, governance and corruption problems are substantial in recipient countries, and this has weakened the potential beneficial effects of aid on economic growth. The seriousness of corruption and governance shortcomings in developing countries is amply evidenced in the Corruption Perceptions Index of Transparency International.[196]

In a study by Carlos Leite and Jens Weidmann, the growth implications of corruption were examined both theoretically in the context of a general equilibrium model and empirically.[197] This study found a significant adverse impact on growth from corruption. Leite and Weidmann focused on the causal effect of rich natural resource endowment as a factor behind corruption, and its derivative negative consequences on economic growth.

A study by Tanzi and Davoodi found countries characterized by high levels of perceived corruption had lower per capita income levels and lower rates of economic growth.[198] In another paper, Tanzi and Davoodi established that corruption negatively impacts the productivity of public investment and shifts spending away from operations and maintenance, because this activity creates less opportunities for graft.[199]

The bias in favor of political over economic activity hurts growth performance. In a 1995 article, "Corruption and Growth," in the Quarterly Journal of Economics, Paulo Mauro found that corruption hurt investment and in turn resulted in a lower rate of economic growth.

Wei similarly determined that corruption negatively affected foreign direct investment.[200] The higher the level of corruption, the greater is the impact on foreign direct investment. In addition, uncertainty concerning the level of corruption weighs particularly heavily on investment. According to Wei, the difference between corruption indices in Singapore and Mexico suggests that corruption raised the perceived marginal tax rate (with corruption thought of as a form of tax) in Mexico by twenty percent.[201] In addition to hurting growth, corruption has a deleterious impact on poverty. This is not surprising as it's the affluent and politically connected who benefit from corruption.

Third, aid organizations are contributing to these problems. It's clear on theoretical grounds that aid in some respects may be exacerbating the corruption in developing countries. For example, funding without firm oversight and strong incentives on the part of the givers will enhance existing corruption.

According to an NBER study by Alesina and Dollar, bilateral aid is driven mostly by the strategic and political interests of donors rather than by the goal of promoting economic development in the developing world. Such aid consequently has a relatively weak link to favorable development outcomes. Only in the Scandinavian countries were aid flows channeled so as to have a significant impact on economic development. In France, Germany, and the United States non-economic considerations were the primary determinants of aid flows.[202]

With multilateral aid organizations, the role of political factors is less clear, but it's not surprising that since such organizations are constituted of members driven by political and strategic interests that such factors are important for these organizations too. In this connection, Robert Barro determined that political-economy variables—comprising IMF quotas that are linked to voting power, and the political and economic proximity to the major shareholding countries of the IMF—are highly correlated with whether a country has a program with the IMF.[203] Political proximity was measured by the degree to which voting patterns were similar in the UN, whereas economic proximity was measured by the amount of trade.

Svensson found an empirical connection between foreign aid and higher levels of corruption in countries with competing social groups.[204] A World Bank report on Sub-Saharan Africa concluded that significant concessional aid flows to Africa greatly increased the opportunities for corruption,[205] while Klitgaard has provided specific and detailed accounts of the link of aid to malfeasance and corruption in Africa.[206]

In addition, aid supplies for bilateral and multilateral givers tend to flow to corrupt countries. For example, another research paper by Alesina found that countries with lower levels of corruption don't receive more aid than those of corrupt regimes. His empirical results were described as robust. In fact, his empirical work suggests that corrupt governments actually received more aid than countries where corruption is constrained to lower levels. This contrasted with foreign direct investment flows and private capital flows, which tended to be more directed to low corruption countries.

This contrast is significant, but it doesn't mean that aid flows are necessarily causing corruption, or that this constitutes an inappropriate policy. High corruption countries are usually the most in need of institutional and economic development, so a case can be made that aid flows should be channeled to these countries. There was, however, "weak evidence" that corruption was higher for countries where aid accounted for a relatively high proportion of government spending relative to domestic revenue sources. This finding, of course, would be consistent with the so-called "voracity effect." Namely, officials in countries highly reliant on foreign aid are more inclined to corruption than if aid accounted for only a small portion of public sector spending. It's interesting that aid from the Scandinavian countries tends to be better targeted and hence may be used more effectively.[207]

A study by Chen and Thomas found that the stop-go character of many IMF programs had an adverse effect on inflation and hurt fiscal and growth performance.[208] As mentioned previously, stop-go performance suggests a weak commitment to buy into the reform agenda. In pursuing its own political and economic agenda, rather than that of the aid community, the country in effect misuses the aid funding.

The connection between centralized fiscal authority and decision-making—which aid tends to bolster—and governance problems and higher corruption is corroborated in a study by Luiz de Mello and Matias Barenstein. In this study they found that decentralized taxation and spending improves governance in both developing and developed countries.[209]

Barro and Lee found that the IMF loan programs in countries tended to hurt democracy in recipient countries.[210] The same study concluded that there are indications that IMF programs have adverse consequences for the rule-of-law. The modus operandi for this was not specified, but it was inferred that enhanced corruption stemming from program involvement might be the key factor.

Governance Problems in Multilateral Aid Institutions

Among the many problems of governance in multilateral aid institutions are three specific syndromes that I will discuss here.

First is the *engagement syndrome.* Aid givers vie with each other to remain engaged, to be part of the club. Competing aid providers don't want to be left out of the game. Developing countries know this and play one aid giver off against another, because each wants to maintain market share. Developing countries know how to play the paper game too. They are disposed toward agreeing to a program even if they know it's unrealistic or won't work, as it will satisfy the aid giver and get them the disbursement of funds desired. As long as they send some positive signals to the aid providers this seems to be enough.

The aid community recognized the genesis of the debt crisis of '70s as in part due to banks pushing funds at developing countries without proper concern for repayment or the proper use of the funds. In the seventies I worked in the International Department in the Chemical Bank of New York and saw this first hand, but this is now a widely shared view of the crisis. The objective for banks in those heady days was expansion, development of market share. Loan officers were rewarded on the basis of the amount of loans they could book. The quality of the loans was hardly an issue.

It's not surprising that developing countries had trouble saying no to loans. It's not easy to push money away. Since banks were more concerned with booking the loans than with the quality, oversight to prevent misuse was unfortunately seriously insufficient. Thus, it is not surprising that many of these loans were put into inappropriate projects and activities, making paying them back difficult.

Multilateral financial institutions do the same thing (the drive is to have programs, remain engaged, and get the money out). The aid community has financial resources that it's mandated to use. The aid community is in the business of providing support to developing countries, so it feels compelled to push out funding, to max out its financial commitment, even if the uses to which that support is provided are questionable. The recipient countries know this, and take advantage of this need to be involved. I have heard some member country officials describe it as "belonging to the Club," that is, donors don't wish to be excluded from a particular country. This wish to belong is pervasive throughout the organizational structure of the aid organizations, but has strong roots especially with those who are most closely involved with the country concerned: the resident representative, the desk officer, the Division Chief with jurisdictional responsibility, the Department Head, and so on. Strong pressure is manifest from the governing board or higher hierarchic levels of aid organizations to make a commitment too. This is particularly the case if certain Board members represent countries with a significant financial stake in the country concerned.

A second syndrome of aid funds are *incentive distortions*. Empirical studies on the incentive distortions of aid organizations is not available, but this is not essential as we are all familiar with the literature on competitive markets and the problems that potentially ensue when actors are not driven by income incentives or profit maximization, particularly in activities involving the lending of money. The public enterprise literature on the problems of multiple objectives is well established. Misplaced incentives at both the institutional level and for the staff comprising these institutions are creating adverse and unintended consequences for governance in recipient countries. Because we don't fully understand what bureaucrats are "really" trying to maximize, it shouldn't be surprising that program outcomes are not as favorable as we would like.

The IMF and other international financial institutions recognize the primacy of the private sector and the importance of the profit incentive, yet we ourselves don't have proper incentive structures in place to ensure that the objectives of development are met. The incentives for individual staff members making up international financial institutions are not linked to good program outcomes.

The incentive structures that drive aid organizations don't establish an association of good program outcomes with career advancement. There are several good reasons for this, some technical and substantive, while others relate to the institutional nature of these organizations. For example, program goals are medium term, while career advancement is based on annual performance reviews. Staff rarely remains working on the same country for more than three years. Mobility is encouraged, so staff changes departments, assignments, and in some cases the nature of their work.

The third syndrome is *accountability shortcomings*. There is little or no accountability if programs don't turn out well. This arises from many factors. First of all, it's difficult to ascertain why a program fails. Was it due to faulty program design, implementation shortcomings on the part of the country authorities, or adverse and unanticipated external factors? Thorough reviews or audits of failures are rarely conducted, and even if they are, they are driven more from an overarching policy or academic perspective than from a desire to determine who was at fault. In essence, even when reviews are conducted, accountability is not at issue.

Accountability is difficult given the complexity of the aid organizations. In any given project or program, many different individuals are involved. Different individuals are involved within an organization, both horizontally and vertically within the administrative hierarchy, and between aid organizations.

Given this, the incentive structures are predicated on "inputs," rather than outputs or effects. For example, the incentive structure rewards the quality of the report underlying the program and focuses on the amount of funding commitment or program engagement. Those individuals responsible for initiating a program or generating a good report are rewarded; those who don't are treated less favorably. Moreover, a good report is not one that necessarily creates a good economic outcome for the country or boosts growth prospects. Rather, it would be one that would be based on generally recognized principles of policy making, but not necessarily in the practical realities in the country concerned. That is, the program could look good on paper, but have little real chance for success. The incentive structure suggests that, for the staff involved, a paper program or even a bad program is better than no program.

Clearly, the negative effects of these governance problems in international financial institutions and in the aid community in general are serious. Shortcomings in aid-organization governance significantly diminish prospects for a real take-off in economic growth in developing countries. These shortcomings erode the credibility of not only the aid providers, but of the member countries involved. In so doing these derivative governance problems reinforce and support institutionalized bad practice and corruption in client states. Corruption in client states is not only accommodated, but encouraged.

Channels or Modalities via Which Aid Givers Can Add to Corruption or Poor Use of Funds

There are multiple channels within which aid givers actually exacerbate corruption. These are as follows:

1. *Constituencies of aid recipients seeking to maximize personal gain.* International aid has created large and powerful developing-country constituencies whose purpose is to extract personal advantage from such aid. The larger the aid flows are relative to the size of GDP or government, the greater the adverse effects of aid on this kind of activity. To the extent that aid is a windfall, it encourages lobbying groups to seek it out and allocate the resulting rents. The appetite for rents is sharpened, and the focus of activity shifts to this easy way of securing money and influence. This approach is much easier than making money through productive activity. In earlier days, rent-seeking economies thrived on the basis of nonmarket arrangements and import substitution policies. In today's world the rent seekers extract their "due" from the aid community. This is where the money is, so this is where the focus is rather than on developing business and promoting growth. The emphasis is on lobbying, exercising influence, on getting a bigger slice of the pie—not on expanding the size of the pie.

2. *Government sector bias.* Foreign aid is biased in favor of the government sector. Aid may lead to an increase in government spending or allow higher levels than would otherwise have prevailed in the absence of aid. However, even where the size of the State is not enlarged, foreign aid tends to increase corruption because government intermediates aid, and hence sees its role enhanced.

Moreover, in addition to the size of government, as measured by its role in spending and revenue collection, the government may be involved in privatization (an act of reducing the size of the government), but this involvement contains significant opportunities for corruption.

The economic argument in public finance literature for a role for the public sector is based on public goods and the need to correct for imperfections in the market. This literature has generally been based on the assumption of no corruption.[211] If corruption is higher in the public than the private sector, an argument could be made that the public sector should be smaller than otherwise would be the case, based on the standard literature. Consequently, the arguments in favor of government's role as a means of correcting for market failure need to be reconsidered.

3. *Bias in favor of political over economic activity.* By channeling aid through a few key institutions or individuals, the latter are favored relative to others, giving such individuals and institutions significant influence. The incentive then is to invest in political capital, rather than human capital, as this is where the return is. The leverage of these individuals and institutions is particularly high when the amount of aid relative to other tax and nontax revenue is high. The connection between politics and economics is so tight in some developing countries that officials must sometimes pay to get a senior position with government. The impact on economic growth is certainly negative because corruption constitutes not only a transfer payment, a bribe, but skews investment away from productive growth enhancing activity. Poverty reduction goals are hurt, as the elite and politically influential gain at the expense of others. In essence, corruption involves reverse targeting.

4. *Concentration of bureaucratic power.* Aid augments and concentrates bureaucratic power. The more intricate and extensive bureaucratic power, the greater is the scope for corruption because officials can use their positions and vested powers for personal gain. The greater licensing and regulation, the more opportunity there is for deriving a quid pro quo in the form of unofficial remuneration.

The link between bureaucratic power and corruption is particularly strong in developing countries, which are of course the countries to which aid is targeted. Relationships based on kinship, tribe, or friendship are much more deeply woven into the cultural fabric in developing countries than in developed countries. In developed countries, bureaucrats are characteristically at arms' length from the people they serve, whereas in most developing countries it's culturally accepted that bureaucrats are supposed to help their friends and relatives.[212] In fact in many developing countries it's considered as a moral obligation to help friends and relatives. The culture of connections and influence is entrenched and more sophisticated in these countries, so pay-offs may not even look like corruption, in that a pay-off may not be explicitly connected with a given favor or even temporally proximate. There may only be an implicit, unspoken, understanding, no formal agreement. In essence an individual's "social capital" is accrued as favors or obligations are earned from others, while obligations to others build up or are worked down over time. This system and set of influences binds behavior, constraining officials from acting with impartiality. It's a mark of certain cultures, an attractive one in that it suggests strong family and friendship ties, but it represents a serious obstacle to effective government and economic development.[213]

The extent to which bureaucracy leads to corruption is dependent on numerous factors, including the extent of discretion in spending decisions; the nature of the tax laws and their implementation; the extent to which goods or services are provided at below market prices; public sector wage levels; use of the civil service for patronage or employer of the last resort; institutional controls and penalties for transgressions; the effectiveness of the judicial system in prosecuting violations; the evenhandedness in the implementation of regulations and laws; and the prevailing contextual culture. Unfortunately, the nature of most of these factors in developing countries conduces to higher levels of corruption than in developed countries. Consequently, aid flowing through this filter of bureaucracy is likely to support and enhance corruption.

5. *Bolsters existing political arrangements and reinforces the status quo.* Aid tends to perpetuate and reinforce existing government connections and arrangements. It's a well-known fact that the longer a government is in power, the more it becomes corrupt. So, by supporting existing political arrangements and regimes by lengthening their time in office, aid can enhance corruption. Prospects for economic growth are thereby diminished, as political change and improvement in the efficacy of government are thwarted. In addition, good governance involves not only selection of governing authority, but its accountability. Weakness on the part of aid givers in holding governments accountable for shortcomings in the handling of aid and in the implementation of reform policies contributes to the governance problem in recipient countries.

6. *Aid supplies tend to flow to corrupt countries.* Aid flows to corrupt countries are greater than to less corrupt states.[214] Of course, we shouldn't conclude that aid is causing corruption simply because more aid flows to highly corrupt countries, as it's not surprising that the countries most affected by corruption are those that are the weakest economically and institutionally. Hence, because these are the countries most in need of assistance, one should not draw the inference that more aid is going to these countries because they are corrupt. Nevertheless the evidence is clear that more aid is going to high corruption countries, and regardless of the rationale driving this, the impact in abetting corruption, or providing adverse incentives, will be similar.

7. *Corrupt countries want more aid.* In addition to the supply driven factor—namely, that aid organizations could be expected to lend more to corrupt countries—there is the demand side of the equation that would conduce to more aid flowing to these countries. The incentive structure would suggest that corrupt governments have poor economic circumstances, as wealth is generated not through production, but through extraction of rent. The appetite for funds at below market cost is particularly strong, as the rents are more enticing.

8. *Financial support delays essential stabilization and reform policies.* Aid, to the extent that it eases the pressures for economic reform and a more efficient use of resources and funds, can delay the implementation of necessary policies. In addition, aid recipients can pretty much pursue their own policy agenda as aid providers are in disarray and unable to marshal significant pressure to keep them on track with a reform policy agenda. Moreover, once bad loans are made, staff of aid-providing organizations involved in the initial decision to grant the assistance have an incentive to cover up the problem and delay an official recognition that a change in course is necessary.

9. *Engagement syndrome.* This refers to the emphasis of aid institutions on maintaining programs—remaining engaged—regardless of the likelihood of a positive effect on the recipient country. The governments of recipient countries understand this well and use the weakness of aid organizations to extract funding without taking the necessary steps to ensure a productive impact on the economy and society. They play aid providers off against one another, generating concern among each that they may be squeezed out of the picture.

10. *Aid agency dependency syndrome.* In certain countries aid agencies have extended such a high amount of loans that they become beholden to the debtors. It's sometimes said if you owe a bank one hundred thousand dollars, the bank owns you; on the other hand, if you owe that bank one hundred million dollars, you own the bank. To forestall a recipient country's default, aid agencies may be constrained to lend more, ever greening their loans, even if they recognize that this constitutes a poor use of funds from both their perspective and the country's. Essentially, corrupt or poorly run governments can gain control of the decision making process in aid agencies regarding lending to them, milking them to support their corrupt practices.[215] This may be called the too-big-to-fail dynamic. The interest of international financial institutions in promoting better policies may be compromised by its interest in getting loans repaid.[216]

This dynamic is similar in effect to the engagement syndrome, but differs in important aspects. In the case of the engagement syndrome, aid organizations are driven by a volitional need to remain involved, whereas in the dependency syndrome they are pulled against their will. In both cases the recipient country exercises leverage over the aid agencies involved, but the degree of leverage is more overt and magnified when the aid agency gets in over its head in debt to a given country. Of course, the dependency syndrome is operative only for countries with large economies, like Argentina, Russia, and Turkey, but not so for smaller developing countries, such as those in Africa.

11. *Reputational considerations of aid organizations.* In the previous example of aid agency dependence syndrome, it's only the countries with large economies that can accumulate a substantial amount of debt vis-à-vis aid providers and thereby exercise a significant amount of leverage over aid organizations. However, small-economy countries can exert leverage, particularly where the amount of their debt to the aid providers is large relative to their GDP. In this case a pull-back in financial commitments from aid providers could result in domestic turmoil and a sizeable negative impact on the poor that could embarrass the aid organizations involved. This might constrain the latter to make loans that they would otherwise prefer not to make.

Another way in which reputational considerations may play a role—and this applies to both large and small countries—is that officials of aid organizations involved in making earlier decisions in programs and financing may want to avoid embarrassment in program failure and/or loan default. To cover up the problem, they may try to provide additional financing to delay the day of reckoning and recognition of the earlier mistake.

12. *Recipient country dependency syndrome.* Dependency-syndrome countries become welfare dependent. The welfare system in the United States in the latter part of the twentieth century created this well-known syndrome of welfare dependency, which entrapped recipients in a seemingly endless cycle of poverty. Foreign aid may

be having a similar effect on the developing world. Foreign aid has created its own constituency in developing countries, which is more focused on milking the aid cow than in taking the necessary steps to kick-start real economic growth based on productive activity. The lessons learned from experience with the welfare system in the United States are of direct relevance here. As a welfare worker in the Bronx of NYC early in my career, I could readily see that only manipulators really benefited from the system. The truly poor didn't have the motivation, energy and intelligence needed to make the system work for them.

It doesn't matter that the money was intended for worthy purposes. The famous saying that "the road to hell is paved with good intentions" is quite germane here. It's not enough to intend funds to be used for certain purposes. The aid process needs to be grounded in reality.

13. *Moral hazard.* By bailing out those who have engaged in bad policies, the aid community is subsidizing such policies and encouraging countries to go this route. Moreover, the moral hazard problem is exacerbated to the extent that more corrupt governments receive more aid than others. The big bailouts are particularly harmful, damaging also the credibility of the aid givers.

14. *Poor donor tracking and auditing.* The inability of aid organizations to track the use of grants and loans to ensure proper usage contributes to corruption in recipient countries. Moreover, even if specific funding support could be tracked, it would be largely meaningless as resources are fungible, and it could free up other money for untoward purposes.

In this connection aid providers suffer from an incentive problem. The fact is that most aid organizations are not preoccupied with repayment prospects, since they are accorded priority status in repayment. Even if projects or programs are unsuccessful, repayment is expected. A commercial creditor would be expected to be a lot more concerned about funds being put to good use, because it would directly affect his prospects of being repaid. An aid-providing institution is pretty much freed from such concerns.

Even in the event of default to an aid organization, bureaucrats representing the organization would remain unconcerned as their jobs and pay wouldn't be on the line. Moreover, in the event of default, the shareholders or supporters of the donor institution would probably be inclined to increase their support to fill the gap.

15. *Blame game.* Reforms are put off as country authorities don't want to make the difficult political decisions of undertaking substantial macroeconomic adjustments. Instead they wait till a crisis is precipitated and then point the finger at the IMF or the foreign community for forcing them to undertake action. The authorities shift the responsibility for the politically costly undertaking to the foreign community. This lack of ownership and responsibility for programs conduces to program failure. If the authorities of a country do not have their heart in the policies they are implementing, they will in all likelihood fail.

16. *Aid lending exacerbates debt problems, fostering disposition to default.* Contractual externalities lead developing countries to take on too much debt. If a borrowing government was to take on debt from only one lender, this bias toward excessive reliance on debt wouldn't be a factor. However, the reality is that there are multiple lenders or investors, and this situation leads to market failure, or a "common agency problem."[217] Over-borrowing tends to be the outcome when a government is dealing with multiple lenders or investors. The new, or last lender in line, is not concerned that the additional lending will create less likelihood for repayment, because he demands a risk premium that is incorporated into the interest rate. The government is unconcerned that debt repayment may be more difficult in the future, as it's more concerned with getting the funding it needs and knows that future problems will likely fall on others. The problem accrues to those creditors who already had outstanding claims with the government, as the value of these claims would be hurt, and for the public as a whole and a government in the future that would have to clean up the mess. These market failure problems would tend to shorten the maturity structure of debt, making the country more vulnerable to

crises. As a result of an excessive accumulation of debt, subsequent governments would find the default option attractive. The incentive to pursue responsible policies would be diminished.

The problem of debt accumulation is exacerbated by aid institutions. Because aid institutions enjoy priority status in repayment, they are more inclined than other creditors to push debt on developing countries. The situation is made worse by the fact that the weakest and most economically troubled countries must rely entirely on official creditors because private market financing is not available to them. Hence the countries that are the most vulnerable are at the most risk of an over-accumulation of debt. It's the official creditors who exercise the least restraint. Unduly high debt levels of course represent a burden on future growth prospects, so it's not surprising that many of these countries are experiencing difficulty in moving onto a higher growth path.

17. *Paper preoccupation.* Aid organizations, as bureaucracies, are in the business of producing reports. Often times unfortunately the report itself is the objective of the institution, rather than bottom-line results in the recipient countries. For example, in Mongolia a priest well known for his productive work on the serious problem of street children was not even contacted by the principal international organization engaged in this issue. In his own words, the organization was "interested in its reports, not children or reality."

18. *The stop-go game.* In the stop-go game the receiving country dissimulates commitment to certain reform objectives and policies to secure the financial support of the aid community. In fact the country remains committed to its own objectives and policies and tries to finance them through dissimulation. Ownership of the reform policies pushed by the aid community is only a façade. The real action is going on behind this front. The game is played through an exercise in time inconsistency. The recipient country commits itself to a reform program receiving in return financial support from the aid community, but this is only an enticement, a trap. Soon the country deviates from the program, causing some aid to cease

flowing. It's difficult, however, for many aid providers to pull the plug, so most aid providers remain engaged, looking for a pretext or rationale to restart their programs. Soon the "transgressing country" gives signs that it will accede to certain reform policies, of course not reversing the damage done in its transgression from the original commitment, and the game is restarted— only to be interrupted again in the not-too-distant future.

19. *Milking political relationships.* A significant proportion of aid, especially bilateral aid, is politically motivated. Such aid is more likely than technically driven aid to exacerbate governance problems in recipient countries. Client states try to milk these political relationships to maximize the funding assistance. For example, Russia in the '90s realized that the West was not inclined to risk worsening its political and economic circumstances, so it was able to get away with minimal reforms and still receive substantial financial assistance.

20. *Heterogeneous oversight-control structures of multilateral aid organizations.* The heterogeneous nature of the boards of multilateral institutions predisposes them to compromise and vote-trading.[218] The intervention of political considerations, of course, diverts multilaterals from the economic objectives that they were created to pursue.[219]

21. *Accountability problem.* Because many institutions are involved in the same program country issues and even within aid organizations many individuals and departments have an input, it's difficult to establish accountability for program failures. A lack of accountability of course eases the incentive to achieve good bottom-line results, which in turn takes the pressure off country officials to use funds in the best possible way. So it's difficult to assess blame for program failure within aid organizations, between them, and for member country officials.

22. *Concessionality enhances the appetite for rent extraction.* Concessionality in itself contributes to the problem of corruption

by increasing the rent accruing to those receiving the funds or to those involved in associated projects. If the interest rate is low, those individuals who receive or control the funds can make an attractive return (the difference between market value and the cost of funds). The windfall rents can be significant given the large amount involved with such assistance.

23. *Protracted formulation process for the programs and inability to adapt in the face of changing circumstances.* Many aid organizations require two or more years to put projects together. By the time these programs are ready for implementation, circumstances may have changed so that such programs are no longer appropriate. Yet once programs develop a certain momentum and have gone through the technical and bureaucratic process of approval, there is a great reluctance to modify or scrap projects. Pushing through projects that are no longer appropriate lends itself to unfavorable outcomes. For example, a rural sector finance project to be intermediated by the banking system may be appropriate in the context of a viable banking system, but it is not in the context of a broken banking system. Yet I have witnessed a regional aid organization pushing funds through a debilitated banking system, which led to severe governance and corruption problems.

24. *Proclivity for crisis intervention.* This is similar to moral hazard, but not quite. Aid providers are particularly drawn to countries in the throes of a crisis. This shouldn't be surprising and in fact is quite justifiable—greater needs should warrant greater support. However, the problem is that many of these crises are policy-driven. Governance problems and corruption lie behind many crises. Consequently, to the extent that the aid organizations are drawn to crisis intervention, they are bailing out or supporting such governance problems.

However an argument can be made that crises are in fact necessary for reform to be adopted. That is there must be policy failure if there is to be sufficient incentive for policy makers to attempt to change the status quo.

25. *Pre-emption of administrative responsibility.* Some aid providers require project administrative units and their own accounting operations outside of the civil service to help to ensure that funds are properly utilized. This can help to forestall corruption where administrative capacity is unreliable. However, over-reliance on this approach can have adverse consequences for governance in recipient countries, as qualified staff may be bid away. The approach takes the pressure off the government to develop its own capacity with financial management, and it makes it more difficult for the government to manage its expenditure program. Over-reliance on long-term fiscal experts can deter governments from developing their own capabilities and responsibility.

26. *Ownership problem.* It's recognized that ownership is a key factor necessary for the success of any economic program, but the channeling of aid as it is currently constituted does not encourage this. In fact, aid providers are pulling recipient countries in different directions. Few countries turn down offers of assistance from donors. The method of operation is to take down as much financial support as possible, trying to satisfy the letter of the agreements with the aid providers, but not the spirit. This is easy to accomplish, because the aid providers' bottom lines are not concerned with the spirit of the agreement. It's the process and engagement that are important, not the outcome.

27. *Technical overload.* It's particularly easy to lose ownership in the shuffle, as most recipient countries are administratively challenged just to keep up with the paper work that the aid organizations are pushing at them. In many cases, particularly for small countries, I surmise that basic loan and aid agreements and technical assistance reports go largely unread, or at least undigested. Information requirements to satisfy aid givers are burdensome and overwhelming. For example, according to Easterly and World Bank Development Indicators for Africa, Tanzania received about one thousand aid missions in one year and the country generated twenty-four hundred reports for the aid givers.[220]

The incentive structure in aid-giving organizations pays no heed to the administrative burdens cast upon aid recipients. These bureaucratic pressures that are in fact placing similar burdens on the staffs of aid organizations have proceeded largely unrestrained. Aid organizations have tried to deal with the by-product rather than the cause, by instead placing an emphasis on capacity building. However, given low wages in aid-recipient institutions, morale problems, and high staff turnover, this attempt to mop up after the problem has not met with much success.

The sheer weight of the work on an overtaxed and technically challenged administrative staff, make it hard for recipient countries to develop a vision or strategic approach of their own. Officials often look like a high-wire circus act in that the performer is juggling many balls while trying to maintain balance. The objectives are principally two-fold: first, to get the money, regardless of the purpose to which it's supposed to be put; and, second, to try to channel the obtained commitment of aid funds so as to maximize the goals of the government, not that of the aid provider. Technical overload clearly works against the development of meaningful ownership.

* * *

CHAPTER 18

Trojan Horse and Role of Technology

The attempt to combine wisdom and power has only rarely been successful and then only for a short time.

~Albert Einstein

No problem can be solved from the same level of consciousness that created it.

~Albert Einstein

Mankind likes to think that he is in control of his own future. He likes the idea of a government endowed with knowledge and foresight making decisions that will lead to a better future for all. We are predisposed to the idea of top-down government. There is something unsettling about being governed by invisible forces, whether the market mechanism or technology. However, only the latter is reality.

Human beings have an inborn need to feel in control of their environment. This has been the case since the beginning of our species. It accounts in large measure for our survival. We can see it in the way we all like to establish a safe and comfortable home, a place in which we are protected and secure.

Arising out of this need, and our hubris, we tend to impart an anthropomorphic aspect to our conception of causation. We associate causation with the effects that result from our actions, like trying to move a table or a chair. Intentionality is part of such actions, and the actions and their effects are localized. In political, social, and economic affairs this intentionality is less apparent, and the effects are not localized. Everything is interconnected, so there is more of a general equilibrium to the way causation works. The "I" disappears, or certainly plays a much diminished role. The role of man and his intentionality become merely part of a larger set of operating forces.

Unfortunately, the liberal is mired in his intentionality. He thinks it enough if he wants something. He doesn't actually have to do it. He has lost connection with the way his intentionality and his actions, to the extent that actions actually materialize, change his environment and the world.

Technology is a Trojan horse. In the Trojan War, the Greek army was encountering difficulty entering the city of Troy to defeat the Trojans. In a cunning move, they built a mammoth wooden horse, filled it with soldiers, and then sailed across the river away from Troy. The Trojans thought the Greeks had given up their attempt to enter the city and pulled the Trojan horse into their city as a prize of war. After the Trojans had gone to sleep that night, the soldiers sneaked out of the horse and opened the gates of the city to the Greek army outside that then destroyed the city and won the war.

We have opened the gates to let technology in, and it has taken us by storm. Government and people are no longer in control. People may think they are in control, but in reality technology and global forces are shaping our destiny. For example, the Puritans never thought their work ethic would lead to the world we live in today and the associated morality. They would be seriously distressed at the prevailing morality in today's world. The Amish in Pennsylvania, however, did not let technology into their world. They still ride in horse-drawn carriages and don't own televisions. Today their culture and morals are much the same as they were back in the eighteenth century, when they settled in this country.

We have no control over the powerful forces of technology, but they are the way to the future. We must learn to ride the horse into the future. Relying on the invisible hand of the market and individual decision-making is the only way. Top-down control and micromanagement will not work. Discretion and institutional intervention will only create problems as they can't capture the complexity of forces at play, especially in a highly dynamic environment.

What then are the forces shaping our world today? Globalization is bringing pressures for international competitiveness to bear; the explosion in information technology is changing the way people work and conduct their lives; the tremendous advances in communications technology has brought the world closer together, diminishing barriers between cultures; immigration has diminished the nation-state; the nanny state and the excessive growth in the power of the State has increased government intervention in our lives; the spreading cancer of collectivist thinking and the growth in government have diminished the role of individuality and resulted in an attendant loss of morality, responsibility, and accountability; individual responsibility has waned while dependency has increased; and a lack of knowledge of history and a sense that one can't play a role in shaping the policies and stances of government mean that the individual has all but thrown up his hands in surrender.

This has led to a situation where the ruling class has taken over, but, while they try to aggrandize themselves and fool themselves and others that they know what they are doing, they really have no idea. We are on autopilot, flying into the great unknown. Forces that we don't understand are dragging us into the future. We can only hope for the best.

Liberalism is taking us in the direction of more government control and planning. It's a dirigiste approach at a time when conscious control from above is more and more folly. Control from above in the form of big government will not work. It's prone not just to mistakes, but to big and costly mistakes.

In an increasingly complex world, intractable to management from above, the only way forward is to rely on decision-making in the private sector. Reliance on the market mechanism will foster continued reliance on accountability and responsibility. The system is responsive to our needs and wants. We will still be on a wild ride into an unpredictable future, but there is really not a more cogent way forward. Today's world is a great deal more complicated than yesterday's. The world is changing fast, and there are many more choices. These choices are much more complex than choices in the past. Perhaps people are getting shell-shocked or are suffering from future shock and are now desperately clinging to a no-longer existent world with less choices and risks. This perhaps explains why so many are willing to buy into the liberal propaganda. The liberal agenda makes no sense on a rational basis and is fraught with potential danger, but many are willing to jump the chasm of doubt to get on board. It's like the snake oil salesman. Everyone knows better than to believe his spiel, but the hope and dose of optimism is too strong to resist.

Liberalism is not just some exogenous disease that has come out of the blue to afflict democracy in America. It is part of the DNA of democracy itself. It has long been known that democracy lends itself to the pandering and the lowering of standards that we now see more and more. It is part of the life cycle of democracy. We can try to fight it off, but it is almost inevitable that overtime democracy will succumb to it.

Moreover, it's difficult to say whether liberalism is bringing about the decline of democracy, freedom, and morality, or whether the latter are in fact engendering liberalism. Both chains of causation are plausible and evident. A weakening in the institution of democracy as it has aged with an attendant overgrowth in the size and influence of government has constricted our freedoms. It's not surprising to see a weakening in moral standards with the decline of religion and the diminished sense of community that has attended urban growth and globalization. So liberalism may be just a symptom of these trends. However, it is clear that there is a conscious dimension to liberalism that is exacerbating these trends. Both influences feed on each other in a vicious circle.

Liberalism uses reductionism to criticize our culture and ascribe oppressive tendencies to our institutions and class structure. According to liberalism, these oppressive tendencies are not driven at the conscious level, but rather at the unconscious level. It's interesting then that the liberal elite sees itself operating above and beyond these unconscious and unseen forces. Liberals think that they can reformulate our society at the conscious level, and that somehow these unseen forces don't affect them. Or perhaps they think that they are smart enough to understand how these forces operate and thereby take steps to neutralize them.

It is ironic that man's intellectual progress has increasingly cast doubt on the rational and emotional freedom of the individual.

Perhaps this intellectual odyssey accounts for the very attenuated role of the individual in today's liberalism. Liberalism is strangely all about determinism, with the individual having no real control of his fate. Yet the ruling elite seem somehow intoxicated with their belief that they can change not only themselves, the nature of man, but the world.

Internal contradiction is the most abiding diacritic of liberalism. Here it manifests itself once again. The inherent elitism, hubris, contempt for the public, and the disconnect from reason and reality are truly breathtaking.

* * *

CHAPTER 19

Concluding Chapter

Equality, rightly understood as our founding fathers understood it, leads to liberty and to the emancipation of creative differences; wrongly understood, as it has been so tragically in our time, it leads first to conformity and then to despotism.

~Barry Goldwater

Democracy and socialism have nothing in common but one word, equality. But notice the difference; while democracy seeks equality in liberty, socialism seeks equality in restraint and servitude.

~Alexis de Tocqueville

America will never be destroyed from the outside. If we falter and lose our freedoms, it will be because we destroyed ourselves.

~Abraham Lincoln

We are fast approaching the ultimate inversion: the stage when government is free to do anything it pleases, while the citizen may only by permission; which is the stage of the darkest periods of human history, the stage of rule by brute force.

~Ayn Rand

The siren call of collectivism and the fear of freedom and responsibility have got a sizeable part of the citizenry under its spell. Dependency and cradle-to-grave protection from the State may seem appealing compared to the hardships of making one's own way in the world, but history tells us that the story doesn't end well. Unfortunately, as Hegel noted, one thing we learn from history is that man never learns the lessons of history.

Liberalism is bankrupt in its origins, means, and effects. Both the psychological and philosophic origins of liberalism are toxic. Its emotional and psychological origins stem from envy, feelings of insecurity, a fear of freedom, a sense of entitlement, a claimant's mentality, an idealism untethered from reality, and greed for power. These psychological roots do not lead to good outcomes. Similarly, its philosophic roots in postmodernism, Rousseau's collectivist ideas, and the mythic mind-set lead to very bad outcomes. The means of liberalism are also bankrupt: the politics of division, complicit legalized theft, and the diminishment of nondiscretionary systems like the rule of law, capitalism, the rules of rationality, and systems of morality and justice. Similarly, the effects of liberalism are devastating: bigger and more dysfunctional government, reduced economic growth and prosperity, continued poverty, high unemployment, budgetary failure, an inevitable debt cataclysm, failure to meet entitlement promises, the erosion of the foundations of democracy, institutional bloat and inefficiency, an expansion of crony capitalism, the degradation of individuality, and a detrimental impact on morality and justice.

Postmodernism is all about difference and otherness, but it's antagonism toward democracy and Western civilization work against the very things it says it supports. Ideas have consequences and the ideas of postmodernism hurt democracy which is the best political paradigm for protecting diversity and otherness. Postmodernism which, a la Foucault, sees oppressive power everywhere, has no constructive proposals for guiding us into the future. It sees only futility, but in destroying constitutional democracy, it is basically creating a void where autocracy is likely to flourish to the detriment of us all.

Rousseau's organic philosophy also leads inevitably to the growth of the State and the diminishment of freedom and individuality. So both postmodernism and Rousseau's organic philosophy lead us toward big government, although the former does not really support this. Likewise the epistemic template of the mythological mindset, which I argued earlier is a very good philosophic representation of liberalism, is fraught with catastrophic outcomes. In its consummate disconnect from reality, liberalism will be like waking up from a dream to confront long ignored realities. Unfortunately, we will only wake up once the realities are truly frightening, at which point it will be too late to do anything about them.

The disease of liberalism is deep-seated, affecting even how the mind works. This accounts for why liberals and conservatives have difficulty talking to one another. So why can't liberals and conservatives understand one another? First, they are living in parallel universes, with one subscribing to an organic view of political economy and the other to an atomistic view. Second, liberals are driven by emotion, conservatives by reason. Third, liberals are idealists, conservatives are pragmatists. Fourth, liberals are unhappy and want change in their personal lives and society, while conservatives are happy in both their personal lives and with the state of society. Fifth, liberals want to be taken care of and want a risk-free environment and future, whereas conservatives believe in achievement, challenge, and surmounting problems and risks. Sixth, liberals believe that social and economic environment determine behavior, whereas conservatives believe in personal responsibility and accountability. Seventh, liberals are driven by outrage at inequity and unequal conditions, whereas conservatives are focused on what works and how to improve it. Eighth, liberals want to be enslaved with choices reduced, while conservatives believe in maximizing choice and enjoy exercising it. Ninth, liberals believe in government meeting their needs and solving problems, while conservatives believe in the private sector and the market. Tenth, liberals don't believe that individuals should be driven by competition and self-interest, preferring to see a society based on cooperation and subordination of self-interest to the general welfare; conservatives on the other hand believe in competition and the development of the self. Eleventh, liberalism in essence is based on a monistic view of the world, whereas conservatives see the world in binary terms. While liberals believe in unity, sameness, and collaboration, conservatives believe in diversity, choice and competition. In its push for conformity, liberalism seeks to suppress those who strive to be different or hold different ideas. In the binary world perspective of conservatives, it's actually good to have an adversarial view and force. The conservative view is Hegelian, seeing conflicting views as natural and helping in the development of a better world order.

Although liberalism proclaims itself to be about the individual and liberty, we have seen that it's really about the diminishment of the individual and the curtailment of liberty as part of a process to enhance the growth, power, and influence of the State. The diacritic of liberalism is its emphasis on collectivism. Liberalism is about the expansion of the State and collective consciousness. Liberal philosophy is organic, placing the whole above the parts, whereas conservative political philosophy is atomistic, placing the individual above the whole. Either approach could theoretically be better than the other. It's important to have a vibrant whole. You could have a polity where individuals are accorded complete freedom and where they thrive, but have an unfavorable integral social situation. Likewise you could have a society as a whole that is thriving, but the individuals comprising it would be miserable and unfulfilled. For example, perhaps the State could be growing in power and sophistication, but the citizenry would be reduced to little more than automatons. Obviously the optimum situation would be one in which both organic society and individuals thrived.

Politics, however, should be about the art of the possible. We need to look at history and use it as a guide forward. History is full of collectivist experiments. The record is a litany of not just failure, but horror.

History is clear about the problem of accumulating power in the hands of the few. It's even clearer about the danger of those who think they know more than others about how they should live. Elitism is just another form of power accumulation. It's but another abuse of the ordinary citizen. Liberalism is all about the pursuit of oppression and the return of man to subjugation and submissiveness. All this is done under the language of liberty and freedom.

Political and institutional failure is brought about by the increasing hegemony of discretion over rules-based systems— such as laws, moral principles, rules of logic, market-based forces, technological forces, and even rules of etiquette. Throughout history men have always sought control over others. It's in our genes. The ruling class is pushing relentlessly to augment its power. Power corrupts, and power in the hands of a few is a menace to society. It's only through relying on rules-based systems that the exercise of discretionary power can be constrained. It's for this reason that the ruling elite is trying to undermine these systems and limit their influence. This is why it's so critical that we support the rule of law, the canons of reason, moral principles, and capitalism. These are the last redoubt against the forces of tyranny that are gaining more and more strength every day.

Institutional overdevelopment and excessive political regulations and interference block and impede economic and technological progress. Nonmarket economies retard progress and adaptation to technological change, whereas market economies unleash these forces. Technology is pushing us into a new era; they are the way to the future. Institutional sclerosis and the increasing hegemony of discretion over rules based systems are retrograde and ill-suited to moving our country forward. The enhanced role accorded to government discretion and intervention is counterproductive and is exacerbating already difficult problems. They are blocking the road to a prosperous future. The world is becoming increasingly complex and difficult to control through top-down planning and management, yet this is precisely what liberalism is trying to do. At a time when institutions are becoming increasingly out-of-date and ill-suited to managing our future, liberals are striving to accord government, the largest institution of them all, more and more control. The dysfunction of government is apparent to all, yet liberals press relentlessly for its expansion. Does this make any sense?

Liberalism is trying to take apart and destroy the current paradigm of democratic-capitalism and replace it with a new socialistic world order run by an "enlightened elite." At a time when technological forces and globalization are already pushing us to the threshold of instability, liberalism is dramatically adding to the destabilization—and is threatening to take us over the edge. Liberals are intent on destroying virtually all of the systems-based stabilizers that have served us so well in the past and that provide us a path into the future. By disconnecting us to our past, liberalism is making the path into the future much more dangerous and uncertain.

Everyone today complains, and rightly so, about black slavery in the past. It should be noted, however, that most of the people in the world today are living under conditions of virtual and abject slavery to their governments and economic need. We in the West are fortunate to be among the few exceptions. Unfortunately, the Left seems intent on bringing us under conditions of economic and political slavery too.

The capitalist system has done more for poverty alleviation since it took root in the middle of the eighteenth century than had been achieved in thousands of years before that. It has transformed the world, improved our health, longevity, and the quality of our lives. People used to live only about forty years, but now can live twice as long. They can now travel around the globe in a matter of hours, whereas even distances of fifty miles were difficult in the past. We now have time, thanks to economic progress, to educate ourselves and life is a great deal less arduous. This is almost entirely due to capitalism. Yet the Left attacks capitalism relentlessly, proposing policies that have led only to tyranny and adversity in the past.

America in particular has played a major role in transforming the world, but the Left seems intent on bringing down one of the greatest nations in history. This will hurt not only this country, but the world.

Liberalism has failed because the conceptual pillars on which it's built are ill-conceived, contrary to reality, and morally bankrupt. Liberalism bases its economic model on heavy state intervention and regulation, when it has been demonstrated both theoretically and empirically that free markets and capitalism work much better—not only from the standpoint of generating economic growth, but in alleviating poverty. Yet liberalism continues to ignore the lessons of history. The historical record of progressive-liberalism is one of consistent failure. It has failed across the gamut in every respect, from the smallest experiments with communes to world-wide redistribution programs. There is not one success to point to. Nevertheless, liberals continue to press the same failed policies.

The issue with liberalism is not even so much about whether this or that policy works or doesn't work. It's about the iron clad laws of arithmetic and commonsense. Do numbers matter? Does the budget need to balance? The government has been spending forty two percent more than the revenues it has been taking in. No rational person would dream of doing this with his personal finances. Do trillion dollar deficits and debt matter? Bankruptcy and the pursuit of unsustainable policies make no sense. Does it make sense to offer people more social security, Medicare, new health care entitlements, and large unfunded pensions to public sector employees if these arrangements are going to go bankrupt? Only the dumb, the financially illiterate, or the insane would say yes. Yet this is what the Democratic Party and liberalism stand for today? This is who they are. Is it any wonder that you cannot reason or conduct rational dialogue with people like this?

It's bizarre, but it seems like we are knowingly destroying ourselves. Perhaps this should not be surprising as much of life is about self-destructive behavior, like drug addiction and alcohol abuse, and not just constructive behavior. Life is about a struggle between these two types of behavior. Since World War II, life-affirming forces predominated and we enjoyed an era of peace and prosperity. Unfortunately, the tide seems to have turned, and self-destructive behavior seems now to be getting the upper hand.

The constraining forces of conscience, morality, and religion have given way to a reign of ego and self-indulgence. Moral relativism has severely weakened traditional life-affirming values and left a void that is being filled by narcissism and greed for power. In Freud's terminology the superego has all but been eliminated from the playing field, so the ego is now untrammeled by conscience, religion, and concern for others.

According to the great American theologian Reinhold Niebuhr, "Some of the greatest perils to democracy arise from the fanaticism of moral idealists who are not conscious of the corruption of self-interest in their professed ideals."[221] Niebuhr recognized that the will for power, ambition, and egotistic fulfillment of potential are a great threat to the well-being of the community. It is only if these selfish forces can be constrained by religion or other forces that communities can live in peace and prosper, and democracies can be sustained.

Unfortunately, the "force of egoistic impulse" is much more powerful than most recognize, and it is almost impossible to suppress. Even if it is held in check at some level, it almost always finds a way around the constraints to achieve its ends in another way. Nowadays this egoistic impulse is rearing its ugly head in the form of liberalism where power is being sought under the guise of altruism. Liberalism, of course, downplays this darker side of human nature as it would expose the power grab that lies in its heart.

Liberalism has ignored process, pragmatics, and incentives, and is rooted in an aversion to reason, empiricism, praxis, and the pursuit of truth. Liberalism's attempt to replace an epistemology based on reason with one based on consensus will set back the progress of man if it succeeds. It's the epistemology of reason, empiricism, and science that has brought about the tremendous progress in the last two hundred and fifty years. It has not only led to an economic transformation of the world, but has served as the basis for freeing man from tyranny. Reason is egalitarian; anyone can have a good idea. The epistemology of reason is fundamental in bringing about liberty. An epistemology based on consensus, on the other hand, is not consistent with individual liberty. It would move us back to an epistemology where the ruling class and the majority define truth. The individual would ineluctably be crushed by the tyranny of the majority. The period of freedom for man, where individuals can truly flourish, has reigned for only several hundred years, but may be drawing to a close. The connection between the reigning epistemology and liberty is a tight one. Once we see epistemology co-opted by the ruling class and the masses, the threat to liberty is quick behind.

Idealism is fundamental to our humanity. However, liberalism has perverted idealism, taking the good intentions of people and putting them in harness to the ruling elite's grab for power. In essence it has transmuted good intentions into a force of evil. For idealism to be constructive, it must be linked to reason and reality, but liberalism has severed this link. As Winston Churchill noted, "A liberal is a man with both feet planted firmly in the air."

Liberalism is based on the moral philosophy of good intentions; it fails because intention is not enough. Consequences count. For liberals, morality is narrowly conceived and based mostly on "fairness," which to the liberal means "equal distribution of income and wealth." It ignores other grounds for morality. More fundamentally, however, liberalism doesn't recognize that its ends-justify-the-means morality is really the antithesis of morality. Even if liberals were successful in creating a classless state, would it be worth the price? Individuality, the dignity of man, and respect for reason and truth would have all been sacrificed—surely a heavy price for the creation of an all-powerful State.

For liberals, man is the measure of all things. This is a selfish view. Liberals speak about their concern for the earth and the environment, but their real interest is in themselves. They are concerned about how we are affecting the environment, because they are worried about the future impact on man. Nature for them is not sacrosanct; it's something to be used for the sake of man. It's just another manifestation of the self-absorbed, selfish core of the liberal mind-set.

Nature, our environment, our cosmic surroundings all eclipse man, who is but a microscopic speck in the universe. We all but disappear in the realm of the universe, yet liberals see man at the center of it all. It seems as though they have returned to pre-Copernican ideas, where the planets all revolved around the earth rather than the sun, and where we were the center of the universe. Here we see the narcissism that lies at the core of liberalism unmistakably revealing itself.

The failure of liberalism to understand the nature of institutions has contributed in no small measure to the failure of liberal policies. Liberals don't understand the inimical effects of liberal policies on institutions and don't understand how institutions work. So it's no surprise that liberal policies are not effectively carried out and implemented. Liberalism has led to inefficient and oversized institutions with too many objectives and too much concentration of power, so the intended effects of liberal policies have consistently failed to materialize.

Liberalism dehumanizes man; it's fundamentally destructive of humanity. The role of the individual is being destroyed. Honor, respect, and character are no longer valued, and man is being stripped of his values through moral relativism. With individuality weakened, and the basis of morality eroded, the ground is fertile for the growth of selfishness, abuse of power, and evil. All this is the result of an ideology purported to be committed to altruism and "goodness."

Liberalism has within it a deeply ingrained bent toward the annihilation of the mind and spirit of man. It strives to transform humans into drones, cogs in the machine of the State. Under liberalism our primary traits would be sameness, conformity, servility, and disposability. In the end, liberalism sacrifices individuality. It just gets in the way. But are not individuality and its development what makes humans so special? The emerging picture is that the ruling elite see the masses as little more than clay to be molded into whatever form they see fit.

Liberalism has a flawed understanding of human nature and government; it has too little faith in man and too much faith in government. Liberals are infected with a deeply ingrained naiveté, understanding man as only interested in doing good. They overlook man's capacity for evil. They fail to understand the danger of vesting too much power in the hands of a few. Their view is that power vested in the hands of a few intellectual elite would be used only for the benefit of man.

Liberalism doesn't understand that man is driven by pleasure, pain, and self-interest (Bentham); and that he is driven by unconscious forces (Freud), not just conscious or rationally driven forces; that he is instinctually aggressive and territorial (Robert Ardrey, *The Territorial Imperative*); and they certainly don't see that man, and most creatures, are hierarchical by instinct and nature. Liberalism understands man simplistically as moldable, plastic. It subscribes to a behaviorism (Skinner), but yet advances policies and practices that reward bad behavior and penalize good behavior. They see man in a Kumbaya ("Let's all just get along") perspective reminiscent of the 1960s' liberal movement: well-intentioned, compassionate, and loving. They don't see man for the complex creature that he is.

Because it misunderstands the nature of man and institutions, liberalism espouses policies that simply don't work. The policies of liberalism actually damage man, rather than improve him. Whereas for Aristotle the most important objective of the State was to provide an environment where man could flourish and achieve his maximum potential, today's liberalism is interested only in subordinating the individual to the State. It's destroying the character and integrity of man. Under liberalism our identity is being obliterated, both as an individual and as a nation.

So, liberalism is working not only to undermine democracy, but more fundamentally to strip man of his nature. It's dehumanizing him as it tries to bring him into submission to the State. Man is destroying himself as he advances liberalism. The process is slow but unmistakable. Certain men are benefitting from the advancement of liberalism today. That is why they are doing it. But man down the road will pay a heavy price. It's a Faustian bargain, but it is another generation that will pay the price. Too many people are supporting liberalism as they buy into the dissimulative rhetoric of compassion and help for the poor, oblivious to the failure of liberal policies and the failure of actions to match the rhetoric. As Michel Foucault said, "As the archaeology of thought easily shows, man is an invention of recent date. And one perhaps nearing its end."

We are destroying ourselves in the name of the State. What is the State? Is it not meant to serve our interests? We are fast becoming the instruments of our own creation—government and technology.

The psychopathologies underlying the incoherency and the malefic nature of liberalism are manifest and shouldn't be underestimated. Liberalism is both a cause and effect of the psychopathology. It produces a culture of dependency and weakness, and it's rooted in envy, anger, and insecurity. It's suffused with cognitive dysfunction. Liberalism has become disconnected from our nature as humans, reason, even the indications of trial and error, the pursuit of truth, serious dialogue, and the basic tenets of morality.

Even President Franklyn Roosevelt, the ultimate icon of liberalism, recognized the corrosive effects of dependency. In 1935, Roosevelt said, "Continued dependence upon relief induces a spiritual and moral disintegration fundamentally destructive to the national fiber. To dole out relief in this way is to administer a narcotic, a subtle destroyer of the human spirit."[222] Rather than rewarding the virtuous, the responsible, and the hard-working, liberalism encourages and enables free riders and parasites. This is hardly a recipe for success.

Egalitarianism is a ruse, a trick to fool the masses into submission. It's amusing that those who consider themselves so superior are so self-righteous and vociferous in their calls for equality. Insincerity is a key hallmark of liberalism. Deliberate lying and distortion preclude the pursuit of reason and the truth; dissimulation is necessary to shield the incoherencies of liberalism from the light of scrutiny.

Reason is viewed as a tool of oppression, as it has served to justify the status quo. In their view people need to behave differently, so they need to think differently. For them, traditional education merely reinforces the existing traditions. The State is needed to redirect and reshape the thinking of people along nontraditional lines. Mao burned books and killed the intelligentsia; Vietnam and Cambodia ran re-education camps. Modern liberals have taken over our education institutions and, rather than teaching critical thinking, just push their agenda. Likewise the mainstream media have been co-opted by liberals. The Left thinks it necessary to make a radical departure from the past, so they recognize the need to destroy the past, including its epistemological, moral, religious, and capitalistic foundations, so that they can build a new system built on an entirely new foundation.

But liberalism's suppression of reason really does not stem so much from ideology, as it does from practical considerations. First, liberalism's historical record of failure cannot stand the light of reason. Second, it is not only the failed record of liberalism that must be shielded, but also liberalism's internal inconsistences and schizophrenic nature. Third, since reason is egalitarian, it must be brushed aside as it works against the elitist grab for power. Fourth, the mindset of reason is not appropriate if the ruling elite wants to enslave the masses, as it is more important to stoke up the emotions of the people. Fifth, reason is not consistent with the group-think and lock-step consensuality required of liberal epistemology. Sixth, there is an institutional bias in government against truth seeking as it limits its power. Seventh, given that liberals only make up 20 percent of the electorate, they have to misrepresent themselves and their agenda to get their way. Deception is justified, however, as it's for a "good purpose" and the masses are too stupid to make use of real information anyway and don't' know what's best for them.

Thus liberalism is severing our connection to the past, rationality, our nature as humans, and the basic tenets of morality. This disconnect is extremely dangerous. Untethered by guidance from reality, our instincts, reason, and basic time-tested precepts of morality, liberalism is leading us into a world of phantasmagoria. We live in a world of seductive illusions, and are now like blind men walking through a minefield. Our vulnerabilities are enhanced by the age of technology. We have become more and more immersed in technologies of simulation and virtual reality, television, and computer and video games that are predisposing us toward fantasy, and are taking us further and further from reality. Our collective memory of the horrors of past history has faded and no longer guides us.

The sacrifice of truth for agenda affects not just society, but goes to the core of the lives of individuals and families. With genuineness and honesty giving way to deceit and dissimulation, trust disintegrates and connection to life in a simple, direct, and alive way is eroded. When we see the warning signs that the pursuit of truth is abandoned, this is like the canary in the mine shaft. The decline of truth and reason tells us that something terribly wrong is happening. It's a warning sign that power is being centralized in the hands of a few, tyranny is in the offing, and that liberty and freedom of thought and expression are at risk.

What is liberalism, if it's not about compassion? This is what liberals are always professing to be at core of their political philosophy. As we have seen, however, liberals are less generous than conservatives in giving to charity, donating blood, volunteering, and in other informal ways of helping people. We have also seen that liberal policies have not worked and that the Left does not care that they have failed. Liberals have made no effort at reforming their failed policies. If liberalism is not about compassion and helping the poor, what is it about? It's about power, pure and simple power, and it's a particularly pernicious power in that it works through deceit and deception. Masquerading as idealism and benevolence, liberalism is a dangerous foe.

Contradiction, perhaps even schizophrenia, is one of the most abiding characteristics of liberalism. While liberals proclaim they are for unity, they practice the politics of division. While they proclaim they are for a classless society, their method of operation is class conflict. While they proclaim that they are for the masses, they are elitist. While they proclaim that they want to help the underclass, their policies actually harm them. While they proclaim that they are for equality, their modus operandi is unequal treatment and special dispensation for their favored groups. While they proclaim that they are for the pursuit of exalted aims, their underlying motivation and their use of base tactics is driven by political greed. While they proclaim that they are striving to create a utopia in the future, they are actually bankrupting future generations and destroying the culture that has underpinned their success. While they proclaim that they are working to create economic justice, they in fact are pursuing policies of economic injustice, as well as social and political injustice. While they proclaim that they are the protectors of morality, their commitment to an ends-justify-the-means approach is the essence of immorality. While they proclaim an interest in advancing liberty, they are actually working to squelch it. While they proclaim that they are against absolutism, they promulgate a dictatorship of moral relativism and march toward a concentration of power. While they proclaim that they are for pluralism and diversity, they push for conformity, sameness, and homogeneity. While they proclaim compassion for the masses, they ignore individual man and hold him in contempt. While they proclaim an anti-materialist agenda, they are in fact driven to steal the wealth of others. While they proclaim themselves tolerant, they practice intolerance. While they see themselves carrying the banner for tolerance and benevolence, they are in fact driven by rage and contempt for those in their way. While they proclaim that those in opposition are extremists, they work to overturn the values and institutions upon which this country was built. While they proclaim the importance of free speech, they practice political correctness. While they proclaim that they want to build a heaven on earth based on harmony, they are in fact fomenting tension and conflict and potentially creating a hell on earth.

Liberalism is in essence a philosophy of denial. We have seen that it is in denial of reality. It is absorbed in how "the world should be," not in how "the world is." It is even in denial of our own human nature and the importance of the individual, and it denies history, tradition, the role of reason, and the danger of accumulation of power. More fundamentally, liberalism is even in denial of its own nature. It pushes for monism, seeking unity and sameness and shunning tension and conflict, but is itself conflicted, binary, and schizoid.

So liberalism is doomed to failure, eventually it will be torn apart by the centrifugal forces inherent in its own internal contradictions. Given these inconsistencies, it's not surprising that liberals are trying to diminish the role of reason in our culture. Blindness toward reality and a disposition toward rage and anger rather than discourse ensure that the day of reckoning cannot be far off. Moreover, liberalism's irresistible primal drive for the organic and collective, which leads to herd-like behavior and thinking ensures that the coming implosion will consume us all.

Liberalism thinks the world is a zero-sum game in that the gain of one group is at the expense of another. This is the politics of negativism and pessimism, and it is rooted in the past. These roots lead to autocracy and tyranny. It's the politics of economic stagnation and the immisseration of the public. Liberalism bases its support on the demanders of government services—the poor, the parasitic, the freeloaders, and the slackers, not on those who create wealth and contribute positively to society. The ideology of liberalism involves a taker mentality, not a giver mentality, so it's no surprise that their "expressed" compassion is an empty sham. This is not the liberalism of John Kennedy, who said in his inaugural speech, "Ask not what your country can do for you, but what you can do for your country." The politics of division, based as it is on taking and not giving, doesn't work in a social welfare state. Liberalism is taking us back to the past, not forward to the future. It's a retrograde political philosophy, leading us toward modern day feudalism.

Thus, liberalism is not just a disease confined to the domain of politics. It has spread throughout our culture. Morality, individual psychology, economics, politics, and epistemology are all intertwined. The poison of liberalism now extends into every interstice of our culture. In this connection a diminishment of the value of hard work, success, responsibility, and accountability has hurt outcomes in economics and politics. Similarly, by devaluing reason and the pursuit and status of truth, liberalism has undermined morality and the practice of politics. What we have now is a vicious circle spiraling out of control toward entropy and decline. The very existence of American democracy and the liberties we enjoy are now under serious threat.

Liberalism is in short a virulent disease. It works incessantly to weaken the host body. Through deconstruction and relativism it's destroying the strengths and values of America and the West. At the same time, the insidious and malefic cells of collectivism are gaining strength. So, while healthy cells are destroyed, they are replaced by the sick cells of collectivism. Does this sound like cancer?

Liberalism preaches altruism, but practices self-interest. It's based on a lack of regard for others. It's like drug addiction: its adherents are self-absorbed, driven by their own needs, and don't care if others are hurt. They want their fix of power and spending NOW, and don't care if government growth gets out of control and debt levels grow unsustainably high and injurious to all, including themselves.

The malefic dynamics are manifest. The mechanics of redistribution are nothing more than legalized theft. If the government was simply taking money from Peter to pay Paul without benefitting itself, this would be problematic enough. It's clear, however, that the government is not a neutral or impartial player in the process. It actively is enhancing its power and influence in the process. It's an accomplice to the crime, it's splitting the loot.

The mania for spending is never-ending. Spending is leading to yet more spending, ever larger debt and expanded government. With larger government, the ruling class is increasing its power and is increasingly disconnected from the rest of the citizenry. The increase in power is feeding upon itself, creating a more centralized and disconnected power center. Its modus operandi of irrationality and lies is inevitably leading to ever greater irrationality and lies. More and more government regulation and interference are leading to more of the same as it must fix and patch its ever growing mistakes and the growing unsustainability of the mess that it's creating.

Voters in the last election placing Obama in office for another four years may have gotten what they want. They want more spending and don't want to pay for it. They are against entitlement reform and curtailing expenditure growth, but are against tax increases, except on others. Bertrand Russell once said, "In a democracy people get the government they deserve." He may very well be right. Our narcissism, denial of reality, and insistence on living beyond our means is a recipe for catastrophe. We will get what we deserve. The only question is when, not if, the ugly denouement will occur and in what form it may occur. But one lesson of history is clear. Evil loves to rear its ugly head during periods of chaos. The horrific wars and mass killings which filled the 20th century are harsh lessons of history which we ignore at our peril. Collectivism seems to have an insatiable appetite for human blood and suffering which should hardly be surprising given that it holds individual life in such low regard.

Liberal policies of unrestrained immigration and cultural relativism are undermining the traditions and foundations of our democracy. As cultural homogeneity has declined, the interests and objectives of different groups have diverged. As interests have diverged, the game has changed from finding consensus and solutions to problems to achieving and exercising power. Everyone is jockeying for power. Before our eyes democracy is being transmuted into nothing more than a raw struggle for power. Reasoning, integrity, and basic values have been jettisoned. Now they're a luxury, apparently, that we can no longer afford.

Liberalism is weakening the forces that have held society together. By trying to bring about abrupt and wrenching change, liberalism is overloading the system, stretching it to the breaking point. The politics of division are adding to pressures on the system. As Abraham Lincoln famously said, "A house divided cannot stand."

H. L. Mencken recognized, "It is mutual trust, even more than mutual interest, that holds human associations together." Yet liberals, through their politics of division, are tearing this trust asunder. Is this a way to build a more perfect society? Trust is the glue holding modern democracies together. Just look at the monetary system. A person accepts money not because it has any inherent value, but because there is an understanding and a bond of trust that determines that money is worth something. Yet even here we see liberalism destroying the foundations of trust as its prodigal monetary and fiscal policies undermine our faith in government and in the value of the money it prints.

In sum, liberalism is wreaking destruction across the board. It's destroying democracy as the size and reach of government expands, power is centralized, and the ruling class detaches from the public. It's destroying individuality and the dignity of man. Honor, respect, and character are no longer valued. All this is the result of an ideology purportedly committed to altruism and "goodness." This is an ideology that doesn't recognize evil even when it's staring it in the face—even in the mirror. In the world of liberalism the only evil is an opposing point of view.

The political system of democracy is prone to pandering, excessive spending, debt accumulation, tyranny by the majority, and to a lowering of standards. These are its weak points, its points of vulnerability. The disease of liberalism attacks all of these weak points. Moreover, whereas the founding fathers emphasized the importance of constraining the power of government, today's liberals are aggressively bringing about a vast expansion in the size and power of government. The assault on America could not be more clear.

Liberalism is a creeping disease, it hardly ever gives ground. It may go into remission for a while, but when it gets an opportunity, which is assured under a two-party democratic system, it expands and metastasizes. It is relentless and ratchets up its influence until soon there is little left of our once healthy body politic. Cancer can often be cured depending on the type, if caught early before it spreads; unfortunately liberalism has spread throughout our socio-economic-political system. As it spreads it is destroying our way of life. George Washington warned, "Government is not reason; it is not eloquent; it is force. Like fire, it is a dangerous servant and a fearful master."

NOTES

࿆

Chapter 2:

1   Tomkins, Silvan.S. "Left and Right: A Basic Dimension of Ideology and Personality." In R.W. White (Ed.) *The Study of Lives.* (Chicago: Atherton, 1963): 388-411.

2   Ibid.

3   "Student Protest Cancels Ann Coulter Canada Speech." *Boston Herald.* March 25, 2010. http://bostonherald.com//news_opinion/international/americas/2010/03/student_protest_cancels_ann_coulter_canada_speech.

4   Johnson, Eliana. "At Columbia, Students Attack Minuteman Founder." *The New York Sun.* October 5, 2006. http://www.nysun.com/new-york/at-columbia-students-attack-minuteman-founder/41020.

5   "Ricci v. Destefano." *Legal Information Institute.* June 29, 2009. http://www.law.cornell.edu/supct/html/07-1428.ZO.html.

6   Podhoretz, Norman. *Why are Jews Liberals?* New York: Doubleday, 2009.

7   Ibid.

8   Ninh, Amie. "Liberal vs. Conservative: Does the Difference Lie in the Brain?" *Time.* April 8, 2011. http://healthland.time.com/2011/04/08/liberal-vs-conservative-does-the-difference-lie-in-the-brain/.

9   Brack, Charles and Xi Zhang. "Conservatives Need More Space than Liberals." *Neuropolitics.* October 2005. http://neuropolitics.org/defaultoct05.asp.

10   Ibid.

11   Carney, Dana R., John T. Jost, Samuel D. Gosling and Jeff Potter. "The Secret Lives of Liberals and Conservatives: Personality Profiles, Interaction Styles, and the Things They Leave Behind." *Political Psychology.* (2008) 29(6), 807-839.

12   Ibid.

13   Bogira, Steve. "Liberals, Conservatives, and Personality Traits." *Chicago Reader.* August 18, 2011. http://www.chicagoreader.com/Bleader/archives/2011/08/18/4462041-liberals-conservatives-and-personality-traits.

14   Cowen, Tyler. "The Personality Traits of Liberals and Conservatives." *Marginal Revolution.* February 25, 2008. http://marginalrevolution.com/marginalrevolution/2008/02/the-personality.html

15   Ibid.

16   Brack, Charles and Xi Zhang. "Conservatives Need More Space than Liberals." *Neuropolitics.* October 2005. http://neuropolitics.org/defaultoct05.asp.

17   Hirsh, Jacob B., Colin G. DeYoung, Xiaowen Xu and Jordan B. Peterson. "Compassionate Liberals and Polite Conservatives: Associations of Agreeableness with Political Ideology and Moral Values." *Journal of Personality and Social Psychology.* (2010) 36(5), 655-664. doi: 10.1177/0146167210366854.

18   Experian Simmons Study. "Republicans and Democrats Like Different TV Shows, Study Says." *Fox News.* November 10, 2010. http://www.foxnews.com/entertainment/2010/11/10/republicans-democrats-like-different-tv-shows-study-says.

19   Bulkeley, Kelly. *American Dreamers: What Dreams Tell Us about the Political Psychology of Conservatives, Liberals, and Everyone Else.* Boston: Beacon Press, 2008.

20   Haidt, Jonathan. "What Makes People Vote Republican? *Edge.* September 9, 2008. http://www.edge.org/3rd_culture/haidt08/haidt08_index.html.

21   Fowler, James. "Why Do People Vote at All?" Comment on Jonathan Haidt "What Makes People Vote Republican?" *Edge.* September 9, 2008. http://www.edge.org/discourse/vote_morality.html#fowler.

22   Bogira, Steve. "Liberals, Conservatives, and Personality Traits." *Chicago Reader.* August 18, 2011. http://www.chicagoreader.com/Bleader/archives/2011/08/18/4462041-liberals-conservatives-and-personality-traits.

Chapter 3:

23   Goldberg, Jonah. *Liberal Fascism: The Secret History of the American Left, from Mussolini to the Politics of Change.* New York: Broadway Books, 2009.

24   Rousseau, Jean-Jacques. *On the Social Contract.* Translated by G.D.H. Cole. Mineola, NY: Dover Publications, 2003.

25   Ibid., 9.

26   Ibid., 25.

27   Berlin, Isaiah. *Political Ideas in the Romantic Age* (Princeton, NJ: Princeton University Press, 2006), 128 – 129.

28   Madison, James. "The Federalist No. 10: The Utility of the Union as a Safeguard Against Domestic Faction and Insurrection, continued." *Daily Advertiser.* November 22, 1787. http://www.constitution.org/fed/federa10.htm.

29   Comte, Auguste. "A General View of Positivism" in *The Great Political Theories.* Vol.2 ed. by Michael Curtis. (New York: Avon Books, 1981), 149-153.

Chapter 4:

30   Rotherham, Andrew. "Fenty's Loss in D.C.: A Blow to Education Reform?" *Time.* September 16, 2010. http://www.time.com/time/nation/article/0,8599,2019395,00.html; Smith, Ben. "Teachers Union Helped Unseat Fenty." *Politico.* September 15, 2010. http://www.politico.com/blogs/bensmith/0910/Teachers_union_helped_unseat_Fenty.html.

31   Barone, Michael. "Busting some Myths about Race and Politics." *The Washington Examiner.* October 27, 2012. http://washingtonexaminer.com/barone-busting-some-myths-about-race-and-politics/article/2511850#.UI6csLp1uSp.

32   Madison, Lucy. "Public-Sector Union AFSCME Now No. 1 Spender in 2010 Election Cycle." *CBS News.* October 22, 2010. http://www.cbsnews.com/8301-503544_162-20020498-503544.html; Barone, Michael. "Public Employee Unions Funnel Public Money to Dems." *The Washington Examiner.* October 25, 2010, 11.

33   Hananel, Sam. "Unions Gearing up to Spend Big in 2012 Elections." *Huffington Post.* February 22, 2012. http://www.huffingtonpost.com/2012/02/22/labor-unions-obama-elections-2012_n_1293173.html; Washington Free Beacon Staff. "Unions Plan to Spend $400 Million to Reelect Obama." *Fox News.* March 12, 2012. http://nation.foxnews.com/president-obama/2012/03/12/unions-plan-spend-400-million-reelect-obama?cmpid=cmty_twitter_Gigya_Unions_Plan_to_Spend_%24400_Million_to_Reelect_Obama.

34   Hananel, Sam. "Unions Gearing up to Spend Big in 2012 Elections." *Huffington Post.* February 22, 2012. http://www.huffingtonpost.com/2012/02/22/labor-unions-obama-elections-2012_n_1293173.html; Van Susteren, Greta and Karl Rove. "Are Democrats and the White House Behind the Union Protests in Wisconsin?" *Fox News.* February 18, 2011. http://www.foxnews.com/on-air/on-the-record/transcript/are-democrats-and-white-behind-union-protests-wisconsin.

35   Davey, Monica and Steven Greenhouse. "Angry Demonstrations in Wisconsin as Cuts Loom." *The New York Times.* February 16, 2011. http://www.nytimes.com/2011/02/17/us/17wisconsin.html?_r=0.

36   Farley, Robert. "Fox Business Network's Eric Bolling Says Wisconsin Teachers Get Compensated Nearly Double Those in Private Sector." *PolitiFact.* February 23, 2011. http://www.politifact.com/truth-o-meter/statements/2011/feb/23/eric-bolling/fox-business-news-eric-bolling-says-wisconsin-teac/.

37   Greenhouse, Steven. "Labor Board Tells Boeing New Factory Breaks Law" *The New York Times.* April 20, 2011. http://www.nytimes.com/2011/04/21/business/21boeing.html?_r=0; Levin, Mark. "Thursday's Mark Levin

Show." *The Mark Levin Radio Show.* April 21, 2011. http://www.marklevinshow.com/Article.asp?id=2167663&spid=41492.

38   Rascoe, Ayesha. "U.S. Approves First New Nuclear Plant in a Generation." *Reuters.* February 9, 2012. http://www.reuters.com/article/2012/02/09/us-usa-nuclear-nrc-idUSTRE8182J720120209.

39   Bedard, Paul. "Poll: Fox, O'Reilly Most Trusted News Sources." *US News.* May 20, 2011. http://www.usnews.com/news/blogs/washington-whispers/2011/05/20/poll-fox-oreilly-most-trusted-news-sources.

40   Berger, Judson. "Boston Herald says White house Cited Months-Old Mitt Romney Op-Ed in Keeping Reporter from Covering President." *Fox News.* May 18, 2011. http://www.foxnews.com/politics/2011/05/18/boston-herald-tiff-white-house-months-old-romney-op-ed/; Graham, Michael. "Did White House Boot Boston Herald? *America Live.* Fox News Network video, 4:56. May 19, 2011. http://video.foxnews.com/v/950878055001/did-white-house-boot-boston-herald/.

41   Crafts, Barbie. "White House Threats: Democrat Lanny Davis Says He Was Threatened, Too." *Examiner.* February 28, 2013. http://www.examiner.com/article/white-house-threats-democrat-lanny-davis-says-he-was-threatened-too.

42   Timmerman, Kenneth R. *Shakedown: Exposing the Real Jesse Jackson.* Washington, D.C.: Regnery Publishing, 2002.

43   Kennedy, Dan. "Facing Facts: Government is Still Less Efficient, More Incompetent than the Private Sector." *Media Research Center.* July 7, 2010. http://www.mrc.org/bailout/facing-facts-government-still-less-efficient-more-incompetent-private-sector.

44   Gasparino, Charles. *Bought and Paid For: The Unholy Alliance Between Barack Obama and Wall Street.* (New York: Penguin Group, 2010), ix-xi.

45   Brooks, Arthur. *Who Really Cares: The Surprising Truth About Compassionate Conservatism.* New York: Basic Books, 2007.

46   Sowell, Thomas. "Liberals or Conservatives: Who Really Cares?" *The Human Events Group: Powerful Conservative Voices.* November 28, 2006. http://www.humanevents.com/2006/11/28/liberals-or-conservatives-who-really-cares/.

47   Brooks, Arthur C.. "A Nation of Givers." *The American Magazine.* March/April 2008 Issue. http://www.american.com/archive/2008/march-april-magazine-contents/a-nation-of-givers.

48   Wolfgang, Ben. "In the Color of Money, Red Staters Outgive Blues." *The Washington Times.* August 21, 2012, 1.

49   Ibid.

50   Mauro, Paulo. "Why Worry About Corruption?" Washington, D.C.: International Monetary Fund (Economic Issues No.6), 1997.

51   Tanzi, Vito and Hamid Davoodi. "Roads to Nowhere: How Corruption in Public Investment Hurts Growth." Washington, D.C.: International Monetary Fund (Economic Issues No.12), 1998, 1, 9, 10.

52   Mauro, Paulo. "Why Worry About Corruption?" Washington, D.C.: International Monetary Fund (Economic Issues No.6), 1997.

53   Drucker, Jesse. "Google 2.4% Rate Shows How $60 Billion Lost to Tax Loopholes." *Bloomberg.* October 21, 2010. http://www.bloomberg.com/news/2010-10-21/google-2-4-rate-shows-how-60-billion-u-s-revenue-lost-to-tax-loopholes.html.

54   Eichler, Alexander. "Apple, Google, Amazon Pay Corporate Income Tax Rate Well Below Official Rate." *Huffington Post.* April 17, 2012. www.huffingtonpost.com/2012/04/17/apple-corporate-income-tax-rate_n_1429955.html; Bar, Zvi. "How General Electric, Apple and Google Maintain a Lower Tax Rate Than You." *Seeking Alpha.* January 11, 2012. http://seekingalpha.com/article/318858-how-general-electric-apple-and-google-maintain-a-lower-tax-rate-than-you.

55   O'Reilly, Bill. "General Electric, NBC News and President Obama." *Fox News.* May 18, 2009. http://www.foxnews.com/on-air/oreilly/2009/05/18/general-electric-nbc-news-and-president-obama?page=1.

56   Carney, Timothy. "Obama pushes myth that fat cats favor the GOP." *The Washington Examiner.* October 25, 2010, 11.

57   Skrzycki, Cindy. *The Regulators: Anonymous Power Brokers in American Politics* (New York: Rowman & Littlefield Publishers, 2003), 49.

58   Ibid.

59   Dettloff, Gary and Michael Hamrick. "Power to Tax, Power to Destroy." *The Washington Times.* June 20, 2012. http://www.washingtontimes.com/news/2012/jun/20/power-to-tax-power-to-destroy/?page=all.

60   "Over-regulated America." *The Economist.* February 18, 2012. http://www.economist.com/node/21547789.

61   Skrzycki, Cindy. *The Regulators: Anonymous Power Brokers in American Politics.* New York: Rowman & Littlefield Publishers, 2003.

62   Dettloff, Gary and Michael Hamrick. "Power to Tax, Power to Destroy." *The Washington Times.* June 20, 2012, B1.

63   "Over-regulated America." *The Economist.* February 18, 2012. http://www.economist.com/node/21547789.

64   Skrzycki, Cindy. *The Regulators: Anonymous Power Brokers in American Politics* (New York: Rowman & Littlefield Publishers, 2003), 49.

65   Ibid., 28.

66   Ibid., 27.

67   Rousseau, Jean-Jacques. *On the Social Contract.* Translated by G.D.H. Cole. (Mineola, NY: Dover Publications, 2003), 25.

68   Ibid., 25.

69   Ibid., 25.

70   Wolin, Richard. *The Seduction of Unreason: The Intellectual Romance with Fascism from Nietzsche to Postmodernity* (Princeton, NJ: Princeton University Press, 2004), 287.

71   Cauchon, Dennis. "Americans Depend More on Federal Aid Than Ever." *USA TODAY.* April 26, 2011. http://usatoday30.usatoday.com/news/nation/2011-04-26-government-payments-economy-medicare.htm.

72   Brownfield, Mike. "Dependence on Government Highest in History." *The Foundry.* February 9, 2012. http://blog.heritage.org/2012/02/09/morning-bell-dependence-on-government-highest-in-history/.

73   "Obama Attacks Job Creators Owners During Roanoke Speech: 'If You've Got A Business, You Didn't Build That.'" *The Inquisitr.* July 16, 2012. http://www.inquisitr.com/277705/obama-attacks-job-creators-owners-during-roanoke-speech-if-youve-got-a-business-you-didnt-build-that/.

74   Mosca, Gaetano. "The Ruling Class" in *The Great Political Theories.* Vol. 2 ed. by Michael Curtis (New York: Avon Books, 1981), 332-337.

75   "Are We Happy Yet?" *Pew Social Trends.* February 13, 2006. http://www.pewsocialtrends.org/2006/02/13/are-we-happy-yet/.

76   Brooks, Arthur C.. *Gross National Happiness: Why Happiness Matters for America and How We Can Get More of It.* New York: Basic Books, 2008.

77   Margasak, Larry. "House Censures Rep. Rangel for Misconduct." *MSN News.* December 2, 2010. http://news.ca.msn.com/top-stories/msnbc-article.aspx?cp-documentid=26594756.

78   York, Byron. "Geithner Can't Explain His Failure to Pay Taxes." *National Review.* January 19 2009. http://www.nationalreview.com/corner/175881/geithner-cant-explain-his-failure-pay-taxes/byron-york.

79   Fee, Gayle and Laura Raposa. "Senator John Kerry Skips Town on Sails Tax." *Boston Herald.* July 23, 2010. http://bostonherald.com//inside_track/inside_track/2010/07/sen_john_kerry_skips_town_sails_tax.

80   McElhatton, Jim. "Biden Collects Rent from Secret Service." *The Washington Times.* July 31, 2011. http://www.washingtontimes.com/news/2011/jul/31/biden-charging-secret-service-cottage-rental/?page=all.

81   Brock, David. "His Cheatin' Heart." *The American Spectator Foundation.* January 1994. http://spectator.org/archives/2012/09/07/his-cheatin-heart.

82   Strassel, Kimberly A. "Trolling for Dirt on the President's List." *The Wall Street Journal.* May 11, 2012, A11.

83   Weber, Joseph. "Romney Donor Bashed by Obama Campaign Now Target of Two Federal Audits." *Fox News.* July 25, 2012. http://www.foxnews.com/politics/2012/07/24/romney-donor-bashed-by-obama-campaign-now-

target-two-federal-audits/. Frank VanderSloot revealed on Fox News that he received an audit notice in June from the IRS and two weeks later received an audit notice from the Labor Department stating that the agency would be looking into records related to foreign workers at his cattle ranch.

84 Rosen, James. "Senate, Presidential Powers Collide in Key Case on Recess Appointments." *Miami Herald.* June 3, 2013. http://www.miamiherald.com/2013/06/03/3431186/senate-presidential-power-collide-in-key-case-on-recss-appointments.html.

85 McConnell, Mitch. "The IRS Scandal and Obama's Culture of Intimidation." *The Washington Post.* May 22, 2013. http://articles.washingtonpost.com/2013-05-22/opinions/39443626_1_obama-administration-disclose-act-government-contract.

86 Elliott, Philip. "Associated Press CEO Gary Pruitt: DOJ's Seizure of Phone Records was 'Unconstitutional.'" *Huffington Post.* May 19, 2013. http://www.huffingtonpost.com/2013/05/19/ap-ceo-gary-pruitt-doj_n_3303296.html.

87 Mirkinson, Jack. "Eric Holder Signed off on Search Warrant for James Rosen Emails: NBC News." *Huffington Post.* May 23, 2013.http://www.huffingtonpost.com/2013/05/23/eric-holder-fox-news-james-rosen-warrant_n_3328663.html.

88 Peterson, Josh. "Report: NSA Internet Spying Program Collected Half-a-Trillion Records in 2012." *The Daily Caller.* June 27, 2013. http://dailycaller.com/2013/06/27/report-nsa-internet-spying-program-collected-half-a-trillion-records-in-2012/.

89 Ibid.

90 Will, George. "How Obama Health Plan Sidesteps the Constitution." *The Washington Post.* June 12, 2011, A19.

91 Ibid.

92 Hamermesh, Daniel S. "Ugly? You May Have a Case." Op ed, *The New York Times.* August 27, 2011. http://www.nytimes.com/2011/08/28/opinion/sunday/ugly-you-may-have-a-case.html.

93 Scruton, Roger. *A Political Philosophy: Arguments for Conservatism.* New York: Continuum Books, 2006; Scruton, Roger (Ed.). *Liberty and Civilization: The Western Heritage: A Collection of Essays from The American Spectator.* New York: Encounter Books, 2010.

94 Gerard, Jeremy. "CBS Gives Rooney a 3-Month Suspension for Remarks." *The New York Times.* February 9, 1990. http://www.nytimes.com/1990/02/09/arts/cbs-gives-rooney-a-3-month-suspension-for-remarks.html.

95 Goldman, Russell. "Juan Williams Calls Firing By NPR 'Chilling Assault on Free Speech.'" *ABC News.* October 21, 2010. http://abcnews.go.com/Politics/juan-williams-thinking/story?id=11937951.

96 Ahrens, Frank. "The Silenced Greaseman." *The Washington Post*. March 9, 2000, C01. http://www.washingtonpost.com/wp-srv/WPcap/2000-03/09/041r-030900-idx.html; Carter, Bill. "Radio Host is Suspended over Racial Remarks." *The New York Times*. April 10, 2007. http://www.nytimes.com/2007/04/10/business/media/10imus.html?_r=0.

97 Allen, George. "The Macaca Incident." *The Political Guide*. October 9, 2012. http://www.thepoliticalguide.com/Profiles/Senate/Virginia/George_Allen/Scandals/The_Macaca_Incident/; Allen, George. "George Allen Introduces Macaca" *YouTube* video, 1:03. August 6, 2006. http://www.youtube.com/watch?feature=player_embedded&v=r90z0PMnKwI.

98 Schwandt, Kimberly. "White House Floating Proposal to Curb Contract Campaign Cash." *Fox News*. April 20, 2011. http://politics.blogs.foxnews.com/2011/04/20/white-house-floating-proposal-curb-contract-campaign-cash.

99 Schwartz, Rhonda, Brian Ross and Chris Francescani. "Edwards Admits Sexual Affair; Lied as Presidential Candidate. *ABC News*. August 8, 2008. http://abcnews.go.com/Blotter/story?id=5441195; Friedman, Emily, Katie Morison and John Griffin. "Timeline: Edwards Affair Through the Years." *ABC News*. June 3, 2011. http://abcnews.go.com/Politics/edwards-scandal-timeline-john-edwards-rielle-hunter-affair/story?id=9621755.

100 Blyth, Myrna. "Remembering Mary Jo." *National Review*. July 20, 2004. http://www.nationalreview.com/articles/211550/remembering-mary-jo/myrna-blyth.

101 Thomas, Clarence. "Clarence Thomas High-Tech Lynching." *YouTube* video, 0:39. March 18, 2008. http://www.youtube.com/watch?v=egTyaIAaqz8.

Chapter 5:

102 "CBO's 2011 Long-Term Budget Outlook." *Congressional Budget Office*. June 2011, xi–x. http://cbo.gov/sites/default/files/cbofiles/attachments/06-21-Long-Term_Budget_Outlook.pdf.

103 Ibid.

104 Liu, Liqun, Andrew J. Rettenmaier and Thomas R. Saving. "How Much Does the Federal Government Owe?" Washington, D.C.: National Center for Policy Analysis Policy Report, no. 338. June 2012. http://www.ncpa.org/pdfs/st338.pdf.

105 Hilsenrath, Jon. "Fed Sets Stage for Stimulus." *The Wall Street Journal*. September 1, 2012, 1.

106 Hall, Ed. "U.S. National Debt Clock." *Brillig*. http://brillig.com/debt_clock/.

107   D'Souza, Dinesh. *The Roots of Obama's Rage*. Washington, D.C.: Regnery Publishing, 2010.

108   D'Souza, Dinesh. *Obama's America: Unmaking the American Dream*. Washington, D.C.: Regnery Publishing, 2012.

109   Smith, Peter J. "Glenn Beck on President Obama's Deep Socialist Roots." *Life Site News*. April 7, 2010. http://www.lifesitenews.com/news/archive// ldn/2010/apr/10040709.

110   Buchanan, Todd. "William C. Ayers." *The New York Times*. http://topics. nytimes.com/topics/reference/timestopics/people/a/william_c_ayers/ index.html.

111   Dettloff, Gary and Michael Hamrick. "Power to Tax, Power to Destroy." *The Washington Times*. June 21, 2012, B1.

112   Ibid., B1.

113   Cox, Chris and Bill Archer. "Why $16 Trillion Only Hints at the True U.S. Debt." *The Wall Street Journal*. November 26, 2012. http://online. wsj.com/article/SB10001424127887323353204578127374039087636. html?mod=WSJ_Opinion_LEADTop.

114   Ibid.

115   Ibid.

116   Meltzer, Allan. "Four Reasons Keynesians Keep Getting it Wrong." *The Wall Street Journal*. October 28, 2011. http://online.wsj.com/article/SB10 001424052970204777904576651532721267002.html.

Chapter 6:

117   Margasak, Larry. "House Censures Rep. Rangel for Misconduct." *NBC News*. December 2, 2010. http://www.nbcnews.com/id/40469225/ns/ politics-capitol_hill.

118   Holcombe, Randall G. *Public Finance and the Political Process* (Carbondale, IL: Southern Illinois University Press, 1983), 98.

119   Mak, Tim. "Gallup Poll: Conservatives Outnumber Liberals." *Politico*. January 12, 2012. http://www.politico.com/news/stories/0112/71385. html.

120   Johnson, J. "International Education Rankings Suggest Reform Can Lift U.S." *U.S. Department of Education*. December 8, 2010. http://www.ed.gov/ blog/2010/12/international-education-rankings-suggest-reform-can-lift-u-s/.

Chapter 7:

121   Eberstadt, Nicholas. "Are Entitlements Corrupting Us? Yes, American Character is at Stake." *Wall Street Journal*. September 1, 2012, C2.

122   Tanzi, Vito. *Government versus Markets* (New York: Cambridge University Press, 2011), 8.

123   Tanzi, Vito. *Government versus Markets* (New York: Cambridge University Press, 2011), 246-247; Afonso, Antonio, Ludger Schuknecht and Vito Tanzi. "Public Sector Efficiency: An International Comparison." *Public Choice.* (2005) 123(3-4), 321-347. doi: 10.1007/s11127-005-7165-2.

124   Reifenrath, Amy. "Cheaters Cost Social Security Billions." *The Oregonian.* December 6, 2008. http://www.oregonlive.com/news/index. ssf/2008/12/disability_fraud_saps_social_s.html; Mariano, Willoughby. "Gingrich Says Large Percent of Social Security Payments are Government Waste." *PolitiFact.* June 24, 2011. http://www.politifact.com/georgia/ statements/2011/jun/24/newt-gingrich/gingrich-says-large-percent-social-security-paymen/; Smith, Shepard. "Senate Report: Quarter of Social Security Disability Benefits Improperly Awarded." *Studio B with Shepard Smith.* Fox News Network video, 2:58. September 17, 2012. http:// www.foxnews.com/politics/2012/09/17/senate-report-about-25-percent-social-security-disability-benefits-improperly/.

125   Koenig, Brian. "CBO: ObamaCare Price Tag Shifts from $940 Billion to $1.76 Trillion." *Yahoo.* March 14, 2012. http://news.yahoo.com/cbo-obamacare-price-tag-shifts-940-billion-1-163500655.html.

126   Friedman, Thomas. "The Uncertainty Tax." *The New York Times.* June 12, 2011, 10.

127   Blackstone, Brian, Mathew Karnitschnig and Robert Thomson. "Europe's Banker Talks Tough." *The Wall Street Journal.* February 24, 2012, 1.

128   Hemingway, Mark. "California Unions Stand in the Way of a Texas-sized Success." *The Washington Examiner.* February 11, 2011, 25.

129   Ibid.

130   Ibid.

Chapter 8:

131   Easterly, William. "The Lost Decades: Developing Countries' Stagnation in Spite of Policy Reform 1980-1998." *Journal of Economic Growth.* (2001) 6(2): 135-157. doi: 10.1023/A:1011378507540; Barro, Robert J. and Jong-Wha Lee. "IMF Programs: Who is Chosen and What Are the Effects?" Cambridge, MA: National Bureau of Economic Research Working Paper No. 8951. May 2002; Corbo, Vittorio, Morris Goldstein and Mohsin Khan (Eds.) *Growth-oriented Adjustment Programs.* Washington, D.C.: International Monetary Fund and World Bank, 1987; Haque, Nadeem and Mohsin Khan. "Do IMF-Supported Programs Work? A Survey of the Cross-Country Empirical Evidence." Washington, D.C.: International Monetary Fund Working Paper No. 98/169. 1998; Przeworski, Adam and James R. Vreeland. "The Effect of IMF Programs on Economic Growth." *Journal of Development Economics.* (2000) 62 (2): 385-421. doi: dx.doi.org/10.1016/S0304-3878(00)00090-0.

132 Easterly, William. "The Cartel of Good Intentions: Bureaucracy versus Markets in Foreign Aid." Washington, D.C.: Center for Global Development Working Paper No.4 (March 2002): 1.

133 Easterly, William. "What Did Structural Adjustment Adjust? The Association of Policies and Growth with Repeated IMF and World Bank Adjustment Loans." Washington, D.C.: Center for Global Development Working Paper No. 11. October 2002.

134 Barro, Robert J. and Jong-Wha Lee. "IMF Programs: Who is Chosen and What Are the Effects?" Cambridge, MA: National Bureau of Economic Research Working Paper No. 8951. May 2002; Corbo, Vittorio, Morris Goldstein and Mohsin Khan (Eds.) *Growth-oriented Adjustment Programs.* Washington, D.C.: International Monetary Fund and World Bank, 1987.

135 Easterly, William. "The Lost Decades: Developing Countries' Stagnation in Spite of Policy Reform 1980-1998." *Journal of Economic Growth.* (2001) 6(2): 135-157. doi: 10.1023/A:1011378507540.

136 Bitler, Marianne and Hilary W. Hoynes. "The State of the Safety Net in the Post-Welfare Reform Era." Cambridge, MA: National Bureau of Economic Research Working Paper 16504. Oct 2010.

137 Schoeni, Robert F. and Rebecca M. Blank. "What Has Welfare Reform Accomplished? Impacts on Welfare Participation, Employment, Income, Poverty, and Family Structure." Cambridge, MA: National Bureau of Economic Research Working Paper 7627. March 2000.

138 Bowman, Sam. "We Need a New Capitalist Revolution: A Young Writer Presents his Provocative Manifesto for Free Markets." *City AM.* September 19, 2011. http://www.adamsmith.org/news/in-the-news/we-need-a-new-capitalist-revolution.

139 Rector, Robert and Rachel Sheffield. "Backgrounder #2607 – Understanding Poverty in the United States: Surprising Facts about America's Poor." *The Heritage Foundation.* September 13, 2011. http://www.heritage.org/research/reports/2011/09/understanding-poverty-in-the-united-states-surprising-facts-about-americas-poor.

140 Terkel, Amanda. "Rick Santorum's Two-Step Plan to End Poverty." *Huffington Post.* December 28, 2011. http://www.huffingtonpost.com/2011/12/28/rick-santorums-poverty_n_1173307.html.

141 Caprara, Collette. "Family Fact of the Week: Closing the Marriage Gap Between Rich and Poor." *The Foundry.* February 9, 2012. http://blog.heritage.org/2012/02/09/family-fact-of-the-week-closing-the-marriage-gap-between-rich-and-poor/.

142 Cardenas, Jose R.. "Hugo Chavez's Legacy of Economic Chaos." *The Washington Times.* February 26, 2013, B1.

143   Hannan, Daniel. *The New Road to Serfdom: A Letter of Warning to America* (New York: Harper Collins, 2010), 82.

144   Garibaldi, Pietro and Paolo Mauro. "Job Creation: Why Some Countries Do Better." Washington, D.C.: International Monetary Fund (Economic Issues No. 20), 2000.

Chapter 9:

145   Coulter, Ann. "Obama's Signature Move: Unsealing Private Records." *The Human Events Group: Powerful Conservative Voices.* August 1, 2012. http://www.humanevents.com/2012/08/01/ann-coulter-obamas-signature-move-unsealing-private-records/.

146   Ibid.

147   Ibid.

148   Clinton, Bill. "Clinton Urges Dems to Question Criticism." October 18, 2006. Quoted in Martin, William. *What Liberals Believe* (New York: Skyhorse Publishing, 2008), 437.

149   Piatelli-Palmarini, Massimo. *Inevitable Illusions: How Mistakes of Reason Rule Our Minds.* New York: John Wiley & Sons, 1994.

150   Newby, Joe. "Democratic Strategist Warns: Mainstream Media 'Enemy of the American People'." *Examiner.* October 1, 2012. http://www.examiner.com/article/democratic-strategist-warns-mainstream-media-enemy-of-the-american-people.

151   Markay, Lachlan. "Undisclosed NBC Conflict of Interest Again Arises in Annual 'Green Week.'" *News Busters.* November 16, 2010. http://newsbusters.org/blogs/lachlan-markay/2010/11/16/undisclosed-nbc-conflict-interest-again-arises-annual-green-week.

152   Ibid.; McGlynn, Katla. "Jon Stewart Rips GE, Obama over Taxes and NBC for Not Covering it." *The Huffington Post.* March 29, 2011. http://www.huffingtonpost.com/2011/03/29/jon-stewart-ge-taxes-video_n_841835.html; Stewart, Jon. "I Give Up – Pay Anything..." The Daily Show with Jon Stewart. *Comedy Central* video, 4:49. March 28, 2011. http://www.thedailyshow.com/watch/mon-march-28-2011/i-give-up—pay-anything—.

153   Lakoff, George and Mark Johnson. *Philosophy in the Flesh: The Embodied Mind and Its Challenge to Western Thought.* New York: Basic Books, 1999.

154   Ibid.

155   Sidanius, Jim, Shana Levin, James H. Liu and Felicia Pratto. "Social Dominance Orientation and the Political Psychology of Gender: An Extension and Cross-Cultural Replication." *European Journal of Social Psychology.* (2000) 30(1): 41-67. doi: 10.1002/(SICI)1099-0992(200001/02)30.

156 Allen, Arthur. "Nature and Nurture." *The Washington Post Magazine.* January 11, 1998. http://www.washingtonpost.com/wp-srv/national/longterm/twins/twins1.htm.

157 Ford, Dennis. *The Search For Meaning: A Short History.* Berkeley: University of California Press, 2007.

158 "Groupthink." *PsySR.* http://www.psysr.org/about/pubs_resources/groupthink%20overview.htm.

159 Lowry, Cheryl. "The Analog-ist: Does the Hive Mind Work Offline?" *Flip the Media.* March 22, 2012. http://flipthemedia.com/2012/03/the-new-groupthink-does-the-hive-mind-work-offline/.

Chapter 10:

160 Blackburn, Simon. *Truth: A Guide.* Oxford: Oxford University Press, 2005.

161 Gorman, Siobhan and Jay Solomon. "Clinton Hits Back at Critics on Libya." *The Wall Street Journal.* January 24, 2013, A6.

162 Ibid.

163 Huemer, Michael (Ed.). *Epistemology: Contemporary Readings.* London: Routledge, 2002.

164 Editorial. "Eric Holder's Long History of Lying to Congress." *Investor's Business Daily.* May 31, 2013. http://news.investors.com/ibd-editorials/053113-658465-eric-holder-repeatedly-lied-to-congress.htm?p=full.

165 Berlin, Isaiah. *Political Ideas in the Romantic Age* (Princeton, NJ: Princeton University Press, 2006), p.127.

166 Klein, Aaron and Brenda Elliott. *Fool Me Twice: Obama's Shocking Plans for the Next Four Years Exposed.* Washington, D.C.: WND Books, 2012.

Chapter 11:

167 Leonhardt, James, L. Robin Keller and Connie Pechmann. "Avoiding the Risk of Responsibility by Seeking Uncertainty: Responsibility Aversion and Preference for Indirect Agency When Choosing for Others." *Journal of Consumer Psychology.* (2011) 21(4): 405-413. doi: ssrn.com/abstract=2015956.

168 Kuligowski, Monte. "A Clear Danger: Obama, a 'Living' Constitution, and 'Positive 'Rights. *American Thinker.* October 2, 2010. http://www.americanthinker.com/2010/10/a_clear_danger_obama_a_living.html.

169 Murdock, Deroy. "Obama Caught Lying about Sequester." *National Review.* February 26, 2013. http://www.nationalreview.com/corner/341553/obama-caught-lying-about-sequester-deroy-murdock.

170 Hanrahan, Mark. "Japan Population Decline: Third of Nation's Youth Have No Interest' in Sex." *Huffington Post.* January 30, 2012. http://www.huffingtonpost.com/2012/01/30/japan-population-decline-youth-no-sex_n_1242014.html.

171 Rand, Ayn. *The Virtue of Selfishness.* New York: New American Library. 1964.

172 Russell, Bertrand. *Authority and the Individual* (Boston: Beacon Press, 1960), 49.

173 Malpas, Jeff. "Death and the Unity of a Life" in *Death and Philosophy.* ed. by Jeff Malpas and Robert C. Solomon. (London: Routledge, 1998), 122.

174 Ibid., 128.

175 Zakaria, Fareed. "Interview with Architect Frank Gehry." *Fareed Zakaria GPS.* CNN Network. September 4, 2011. http://transcripts.cnn.com/TRANSCRIPTS/1109/04/fzgps.01.html.

176 Fromm, Erich. *Escape From Freedom* (New York: Henry Holt and Company, 1969), 154-155.

177 Peterson, Josh. "Report: NSA Internet Spying Program Collected Half-a-Trillion Records in 2012." *The Daily Caller.* June 27, 2013. http://dailycaller.com/2013/06/27/report-nsa-internet-spying-program-collected-half-a-trillion-records-in-2012/.

Chapter 13:

178 Munro, Neil. "Polling Shows Little Gain for GOP from Immigration Reform." *The Daily Caller.* January 30, 2013. http://dailycaller.com/2013/01/30/polling-shows-little-gain-for-gop-from-immigration-reform/#ixzz2M4MUK2ve.

179 Dinan, Stephen. "Slow Path to Progress for U.S. Immigrants." *The Washington Times.* August 8, 2012.

Chapter 14:

180 Russell, Bertrand. *Authority and the Individual* (Boston: Beacon Press, 1960), 65-66.

181 Rawls, John. *A Theory of Justice,* Revised Edition (Cambridge, MA: The Belknap Press of Harvard University Press, 1999), 23.

182 Ibid., 13.

183 Ibid., 64.

Chapter 15:

184 Strauss, William and Neil Howe. *The Fourth Turning: An American Prophecy* (New York: Broadway Books, 1997), 325.

185 Dupre, Ben. *50 Philosophy Ideas You Really Need to Know* (London: Quercus Publishing, 2007), 98.

186 Haidt, Jonathan. "What Makes People Vote Republican?" *Edge.* September 9, 2008. http://www.edge.org/3rd_culture/haidt08/haidt08_index.html.

187 Ibid.

188 Ibid.

Chapter 16:

189 Taleb, Nassim Nicholas. *"The Black Swan: The Impact of the Highly Improbable."* New York: Random House, 2010.

190 Taleb, Nassim Nicholas. *"Antifragile: Things That Gain from Disorder."* New York: Random House, 2012.

191 Ibid.

192 Russell, Bertrand. *Authority and the Individual.* Boston: Beacon Press, 1960. p.75.

193 Tanzi, Vito. "Complexity and Systemic Failure." *Transition and Beyond.* ed. by Saul Estrin, Grzegorz W. Kolodko and Milica Uvalic . (London: Palgrave, 2007), 229-46; Tanzi, Vito. *Government versus Markets* (New York: Cambridge University Press, 2011), 332.

194 Acemoglu, Daron and James Robinson. *Why Nations Fail: The Origins of Power, Prosperity and Poverty.* New York: Crown Publishing Group, 2012.

Chapter 17:

195 By aid, I mean bilateral aid, multilateral aid, both loans and grants, and technical assistance and debt forgiveness.

196 "Corruption Perceptions Index 2010." *Transparency International.* 2010. http://files.transparency.org/content/download/132/531/2010_CPI_EN.pdf.

197 Leite, Carlos and Jens Weidmann. "Does Mother Nature Corrupt? Natural Resources, Corruption, and Economic Growth," *Governance, Corruption, and Economic Performance.* ed. by George T. Abed and Sanjeev Gupta. Washington, D.C.: International Monetary Fund, 2002.

198 Tanzi, Vito and Hamid Davoodi, "Corruption, Growth, and Public Finances." *Governance, Corruption, and Economic Performance.* ed. by George T. Abed and Sanjeev Gupta. Washington, D.C.: International Monetary Fund, 2002.

199 Tanzi, Vito and Hamid Davoodi. "Corruption, Public Investment, and Growth." Washington, D.C.: International Monetary Fund Working Paper No. 97/139. 1997.

200 Wei, Shang-Jin. "How Taxing is Corruption on International Investors?" Cambridge, MA: National Bureau of Economic Research Working Paper No. 6030. May 1997.

201 Gupta, Sanjeev, Hamid R. Davoodi and Rosa Alonso-Terme. "Does Corruption Affect Income Inequality and Poverty?" in *Governance, Corruption, and Economic Performance.* ed. by George T. Abed and Sanjeev Gupta. Washington, D.C.: International Monetary Fund, 2002.

202 Alesina, Alberto and David Dollar. "Who Gives Foreign Aid to Whom and Why?" Cambridge, MA: National Bureau of Economic Research Working Paper No. 6612. 1998.

203   Barro, Robert J. and Jong-Wha Lee. "IMF Programs: Who is Chosen and What Are the Effects?" Cambridge, MA: National Bureau of Economic Research Working Paper No. 8951 (2002): 1-37.

204   Svensson, Jakob. "Foreign Aid and Rent-Seeking." *Journal of International Economics.* (2000) 51(2), 437-461. doi: 10.1016/S0022-1996(99)00014-8.

205   World Bank. *Sub-Saharan Africa: From Crisis to Sustainable Growth* (Washington, D.C.: World Bank, 1989), 27, 61.

206   Klitgaard, R. *Tropical Gangsters.* New York: Basic Books, 1990.

207   Alesina, Alberto and Beatrice Weder. "Do Corrupt Governments Receive Less Foreign Aid?" Cambridge, MA: National Bureau of Economic Research Working Paper No. 7108. May 1999.

208   Chen, Chuling and Alun Thomas. "An Evaluation of Fund Programs in the 1990s: The Importance of Taking Explicit Account of Stoppages." Washington, D.C.: International Monetary Fund Working Paper, forthcoming. 2003.

209   de Mello, Luiz and Matias Barenstein. "Fiscal Decentralization and Governance: A Cross-Country Analysis." in *Governance, Corruption, and Economic Performance.* ed. by George T. Abed and Sanjeev Gupta. Washington, D.C.: International Monetary Fund, 2002.

210   Barro, Robert J. and Jong-Wha Lee. "IMF Programs: Who is Chosen and What Are the Effects?" Cambridge, MA: National Bureau of Economic Research Working Paper No. 8951 (2002): 32.

211   Tanzi, Vito. "Corruption, Governmental Activities, and Markets." Washington, D.C.: International Monetary Fund Working Paper No. 94/99 (1994): 2.

212   Ibid.

213   Ibid.

214   Alesina, Alberto and Beatrice Weder. "Do Corrupt Governments Receive Less Foreign Aid?" Cambridge, MA: National Bureau of Economic Research Working Paper No. 7108. May 1999.

215   Ramcharan, Rodney. "Reputation, Debt and Policy Conditionality." Washington, D.C.: International Monetary Fund Working Paper No. 03/192. 2003.

216   Ibid.

217   Tirole, Jean. "Financial Crises, Liquidity, and the International Monetary System" (Princeton, NJ: Princeton University Press, 2002), 92-94.

218   Ibid., 118.

219   Hansmann, H. *The Ownership of Enterprise.* Cambridge, MA: Belknap Press of Harvard University Press, 1996.

220   Easterly, William. "The Cartel of Good Intentions: Bureaucracy Versus Markets in Foreign Aid." Washington, D.C.: Center for Global Development Working Paper No.4 (March 2002): 20.

Chapter 19:

221   Niebuhr, Reinhold. "The Children of Light and the Children of Darkness" in *The Great Political Theories*. Vol.2 ed. by Michael Curtis. (New York: Avon Books, 1981), 421.

222   "Factsheet #82: Welfare Reform The Next Steps." *The Heritage Foundation*. March 17, 2011. http://www.heritage.org/research/factsheets/2011/03/welfare-reform-the-next-steps.

26157029R00236

Made in the USA
Lexington, KY
19 September 2013